RFK and MLK

RFK and MLK
Visions of Hope, 1963–1968

PHILIP A. GODUTI, JR.

McFarland & Company, Inc., Publishers
Jefferson, North Carolina

LIBRARY OF CONGRESS CATALOGUING-IN-PUBLICATION DATA

Names: Goduti, Philip A., 1974– author.
Title: RFK and MLK : visions of hope, 1963–1968 / Philip A. Goduti, Jr.
Description: Jefferson, North Carolina : McFarland & Company, Inc., Publishers, 2017. | Includes bibliographical references and index.
Identifiers: LCCN 2017020794 | ISBN 9780786476725 (softcover : acid free paper) ∞
Subjects: LCSH: Kennedy, Robert F., 1925–1968. | King, Martin Luther, Jr., 1929–1968. | United States—Politics and government—1963–1969. | African Americans—Civil rights—History—20th century. | Civil rights movements—United States—History—20th century.
Classification: LCC E840.8.K4 G579 2017 | DDC 323.1196/07300904—dc23
LC record available at https://lccn.loc.gov/2017020794

BRITISH LIBRARY CATALOGUING DATA ARE AVAILABLE

ISBN (print) 978-0-7864-7672-5
ISBN (ebook) 978-1-4766-2872-1

© 2017 Philip A. Goduti, Jr. All rights reserved

No part of this book may be reproduced or transmitted in any form or by any means, electronic or mechanical, including photocopying or recording, or by any information storage and retrieval system, without permission in writing from the publisher.

Front cover: Martin Luther King, Jr., and Attorney General Robert F. Kennedy (center) with Vice President Lyndon B. Johnson and civil rights leaders, June 22, 1963 (Abbie Rowe, White House Photographs, John F. Kennedy Presidential Library and Museum, Boston)

Printed in the United States of America

McFarland & Company, Inc., Publishers
  Box 611, Jefferson, North Carolina 28640
  www.mcfarlandpub.com

For Alyssa, Alex, Olivia and Sam

I have come to understand that the **hope** *President Kennedy kindled is not dead but alive. It is not a memory, but a living force. The torch still burns, and because it does, there remains for all of us, the chance to light up the tomorrows, and to brighten the future.*—Robert F. Kennedy, Free University, Berlin, June 26, 1964

I believe that even amid today's mortar bursts and whining bullets, there is still **hope** *for a brighter tomorrow.*—Martin Luther King, Jr., Nobel Peace Prize Acceptance Speech, December 10, 1964

In the glow of the lamplight on my desk a few nights ago, I gazed upon a wondrous sign of our times, full of **hope** *and promise of the future.*— Martin Luther King, Jr., Montgomery, Alabama, March 25, 1965

Most important, we must impart **hope**—**hope** *for progress, fulfilled as quickly as circumstances permit.*—Robert F. Kennedy, Address to the International Police Academy Regarding America's Role in Vietnam, July 9, 1965

Each time a man stands up for an ideal, or acts to improve the lot of others, or strikes out against injustice, he sends forth a tiny ripple of **hope***, and crossing each other from a million different centers of energy and daring those ripples build a current which can sweep down the mightiest walls of oppression and resistance.*—Robert F. Kennedy, Day of Affirmation Speech, University of Capetown, Capetown, South Africa, June 6, 1966

Our only **hope** *today lies in our ability to recapture the revolutionary spirit and go out into a sometimes hostile world declaring eternal hostility to poverty, racism, and militarism.*—Martin Luther King, Jr., "Beyond Vietnam," April 4, 1967

Table of Contents

Acknowledgments   ix

Preface   1

Introduction   4

Prologue—"Jack's Been Shot"   11

Part I. America in the Wake of Tragedy, 1963

1: November 22, 1963   23

2: "Let Us Continue"   38

Part II. Forging a New American Identity, 1964

3: Finding a Voice   49

4: "The Hearts and Minds of Youth"   65

5: "The Clock of Destiny Is Ticking Out"   78

6: Freedom and the World   100

7: New Awakenings   122

Part III. Marching On and Hitting Full Stride, 1965–1966

8: Selma   135

9: Bloody Sunday and the Aftermath   146

10:	"The Crises of the Moment"	167
11:	Urban Crisis, Voting Rights and Watts	183
12:	"Ripples of Hope"	200

PART IV. VISIONS OF AMERICA, 1967–1968

13:	"A Coalition of Conscience"	221
14:	"Beyond Vietnam"	239
15:	"A Newer World"	255
16:	1968	269

Epilogue—Selma, 2015	281
Chapter Notes	285
Bibliography	299
Index	301

Acknowledgments

This book is the culmination of four years of research that would not be possible without the help of many wonderful people. The John F. Kennedy Library, Lyndon B. Johnson Library and the King Center Digital Archives were vital sources for bringing together the voices of these individuals as I explored the sixties. Indeed, the *New York Times* archive played a substantial role in analyzing the reaction of the people as the issues discussed in this book unfolded amid the tumultuous 1960s. While they were not the only sources of research, all four stand out as a reminder that there are many people who come together to make sure that the past stays alive and continues to be examined by historians, writers and students for generations.

I am also very appreciative of the people at Quinnipiac University who have continued to encourage me to teach and write about history. The Department of History has been wonderful to work with for the past 17 years. I am very appreciative for the guidance of Professors Kathy Cooke, David Valone and Jill Fehleison. Professor Emeritus Ronald Heiferman continues to be my adviser in all things history. I am lucky to have his guidance in this profession and life. I am also very grateful to Associate Vice President for Public Relations John W. Morgan who continues to get my work out there so that I am part of the conversation. It is wonderful to work in a profession where people are supportive and believe in my work. Words cannot express how much that factors into the production of this and other projects.

I am very grateful for the support that I am given by my colleagues at Somers High School. I am lucky to be working with these talented professionals every day. I especially appreciate the encouragement from my department members: Kristen Angelica, Andrew Drummey, Marc Dzicek and Matthew Macaluso. Our daily conversations keep history alive for me, and I have endeavored to bring that into this book.

My family has always encouraged me to continue in my pursuits, and for that I am grateful. My mother Rosemarie Goduti, Uncle John Mendes and Aunt Sharon Mendes are all very supportive as I continue to write about the past. I have been blessed with a wonderful family that has always been there to encourage me.

Writing a book takes a great deal of time and energy. I could not do this without the support of my wife, Alyssa Goduti. She has sacrificed time so I could sit at my desk and delve into the past. As my muse, her guidance has helped me craft a narrative of a period in history that I think is important. My children, Alexander, Olivia and Samuel are major inspirations when I write history. It has always been my goal to write a book that they will someday read and gain a deeper understanding and appreciation of the past. I write for Alyssa, Alex, Olivia and Sam more than any others, which is why I dedicate this book to them.

Preface

Robert F. Kennedy and Martin Luther King, Jr., shared a vision for America that empowered young people and challenged the status quo, hoping to pave the way for future change. Their strong rhetoric and action led others to follow them and work toward creating an America that included all races and ideas. Indeed that effort is evident in the early part of the twenty-first century. The journey they took had an impact on the nation, inspiring future leaders and blazing a new path for American society.

This book is the result of many conversations with students and colleagues about the Kennedy assassination and the impact it had on American history. Those conversations in the classroom led me to reflect on this period and how that event played a role in shaping American society. To be sure, the death of a young, inspirational leader was a catalyst for many Americans to reconsider where the nation was headed and the role that they played in it. The 1960s was a period in American history where many people questioned authority. The rights revolution had its seeds in the fifties, blossomed in the sixties, and came into full bloom as Americans embarked to define those rights in the twenty-first century. The period that this book covers is an especially difficult and confusing era in American history. It is with great diligence that I endeavor to contribute to that time. After considering the varied perspectives of the period, I found myself seeing the events in the wake of the assassination through the eyes of Robert F. Kennedy and Martin Luther King, Jr.

Poverty, the Vietnam War and civil rights were issues that Kennedy and King made a priority to address. They both played a role in shaping American attitudes on those topics in the final years of their lives. With that notion in mind I ventured to write a book that would consider which of those issues moved America from the conservative 1950s to the radical 1960s. Was it the Vietnam War that changed conventional thinking to question government action and its role in the world? Indeed, this is a theme that has carried over into the twenty-first century as America deals with the vestiges of such Cold War ventures. To be sure, the conversation of the sixties led many in the nation to question the morality of war. Perhaps it was the civil rights movement that moved people to organize and protest the issues that they believed were hurting America. Certainly, civil rights is still an important struggle in the twenty-first century, with movements like "Black Lives Matter" challenging authority in the wake of tragic events. The election of President Barack Obama seemed to be a turning point, but on the threshold of the twenty-first century there are still so many complex issues surrounding the racial tension in the nation. Or, finally, was it the issue of poverty? This is something that has stymied lawmakers since the birth of the republic. Certainly, extreme wealth and the role it plays in American society is a major issue in the twenty-first century and something that King and Kennedy wanted to address in the sixties.

After exploring all of those topics I have concluded that it was a myriad of issues, ranging in intensity, with poverty, the morality of war and civil rights as central motivators that moved America into a new period in its history, where it would question authority and lay the groundwork for future generations. In all of that, however, Kennedy and King were there, speaking out and challenging the social norms that created this nation in the middle of the twentieth century, when the seeds for the next generation were being planted so that future generations could consider their place in the history of the nation, indeed the world.

The presidency of Barack Obama also played a role in this book. As the first Generation X president, President Obama was influenced by the rhetoric of these two men. Throughout his presidency, Obama had done a great deal to change the attitudes toward America, stressing a path to peace in his Nobel Peace Prize acceptance speech in 2009, ending the war in Iraq and acknowledging the need to effectively combat climate change. He is the embodiment of the times that these two men, and many others, shaped, and his presidency is a product of that period. To be sure, President Obama's leadership was polarizing to some degree, but so were the times in which Kennedy and King made their presence known to the world.

Robert Kennedy and Martin Luther King were not alone in the quest to address the issues of their time. They were joined by Lyndon Johnson, Betty Friedan, John Lewis, Gloria Steinem, Stokely Carmichael and many others who were just as vocal and impactful as they were. However, with the exception of President Johnson, no other person was as recognizable as these two men. Kennedy, the brother of a fallen leader, came to symbolize what remained of the New Frontier while in the process he discovered his own voice, empowering people throughout the world. Martin Luther King, Jr., the Nobel Peace Prize winner and advocate of nonviolent protest, emerged in the wake of the Kennedy assassination as someone who would lead people to challenge the racist institutions of this nation using the power of love. They were both extraordinary people who lived extraordinary lives.

Robert Kennedy and Martin Luther King, Jr., lived parallel lives, meeting at the crossroads of history, where America experienced a series of cathartic events that led to the formation of a new society. This story is about how those events and these two men's reaction to them shaped the national discourse, affecting not only their times but also the times that followed. This book highlights those moments in history where their ideas converged, almost poetically, to shape the future and make sense of a confusing time for the nation.

Introduction

The rhetoric of Robert Kennedy and Martin Luther King has been quoted by numerous people to commemorate different occasions. Their ideas, passion and iconic presence in the transformative decade of the 1960s are something for scholars to ponder as we make sense of that confusing period. Exploring the significance and power of their words will help historians understand the impact that they had not only on their own time but on the days that followed. Their ideas contributed to a new American conscience, which led to an awakening of a new identity in America when the sixties came to a close. The nation confronted civil rights issues and the growing war in Vietnam. Those events shaped people, while Kennedy and King tried to address those problems using new methods that challenged the status quo. They were visionaries. This book will explore the writings, speeches and actions of Robert F. Kennedy and Martin Luther King, Jr., in an effort to explore how their words affected American society. Their journey had its roots in the 1950s, but the assassination of President John F. Kennedy created a void in leadership that both Kennedy and King filled for many Americans.

The assassination of President John F. Kennedy set the tone for the rest of the decade and laid the foundation for what would become a new American identity. From 1960 to 1963, America experienced a great deal of growth socially, politically and globally. The Kennedy brothers sent a bill to Congress that would outlaw segregation and support the civil rights movement, more than any other president since Lincoln, affecting the climate in the country for future change. President Kennedy's forbearance over the military, coupled with the keen advice he was given by members of his cabinet, brought America out of that period without a nuclear exchange. There was also a strong political divide in the nation, rooted in liberalism accompanied by a growing conservative movement in opposition. In his short time in office, President John F. Kennedy dealt with more crises than any modern president except Franklin D. Roosevelt. His assassination marked the end of his "New Frontier," yet the issues that were so pervasive in his life were still there in the wake of his death. That event, however, would compound these issues and push America in a new direction.

At the threshold of a new decade, John F. Kennedy symbolized all that America hoped to be. Serving in World War II and standing firm as a cold warrior in the Senate, Kennedy came into the White House ready to ignite, as he said, that torch that "has been passed to a new generation of Americans." In his thousand days in office he confronted the Soviet Union over Berlin and Cuba and told Americans that civil rights was a moral, not a political, issue, laying the foundation for future generations to remake America. As he prepared for his reelection in 1964, that youthful, progressive, charmingly witty, politically savvy version of the presidency came to a sudden halt on November 22, 1963.

The assassination of John F. Kennedy had reverberations that irrevocably changed the nation in its wake. Lee Harvey Oswald, Jack Ruby, John, Jr., saluting his father and Jackie dressed in black led by Robert Kennedy are all symbols that have been seared into the mythology of what actually happened those four days in November. Conspiracy theories and testaments to what the Kennedy years meant have been written by authors for the past fifty years. More than fifty years later people are still invoking Kennedy's vision for America and consider how he would have handled the issues that have defined us since his murder at Dealey Plaza.

In the wake of World War II America seemed invincible. American determination and ingenuity defeated the Nazis and the militaristic Japanese, proving to the world that democracy and self-determination were at the core of progress and success. The people of the United States gave the world an "Arsenal of Democracy" that turned the tide of the war. The forties were followed by a decade that built on that dominance, and that generation seemed unstoppable. When Lee Harvey Oswald, a warehouse worker, shot and killed President John F. Kennedy, the leader of the free world and arguably the most powerful man in the world, it became clear to many Americans that they were not, in fact, invincible. Americans were shocked and experienced strong emotions for this person whom they never met. That death, like that of a close family member, changed Americans. However, since this death was an international event, it had a similar effect on American nationalism and identity.

In an effort to trace the path that America took in the wake of the Kennedy assassination, this book will follow Robert F. Kennedy and Martin Luther King in the aftermath of that tragedy until 1968. In addition, the perspective of Lyndon Johnson will play a role in exploring this period in

American history. All three men had a hand in shaping that period. It is fair to say that their contributions paved the way for greater change in the nation. This study will delve into the workings of the Senate and White House as they debated the Gulf of Tonkin Resolution through the perspective of Kennedy and Johnson. It will also consider the many civil rights issues under King's watch as the primary leader of the movement. Since Vietnam and civil rights played such a prominent role in those years, an analysis of these individuals could provide some important insight. In a larger sense they were part of a cathartic transformation that brought America into an awakening.

Robert Kennedy had a unique vantage point. The loss of his brother and his role as attorney general provides insight not only into the grief the nation endured, but also the problems that plagued American society. Kennedy was there to witness the racial divide in the country from the early days in Greensboro, North Carolina, to the harrowing standoff at Selma to the tragedy of Dr. King's death. He was also present in the Cabinet Room for the early days of Vietnam under his brother's administration to his days in the Senate when the first troops landed in 1965 to American's experience of the Tet Offensive in 1968. Bobby was a witness to the travails that shaped this nation at a crucial time, and his perspective can give historians insight into those events.

Martin Luther King, Jr., did more to focus the nonviolent philosophy of the civil rights movement than any other leader. His skillful use of the tactic paved the way to influence not only African American civil rights, but also other movements in the nation. His vision continues to serve as a lightning rod for change—blazing a path into the twenty-first century. This book will look at both his rhetoric and his actions in the wake of John Kennedy's tragic death. The Civil Rights Act of 1964 and the Voting Rights Act of 1965 are testaments to his unwillingness to give up in the face of hardship. To be sure, King's words have been etched in stone, moving future generations to aspire to his vision, helming the nation to achieve its lofty ideals of freedom and equality.

On another, related, front, this book will delve into the impact of the Vietnam War as well as how American leaders debated and ultimately implemented their policy in Southeast Asia. The war affected a generation of Americans differently than any other fought by Americans. This book will explore how that war contributed to the distrust of and disillusionment in the U.S. government as it perpetrated its policy in Vietnam, which is something unprecedented in U.S. history, and laid the foundation for subsequent generations to rethink the government's actions in future wars.

The assassination was something that shut down the nation for four days. People gathered on the street as the flag-draped casket was pulled by horses to Arlington National Cemetery. Dressed in black and holding Jacqueline Kennedy's hand, Robert Kennedy ushered his brother to his final resting place, at the foot of Robert E. Lee's home, where a flame still burns today, and not far from where he would eventually rest after his own assassination in 1968. The nation saw Robert Kennedy as the heir to the Kennedy legacy, a reminder that there was a time when the Kennedy brothers had a vision for the nation. He had enormous pressure from the American people as well as his family to take up this mantle, despite his grief, while at the same time to discover his voice and cause separate from his fallen brother, even though it pained him to do so.

Robert Kennedy stayed on as attorney general despite the feelings he had for Lyndon Johnson. The Kennedy agenda was still before Congress, and LBJ had the ability to get some of it passed. While RFK showed public support for Johnson, he also had a private contempt for the man who now occupied his brother's office. He stayed on at the president's urging, but it would not be long before Bobby looked to make his own mark. On August 22, 1964, Robert Kennedy announced to the world that he would run for senator of New York. This study will discuss that candidacy and how Robert Kennedy used his office to make a difference in the lives of the dispossessed and to expose injustice, not only in America but throughout the world. His actions were part of a larger movement that sprang from his brother's rhetoric, which Robert Kennedy tried to make reality in the wake of his brother's murder. That quest would bring him to Bedford Stuyvesant in Brooklyn to help the impoverished and to South Africa to confront apartheid, culminating in a run for the presidency in 1968.

In many ways Robert Kennedy was the embodiment of his times. Prior to his brother's murder he was cautious politically, considering the ramifications on any stand for human rights. After his brother died, he had an awakening wherein he embraced the cause of others and searched for his own voice. The nation went down a similar path. The American people screamed for the Beatles' "I Saw Her Standing There" in 1964, then embraced the Doors' "Light My Fire" in 1968. That generation had its own evolution in which they disregarded caution and embraced change. This was a new America, born from the ashes of November 22, 1963. This rebirth contributed to the relentless vilification of Lyndon Johnson and his policy in Vietnam as the casualties were part of dinner-table chatter and classroom debates, diminishing and forever altering America's place in the world.

Martin Luther King and the Kennedy brothers worked to change the climate of the nation together in those early days of the 1960s. In the years that John Kennedy was in office, more had been done for civil rights than at any other time in American history, save the end of the Civil War. King was twenty-six when he was thrust into the national spotlight. He was chosen by the Montgomery Improvement Association to lead a boycott of the buses. Suddenly this young preacher with a doctorate from Boston University was a national leader on civil rights.

King was committed to nonviolent direct action and challenged segregation in the South with this tactic. He was very successful at Montgomery but stalled somewhat as his new group, the Southern Christian Leadership Conference (SCLC), worked to make its name in the movement. He encountered great success when the Kennedys were in office. He supported the Freedom Rides, challenged Bull Connor in Birmingham and led the March on Washington. While the movement was largely grassroots in nature, King emerged as a natural leader.

After the March on Washington in August 1963, Martin Luther King, Jr., solidified his place as the leader of African Americans in this nation. Indeed there were many who made that claim, but it was clear that King had the support of the majority of African Americans. Many historians consider his "I Have a Dream" speech as the greatest speech of the twentieth century, second only to Lincoln's "Gettysburg Address" in American history. King's vision for America was tested in the days after Kennedy's assassination. Despite the passage of the Civil Rights Act in 1964 there were still many injustices in the nation. This book will analyze what role Dr. King played in shaping the civil rights movement further, giving it a voice that survives into the twenty-first century. Like Johnson and Kennedy, King was someone who affected the period. He was at the center of voting rights, supporting Freedom Summer, marching in Selma and empowering the impoverished. He and Robert Kennedy shared their concern over the plight of the dispossessed and spoke out against Vietnam.

Martin Luther King, Jr., was a world figure that inspired millions. He is the only nonpresident to have a monument on the National Mall, among Lincoln, Jefferson, FDR, and Washington. Like Lyndon Johnson and Robert Kennedy, he found himself in a place where he could affect change in the wake of the president's assassination. For years many civil rights leaders challenged King's leadership. After the March on Washington, the Civil Rights Act of 1964, a Nobel Peace Prize, and the Voting Rights Act of 1965, it was apparent that he was the one to bring about the change he preached in his "I Have a Dream" speech. His subsequent actions, culminating with his death in 1968, set in motion a movement in the United States that continues to generate momentum.

Lyndon Johnson was a Texas politician who was inspired by FDR's New Deal. He wanted to bring those types of programs to the people of

Texas, creating opportunities for everyone. He started in the House of Representatives and moved on to the Senate. He had a storied career in both houses getting legislation passed and strong-arming people into seeing things his way. In 1960 he ran for president, but he lost to Kennedy in the primaries. When the convention came around, much to the chagrin of John and Robert's father Joseph Kennedy, Johnson was selected to run as the vice president. JFK knew that he needed Johnson in the South and that he would deliver. This move secured LBJ's place in history. After John Kennedy was murdered, Johnson took over the presidency, inherited the Kennedy agenda with all its issues, and tried to bring those ideas that he had as a young congressman not only to Texans but the whole nation.

Civil rights and Vietnam remained at the forefront for LBJ. He inherited both of them from JFK. In the case of civil rights, the Kennedy brothers worked hard to change the climate of the nation. In 1961 Johnson would never have been able to pass the type of civil rights bill he signed in 1964. After the Kennedy brothers and the civil rights leaders brought those issues out, it was possible for Johnson to push the 1964 bill through Congress, making history. Vietnam, on the other hand, was never a priority for John Kennedy. He was more concerned with the Soviet Union. That said, Kennedy believed it was worth sixteen thousand Americans advising the South Vietnamese. Johnson may have inherited that situation, but it was his actions that escalated the war, making it difficult for him to pass his domestic program that he always dreamed of. This book will explore Johnson's Cabinet Room as they debated America's involvement in Vietnam in the wake of Tonkin and Pleiku in an effort to gain a deeper understanding of Johnson's actions in the context of the sixties.

Lyndon Johnson can be credited with implementing the greatest domestic agenda since the New Deal. His Great Society and the War on Poverty reinvigorated liberalism. As a result, it also emboldened the conservative movement. Were it not for his political prowess, those bills would never have made it through Congress. His vision for America, however, was in danger as the nation sent more troops to fight in Vietnam. Lyndon Johnson galvanized the nation. His actions in Vietnam led to a march of protest against the U.S. government. Since then, the United States has experienced similar movements, but nothing that would change the nation in that manner. In addition, his domestic program continues to generate debate in Congress and on the air waves.

The nation did not embrace Johnson in the same spirit that they did the New Frontier. The assassination affected the nation in a negative way for Johnson in that the people were even more inspired by JFK in his death than when he was alive. Johnson was nothing like Kennedy. Americans naturally moved away from him as a way of rejecting someone who tried to replace their fallen leader. Every president after JFK endured a great deal of scrutiny, arguably more than any other in the history of the presidency. Part of this feeling was the distrust that Johnson sowed with Vietnam, and later it was compounded by Richard Nixon's actions in the Watergate scandal as well as the exposure of the Pentagon Papers, to name a few. The nation was changing. No longer would it turn a blind eye to indiscretion and negligence. The American people looked to hold their leaders accountable.

This book looks to illuminate how the period from 1963 to 1968 changed America, generating movements and philosophies that shifted American thought, in essence creating a new American identity. Gone were the days of the western frontier or American factories that embodied true Americanism. While those events and contributions are still a part of the American spirit, the world saw a new nation emerge after John F. Kennedy's murder. This period gave birth to a generation that would move America from a producer of goods to a consumer-driven economy; from a racist, discriminating society to a nation accepting of differences; from a nation that saw war at times as the only option to one that did its best to stay away from war; from a political atmosphere that banded together in the first half of the twentieth century to one that polarized the nation into the twenty-first century.

America has gone through several transformations in its history, with each era building on the previous one. The sixties were not any different than those eras. The period from 1963 to 1968 was a bridge where America found new voices, economic thought, military know-how, political philosophies and pop-culture that served as a foundation for the subsequent decades. In fact most of what people view as "the sixties" did not make an appearance until after Kennedy's death. The major movements, rooted in antiwar protest, gained momentum post-assassination. The Beatles, the Doors, Bob Dylan, Janice Joplin and Woodstock also came in the aftermath. The years 1960 to 1963 were much like the fifties, rooted in Cold War ideology. Even Robert Kennedy transformed in appearance from a short-haired, close-cropped haircut to a shaggy one. America changed not only ideologically, but also physically. The nation was at a crossroads that would define the next three decades until another event, in the early morning of September 11, 2001, started a new era in American history.

Prologue—"Jack's Been Shot"

On March 2, 1966, the Rev. Dr. Martin Luther King, Jr., sent a letter to Senator Robert F. Kennedy to "applaud" him for a statement he made on the Vietnam War. "You have expressed a political philosophy for an era," King wrote. "In the past two decades the radical transformation of the world has not evoked a rational and realistic system of ideas that correspond to altered world relationships." King had been battling racism as the leader of the movement. His mention of "rational and realistic system of ideas" spoke to the fact that he looked for those qualities in political leaders that were lacking in the South. To be sure, the embattled civil rights leader was looking for hope that someone could complement his ideals for the new world. While Robert Kennedy and King did not always see eye to eye, as they grew in their leadership roles, they became closer in their philosophies of where America needed to go as they moved forward. "Problems have been approached piece-meal, in isolation and, unhappily, without creative or bold imagination," King wrote. It had been nearly three years since John F. Kennedy had been assassinated, and the world was still dealing with the vestiges of that tragedy.

King believed that President Kennedy had an impact on the civil rights movement, and his loss had an effect on the movement. King wrote, "Former President Kennedy, your great brother, carried us far in new directions and his concept of a world of diversity; your position advances us to the next step which requires us to reach the political maturity to recognize and relate to all elements produced by the contemporary colonial revolutions." The nation, indeed the world, was changing. King and Kennedy were at the center of such change. As the sixties continued to take shape, they would play a significant role in shaping a new American identity. "Years of struggle have demonstrated that the new elements, no matter how repugnant their politics ... are a viable force." King was impressed with Kennedy's "doctrine of sharing power and responsibility by affirmative action on our part. This policy served us well in partially abating tensions evoked by integration problems in the United States." King suggested that he apply that principle to international relations. He finished, saying, "I hope your leadership will prevail with the majority of the nation and I shall continue to do whatever I am able to assist toward that end."[1]

Robert Kennedy responded to King's letter on March 31, 1966, saying, "You may well flatter my statement. But I agree with your profound insight that we are now called upon to work in the world politically—to see interests of all people as interests which must be reconciled, in a manner which does violence to the central interests of as few people as possible." Kennedy's vision for the nation included a larger role in world affairs. He understood the responsibility the nation had to lead. With the Vietnam conflict finding its stride, Kennedy continued to share his vision for the world: "I think—and certainly I hope—that we can preserve our basic values of freedom and dignity, indeed extend them throughout the world, without incessant military conflict with those whose more immediate interests are different from our own." At this point, Kennedy was at an ideological crescendo of finding his voice, speaking out against the Vietnam War, focusing on a policy that did not advocate the use of force. In just a couple of months after this letter, Kennedy would go to South Africa, giving the message that he is most known for, opposing apartheid and discrimination, showcasing his vision of hope for the world.

While Kennedy had his own beliefs and at one point saw King's vision as impractical, by 1966 he had come full circle and was now a part of King's movement. "And I would add if we succeed in this effort," he wrote, including himself, "much of the credit will be due to you and your colleagues in the Civil Rights Movement." Bobby not only acknowledged the movement; he emphasized the role that King played and applauded it. He went further:

> You have taught us a great deal about reconciling opposed interests within our own country; your statement of 1960, that you were concerned not with the "New Jerusalem," but with "the New Atlanta, the New Birmingham, the New Montgomery, the New South," was in my judgement a landmark in American history.

Kennedy believed that this notion was "a commitment to solve our problems not by escaping to the North or to the West but by facing our conflicts and resolving them where we stood." He concluded that if what he had witnessed on his recent trips to Mississippi and Alabama was any indication, "your future success in the South is assured." He thanked him for the letter and "for the deep perception it contained, and for its kind thoughts."[2]

These two giants of the sixties did a great deal to help the nation heal from the tragic death of President John F. Kennedy. Together, they also shaped the rhetoric that would inspire Americans and drive the nation toward a new era, one that would embrace rights and peace more so than any other moment in the history of the nation. They were affected by the rights movements of the decades, the Vietnam conflict and the stark reality that death was always lurking around the corner when people embark on such magnificent change. These letters do not tell the full story. They show an exchange between two leaders after they have found their voice and endured great hardship and tragedy. The tone and camaraderie in these letters was not there when these two men came across each other in the history.

In 1960 there was a young preacher fighting to change the nature of men and a nation, looking for support from a government that had historically turned its back on its own citizens for nearly one hundred years, who believed that nonviolence was the best route to confront the violent nature of segregation. On the other side was a young campaign manager who believed that he fought communism and corruption in the Senate, living to serve his older, charismatic brother, with a family burden to bear and the prospect of disappointing them if he was unsuccessful. These men, speaking six years after their initial meeting in history, had come a long way to shape a nation. They only had two years left and would continue, until the day they died, to serve their cause.

The Kennedy assassination would do even more to bring these men into the history books. In that vacuum of leadership, they were there to take the torch, as JFK said, and carry on those ideals that had shaped the New Frontier. While it took them time to establish their own voice, that vision played an important role in American history. To be sure, it was a moment that Americans would not forget. People remembered where they were and when they heard about it, what they were eating, whom they were speaking to, what was on television or the radio when it was interrupted to tell the world what had happened. It was an event that shaped a generation, creating a different America in its wake, moving from an age of innocence and wonder to disbelief, distrust and war.

Robert F. Kennedy stopped home for lunch at Hickory Hill, his home in Virginia, when he found out. He wanted a break after attending meetings on organized crime and was with Robert Morgenthau and Silvio Mollo, who were members of the criminal investigation division of the Department of Justice. Just as they were leaving, they saw some commotion on the side of the house, where some workers heard a news report on the radio. At the same time the phone rang and Ethel Kennedy called Bobby in. It was J. Edgar Hoover, the director of the FBI. Kennedy listened for a brief period and hung up. He could not speak for a few seconds. The look of "shock and horror" prompted Ethel to go to him. He finally said, "Jack's been shot. It may be fatal."[3]

Robert F. Kennedy's brief period in American history coincided with one of the most tumultuous times in the history of the United States. He came on the scene in the 1950s, working for Senator Joseph McCarthy and later Senator John McClellan's "Rackets Committee." He sat alongside his famous brother, then Senator John F. Kennedy, and questioned union bosses and mobsters. The venture garnered media attention, and the "Kennedy brothers," as they became to be known, arrived on the national scene. Bobby Kennedy never wavered and always looked for justice. These were formative years for the younger Kennedy. The experiences shaped his beliefs, strengthening moral codes that he would build on later in life. "My biggest problem as counsel is to keep my temper," Robert Kennedy said later of his time on the committee. "To see people sit in front of us and lie and evade makes me boil inside. But you can't lose your temper—if you do, the witness has gotten the best of you."[4] He went after Teamster boss Jimmy Hoffa and Chicago crime boss Momo Salvatore Giancana. When Giancana refused to answer questions and pled the Fifth Amendment as his defense, Robert Kennedy said, "Would you tell us anything about your operations or will you just giggle every time I ask you a question?" Giancana responded, "I decline to answer because I honestly believe my answer might tend to incriminate me." Kennedy quickly said, "I thought only little girls giggled, Mr. Giancana."[5] His audacity was legendary, but it was rooted in the notion that justice was on his side. When he became attorney general for his brother's administration, that sense of morality would be both challenged and discovered anew.

King entered the national scene with the Montgomery Bus Boycott in 1955. He led the Montgomery Improvement Association to challenge the segregation of the buses in the city after Rosa Parks refused to stand up, challenging the status quo that had been so pervasive since the end of the Civil War. King was threatened, his house bombed and his family harassed. He came out of this experience in the forefront of the movement, changing the direction and philosophy to one of nonviolent direct action. Despite the many threats to his life, he continued to say that love would be the only weapon against hate. When a crowd gathered outside his home in the wake of the bombing that threatened not only King but also Coretta Scott King and their newborn baby, King emphasized his commitment to nonviolence in his address to the people:

> Don't get panicky. Don't do anything panicky. Don't get your weapons. If you have weapons, take them home. He who lives by the sword will perish by the sword.

Remember that is what Jesus said. We are not advocating violence. We want to love our enemies. Be good to them. This is what we must live by. We must meet hate with love.[6]

That response is indicative of his relentless pursuit to fuse nonviolent tactics in the struggle of equal rights. King was in the forefront of that new type of protest that would inspire young people especially to pick up this tactic and stand up to oppression and violence in the name of segregation.

Robert Kennedy's first experience with injustice came during the election of 1960 when four college students challenged segregation at a Woolworths in Greensboro, North Carolina. While he was removed from that act, the event would eventually affect his brother's pursuit of the White House when Martin Luther King, Jr., was arrested in Atlanta for participating in what would be termed as the sit-in movement, which sprang from that day in North Carolina. This was the first time that the two leaders crossed paths. While they did not meet face to face at this point, the episode played a major role in the election.

The presiding judge refused to grant bail to King due to a previous traffic violation. At the suggestion of Harris Wofford and Sargent Shriver, advisers to the campaign, John F. Kennedy called Coretta Scott King, saying, "I want to express to you my concern about your husband. I know this must be very hard for you." He went on, "I understand you are expecting a baby, and I just wanted you to know that I was thinking about you and Dr. King. If there is anything I can do to help, please feel free to call on me."[7] It was a short phone call, a candidate reaching out to the wife of an embattled leader. To be sure, it was symbolic that John F. Kennedy did not agree with the segregationist governments in the South, and the phone call was akin to saying that the judge and the institution that had imprisoned King was wrong. Robert Kennedy was furious. John Seigenthaler called Wofford and Shriver on behalf of Robert Kennedy, saying, "Bob wants to see you bomb throwers right away."[8]

Robert Kennedy understood that the election was going to be close. Politicians in the South did not want to see anyone in the White House who was friendly to civil rights leaders. He said to Shriver and Wofford, "Do you know that three southern governors told us that if Jack supported Jimmy Hoffa, Nikita Khrushchev, or Martin Luther King they would throw their states to Nixon? Do you know that this election may be razor close and you have probably just lost it for us?"[9] However, when Robert Kennedy was told that the judge denied Martin Luther King bail, his tone changed. Robert Kennedy responded, "How could they do that? You can't deny bail on a misdemeanor."[10] Eventually his desire to see justice prevail would overcome his political ambition. The impetuous campaign manager stopped thinking about the election and realized that King had been treated horribly. Robert Kennedy called the judge and said, "Are you American? Do you know what it means to be an American? You get King out of Jail."[11] King was released on bail, and the Kennedy brothers would win one of the closest elections in history.

Martin Luther King and Bobby would come together again in history. Little did they know that their relationship would inspire millions of Americans. That story was an important element of the sixties and would prove to shape not only the times that they lived in, but also the decades that followed—having a ripple effect that continued into the twenty-first century. These first instances of their partnership highlight the fact that they agreed on the injustices that the South employed to maintain its oppressive regime and deny African Americans their rights as guaranteed by the Constitution. They were also still finding their voice and considering where their ideas fit into the movement. The years that followed the election would prove to bring them even closer to finding a common voice.

After Robert Kennedy served as campaign manager for his brother's campaign in 1960, he was appointed as attorney general of the United States. This gave him the unique opportunity to act on what he saw as an injustice. In his first speech as attorney general, Robert Kennedy addressed the University of Georgia Law School on May 6, 1961. He said in that speech, "We know too that throughout the long history of mankind, man has had to struggle to create a system of law and of government in which fundamental freedoms would be linked with the enforcement of justice." He went on, "We know that if one man's rights are denied, the rights of all are endangered."[12] Robert Kennedy believed in a world that embraced the law. His privileged upbringing, however, fostered a naïveté that made it difficult for him to see the world as it was—not right and wrong, but shades of gray. In his time as attorney general the younger Kennedy was involved in events that would lay the groundwork for the rest of the sixties, indeed the century. The civil rights movement would bring Kennedy and King together again at a moment in history where the nation began its road to changing the fabric of societal norms, ushering in an age that fostered the rights of minorities, leading to an era where the majority of minority groups would become a force in politics and social change.

As John F. Kennedy's closest confidant, Robert Kennedy was always present when there was an important decision to be made on foreign policy. After the Bay of Pigs, a CIA-led operation to oust Castro, JFK called on his brother to help him make most decisions. John Kennedy's distrust of the military establishment went back to his days in the navy while stationed in the South Pacific during the Second World War. After an incident where a

Japanese destroyer rammed into Lt. John F. Kennedy's patrol boat *PT 109*, he wrote home saying, "People get used to talking about billions of dollars and millions of soldiers that thousands of dead sound like a drop in the bucket. But if those thousands want to live as much as the ten I saw—they would measure their words with great, great care."[13] Bobby Kennedy shared his brother's concern over military power after the Bay of Pigs. He looked not only to advise his brother but also to guard JFK's legacy. Indeed, Robert Kennedy was not blind to the importance of the events that shaped John Kennedy's one thousand days in office.

Before a pivotal meeting with Soviet premier Nikita Khrushchev at Vienna in 1961, Robert F. Kennedy was challenged by civil rights groups on the issue of segregation in the South. Confronted with his first major issue of rights, Robert Kennedy looked to the law to lead the way. America was not ready to fully embrace civil rights in 1961. The Congress of Racial Equality (CORE) and the Student Nonviolent Coordinating Committee (SNCC) tried to desegregate the bus system. They were called Freedom Riders, and they encountered major resistance in Alabama. They were beaten in Birmingham and Montgomery. One of the buses they were riding was torched by the Ku Klux Klan in Anniston. Robert Kennedy sent John Seigenthaler, a Justice Department official, who was also beaten by the same mob that attacked John Lewis in Montgomery, to help these civil rights warriors. It culminated in a face-off at the First Baptist Church in Montgomery. The Kennedys were hoping that the governor of Alabama, John Patterson, would intervene and send relief. He refused, believing that the Freedom Riders were unwanted in Alabama. Kennedy acted by sending in U.S. Marshals. Martin Luther King came to Montgomery, where his first pastorship was, to support the Riders. He arrived at the First Baptist Church and encountered an angry mob outside. Once again, Kennedy and King found themselves connected in history.

Dr. King, Ralph Abernathy, John Lewis and many others were held up in the church while a mob outside threw Molotov cocktails and bricks at the building and yelled racial slurs. Kennedy and King had a conversation on the phone during the incident. In an effort to break the tension, Kennedy said, "There were our people down there, and as long as he was in church, he might say a prayer for us." Kennedy remembered, "He didn't think that was very humorous." Kennedy said that King "rather berated me for what was happening to him at the time. And I said to him that I didn't think that he'd be alive if it wasn't for us, and that we were going to keep him alive, and that the marshals would keep the church from burning down." In fact King reminded Kennedy that the mob was getting more violent and was threatening the people in the church. "We're going to have a bloody confrontation," he said to Kennedy.[14] At the behest of Kennedy, Patterson sent in the National Guard to escort the Freedom Riders, Dr. King and others to safety. The incident awakened Robert Kennedy to the evils of segregation and racism. It was the first step on a road that would eventually lead him to embrace the plight of others. For King, it contributed to his status as the civil rights leader for the nation, paving the way toward the Nobel Peace Prize.

In the same year of the Freedom Rides John F. Kennedy was confronted with the first major foreign policy crisis of his administration after the Bay of Pigs. After his meeting with Khrushchev in Vienna, JFK was challenged by the Soviet Union on access rights to Berlin with the truculent act of putting a wall up in between East and West Berlin as a way to stop the flow of refugees from the east to the west. After the failed attack at the Bay of Pigs in Cuba, John F. Kennedy needed a strong response to Soviet posturing and building the Berlin wall that would symbolize the differences between the Soviet Union and the United States to the world. Indeed, Cold War polemics called for such a response. JFK brought up the reserves and ordered the military to defend West Berlin. It seemed that the world was going to war. Robert Kennedy was by his side for the whole crisis. It was Bobby's back-channel correspondence with Georgi Bolshakov, a Khrushchev emissary, that helped ease the tension between Khrushchev and Kennedy, bringing the nation away from the brink of war.[15]

As if the Freedom Riders and the standoff in Berlin were not enough, 1962 proved to be the most important year in the short-lived Kennedy presidency. In an effort to continue the challenge against segregation, James Meredith challenged the University of Mississippi segregation policy. Bobby Kennedy and Ross Barnett squared off publicly with charged rhetoric and privately in telephone calls that eventually involved President Kennedy. This time Nicholas Katzenbach, the deputy attorney general, stood resolute on the Ole Miss campus, on Bobby Kennedy's orders, to protect Meredith at all costs, despite the growing riot that would ultimately kill people and bring the army back to the South.[16] His actions, with JFK's support, contributed to the America understanding of the race problem and the desire to do something about it. The Kennedy brothers were slowly shifting the climate in America to accept civil rights on a broad scale, forever changing not only the political landscape, but also the very fabric of American society.

In the days following the Ole Miss crisis, Robert Kennedy was once again thrust into the throes of history, contributing to a decision-making process that had the potential to change the world. Nikita Khrushchev installed nuclear missiles in Cuba hoping to push John Kennedy on Berlin.

When JFK found out he immediately called his brother to be by his side. For thirteen days the so-called "EXCOMM" debated what to do about the missiles, which represented a threat to the security of the United States. Robert Kennedy and Secretary of Defense Robert McNamara had pushed for a blockade of Cuba, while the military and other advisers favored an invasion of the island. RFK and McNamara won the day, and JFK blockaded the island in order gain time to weigh other, diplomatic options.[17]

The crisis culminated in a meeting between Robert Kennedy and Soviet ambassador Anatoly Dobrynin. Robert Kennedy wrote a memo discussing his role in the meeting. He said, "Mr. Khrushchev and he had misled us. The Soviet Union had secretly established missile bases in Cuba while at the same time proclaiming, privately and publicly, that this would never be done. I said those missile bases had to go and they had to go right away." Playing an unprecedented role for an attorney general, he told Dobrynin with regard to an exchange of missiles in Turkey for missiles in Cuba that there could be "no quid pro quo—no deal of this kind could be made. This was a matter that had to be considered by NATO and that it was up to NATO to make the decision." He went on to say that it was "completely impossible for NATO to take such a step under the present threatening position of the Soviet Union."[18] The missiles in Turkey and a pledge not to invade Cuba was the carrot that Khrushchev needed to withdraw the missiles in Cuba. Robert Kennedy was at the center of the most dangerous moment of the Cold War.

While Kennedy did not make it public that the United States would not invade if the missiles were removed, there was, however, a secret deal to remove the missiles in Turkey five to six months later. Kennedy wrote to his brother, "Per your instructions I repeated that there could be no deal of any kind and that any steps toward easing tensions in other parts of the world largely depended on the Soviet Union and Mr. Khrushchev taking action in Cuba and taking it immediately." He finished by saying that he needed an answer the next day or otherwise there could be "drastic consequences."[19] Khrushchev cabled President Kennedy the next day and said he would withdraw the missiles. Robert Kennedy served as a messenger to the Russians at a crucial time in the Cuban missile crisis. This extraordinary period in history was still not over as RFK still had to confront America's inner demons in the South in 1963.

America continued to struggle with the race issue and Robert Kennedy and Martin Luther King, Jr., became allies in the struggle for civil rights. In April 1963 Martin Luther King exposed the vicious tactics of Birmingham's Eugene "Bull" Connor. King led a movement to desegregate what many people saw as the most graphic and oppressive symbol of segregation in the South. John and Robert Kennedy watched as the news agencies shared pictures of German shepherds biting into the stomachs of marchers and children getting bulldozed by powerful fire hoses that took the mortar off the sides of brick buildings. It was the final awakening that the nation and the Kennedy brothers needed to make their move. Robert Kennedy recalled later, "What Bull Connor did down there, and the dogs and hoses and the pictures with the Negroes, is what created in the United States that more needed to be done."[20] Birmingham was what Robert Kennedy needed to begin legislation to eradicate segregation from the United States. RFK recalled, "Well, now we had to do something to deal with this kind of problem, and the country wanted something done and would support action being taken. So that's why we moved in the direction that we did."[21]

It was in Birmingham that Martin Luther King wrote his eloquent defense of his actions in the movement and how he felt that African Americans could not wait any longer for full equality under the law. "We know through painful experience that freedom is never voluntarily given by the oppressor; it must be demanded by the oppressed," he wrote. In a response to his critics, King said, "Frankly, I have yet to engage in a direct-action campaign that was 'well timed' in the view of those who have not suffered unduly from the disease of segregation." This letter has been lauded by many scholars as King's greatest defense of the movement. To be sure, it played a big role in helping his contemporaries, who were critical of his actions, understand his philosophy. "For years now I have heard the word 'Wait!' It rings in the ear of every Negro with piercing familiarity. This 'Wait' has almost always meant 'Never.' We must come to see, with one of our distinguished jurists, that 'justice too long delayed is justice denied.'"[22] The "Letter from Birmingham Jail" was a turning point for King. It also seemed clear in the wake of the Birmingham campaign that Robert Kennedy had evolved in his views of the civil rights struggle.

Robert Kennedy moved from a reluctant politician on issues of race to a civil rights advocate determined to change the situation in the United States. In a May 17, 1963, speech he said, "The American Negro is only beginning to raise his voice in protest. His protest is justified, and our responsibility is clear."[23] The following month RFK orchestrated the integration of the University of Alabama with Vivian Malone and James Hood. As soon as they were safely enrolled, despite the defiant actions of George Wallace, Bobby and his most trusted adviser, Burke Marshall, implored John Kennedy to say something definitive on the race issue in the country. They prevailed and JFK sent legislation to desegregate the nation. In his June 11, 1963, speech to the nation, which RFK helped to write, JFK said he would desegregate public facilities. The Civil Rights Bill was sent to Congress and in August of that year civil rights leaders marched on Lincoln Memorial demanding its passage.

On the precipice of that fateful day in November 1963, Robert Kennedy and Martin Luther King were at a crossroads in their public lives. After the tumultuous period of the early sixties, they were poised to make a difference in the days that followed. To be sure, the assassination of John F. Kennedy changed that dynamic. After King's eloquent "I have a Dream" speech that defined a movement, the nation was moving toward greater acceptance of racial equality. It was the pinnacle of the civil rights movement. While most of it was the result of people like John Lewis, Medgar Evers, Bayard Rustin, Martin Luther King, Diane Nash, Ella Baker and Rosa Parks, history cannot ignore that the awakening of Robert Kennedy's desire for justice played a role in that historic triumph for equality. Indeed, Bobby Kennedy had every intention to usher that bill through Congress for his brother to sign. But that would never happen.

PART I. AMERICA IN THE WAKE OF TRAGEDY, 1963

1

November 22, 1963

I

"The President's dead."

On November 22, 1963, Robert F. Kennedy had to endure not only the death of his president but also his best friend and brother, someone he looked up to as a boy and wanted to be like when he entered the navy. FBI Director J. Edgar Hoover called around 2:30 p.m. and said, "The president's dead." RFK looked at Ethel and said, "He had the most wonderful life." In his short tenure in the White House, John F. Kennedy set in motion a path that would have reverberations after his death. In that instant, Robert F. Kennedy became the standard-bearer for the family and the New Frontier.

Of course, John Kennedy's death had greatly affected Bobby. His biographer Evan Thomas writes that RFK "embraced his children as they returned from school and gently comforted them. His grace was touching, but a veneer. Grief would descend over Kennedy like a veil. In time, from long suffering would come transcendence and wisdom."[1] When Hoover called about JFK's death, RFK recalled, "I think he told me with pleasure." Hoover's voice was flat, "not quite as excited as if he were reporting the fact the he had found a communist on the faculty of Howard University."[2] This new reality had an effect on Bobby that would shape the rest of his life.

In his brief time on his own, Robert Kennedy would come to mean something to a nation that not only grieved for a lost leader, but also struggled with the issue of race and the crisis in Vietnam. Some people saw him as the light they could follow and remake the country, despite the fact that JFK was no longer among them. Bobby was nothing like his brother and would slowly, almost begrudgingly, accept this new role, bringing into the spotlight and revitalizing a political discourse that his brother had started in 1960.

As he paced back and forth on the lawn beside his house awaiting word of his brother's fate, Robert Kennedy recalled that he had received a letter from someone in Texas prior to that trip. The letter said that JFK should not go to Dallas because someone would kill him. He forwarded the letter to Kenny O'Donnell, Special Assistant to President Kennedy, but never thought that it would happen. "I thought it would be me," he said to Edwin Guthman later. "There is so much bitterness. I thought they would get one of us, but Jack, after all he'd been through, never worried about it."[3]

Jack Kennedy had been a sick boy. He overcame his illness, served in World War II, published two books (one of them won the Pulitzer Prize), and ran successfully for the House of Representatives and the Senate, culminating in a successful bid for the presidency in 1960. Addison's disease, as well as other ailments, had plagued his body to the point where he was given last rites on several occasions. He was not supposed to be in the White House. His older brother Joseph Kennedy was the presumptive politician, but a mission in World War II had claimed Joe's life. JFK had decided to run not because of his fallen brother, but because of his desire to affect events in the world. In the wake of yet another tragedy in the Kennedy family, Robert Kennedy was presented with a similar fate that his famous older brother was in 1944 when the Army Chaplain knocked on the door in Hyannis Port to inform the family of Joe Kennedy, Jr.'s death.

Robert Kennedy's loss was also the nation's. As the country tried to make sense of John F. Kennedy's death, it changed. The nation, in the middle of its grief, started to see the world differently. A young inspirational leader had been torn away and now they had to deal with that loss. John F. Kennedy symbolized the future, looking to the stars, staring down the Soviets and moving America into a New Frontier. In addition to this tragic loss, Robert Kennedy's relationship with now-President Lyndon Johnson was tense, and he knew that he did not have the power that came with his brother in the Oval Office. This new dynamic immediately had an effect on the role Robert F. Kennedy played in government.

Robert Kennedy wanted to know if there was more to the murder than the lone assassin. Kennedy asked John McCone, the director of the CIA, to come by Hickory Hill, Robert Kennedy's home in Virginia. He asked McCone if the CIA had anything to do with JFK's death. McCone, like Robert Kennedy, was very religious, and RFK had allegedly asked him about the CIA's involvement in such a way that it invoked their shared belief in Catholicism. Under that premise, McCone swore that the CIA did not have any role in the tragedy. Kennedy went further, becoming obsessed to some degree, and looked for a Cuban or mafia connection. He found nothing. Bobby Kennedy was suddenly thrust into the patriarch role of the family.[4]

Robert Kennedy and Lyndon Johnson's relationship was complicated on many levels. Jeff Shesol writes in his book *Mutual Contempt: Lyndon Johnson,*

1: November 22, 1963

Robert Kennedy and the Feud that Defined a Decade that "the rivalry between LBJ and RFK was of a different magnitude—and of greater importance— than any of the postwar era. Their antagonism spawned political turf battles across the United States. It divided constituencies the two men once shared and weakened their party by forcing its members to choose between them."[5] In the wake of his brother's death, Bobby Kennedy had to suddenly accept the reality that Lyndon Johnson was president of the United States. That reality hit home almost immediately after Kennedy found out about his brother's death. It was more than accepting a new leader taking over for his brother. Robert Kennedy believed that Johnson was not worthy.

Robert Kennedy and Lyndon Johnson's relationship dated back to the Senate when Bobby worked on the "Rackets Committee." However, the heart of the rift between the men actually took place at the Democratic National Convention in 1960. It was a great triumph for the Kennedy campaign and a defeat for Johnson who came into the race too late to be a true contender. In a last-minute effort to gain ground on what he viewed as a young, inexperienced candidate, Johnson challenged John F. Kennedy to a debate at the convention and had John Connally leak to the press that John Kennedy suffered from Addison's disease.[6] Both maneuvers backfired. JFK performed brilliantly at the debate, and Bobby never forgave Johnson for leaking the Addison's disease to the press.

The selection of JFK's vice president was very important. The 1960 election would be razor close. The Kennedys knew that JFK's youth and Catholicism were an issue in the election, and they needed some leverage in the South. They needed Lyndon Johnson. While Bobby considered Missouri senator Stu Symington and chairman of the Democratic National Committee Henry "Scoop" Jackson, the politically astute Jack Kennedy thought otherwise. In fact, JFK remarked to Walt Rostow in 1958 that Johnson had "the most legitimate claim in the party for the election." Kennedy knew that a southerner would be tough to elect. "It's too close to Appomattox," he said.[7] Jack Kennedy was also aware of Johnson's great ego. "Of course I want Lyndon Johnson," Kennedy said to Tip O'Neil at the convention. "The only things is, I would never want to offer it to him and have him turn me down. I would be terrifically embarrassed. He's the natural. If I can ever get him on the ticket, no way we can lose."[8]

The issue of Lyndon Johnson on the ballot was a source of tension between RFK and JFK. John Kennedy had gone off to offer Johnson the spot. He came back to the hotel room to tell Bobby what happened.

"You just won't believe it," JFK said

"What?" Bobby asked.

"He wants it."

"Oh my God."

"Now what do we do?" JFK asked.[9]

Robert Kennedy remembered in 1964, "So the thing is that we spent the rest of the day—and we both promised each other that we'd never tell what happened." Laughing, he continued, "But we spent the rest of the day alternating between thinking it was good and thinking that it wasn't good that he'd offered him the Vice Presidency and how we could get out of it."[10]

The brothers went back and forth on the matter. On the one hand they thought he should be on the ticket because "he would be so mean as majority leader," Bobby recalled. They also felt that by having him on the ticket they would be able to "control him." But after the back-and-forth, Robert Kennedy recalled that his brother ultimately wanted LBJ off the ticket. "Well we finally decided by about two o'clock that we'd try to get him out of there and not have him because Jack thought he would be unpleasant with him … and if we could get him to withdraw and still be happy that would be fine."[11] What happened after this discussion affected Robert Kennedy and Lyndon Johnson's relationship for the rest of their lives.

Robert Kennedy made two trips by his recollection to see Lyndon Johnson. The first one was "to sort of feel him out." The second trip was when he tried to get LBJ off the ticket. Bobby remembered that "there were just two of us there." Sam Rayburn had been at the first meeting but not at the second, according to Robert Kennedy's recollection, which was five years later. LBJ sat on the couch in his room and Bobby was at his right. "I remember the whole conversation," Bobby said in 1965. "So I went down to see if I could get him to withdraw, and, obviously with the close relationship between my brother…. I wasn't going down to see if he would withdraw just as a lark on my own."[12] Indeed, the account of this exchange between Johnson and the Kennedy brothers has been explored to the point where there is no clear story of who said what. It seems clear, however, that the brothers were trying to get Lyndon Johnson off the ticket while at the same time save political face.

According to Robert Kennedy, the brothers had worked out a story saying that "there's going to be a lot of opposition" for Johnson. He continued with his conversation, saying that it was going to be unpleasant,

> that it was going to focus attention, and we were going to have trouble with the liberals, and they were going to get up and fight, and the president didn't think that he wanted to go through that kind of an unpleasant fight, but the president wanted to have him play an important role, and he could run the party.[13]

In addition they were going to suggest that in eight years he could run for the presidency and have the "machinery" he needed to win. Bobby was clear in 1965 that at the convention his brother "wanted to get rid of him."[14]

Robert Kennedy remembered Johnson's reaction, saying, "He is one of the greatest sad-looking people in the world. You know he could turn that on; I thought he burst into tears." LBJ got emotional at the thought of leaving the ticket. RFK remembered, "He just shook, and tears came into his eyes, and said 'I want to be vice president, and if the president will have me, I'll join with him in making a fight for it.'" Bobby was taken aback. Clearly he saw no way out. So he replied, saying, "Well, then that's fine. He wants you to be vice president. We want you to know."[15] This humiliating experience left an indelible mark on LBJ. The fact that he had to nearly beg for a spot to Bobby, someone whom LBJ believed did not put in the time to be in that position, was never lost on Johnson and would haunt their relationship for the rest of Bobby's life.

These events were at the heart of the rift between Johnson and Robert Kennedy. Jeff Shesol writes, "The story of the 1960 Democratic National Convention—and the real beginning of the Johnson-Kennedy feud—is a convoluted chronology of misreadings, miscommunications, and missed connections."[16] Bobby even went as far as saying after his brother died, "There were only three persons who knew the whole story, and now one is gone. I guess it will have to wait until Lyndon and I write our memoirs."[17] Robert Caro writes, "Lyndon Johnson never forgot or forgave, could never, until he died, stop talking about, Robert Kennedy's visits to his hotel room during the 1960 Democratic convention to try to force him off the ticket."[18] Arthur Schlesinger asked Robert Kennedy why Johnson had a different version of the story. "It's wrong," Bobby said. He went further saying that Johnson "lies all the time. I'm telling you, he just lies continuously about everything. In every conversation I have with him, he lies. As I've said, he lies even when he doesn't have to lie." Kennedy laughed at the last comment.[19]

To add injury to insult, Lyndon Johnson was at a loss that he could not get Bobby Kennedy to embrace him the way others in politics had for years. After a White House dance in 1961, Johnson remarked, "Bobby, you do not like me.... Your brother likes me. Your sister-in-law likes me. Your Daddy likes me. But you don't like me. Now, why? Why don't you like me?"[20] Robert Kennedy did not like LBJ, and it was ever apparent in the wake of his brother's death. He once characterized LBJ as "mean, bitter, vicious—an animal in many ways." Johnson saw Bobby as a "grandstanding little runt."[21] Indeed, until 1964 RFK had not won an election in his own right. For LBJ that was an important distinction if someone wanted a seat at the table of politics.

This rivalry in the wake of the assassination contributed to the state of affairs of the United States. Robert Kennedy and Lyndon Johnson were seen as the heirs of a fallen leader—one was symbolic while the other was constitutionally driven. Like something from one of Shakespeare's plays, they stood to have great influence on the era, and they were in competition over who would have the greatest impact. In many ways it was a failure to lead for both men. If Lyndon Johnson could only look beyond his insecurities and consider Robert Kennedy as a viable adviser, he may have had even more political power. On the other hand, if Bobby had accepted that American politics needed people like Johnson to make things work he may have played a larger role at the center rather than learning how to affect events from the sidelines. Indeed, John F. Kennedy understood both principles and made decisions where he utilized both Lyndon Johnson's political prowess and Robert Kennedy's moral compass. The two men could have been a force, leading the country through what would be a major transition. Instead their feud contributed to the instability of American society.

Like Robert Kennedy, Lyndon Johnson was someone who wanted to make a difference. He commented once, "Some men want power simply to strut around the world and hear the tune 'Hail to the Chief.' Others want it simply to build prestige ... and to buy pretty things. Well I wanted power to give things to people—all sorts of things to all sorts of people, especially the poor and the blacks."[22] Johnson had his opportunity to wield power and make a difference. However, he had to contend with Bobby Kennedy. Jeff Shesol writes that RFK and LBJ were "competitors for the legacy of the martyred JFK, dueling heirs to the Kennedy throne."[23] Robert Kennedy had a great deal of influence on the fallen president, and it stood to reason that the men who followed JFK would flock to Bobby, not Johnson. Lyndon Johnson once remarked to a reporter when he was serving as vice president under President Kennedy, "Every time they have a conference don't tell me about who is the top adviser. It isn't McNamara, the Chiefs of Staff, or anybody else like that. Bobby is first in, last out. And Bobby is the boy he listens to."[24]

II

"Calling Bobby was really wrong."

The phone rang again at Hickory Hill an hour after Hoover's message that the president had died. This time the phone call was from Lyndon Johnson from Dallas. LBJ was talking about the potential of a worldwide plot. He said, "A lot of people down here think I should be sworn in right away. Do you have any objection to that?"[25] Still dealing with the shock,

Robert Kennedy recalled later, "I was sort of taken aback at the moment because I didn't think—see what the rush was." He went on to say, "I thought, I suppose, at the time, at least, I thought it would be nice if the President came back to Washington [as] President Kennedy."[26] Of course John Kennedy did not lose that distinction when he died or when Johnson was sworn in. Bobby's remark speaks to his emotions surrounding the event. Johnson was talking about a worldwide conspiracy and wanting to show the world that he was in charge. In fact, Johnson became president immediately after Kennedy died. The office, according to the Constitution, automatically transferred to the vice president. Johnson, however, may have had different motives for the call to Kennedy. The famous picture of Lyndon Johnson being sworn in with the somber Jackie by his side was not necessary.

Lyndon Johnson understood the gravity of the situation, but it was not unprecedented for a president to die in office, whether by assassination or natural causes, and a vice president to resume the duties of that office. It was, however, the first such act in an era where the press and the media played such a prominent role in American society. The photo from Air Force One was meant to tell the American people, indeed the world, that the United States had strong leadership even in the wake of this major tragedy.

Robert Kennedy wanted to serve his country but clearly struggled with the loss of his brother, as most people would in a situation like this. He recalled later that Johnson "began to ask me a lot of questions about who should swear him in. I was too confused and upset to talk to him about it."[27] Kennedy said that he would look into it and get back to Johnson. Lyndon Johnson did very little without thinking about the political outcome. It seems very logical that he was looking not only to gain RFK's support, but also to make it clear to the young attorney general that he was president and the tide had turned.

Johnson biographer Robert Caro writes that Johnson's insecurity may have played a role in the phone call to Robert Kennedy. He writes, "He seems to have felt even in this first hour that the best way to legitimize his ascent to the throne, to make himself seem less like a usurper, would be to demonstrate that his ascent had the support of his predecessor's family."[28] If that were truly his motive, he was mistaken to involve Bobby, especially so soon after the murder, because it drove Robert Kennedy further away from Johnson.

Nicholas Katzenbach, the deputy attorney general, helped Bobby Kennedy find the correct wording of the oath and whether it was necessary for Johnson to take it. Katzenbach reassured Robert Kennedy that Johnson did not have to be sworn in right away, but given the "symbolic significance," it was desirable. He also told Kennedy that any official who can administer an oath could give it.[29] The two men called back Johnson and recited the oath of office over the phone. Bobby started but then handed the phone to Katzenbach. It was a moment that Robert Kennedy did not have to attend to. Johnson could have called any government official. In fact, Katzenbach was available without going through Kennedy. Katzenbach was appalled at Johnson's phone call and said later, "Calling Bobby was really wrong."[30]

The fact that calling the attorney general, the leading legal counsel to the president, was wrong speaks to the uniqueness of the situation. Never had there been brothers in a cabinet-level position and the presidency. This was the first such situation, and it added to the complexity of the aftermath. Johnson remarked later that Robert Kennedy was "very businesslike, although I guess he must have been suffering more than almost anyone except Mrs. Kennedy." Judge Sarah T. Hughes arrived at 3:38 p.m. and Johnson put his hand on John F. Kennedy's bible and was sworn into the office of the president of the United States.[31] He stood next to Jacqueline Kennedy, who was still in her famous pink suit. After the oath was administered, Air Force One took off for Washington, D.C., carrying a new president and a fallen one home.

As the plane made its way to Washington, Johnson, in the same part of the plane that he took the oath, started to organize his thoughts as to the next step. He did not want to get into the presidency in this manner, but he needed to be prepared. He jotted down on a piece of paper, "1. Staff; 2. Cabinet; 3, Leadership."[32] He communicated back to Washington saying that he wanted a meeting with the cabinet and the White House staff. He recalled later, "I needed that White House staff. Without them I would have lost my link to John Kennedy, and without that I would have had no chance of gaining the support of the media or the Eastern intellectuals. And without that support I would have had absolutely no chance of governing the country."[33] Johnson had always worried that his Texas roots would hurt his chances with the East Coast. He was right. Having a connection to the Kennedys helped bridge that divide. However, when Johnson tried to speak to Kenny O'Donnell, who was on the plane with Mrs. Kennedy in the rear with the coffin, about arranging a staff meeting, he said to Bill Moyers, a Johnson aid, that he "didn't have the stomach for it." In addition, the cabinet meeting had to be held the next day because many of them were on a plane over the Pacific.[34] While Johnson's attempt at demonstrating leadership and resolve on the surface was genuine, it was stalled by the reality that many of the men who were brought to Washington by JFK were still yearning for a Kennedy in the leadership role he now occupied.

III

"This is what is going to happen to me."

Martin Luther King, Jr., was sitting at home when a news flash came across the television saying that President Kennedy had been shot. He yelled upstairs to his wife, Coretta, saying, "Corrie, I just heard that Kennedy has been shot, maybe killed." The two sat in front of the television, like the rest of the nation, waiting for word on Kennedy's condition. King commented to his wife at that time, "I hope that he will live, this is just terrible." He went on to say, "I think if he lives, if he pulls through this, it will help him understand what we go through." After Walter Cronkite announced to the world that Kennedy had fallen, King was very quiet at first. He turned to Coretta and said, "This is what is going to happen to me. This is such a sick society."[35]

In the wake of Kennedy's death, King spoke with his advisers and issued a statement regarding the assassination: "I am shocked and grief stricken at the tragic assassination of President Kennedy." He went on to state,

> He was a great and dedicated President. His death is a great loss to America and the world. The finest tribute that the American people can pay to the late President Kennedy is to implement the progressive policies that he sought to initiate in foreign and domestic relations.[36]

King knew that this could have ramifications for the movement. He was also affected by the death of Kennedy personally. Yolanda King, the oldest of King's children, came home from school and jumped into his arms saying, "Oh, Daddy, now we will never get our freedom." King wanted to make it better for his daughter and said, "Now don't you worry, baby. It's going to be all right."[37] Yolanda King saw JFK as a beacon for freedom. Many did not know that it was Bobby, more than any other adviser, who led President Kennedy to embrace civil rights as a moral issue. Dr. King, like Robert Kennedy and Lyndon Johnson, was a voice that had the potential to help the nation navigate through their grief and accept the reality that the nation was different in the wake of the assassination.

Dr. King had a connection to the Kennedy White House. Those triumphs that he led were as much part of the Kennedy years as they were of his. Robert Kennedy and Martin Luther King had a role to play in the wake of the tragedy. It was imperative that King continue his leadership in the movement. The Civil Rights Bill was still before Congress, and it was vital to the movement that it pass. King moved the American people to embrace the Civil Rights Act of 1964 and the Voting Rights Act of 1965 as law. It was also Bobby Kennedy who needed to continue to work with King. To be sure,

Bobby learned a lot from King and others in the movement. Those triumphs that King and others spearheaded affected the young attorney general. As he embarked to realize his own ambition, the struggle continued to play a pivotal role in that evolution.

King was a major voice in the sixties that would inspire many Americans in different ways. King's comments in the aftermath of this national tragedy were important and, to some extent, even expected by some. David Garrow writes that King "was deeply disturbed by John Kennedy's death. He believed the assassination reflected not just one man's deed but a larger and more tragic national climate of violence."[38] Indeed, King's own words in the presence of Kennedy's death were of what would eventually happen to him in 1968. The nation was in a very violent state and it needed leaders to guide it through. America was experiencing a catharsis and unfortunately would have moments of extreme violence in the midst of changing the status quo.

As the Kings were dealing with the tragedy of Kennedy's death, Robert Kennedy was at Andrews Air Force base waiting for his brother. When Air Force One touched down, the press was focused on the rear of the plane where JFK's coffin was supposed to be unloaded. Bobby went to the front of the plane, entered at the cabin and went in saying, "I want to see Jackie." He walked by Johnson and went straight to Jackie, hugging her and then leading her off the plane without a word to the new president.[39] Jeff Shesol argues that the "brush-off wounded [LBJ] deeply."[40] Johnson had no choice but to move on from the incident. He also did not want to offend the family and never let it be known publicly that he was hurt by Bobby. He later told Cronkite that he didn't remember the incident. "I would have thought that the natural thing to do was go as quickly as you could to the widow, Mrs. Kennedy, and to try to console her and give her strength." He went on to say, "I would have found nothing improper in it."[41] LBJ made a statement on the tarmac at Andrews saying,

> This is a sad time for all people. We have suffered a loss that cannot be weighed. For me, it is a deep personal tragedy. I know that the world shares the sorrow that Mrs. Kennedy and her family bear. I will do my best. That is all I can do. I ask for your help—and God's.[42]

LBJ boarded a helicopter that would take him from the airport for the first time as Commander-in-Chief.

In the helicopter Johnson had George Ball, McGeorge Bundy and Robert McNamara on board. He asked if there were any issues as a result of the assassination that needed immediate attention. Then he got very close to them and said, "President Kennedy did something I could never have done. He gathered around him the ablest people I've ever seen—not his friends, not even the best in public service, but the best anywhere. I want you to stay. I need you. I want you to stand with me."[43] With that statement Johnson started to make decisions that would affect his presidency. He wanted to continue with the Kennedy agenda, but he also wanted his own. He knew that he needed the "Kennedy aura" to get done what needed to get done as president. These three men would stay at their posts and have a further impact on history.

Robert Kennedy spent that night in the Lincoln Bedroom at the White House to be close to Jackie and the kids. It was the beginning of a period in his life where he would search for the meaning in the aftermath of the assassination. Robert Kennedy began his journey to find his own voice and lead in his own right that evening in the Lincoln Bedroom. Charles Spalding brought him a sleeping pill. "God it's so awful. Everything was really beginning to run so well," Bobby said. As Spalding was leaving he heard Bobby behind the closed door, sobbing, saying, "Why, God?"[44]

IV

"So by this time I was rather fed up with him."

The issues between Robert Kennedy and Johnson had evolved rather dramatically in those days after the assassination. Kennedy recalled in 1964 a comment that LBJ made to Pierre Salinger after the assassination. Allegedly LBJ had said that John Kennedy was murdered as retribution for JFK's role in the death of Rafael Trujillo of Yugoslavia and Ngo Dinh Diem of South Vietnam. Johnson, RFK recalled, spoke of

> divine retribution. He said that, and then went on, I think, and talked and said that's what happened, and that when he was growing up one of the—somebody that he knew who had misbehaved ... was on a sled or something and hit his head and became crosseyed. And he said that was God's retribution for people who were bad and so you should be careful of crosseyed people because God put His mark on them, and that this might very well be God's retribution to Kennedy for his participation in the assassination of these two people.

The interviewer had never heard that story. There was a long pause and then Bobby commented, "But otherwise it's a friendly relationship."[45] To be sure, RFK and LBJ were extremely important in the years following the assassination. For Robert Kennedy to bring up this story points not only to the tense relationship between him and Johnson but also the complicated nuances that existed between them. It was a series of smaller incidents that plagued their relationship. Those events would not end, and the relationship continued to sour.

Beyond the politics, Robert Kennedy had major issues with Johnson that even stemmed from the day his brother was assassinated. He remembered in May 1964, not long after his brother's death, "There were four or five matters that arose during the period of November 22nd to November 27th or so that, which made me bitterer, unhappy at least with Lyndon Johnson. And, uh, these events involving the treatment of Jackie on the plane trip back and all that kind of business."[46] The day after the assassination Bobby went to the Oval Office to clear out his brother's belongings at 9:00am. He found Evelyn Lincoln sobbing in the hallway. Johnson was in the office and had told Lincoln to clear her things out of for his secretaries. His brother's rocking chair was in the hallway upside down. It had been removed so the rugs could be cleaned while JFK was away in Dallas. It remained in the hallway, serving as a symbol that his brother would never sit in it again.[47]

Robert Kennedy saw this action as an issue not only with the people who supported Kennedy, but also the family. "He came to the White House on Saturday and started moving all my brother's things out Saturday morning at nine o'clock."[48] Johnson saw Kennedy in the hallway and waved him in, saying, "I need you more than he needed you."[49] The conversation was short. "I don't want to discuss it," Kennedy said. He asked Johnson if he could wait. Kennedy recalled saying "it was going to take us a period of time to move out of here, and I think, maybe, can't you wait? He said, well, of course, and then he started to explain.... McNamara had told him he had to move in. Dean Rusk told him he had to move in because the world would fall apart.... He didn't want to move in and everybody told him he should move in."[50] Robert Kennedy did not care. In fact his unresponsiveness to LBJ's explanation prompted Johnson to move back to the Executive Office Building. When he was questioned by his staff about this decision, that it would lead to the American people lacking confidence, Johnson said sharply, "People will get confidence if we do our job properly ... stop this. Our first concern is Mrs. Kennedy and the family."[51]

It seemed that Lyndon Johnson was uncertain in those days following the assassination where his place was within the administration, which was strange given the fact that he had a right to the office. It also speaks to the power that Robert Kennedy had just after the assassination. Johnson was still surrounded by Kennedy's men and needed to assert himself so he could bring in his own people. Bobby Kennedy, he felt, was someone who was constantly lurking in the background. He said later that he truly believed that Bobby "seriously considered whether he would let me be president, whether he should really take the position [that] the vice president didn't automatically move in. I thought that was on his mind every time I saw him in the first few days."[52]

In an attempt to grab the reins of leadership, Johnson had a cabinet meeting that morning. Kennedy didn't want to go. As the meeting started, the attorney general's chair remained empty. RFK recalled later, "I was upset about what had happened on the plane and [by] the fact that he came into the office. So by this time I was rather fed up with him.... But I went by and Mac Bundy said it was very important that I come to the cabinet meeting."[53] As Kennedy entered the room, several people rose to their feet, but Johnson stayed seated.[54] Johnson was upset that Bobby came in late and even commented to one other cabinet member that he did it on purpose to spoil the effect of the first cabinet meeting.[55]

Of course, in the midst of the crisis, like so many other times in American history, the country wanted to hear from the president of the United States. Johnson wanted to address Congress, but he felt that he should wait until after the funeral and do it on Tuesday, November 26. Bobby wanted him to wait one more day. Bundy went to RFK and said that the president wanted Tuesday. "Well, the hell with it," Bobby shot back. "Why do you ask me about it? Don't ask me about what you want done—you'll tell me what it's going to be anyway. So go ahead and do it." When Bundy was unsuccessful, LBJ sent Shriver, Kennedy's brother-in-law, to sway his mind. "Why does he tell you to ask me? Now he's hacking at you. He knows I want to wait until Wednesday." Shriver went to LBJ and said, "Bob prefers to wait a day, unless there are overriding reasons for having the address earlier."[56] LBJ acquiesced and planned for the speech on Wednesday.

V

"He came to see the moral issue."

Martin Luther King, Jr., gave a eulogy in his church on November 24, saying, "Men everywhere were stunned into [somber] confusion at the news of the [assassination] of [President] John F. Kennedy. We watched the 35th President of our nation go down like a great cedar." King went on and talked about the "stunning blow" to the nation. "I was always impressed," he told his congregation, "with his ready knowledge of the world situation. In a period of change the nation has lost a leader who was unafraid of change." He said of the civil rights that Kennedy "met the issue with forthrightness and courage" and that "he came to see the moral issue" in the movement.[57]

On November 24, 1963, John F. Kennedy was taken to the Capitol Rotunda to lie in state for the world to come and pay their respects. With flags at half-mast, the nation prepared to say good-bye to President Kennedy. Orange leaves carpeted the ground and rain slowly fell from the sky. People lined the streets as the flag-draped caisson was taken from the White House, pulled by horses, with the black horse in the rear, a symbol of a fallen leader. Bobby, Jackie, Caroline and John, Jr., followed. Drums played in the background as mourners climbed statues to get a better glimpse of Kennedy's procession.[58]

They arrived at the rotunda, bringing the casket to a place where Lincoln and Roosevelt had been when they died in office. The band played a somber tune while Jackie, donning her black veil, with Bobby and the rest of the family following, walked up the steps of the grand plaza to the dome. President Johnson laid a wreath at the base of the coffin, Jackie and Caroline knelt by the side and said a prayer. Dressed in blue and holding their mother's hand, Caroline and John, Jr., walked down the steps of the Capitol. Bobby stood tall, with a piece of paper in his hand, dressed in the black tie that he would wear for months after the death of his brother.[59]

In the midst of the services on that day, Jack Ruby shot and killed Lee Harvey Oswald, the president's assassin. Johnson informed Kennedy about the incident. LBJ then said that as the chief law enforcement officer in the nation, "You've got to do something, we've got to do something. We've got to get involved. It's giving the United States a bad name in the rest of the world." RFK saw it is as insensitive for LBJ to call on RFK's role as attorney general at this particular moment. The fact that these events may have been an embarrassment to the United States, RFK remembered, "wasn't, it couldn't be, the thing foremost in my mind."[60]

The next morning, with flags still at half-mast, President Kennedy was taken from the rotunda in the same flag-draped caisson. The horses took Kennedy through the streets of Washington where, once again, mourners lined the streets and the band played behind Kennedy's casket, marching to the White House to hear a choir sing on the lawn. He went from the White House to St. Matthews Church, where they had a mass for burial. The family marched together, in a wave of black, led by Jackie and the children, dressed again in their light blue jackets. Bobby and Ted were in the forefront as the archbishop led the casket into the church.

While his father made his way to his final resting place, at the foot of the Robert E. Lee house, where the eternal flame still burns today, John F. Kennedy, Jr., stood apart from his family for a moment that has been enshrined in history. Wearing his blue coat, wiping tears from his eyes, he brought his hand to his temple and saluted his father. The world gasped at such an act by a little boy who turned three years old on the day that he buried his father. It epitomized the emotion of the time, captured in the act of a little boy who just lost his father and was burying him on his birthday.

The procession made its way to Arlington National Cemetery, passing Lincoln Memorial, going over the bridge. As the people came to the majestic lawn at Arlington, where gravestones stood in unison, like the terra-cotta soldiers of ancient China, bagpipes played and soldiers adorned the landscape. Jets flew over, paying homage to a fallen leader. Bobby, holding Jackie's hand, took a seat by the coffin as they stretched the flag. They all prayed. He was blessed by the priest, and the honor guard took their posts. A twenty-one-gun salute honored him, taps played, the flag was folded and the eternal flame was lit by Jackie.[61] Later than night, after the guests had left the White House and it was just the immediate family, Bobby turned to Jackie and said, "Shall we go visit our friend?" They went together, across the bridge, to Arlington, knelt beside the flame and prayed.[62]

2

"Let Us Continue"

I

"The times cried out for leadership."

On Monday, November 25, at 9:20 p.m., Dr. King spoke to Lyndon Johnson on the phone regarding the Civil Rights Bill. Johnson commented on some of King's remarks that had been broadcast earlier that day: "I've been locked up in this office and I haven't seen it. But I wanted to tell you how grateful I am, and how worthy I'm going to try to be of all your hopes." King thanked Johnson and acknowledged "what a difficult period this is." To that Johnson replied, "It's a—it's just an impossible period. We got a budget coming up that's—we got nothing to do with it, it's practically already made. And we got a civil rights bill that hadn't even passed the House." He went on, saying that Hubert Humphrey wanted to go home and they were all going to wait until the next session to deal with these issues. "But we'll just keep them there next year until they do," Johnson said, "and we just won't give up an inch."[1] Johnson wanted to show King that he planned to support Kennedy's legislative agenda, but he emphasized the importance of the Civil Rights Bill that Kennedy proposed the previous June.

King appreciated what Johnson was saying. It was, after all, his first conversation with him as President of the United States. "Well, this is mighty fine," King replied. King went on to stress his own position on the meaning of Kennedy's death to the cause of civil rights. "I think it's so imperative. I think one of the great tributes that we can pay in the memory of President Kennedy is to try to enact some of the great progressive policies that he sought to initiate." Johnson said that he planned to support them all. "And I'm going to do my best to get other men to do likewise, and I'll have to have you-all's help." He emphasized to King, "I never needed it more than I do now." They parted on good terms with Johnson inviting King to the White House.[2]

After Kennedy's funeral, Dr. King took a moment to reflect on John F. Kennedy's legacy. On November 26, after receiving an award, King spoke at the Freedom House Annual Dinner and characterized Kennedy's death as "one of the most shocking and humble tragedies that has ever befallen our nation." He wanted to accept the award by paying tribute to Kennedy whom he called a "national hero and a symbol of man's timeless quest for peace and freedom."[3] The speech came just before Lyndon Johnson's remarks and speaks to King's growing influence in the wake of the March on Washington just five months prior, which culminated in a meeting with JFK at the White House.

King believed that John F. Kennedy had the ability to lead the nation in time of great turmoil. "In a period of change the nation has lost a leader who was unafraid of change. He came to the presidency in one of the most turbulent and cataclysmic periods in human history." King characterized the problems of the world as "gigantic in extent and chaotic in detail." The issues were far reaching, involving both international and domestic issues. "John Kennedy met these problems with a depth of concern, a breath of intelligence, and a keen sense of history. He had the courage to be a friend of civil rights and a stalwart advocate of peace." King said that the grief of the many millions of people revealed "that President Kennedy had become a symbol of people's yearnings for justice, economic well-being and peace, as well as the importance of a commitment to moral values."[4]

Since Kennedy had started to embrace the civil rights cause toward the end of his life, he became a symbol of the movement and even an advocate for the change that King had hoped to usher into American society. King even went as far as to quote JFK's June 11, 1963, civil rights address. He took his message beyond Lee Harvey Oswald's actions on November 22 and spoke to the climate that contributed to the assassination. "Our late president was assassinated by a morally inclement climate. It is a climate filled with heavy torrents of false accusations, jostling winds of hatred and raging storms of violence."[5] The climate that King referred to was something that he believed not only contributed to Kennedy's murder but also continued to stymie the civil rights movement. King believed that this atmosphere needed to be addressed and Kennedy's death was another example of that climate.

In some ways King, like Robert Kennedy, was trying to understand and come to grips with the reasons why John Kennedy, a man who was trying to do good, was killed. He blamed the "climate" of the nation as much as Oswald. Indeed, the "climate" of this nation had laid the foundation for some of our greatest tragedies. "It is a climate where men can not disagree with our being disagreeable, and where they express dissent through violence and murder." That was the climate of the segregationist south that King had lived with his whole life. This was the climate that Robert Kennedy and Martin Luther King were trying to change when they, themselves, were murdered in 1968. It was also the same climate that led to the Civil War in 1860. King wanted to promote an atmosphere where people could talk about differences and come to a compromise without violence or bloodshed. To be sure it was a bedrock principle of the early history of the United States.

The New Frontier served as a bridge between the fifties and sixties, Kennedy's death, an attack on the New Frontier and all its aspirations for the people that it hoped to serve, brought a more dangerous climate to the nation. "It is the same climate that murdered Medgar Evers in Mississippi and six innocent Negro children in Birmingham, Alabama," King said. But he didn't point the blame of that climate on one person. "So in a sense we are all participants in that horrible assassination that tarnished the image of our nation."[6] His hope was to lead the nation and create a new climate from the ashes of this tragedy. King's actions in the wake of the assassination complemented Robert Kennedy. They both wanted to empower America's youth in the hopes that it would lead to lasting change.

King believed that Kennedy's murder was a symptom of a larger societal issue that plagued the nation. In the hopes of inspiring people to lead the charge for change, he pointed out how the actions of the national community contributed to this climate. This act was a symptom of a larger problem. He condemned society for its apathy and listed the offenses.

> By our silence, by our willingness to compromise principle; by our constant attempt to cure the cancer of racial injustice with the vaseline of gradualism; by our readiness to allow arms to be purchased at will and fired at whim; by allowing our movie and television screens to teach our children that the hero is one who masters the art of shouting and the technique of killing; by allowing all these developments we have created an atmosphere in which violence and hatred have become popular past times in many quarters of our nation.[7]

King found meaning in Kennedy's death. He hoped that it would serve as a catalyst for the nation, something to unite people and start the change he hoped to usher into American society. In his spiritual quest to find meaning in JFK's murder, he found a way to empower people and foster change.

Kennedy's assassination, according to King, was an important message to the nation. Where Robert Kennedy looked to the Greeks, King looked to his own spiritual beliefs. Kennedy's death "has something to say to every politician who has fed his constituents the stale bread of racism and the spoiled meat of hatred. He has something to say to every clergyman who had observed racial evils and remained silent behind the safe security of stained glass windows." Looking deep into the "climate" of the nation, which was something that Kennedy wanted to change, King talked about the "profound truths" that Kennedy's murder illuminated to the world. "He said to all of us that the virus of hate that has seeped into the reins of our nation, if unchecked, will lead inevitably to our moral and spiritual doom."[8]

Martin Luther King's words played a vital role in comprehending the enormity of the tragedy that had befallen the American people. King not only appealed to African Americans; he also inspired White America, becoming the bridge that Kennedy had started to embody just prior to his murder. This was an important distinction with the nation trying to overcome the racial divide that had plagued it since 1619, when the first slave ships docked in Jamestown, Virginia. To be sure, the climate of hate contributed to Kennedy's murder. King was on the threshold of his own legacy. His actions as a leader in the movement led the Nobel Committee to grant him the Peace Prize. That award signified that King was making progress not only toward easing the racial tension in the nation but also the same vitriol that contributed to Kennedy's assassination. His message inspired Americans and helped people see that America still had much to do before his dream would be realized.

For King the future held a battle to "rid our nation of the vestiges of racial segregation and discrimination." He proclaimed, "Our goal is freedom," and went on to link Lincoln's immortal words in the Gettysburg address to Kennedy's passing. "We are challenged to see that John F. Kennedy does not die in vain," he said, alluding to the words in the address. Calling Kennedy a "noble servant of humanity," King wanted to continue toward a civil rights act and "all of the progressive policies which he sought to initiate." King said that if the nation does this with "vigor and valor, the forces of insecurity, the doubts clouding our future, will be transformed into radiant confidence, into glowing excitement to reach creative goals, and into an abiding moral balance where every man will respect the dignity and worth of human personality."[9] Before Johnson linked the passage of the Civil Rights Bill to JFK's legacy, King did, laying the groundwork for the passage of the act.

King linked this journey of the nation to an ultimate goal—a day of jubilation. "When this day comes the hanging discards of our nation will be transformed into a beautiful symphony of brotherhood, and men everywhere will know that America is truly the free and the home of the brave."[10] Coming on the cusp of a national tragedy, King's words looked to heal the nation but also pointed to where it needed to go to find some solace. On a larger note, he was hoping to find some meaning in Kennedy's death. He believed that the nation was ready for change, and Kennedy had started them on that path. King was ready to lead the nation into a new phase of the civil rights movement. Robert Kennedy was ready to go with King. Together they would usher in the largest rights revolution that the nation would ever see. At the heart of that movement were young people who heard their words and used them as a way to empower Americans. King's words set the stage for Lyndon Johnson. The president's first major address was one of his most important and in some ways complemented King's vision for the nation.

On November 27, 1963, Lyndon Johnson walked into a joint session of Congress amid a standing ovation from the whole room, which continued for some time as he looked at his notes. Then the gavel sounded and he was introduced as "our former colleague the president of the United States." The room erupted again.[11] Johnson exuded poise and confidence, echoing the fallen president's ideals while asserting the same principles of his own. It was a historic speech in the wake of a historic crisis that would shape America in its aftermath. Indeed Lyndon Johnson followed up on JFK's program, but after the Civil Rights Act of 1964, the New Frontier ceased, and LBJ became the lightning rod for what would come out of his administration.

Lyndon Johnson had a lot riding on this first major address in the wake of the assassination. He recalled later, "A nation stunned, shaken to its very heart, had to be reassured that the government was not in a state of paralysis." He went on to say, "I had to convince everyone everywhere that the country would go forward.... Any hesitation or wavering, any false step, any sign of self doubt, could have been disastrous." He concluded, "The times cried out for leadership."[12] Like King the day before, Johnson stressed the importance of the event but also wanted to see meaning in the tragedy. Not only did he have to show strong leadership, he needed the support of the people in his government.

Johnson knew that his effort went beyond assuaging a grieving nation. "I knew how they felt," Johnson said of Kennedy's staff. "The impact of Kennedy's death was evident everywhere—in the looks of their faces and the sound of their voices. He was gone and with his going they must have felt that everything had changed. Suddenly they were outsiders just as I had been for almost three years, outsiders on the inside." Johnson understood this new wrinkle in the New Frontier because he had been in the shoes of the men who followed Kennedy. "The White House is small, but if you're not at the center it seems enormous."[13] The Kennedy cabinet was an important piece to help him lead effectively. While LBJ understood that with most of them, he lost that with the most pivotal person, Robert Kennedy.

He started his speech saying, "All I have I would have given gladly not to be standing here today." Johnson touched on the achievements of the

Kennedy years and the tenacity of a grief-stricken nation. "Today John Fitzgerald Kennedy lives on in the immortal words and works that he left behind. He lives on in the mind and memories of mankind. He lives on in the hearts of his countrymen." Johnson was sure to bring all the success of the New Frontier into his speech.

> The dream of conquering the vastness of space—the dream of partnership across the Atlantic—and across the Pacific as well—the dream of a Peace Corps in less developed nations—the dream of education for all of our children—the dream of jobs for all who seek them and need them—the dream of care for our elderly—the dream of an all-out attack on mental illness—and above all, the dream of equal rights for all Americans, whatever their race or color—these and other American dreams have been vitalized by his drive and by his dedication.

The speech was meant to not only soothe the nation, but also empower his administration and demonstrate to the world that the United States was still a force. He was met with applause after he cited "equal rights for all Americans." In a rally cry for action, pushing the JFK agenda, Johnson said, "And now the ideas and the ideals which he so nobly represented must and will be translated into effective action."[14] The chamber erupted into applause. It was their time to do something to help the nation.

Johnson was at his best when the country needed him most. They had just laid John F. Kennedy to rest, but LBJ was determined to take this moment and demonstrate to the world that he intended to meet this tragedy with action. Robert Caro writes,

> The manner in which he spoke of his grief—the moving first line of the speech and the apparent sincerity and deep, solemn emotion with which he delivered it, together with the many lines thereafter in which he spoke of John Kennedy—accomplished what may have been the most difficult feat of all: to convince even men and women who, long familiar with Johnson and his ambitions as well as with his ostracism by the Kennedys, had not been disposed to accept his sincerity.[15]

He invoked JFK's powerful inaugural in an effort to not only show a link between the administration, but also the same vigorous, forceful manner in which his predecessor demonstrated on the steps of the building where he was giving his speech. Seizing that moment, LBJ understood the power of the Kennedy legacy and planned to use it as a driving force to enact legislation. "But let us begin," JFK pled to the country in 1961. Johnson wanted to invoke Kennedy's ideals. "Today, in this moment of new resolve, I would say to all my fellow Americans, let us continue."[16] His voice was timid, almost quivering at times, with moments of strong rhetoric—emphasizing his point, exuding strength and determination.

Lyndon Johnson understood politics and the power that the Kennedy mantle held to get legislation passed. "Our most immediate tasks are here on this Hill," he said. Perhaps the greatest link to such a strategy was how he tied Kennedy's legacy to civil rights.

> First, no memorial oration or eulogy could more eloquently honor President Kennedy's memory than the earliest possible passage of the civil rights bill for which he fought so long. We have talked long enough in this country about equal rights. We have talked for one hundred years or more. It is time now to write the next chapter, and to write it in the books of law.[17]

Johnson's insistence that passage of the Civil Rights Bill was tied to Kennedy's legacy and vision for the nation points to the role that the Kennedy's had in the passage of that bill. In addition, his rhetoric is similar to Kennedy's message from June of that year. While Johnson should get credit for moving the legislation through Congress and building on the strength of the bill, Kennedy should be recognized for the spirit of the law that would come to help so many Americans. In addition, Martin Luther King had alluded to passage of it in his statements following Kennedy's death. This was the "progressive" policy that he wanted LBJ to follow up on.

Johnson talked about a tax bill and the importance of education for the nation. He demonstrated to the nation, indeed the world, that he had the ability to lead. Caro writes, "The speech reminded journalists and Congressmen as well that in fact he *had*, for six years, gotten Congress to do it." Johnson appealed to everyone there: "The need is here. The need is now. I ask your help." This is one of Johnson's best, most motivational and inspiring speeches. He succeeded in reassuring the nation that he was in charge and the government would continue, but he did it in such a way that paid homage to a fallen leader. His sincerity seemed evident, and the nation followed him, electing him in his own right overwhelmingly in 1964. "The time has come for Americans of all races and creeds and political beliefs to understand and to respect one another," he said.[18] His speech was meant to unite the nation as well as to continue with a legislative agenda that was stalled. His plea for help did not make him look weak—it made him look human. It had a similar tone that "Ask not" did for JFK in 1961.

Sitting next to Robert McNamara, with the rest of the cabinet, was Robert Kennedy. His hands were folded in his lap as he listened to Johnson talk about his brother. Still dressed in black, he stared ahead, statue-like. In the coming months Robert Kennedy would deal with the loss of his brother and reinvent himself for the nation. He found strength in the legacy of his brother and embraced a new message that attacked poverty and empowered America's youth. Indeed, his rhetoric was something that shaped the sixties and put in motion a revolution that would change the nation.

II

"My brother barely had a chance to get started."

Robert Kennedy went back to work on December 6. He took long walks and went home for lunch, slowly getting back into his life at the Justice Department. He looked at pending cases, which included his old nemesis Jimmy Hoffa, who was being investigated for jury tampering.[19] Robert Kennedy lost weight due to his grief. His clothes no longer fit. He was concerned that his pursuit of dangerous, evil men may have been partly to blame for the death of his brother.

At a Christmas party held by Mary McGrory, the *Washington Evening Star* columnist, amid the laughter, a small six-year-old African American boy ran up to Bobby and said, "You're brother is dead." The room became silent and the boy, scared, started to cry. Kennedy knelt down, hugged the boy and said, "That's all right. I have another."[20] He started to become outwardly compassionate and caring about others. Embracing this child was a public example of the beginning of this transformation. He slowly found his place in the new government, eventually coming out from under it to be his own force. Kennedy started to look at the plight of others and how he could make a difference.

Arthur Schlesinger and Richard Goodwin met with Robert Kennedy on December 13, 1963. Bobby believed that he and other Kennedy loyalists had a certain amount of political power until Election Day 1964. Kennedy felt that they must "use that power in these months to the best possible advantage." He wanted everyone who believed in the Kennedy program to "stay in close touch and not let them pick us off one by one. I haven't the answer in detail yet, but I am sure that the fundamental principle now is collective action." He stood up at his desk, looked at Schlesinger and Goodwin and said "Sure, I've lost a brother. Other people lose wives.... But that's not what's important. What's important is what we were trying to do for this country." Kennedy wanted to continue his brother's vision for the nation. "My brother barely had a chance to get started—and there is so much now to be done—for the Negroes and the unemployed and the school kids and everyone else who is not getting a decent break in our society. This is what counts."[21] Kennedy started to take on the ideals that would empower him later in life, indeed to become a part of this new decade that would usher in so much change.

Robert Kennedy did not believe that Lyndon Johnson embodied the ideals of the New Frontier. "The new fellow doesn't get this," he continued to Schlesinger and Goodwin. "He knows all about politics and nothing about human beings."²² Bobby believed he was someone who could lead in the absence of his brother. He was trying to find a way to do it without politically hurting himself or the party. "I haven't talked to [Johnson] yet. I don't feel mentally or physically prepared to do so yet. When I talk to him, I am ready to be tough about what we must have."²³ Bobby saw this as a battle between two methods of leadership, two ideals that had the potential to change the nation. He still did not understand that the center of power had changed. He may have had political power, but Johnson was president. Lyndon Johnson capitalized on the Kennedy aura to get programs through Congress, invoking JFK's legacy in the process, but taking full credit when it finally passed as his own. For Kennedy, this was a confrontation that he needed to prepare. Kennedy concluded by saying that the people in Washington "didn't come here just to work for John Kennedy, an individual, but for ideas, things we wanted to do."²⁴

Robert Kennedy was right. The New Frontier was larger than JFK. It had far-reaching effects into civil rights and foreign policy while JFK was alive. The nation was charted on a path to accept African Americans into society, laying the groundwork for a larger rights revolution as a result. John Kennedy also proposed peace and started to move the nation's foreign policy in that direction. It had the potential to do even more in the wake of his death. Despite these factors, Bobby struggled with how he would take those ideals and lead with them—making it his cause. The nation, however, was different. The assassination was the catalyst of that change. Bobby, like the nation, was also changing, looking to move in a new direction.

While Bobby contemplated the way he could keep New Frontier ideals alive, Martin Luther King, Jr., considered the role that Lyndon Johnson would play in the movement in a draft, which included handwritten notes, of an article for the *New York Amsterdam News*. The article was entitled "Our New President" and it considered the fact of Johnson's southern roots and what that meant for the movement. It posed the question, with a southerner in the Oval Office, "are the chances of the Negro for full emancipation, better or worse?" In an effort to foment good intentions toward Johnson, King asked his readers to look beyond "the same kind of provincialism that causes the Negro to suffer." He went on to say, "We can not afford the luxury of prejudice to discount Lyndon Johnson's true worth just because he happens to be from the south."²⁵

King acknowledged that Johnson had a "better than good" civil rights record and commended his "unique and skillful experience as Senate Majority Leader." He hoped that experience would elicit "more results than we would ultimately expect." Of course Johnson's ability in the Senate had a profound effect on the civil rights movement. Moving into the start of 1964 the new president stood on the precipice of great change in many areas—in both domestic and foreign policy.

Particularly interesting was King's endorsement of Johnson where he believed that "it seems abundantly clear he means business" on civil rights and may be able to reason with men like George Wallace, who dismissed the Kennedys as outsiders, not able to understand the issues of the South from their privileged, New England background. Johnson was much more "down to earth" and came from the southern culture. "This is an interesting turn of affairs," King wrote. King acknowledged Johnson's insistence on the passage of the Civil Rights Bill in his first speech to a joint session of Congress as running the "gauntlet of political suicide." He said it was "courageous and heroic." King finished the piece, in his own handwriting, saying that Johnson was now a speaker for the nation, not one region in the Senate. "His goal must not be to help certain people, but all people." King's goal was to work with Johnson while Kennedy's strategy was to outlast him and regain the post that his brother lost. King's efforts were carefully thought out, demonstrating not only his political prowess but also the hope he wanted to inspire. The Civil Rights Act was something that he wanted LBJ to sign into law. King needed both Johnson and Bobby Kennedy to get it passed.

In an effort to further the cause of the passage of the Civil Rights Act, King talked in a speech about the issues of segregation in Atlanta, Georgia. He called Atlanta "an island of moderation in the midst of a tempestuous ocean of defiance" of the *Brown* decision of 1954. He said because of this position Atlanta has established a reputation "as a program of racial harmony and the epitome of social progress." Despite that reputation, King said that Atlanta had fallen behind major southern cities "in progress toward segregation."[26] King used every available tactic to bring to the forefront the need for the law. Indeed, his persistence and ability to craft rhetoric paved the way closer to the passage of the act. To some extent Johnson needed King to keep bringing the inadequacies within American society to light.

Given that Atlanta was his home, King was not there to admonish or embarrass the city. He wanted to "call Atlanta back to something noble and pleas with her to rise from the dark yesterdays of racial injustice to bright tomorrows and justice for all." King's words and actions spoke to the vision that he had for the nation. Indeed, there was no greater need for his own family than to desegregate his home city. He went into detail on the disparities in Atlanta, from public schools to restaurants to hotels to neighborhoods in the suburbs to hospital beds. "We are determined to be free, and we are determined to achieve that freedom now." King's determination was something that the movement stood on. "It is as old as our fore parents' revolt against the evil system of slavery and as modern as our willingness to face the sharp teeth of vicious dogs, the brutal hands of the inhuman policemen, and the staggering waters of powerful fire hoses."[27]

At the heart of King's message was that the movement was not going to quit. He pointed to the fact that history was filled with tragic stories of privileged groups not giving up their place in society. "Freedom is never voluntary given by the oppressor; it must be demanded by the oppressed," King said. "Our goal is freedom." He believed that the nation and the city would find freedom for African Americans. He finished his speech with the words of former slaves: "Walk together children, don't you get weary. There is a great camp meeting in the promised land."[28]

Lyndon Johnson sent Robert Kennedy a message for the new year of 1964: "I know how hard the past six weeks have been for you," he started the telegram. "Under the most trying circumstances your first thoughts have been for your country. Your brother would have been very proud of the strength you have shown. As the new year begins, I resolve to do my best to fulfill his trust in me. I will need your counsel and support."[29] Lyndon Johnson did not like Robert Kennedy, but he did try to connote a working relationship with the man. Bobby was not as gracious.

As the decade continued, 1964 would prove a pivotal year for the nation. While civil rights was still in the forefront, Vietnam lurked in the shadows, plaguing Johnson's efforts as he embarked on a "War on Poverty." Kennedy and King went further to establish their voice while one would win his first national election and the other a Nobel Peace Prize. It was an important moment in American history and it started the nation on a path to embrace new ideals.

PART II. FORGING A NEW AMERICAN IDENTITY, 1964

3

Finding a Voice

I

*"I know you're president,
and don't ever talk to me like that again."*

Robert Kennedy took a trip to Tokyo in January 1964 to meet with President Sukarno of Indonesia about a crisis in Malaysia. Prior to the meeting RFK made a speech at Waseda University in Japan. To a packed auditorium and people standing outside in the rain listening on loud speakers Kennedy gave the speech without any notes. There were tears in the eyes of many of the Japanese as they listened to him talk about his brother. "He was not only president of one nation he was president of young people around the world. If President Kennedy's life and death are to mean anything, we young people must work harder for a better life for all the people in the world." The place exploded with applause, the sounds of cheers reverberating throughout the auditorium, while students rushed toward him, hoping to shake his hand.[1] Kennedy's strategy was to empower the young people of the world. This would become a major point of his rhetoric. At Tokyo, however, Robert Kennedy was just realizing his vision and how he could achieve it. MLK had a major head start—he knew what he wanted and how to achieve it. That hope to change America's climate was something that they both shared.

Kennedy met with President Sukarno after the speech. "Did you come to threaten me?" Sukarno asked. "No. I've come to get you out of trouble," he replied.[2] Kennedy implored Sukarno to find a peaceful way to end the crisis. "Why not negotiate? If it doesn't work out, you can always go back to shooting and killing."[3] He was able to get Sukarno to agree to a ceasefire. The caveat was that the Malaysians had to as well.[4] The result of this meeting demonstrated that Robert Kennedy had respect internationally and was still able to contribute to American foreign policy. In addition, it was clear that not only did people want to hear him, but also leaders from other countries.

From Japan, Robert Kennedy went to South Korea to meet American and South Korean soldiers at the 38th parallel, and then he went to Manila. With cheering students overwhelming his car, Kennedy proceeded to speak at the University of the Philippines and received an honorary degree. "President Kennedy had a particularly close relationship with young people," Kennedy said, this time with prepared remarks. It was the start of a rhetoric that hoped to inspire the next generation. He invoked his brother's ideals that the answer to problems around the world come from "the educated man." He went on, saying, "There is no question that in these dangerous days for all of us, that this planet has grown so small that we are as one."[5]

Like his brother, Robert Kennedy emphasized the importance of participation. "We have a responsibility to offer an alternative, to know what we are talking about, to think of our ideals and know what's behind them."[6] While there was still extreme grief and sorrow in his life, Robert Kennedy took his brother's philosophy and articulated it in his own way. In fact he said it himself that there were ideals bigger than his brother, and he wanted to keep that rhetoric alive. That effort was what propelled his rhetoric to new heights. The introspective nature of his remarks was an example of the journey that Robert Kennedy had been taking to understand the meaning of the events of 1963. He wanted to create a new society. He had witnessed destruction and experienced great loss. It was his way to honor his brother's contribution to the world while at the same time finding his own voice.

This trip demonstrated to Robert Kennedy and others that not only was he going to continue the work of the New Frontier, but he could also carry the ideals of JFK's rhetoric in his speeches. "So if there is anything that can be gained," he said in his speech at the University of the Philippines, "not just for the people of my own country in the United States, but really the people all over the world, and particularly the young people, by the life and death of President Kennedy, it's the fact that we must participate."[7] Edwin Guthman wrote that Bobby was "speaking from his heart, not his mind, groping to find some meaning to the President's death, trying to put it into words."[8] Indeed, Kennedy, like America in many ways, was at a crossroads. He needed to find himself. This trip, it seems, gave him an idea of how he could matter to people the way his brother did to so many. After he concluded the speech the place erupted in applause. Bobby stood motionless. Kennedy said to Schlesinger, "I hadn't wanted to go on that trip, but afterwards I was glad I had."[9] While Kennedy assumed his work at the Justice Department he still was not back in the swing of things yet. His great nemesis from his rackets committee days, Jimmy Hoffa, had finally been convicted and sent to prison. Kennedy commented that it was "nothing to celebrate."[10]

In those immediate months Robert Kennedy was trying to figure out his place in the world. He empowered young people and students across the world. This would become a big part of his rhetoric and legacy following JFK's death. The strength of America's youth to foster change in the 1960s is evidence that Bobby understood their power and wanted to harness it as a force moving forward with New Frontier ideas.

For President Johnson, 1964 was an important year, as he was gearing up for his run for the presidency. As any good politician would have done, he was making sure that Robert Kennedy would be an asset for his run and not someone who would be detrimental. Guthman remembered that Paul Corbin, a member of the Democratic National Committee and a friend of Kennedy, tried to get Bobby's name on the ticket for the vice president spot, and that did not go over well with Johnson. He suspected that Robert Kennedy had something to do with that.

On February 11, 1964, Lyndon Johnson called Robert Kennedy into the Oval Office after a cabinet meeting to complain about Paul Corbin. Corbin tried to get Bobby written in on the primary ballot as the vice president nominee in New Hampshire. LBJ wanted Corbin fired. RFK protected Corbin saying that he was a JFK appointee. Johnson disregarded the plea and said, "Do it," and then added, "President Kennedy is not president anymore. I am." Robert Kennedy remembered later that "it was a bitter, mean conversation." He added, "It was the meanest tone I've heard." Kennedy fired back to Johnson, "I know you're president, and don't ever talk to me like that again."[11] This is a relationship that Johnson needed desperately if he was truly going to use the legacy of the fallen president to pass legislation and guarantee his election in 1964. While he was coy with Kennedy and wanted to show him who was in charge, Bobby had a great deal of power with the people, and that would come into play in the years to come. But at the start this was a difficult relationship and something that the people would not fully realize until years after they were both dead.

In that same February 11 meeting, Johnson said that he sent Bobby to Indonesia "to keep things equal" for those looking for the vice president position. Kennedy responded, knowing that he would have to pay back any favors from the Johnson, "Don't ever do a favor for me again." Kennedy remarked to Guthman after that meeting, "I'll tell you one thing, this relationship can't last much longer."[12] Guthman wrote, "During this period a great amount of backbiting and rumor peddling fed the mistrust of both President Johnson and Bob." Guthman continued, "It did not arise from the friction or misunderstanding between Bob's staff and the new men Johnson brought into the White House."[13] Robert Kennedy had been contemplating a new role in government, and the souring relationship between him and Johnson might have been all that he needed to bring him to the next phase in that development. At the heart of Robert Kennedy's quest was his need to keep his brother's ideas alive. The New Frontier was a legacy that he thought would get lost with Johnson at the helm. The relationship grew more contentious as rumors regarding the 1964 election spread.

Apparently a story got to Johnson, through the FBI, that Guthman and others were going to nominate RFK for the presidency. It was not true. Despite that fact, it had an implication on the relationship with Johnson. "The President was furious," Guthman recalled. Kennedy "was amazed that President Johnson would put any credence in such a report, and of course he was miffed at the FBI." The report not only had ramifications on the LBJ–RFK relationship but also between Hoover and RFK.[14] Guthman wrote that RFK understood Johnson to some degree. Indeed they both had presidential aspirations and wanted to lead in their own right. Hoover was another story. RFK also recognized that he was no longer in the same place he was prior to the assassination and suffered from diminished political power. Hoover historically fed on power and he looked to Johnson as a result, instead of Kennedy.[15]

Guthman remembered thinking highly of the FBI going into his work at the Justice Department. It stemmed from his time in Seattle as a reporter. That respect remained when he left the Justice Department. He did not, however, feel the same way about Hoover. Guthman recalled that he became "disenchanted with Hoover as Hoover aged. [He] had become increasingly oppressive to the agents—and his inability to get along with men who honestly disagreed with his views; and finally by his treatment of Bob after the assassination, which seemed to me to be cruel."[16] Robert Kennedy remembered "his conversations with me on November 22nd were so unpleasant.... I don't, can't go into all the details of that, just that the tone in his voice and the information and what he was giving me was.... I mean it wasn't the way you would, under the circumstances, I thought an individual would talk."[17] Overall Robert Kennedy's experience to start 1964 was representative of how the administration would treat him. As the year progressed he continued to reshape his image and took some of his brother's ideals—incorporating them into his own rhetoric.

II

"Why did you die?"

Robert F. Kennedy addressed a group at the Joseph P. Kennedy Awards dinner in New York on February 5, 1964. He started the speech discussing the issue of "mental retardation," as it was called then, and talked about what President Kennedy had wanted to do to help those who were developmentally disabled. Kennedy said that all of them present at the dinner, as well as his fallen brother, "were strengthened in our determination to bring all the resources of knowledge, skill and compassion to the prevention of mental retardation and to aid and assist the five and a half million already afflicted." He continued, "Those here tonight are the people President Kennedy was counting on to lead this effort."[18] Still trying to lead the charge of the New Frontier, Bobby invoked his brother and the vision they shared for the nation.

In many ways Bobby understood the plight of the disadvantaged now more than ever. His experiences in office as well as the loss of his brother had affected him in ways that he did not yet understand. Bobby's speeches gave insight into the emotions his generation had a difficult time conveying to others. Kennedy said, "Millions of Americans had been condemned to a life of despair." He characterized them as the "forgotten nation—a nation of men and women who had been crippled through no fault of their own and their fellow citizens, except for their heartbroken families, hardly knew they existed." Kennedy wanted to raise awareness of this issue to the American public. This dinner, he said, was part of the effort to do that. Indeed, this was something personal to Kennedy, as his own sister, Rosemary, was among the "afflicted" he referred to in his speech. Kennedy said that much has been done to raise awareness as well as research in this field, but there was still more to do. "Because only if the fortunate—help those who are afflicted, can [there] be any hope for the future for any of us. It is our responsibility towards our fellow human beings that we engage in this work."[19] This was an example of the new rhetoric that Bobby was trying to channel. His words were meant to comfort but also inspire action, which was how the New Frontier tried to attack the issues in American society. Indeed, the Kennedy administration learned how to use rhetoric effectively, and Robert Kennedy was not only a witness, but he also helped craft the imagery that has sustained for so many years since the inaugural in 1961.

In March 1964, RFK, Jackie and others spent some time at the Caribbean island of Antigua as guests of Rachel Lambert "Bunny" Mellon. Jackie gave Bobby Edith Hamilton's book *The Greek Way* on this trip.

Kennedy became enthralled with Greek poets and historians, finding some solace in their view of the world. He dove into the world of Herodotus, Aeschylus and others.[20] Kennedy was lost, looking for some logical meaning behind his brother's death. But he could not find it anywhere, not even in his own faith, which he was devoted to on many levels. Evan Thomas argues that the Greeks brought RFK back to the point where he understood his obligation to "serve the state." From the tragedies he found solace and a deeper understanding of life.[21] Indeed, these stories brought his own experiences into perspective. His convictions were now built on tragedy and the events that shaped not only his life, but many in America. In the winter and spring of 1964 Kennedy put himself in an exile, looking for meaning.[22] This changed his outlook on life and brought him closer with the people in the nation whom he would fight for later in his career.

On St. Patrick's Day in 1964, Robert Kennedy agreed to give a speech to the Friendly Sons of Saint Patrick in Scranton, Pennsylvania. When RFK's private plane, *The Caroline*, landed, more than two thousand people broke the police lines and wanted to see RFK.[23] In his address Robert Kennedy talked about how the Irish had come to the United States prior to the Civil War, saying, "They left behind hearts and fields and a nation yearning to be free." Kennedy had tried to identify with those who were disadvantaged in his address. "But no one familiar with the story of the Irish here would underrate the difficulties they faced after landing in the United States. As the first of the racial minorities, our forefathers were subject to every discrimination found wherever discrimination is known."[24] This was not the first time he had tried to connect racial discrimination to his family story. During the Freedom Rides Kennedy had spoken to civil rights advocates and used this experience as a means to connect with them. It was not something, however, that African Americans would not acknowledge as the same. After all, at least Kennedy's forefathers were free and not enslaved by law.

In his speech Robert Kennedy hoped to make a connection between the disadvantaged and his ancestors. To be sure, there was a connection, but it was often lost on the crowd given the fact that Kennedy himself came from a great deal of wealth and privilege. Kennedy went on to say that the "Irish have survived persecution in their own land and discrimination in ours. They have emerged from the shadow of subjugation into the sunlight of personal liberty and national independence." He continued, "Indeed, Ireland's chief export has been neither the potatoes nor linen, but exiles and immigrants who have fought with sword and pen for freedom around the earth." This speech seems to have empowered Kennedy. In the wake of his brother's death he struggled, looking to the Greeks for some solace and explanation. This speech touched on something that his family identified and drew power from. Indeed, the plight of the Irish was a badge that he wore to let others know that he understood the plight of the disadvantaged.

Kennedy started to craft his own voice in this speech. He said, "Today the Irish enjoy their freedom at a time when billions of people live in deprivation and despair under totalitarian dictatorships stretching eastward from the Wall in Berlin to the troubled borders of South Viet Nam." He continued, "I know of few in our land—and I hope none in this room—who would ignore threats to peace and freedom in far off places." Kennedy's allusion to the Cold War threats was his way of testing his own abilities to talk about these things in the same public way that his brother did. He wanted to be on a larger stage, and this was a good place to test that out. He said, "No problem weighs heavier on the conscience of free men than the fate of millions held in iron captivity."

Beyond the Cold War, Kennedy went further to distinguish his views on civil rights. "I would hope that none here would ignore the current struggle of some of our fellow citizens right here in the United States for their measure of freedom." In the hopes of making a link between the plight of civil rights leaders and the Irish, he harked back to the travails of Irish Catholics in the seventeenth century. He said that his time in the Justice Department was spent looking at the rights of others. "There are Americans who—as the Irish did—still face discrimination in employment—sometimes open, sometimes hidden. There are cities today that are torn with strife over whether a Negro should be allowed to drive a garbage truck; and there are walls of silent conspiracy that block the progress of others because of race or creed, without regard to ability." Of course, Kennedy was also trying to gain support for the Civil Rights Act that was making its way through Congress. The civil rights movement was in full swing. Dr. King was also trying to get the same legislation passed. The two men shared the belief that the government could make a difference in the effort to achieve freedom and equality for all.

Kennedy said that the greatest threat to freedom, however, was communism, "a tyranny that holds its captives in vice like subjugation on a global scale. For nearly twenty years we and our Allies have striven to halt the communist advance." In a divergence from the usual diplomacy, Kennedy spoke to America's allies who did not recognize the same freedoms the United States does.

> It is easy for us to believe that the imperialism of the west was infinitely preferable to the tyranny of communism. But the sullen hostility of the African and Asian colonial nations have shown us that not all hold the same view. The bloody struggles for liberty from the sands of Algeria and the steaming jungles of Indonesia and Viet Nam proved that others would make the same sacrifices to throw off the yoke of imperialism today that the Irish did more than half a century ago.

With American in transition, this quote speaks to the struggles of American foreign policy and how he planned to approach them.

Kennedy ended this speech on a personal note. He spoke about Irish legend Owen Roe O'Neill's death. He quoted a poem that spoke about the grief the Irish people felt in the wake of O'Neill's death. When he practiced this speech, Kennedy would not be able to finish the last lines of the poem because he thought of his fallen brother.

> We're sheep without a shepherd
> When the snow shuts out the sky
> Oh! why did you leave us Owen?
> Why did you die?

Guthman recalled that he reworked the speech to leave out the poem. Kennedy asked, "Why did you do that?" Guthman said, "You'll never get through it. You don't have to put yourself through that." Kennedy responded, "I've been practicing in front of a mirror. I can't get through it yet—but I will."[25] Guthman wrote that RFK was trying

> to demonstrate the public and key political support that impress occupants of the White House and, in this instance, might lead President Johnson to conclude that Bob's vote polling power in the north and west would more than offset the liability he would be in the south.[26]

Guthman also wrote that the experience in Scranton had an impact on RFK. Kennedy found himself in the midst of a vice president race—despite the fact that he knew he couldn't do it and that LBJ wouldn't want him. "I'd be climbing the walls in three months," he said.[27]

Kennedy's speech articulated his position on Cold War and civil rights issues. It was his moment to come out to the public and begin to lay out his vision for the nation on his own. It was clear that Johnson was going to omit him on the ticket as the vice president. Kennedy would have to find another way to impact the events in the nation. This speech was his first attempt to articulate his beliefs in a meaningful way.

The *Rocky Mountain News* out of Colorado published a story on March 22, 1964, saying that Ted Kennedy praised Lyndon Johnson in his remarks, which even hinted at Bobby in the VP race. Ted Kennedy made it clear to the reporter that the Kennedys "are going to continue to be public servants." He even went as far as to characterize reports that there was friction between Bobby and LBJ as "fabrications." He invoked his fallen brother's ideals that Colorado can demonstrate to the nation that "the west is not the stronghold of reaction but progress ... not the home of extremism but of common sense." He said that "the people of this state are not just for themselves but for each other and that the spirit of the New Frontier lives on."[28]

Ted Kennedy's comments not only speak to his support of New Frontier idealism, but also to a revitalization of liberalism that the Kennedys are linked to and that would polarize politics going into the twenty-first century. Ted Kennedy spoke in support of the War on Poverty, going as far as to say that JFK wanted similar programs. He also said that he believed a civil rights bill was eminent after some debate in Congress. He pushed for strong legislation to help western projects. "Shoes and textiles of Massachusetts couldn't be sold without a strong economy in our west."[29] Ted Kennedy's support of the president's program was an indication that Bobby was finally ready to make a move. To be sure, the fact that Ted Kennedy showed solidarity with LBJ was an important element. It was up to Lyndon Johnson if he wanted Bobby on the ticket or if the political establishment would be able to pressure LBJ to do it.

Robert Kennedy was interviewed by Jack Paar in March 1964. The questions mostly focused on the future Kennedy Library and how Jackie and the kids were doing in the wake of the tragedy. He told stories of Ted Kennedy, in the aftermath of the assassination, telling John and Caroline stories at night and Dave Powers, a Kennedy adviser and close friend, going to see the kids at midday. In the course of the interview Paar asked Bobby what was in his future. "Well, I thought a lot about what the future would be a good deal during December, and I finally decided in the first week of January that I would put that off, that I would stay as attorney general through the election and then I would just decide what I was doing afterwards." There were many in the Democratic Party, however, that felt differently, and they would be sure to pressure Kennedy to make a decision as to what role he would play in American politics. Nevertheless, Kennedy made it clear that he was "not prepared to decide yet."[30] This was a critical moment for the young Kennedy. Much like the period between serving Senator Joseph McCarthy and Senator John McClellan, Bobby was waiting, looking for something that would occupy his passion and desire to do something for the nation. As he engaged in this quest, Kennedy continued to make speeches, finding his own voice while at the same time continuing with what he believed were his brother's ideals.

In his statement to the Clergymen's Association, Martin Luther King commended the "door-to-door" efforts of voter registration. King liked the turnout and said, "The enemies of civil rights have a way of exaggerating problems in Washington's Negro community and using them to reflect adversely upon the Negro struggle throughout the country."[31] The vote was an important issue. As the spring turned into summer, students and civil rights leaders from all over the country readied themselves for a battle in Mississippi. It proves that the nation was at odds with its fundamental ideals. Beyond the egalitarian spirit that it was constantly at odds with, the democratic ideals of the republic were at stake. King and others hoped to make that issue a part of the rhetoric until all citizens, regardless of race, would be able to enjoy the full fruits of rights that had been given to them by God.

III

"This program calls for a total attack on the cycle of poverty."

While going through JFK's materials, Bobby found a scrap of paper from one of the last cabinet meetings that had the word "poverty" written on it several times and circled. Kennedy took it to represent part of JFK's legacy and had it framed and displayed in his office at the Justice Department.[32] Perhaps the religious RFK needed a sign from the grave where he should go in the wake of the tragedy. How would he define himself for the world in a way that was distinctive but also honor the memory of his fallen brother? Indeed, the push to end poverty was very pervasive in the late sixties. Both Johnson and Kennedy wanted to attack this issue, and it does become a part of their legacy in history. King also took it on as his own movement after the Selma campaign in 1965.

In his first State of the Union address on January 8, 1964, Lyndon Johnson outlined for the American people his vision for the nation. He incorporated two important issues that would be entwined both with JFK's legacy and his own—civil rights and an attack on poverty. Johnson started his speech saying,

> Let this session of Congress be known as the session which did more for civil rights than the last hundred sessions combined; as the session which enacted the most far-reaching tax cut of our time; as the session which declared all-out war on human poverty and unemployment in these United States.

He went on to address the issues of health care and infrastructure needs for the nation as well as foreign aid and an education program. In short, he outlined what history would term the Great Society. Johnson's ambitious agenda paved the way for change, but it also acknowledged John F. Kennedy's presidency, saying, "Let us carry forward the plans and programs of John Fitzgerald Kennedy—not because of our sorrow or sympathy, but because they are right."[33] Not only did he use Kennedy's legacy to get these programs past Congress, but he gave credit to JFK as someone who came up with these options that redefined American liberalism.

Johnson pledged a "progressive administration." At the heart of the message were the two issues that haunted the nation before Vietnam altered it forever. "Unfortunately," he said, "many Americans live on the outskirts of hope—some because of their poverty, and some because of their color, and all too many because of both. Our task is to help replace their despair with opportunity." That was the prelude to his ultimate declaration that said, "This administration today, here and now, declares unconditional war on poverty in America. I urge this Congress and all Americans to join with me in that effort." His effort was in the sprint of New Frontier ideas, but it also hoped to do more.

Johnson understood that this effort would take time and acknowledged, "It will not be a short or easy struggle, no single weapon or strategy will suffice, but we shall not rest until that war is won." In a new approach to liberalism, hoping to pay homage and enhance FDR's New Deal, he said, "The richest Nation on earth can afford to win it. We cannot afford to lose it. One thousand dollars invested in salvaging an unemployable youth today can return $40,000 or more in his lifetime."[34] This speech set in motion an effort to create government programs to help the disadvantaged. Indeed, it was unprecedented and proposed in the midst of a wave of affluence. Johnson hoped to create his own legacy while at the same time inspiring others the way FDR had shaped his own belief in government. In early 1964 it seemed that a Johnson presidency meant to revitalize America, infusing it with programs that would help Americans for generations. Vietnam was not a part of that equation. Johnson had never planned for a war to be his legacy.

The "War on Poverty," as it would be known, complemented the efforts of the civil rights movement. It also became an important piece of the vision that both Robert Kennedy and Martin Luther King had for the nation. Kennedy supported the War on Poverty that Lyndon Johnson was waging not only because he believed in it and shared the same values, but also because it was originally a part of John F. Kennedy's agenda before he died. The day before his younger brother Ted would give his maiden speech on the floor of the Senate, Robert Kennedy addressed the House Committee on Education and Labor in support of LBJ's initiative. "This program calls for a total attack on the cycle of poverty, frustration and dependency in which too many of our fellow Americans are caught—millions of people who have been pushed to the wall and largely forgotten."[35]

This plight was something that Kennedy would embrace throughout the rest of his life, and it would be a major part of his agenda in his run for the presidency in 1968. "This program seeks to bring hope to the hopeless, dignity to the deprived and self-respect to people who have none." He invoked his brother in the opening saying that JFK was "totally committed to confronting and dealing with these problems, and involving the national administration to a greater extent than ever before." Robert Kennedy said that his brother "saw the national administration's role as provisional leadership, pointing the way, firing answers and stimulating local communities, states and private interests to step up their efforts to run their own programs." RFK was ushering in a new kind of liberalism and hoped to define it for the next generation of Americans. Lyndon Johnson's program was an important part of this transformation in American politics. Indeed, it played a major role in bringing the American identity into a new era.

In the hopes of tying his endeavors to the Democratic Party, Robert Kennedy understood the importance of such programs for the people of the nation.

> Our system is fiercely competitive. This has produced an affluent society and gives Americans unparalleled opportunities for achievement. But if a person is uneducated or poorly educated, or is handicapped by poor health, old age, or race or religion, he cannot compete; and the gap between the prosperous world and his poverty will widen.[36]

In the wake of World War II, the United States emerged as one of the greatest societies in history, offering many new opportunities for social mobility. As the nation moved into a new era in politics and a challenge to liberalism was on the horizon, Robert Kennedy looked not only to extend those programs but also to redefine them for future generations. His speech before the House of Representatives focused on how these new bills could help young people. He referred to the success of the Committee on Juvenile Delinquency and Youth Crime, Washington Action for Youth and a halfway house program launched by the Bureau of Prisons. He told the stories of young people who were helped by these groups and how the House needed to continue to fund these programs not only because it would help these adolescents but because it was the future of the country. All of this rhetoric reshaped his image to the nation, paving the way for a campaign, reimagining the New Frontier.

This issue was linked to Kennedy's empowerment of America's youth. Attacking poverty would help many young people achieve new heights. Kennedy remarked, "For each success story there are ten examples of where only a surface has been scratched." He highlighted Harlem, New York and Charleston, West Virginia, as two examples of communities that "are trying to do something about those problems and are getting some help from the federal government." He went on to cite statistics of the grueling circumstances in those communities and the disadvantages children have growing up in them. In a voice that he would someday fully embrace and make a part of his campaign for the presidency, Kennedy said, "These are the cycles of despair that our nation must cope with. These are some of the complex, interwoven problems that we set out to deal with in the [Juvenile Delinquency Act] three years ago."[37] Kennedy was not only supporting Johnson's measure before Congress; he was also pointing to his brother's success. More importantly, he saw juvenile delinquency linked to poverty and saw this measure as a way to empower young people. This legislation was passed under JFK's watch, and Robert Kennedy wanted it known that it had done a lot to help people, which was becoming more and more his own mantra that he would embrace.

Kennedy looked not only to give children better education opportunities but also to help their families find some way to improve themselves. His speech spoke to the hope that by attacking poverty it also attacked the issue of rights. "We have concentrated on changing an environment which breeds hopelessness and defeatism—in which a young person is unable to move the institutions which affect him; in which he comes to feel that everything is closing in on him—that he is powerless in a hostile world." Kennedy continued saying that "There is no one cause of delinquency—and poverty." The complexities behind the poverty issue in a nation that was so "affluent," as Kennedy pointed out in the beginning of his testimony, are many.

> These factors do not exist in isolation; they exist together, and reinforce one another. And together they overwhelm the young person. A program to deal with youth cannot merely change one or a few of these conditions. It must be a total attack on the problems of inadequate adults, illiteracy, infant mortality, dilapidated and crowded housing, inadequate community services, crime, unemployment, and mental illness.

He concluded that in order to usher in these changes this effort must be done with a combination of the federal government stimulating "local action." This testimony provides insight into the issues that Kennedy saw as paramount for the government to address. To be sure, this preview is something that we can use to unwrap his vision for the nation and how that drove not only his work but also that of the people that followed him.

Kennedy went on to speak about the different elements of the act and how groups could work together. At the heart of his testimony was a plea that in order to make America an even greater nation the federal and local government needed to play a role to help the disadvantaged, which was an ideal of the Great Society. Kennedy said that the bill

> represents a broad attack on poverty, and its parts fit well together. The great challenge that we have as a nation is to solve this problem. The Federal government, the states, local communities, private organizations and individual citizens must join together. If we can do what we have done around the world in Europe, in

Latin-America, in Africa and Asia, and then find we cannot effectively wipe out poverty here, then we will have failed as a society.

This challenge was representative of the Kennedy idealism that was so pervasive in the Camelot Period. Robert Kennedy invoked those ideals in an effort to pass this legislation. He was also refocusing these notions in the wake of his brother's death in the hopes of recapturing some of the ideals that made his brother's administration different and captivating. He finished, saying, "There are children without half a chance, without proper food, without proper medical care. There are fathers who are unable to work because of illness or lack of training. There are mothers and senior citizens—all important, all individuals, who feel the pain of hunger and despair and degradation."[38]

Robert Kennedy was experiencing a reawakening of sorts. He had great compassion for people who suffered. From his dark malaise in the wake of his brother's death rose from the ashes a progressive liberal who wanted to help the disadvantaged. The speech was more than support of Johnson's programs; it was a realization of his own vision for the nation, which he embraced moving forward and made a part of his family's legacy to American history.

As America stood on the precipice of great change, Robert Kennedy attempted to help the nation see the problems they were confronting not only in the wake of JFK's death, but also as 1964 became the year where all movements would ignite and explode into 1965. This was the heart of his philosophy, looking to deal with problems in new ways, promising a new American society. Indeed, it mirrored his own brother's rhetoric. What Kennedy, and others from this period, did accomplish was bringing to the forefront the issues of poverty and race. Further, by empowering the youth through his rhetoric he set the stage for rights groups to take advantage of this new world and promote their ideals to help this growing society. The next day his brother Ted stood on the floor of the Senate and gave his maiden speech about civil rights.

IV

"His heart and soul are in this bill."

It must have been an emotional moment for the young senator from Massachusetts, Edward M. Kennedy. Life had not yet interfered with what had the potential of a storied political career. He would become, as some would call him, "the Lion of the Senate." It was appropriate and altogether fitting that the first time he officially spoke out was in support of his fallen brother's civil rights bill. "Mr. President," he said, "it is with some hesitation that I rise to speak on the pending legislation before the Senate." Ted Kennedy said,

> A freshman senator should be seen, not heard; should learn, and not teach. This is especially true when the Senate is engaged in a truly momentous debate, in which we have seen displayed the most profound skills of the ablest Senators, in both parties, on both sides of the issues.[39]

Indeed there was a great deal of support and debate on this bill. Kennedy spoke about the discussion, saying how impressed he was that the leaders of the country were committed to finding a national consensus on the issue.

Ted Kennedy appreciated the nature of the issue and felt compelled to comment on it. He recalled in his memoir that the passage of the bill "in the Senate remained far from a sure thing. No important civil rights legislation since Reconstruction had ever made it past the stone wall of southern resistance."[40] He realized that by taking the floor so early in his career he was breaking tradition. "But it seemed to me that civil rights was *the* issue and this was *the* time. I was increasingly involved in both the substance of the discussion and the debate and felt that it was very important to speak out."[41] He continued on the floor of the Senate with his testimony, saying,

> I believe that the basic problem the American people face in the 1960s in the field of civil rights is one of adjustment. It is the task of adjusting to the fact that Negroes are going to be members of the community of American citizens, with the same rights and same responsibility as every one of us.[42]

Kennedy spoke from the perspective of Massachusetts and stressed that the state had done a great deal over the years to embrace different groups of people. "We have not suffered from this effect," he said. "Indeed, we have been strengthened."

At the heart of his comments was the notion that legislation would do more to make America a stronger nation. He understood the gradualistic nature of the legislation.

> It is true, as has been said on this floor, that prejudice exists in the minds and hearts of men. It can not be eradicated by law. But I firmly believe a sense of fairness and goodwill also exists in the minds and hearts of men, side by side with the prejudice; a sense of fairness and goodwill which shows itself so often in acts of charity and kindness toward others.

This hope was something that the Kennedy brothers shared with Dr. King's vision of the nation—that people would someday find a way to accept everyone for who they were. Kennedy believed that the bill had "deep moral implications for the individual and his society." To be sure, the Civil Rights

Act would have major implications that would continue into the twenty-first century.

In his final plea to the Senate, Ted Kennedy invoked his brother's spirit. Indeed, Lyndon Johnson did the same thing in his address to Congress. It was important to link the bill to John F. Kennedy, which makes that measure even more a part of his final legacy to the nation. "My brother was the first president of the United States to state publicly that segregation was morally wrong," Ted Kennedy said.

> His heart and soul are in this bill. If his life and death had a meaning, it was that we should not hate but love one another; we should use our powers not to create conditions of oppression that lead to violence, but conditions of freedom that lead to peace. It is in that spirit that I hope the Senate will pass this bill.

Kennedy's speech brought into perspective the history behind this bill. His reference to the "minds and hearts of men" was something that both Robert Kennedy and Martin Luther King referred to in their speeches. Indeed, it was a difficult charge to try and change human nature. This bill, however, had the potential to do exactly that, or so the Kennedys and King would argue. It certainly played a role in shaping a new America.

On a larger note, Ted Kennedy's maiden speech puts into sharp focus the significant role these brothers played in changing the climate of the nation. All of them stood up publicly and demanded that every American had a legal right to the same protection under the law. There is no historical parallel in American history where three brothers led the charge for a bill. To be sure the issue of equality under the law was more than a stand on an issue for the Kennedy brothers. It became their longest, lasting legacy. John F. Kennedy's June 11, 1963, address on civil rights set the tone. It was followed by the support of his attorney general, Robert Kennedy, in a variety of forms, ranging from testimony in front of Congress to assisting civil rights groups going back to 1960. Finally, Ted Kennedy's maiden speech was the last piece that brought all three brothers together in one bill that looked to change the nation to be more inclusive of its citizens. The Civil Rights Act was as much a Kennedy brothers piece of legislation as it was Johnson's—the man who signed it.

4

"The Hearts and Minds of Youth"

I

"They will prevail."

Robert Kennedy's message in 1964 would catapult him into the race for a Senate seat. While he was reluctant to embrace this opportunity, it would inevitably lead him to find a place where he would be on his own and able to give his own ideas. Robert Kennedy saw America's youth as an important force that would move America, indeed the world, in a new direction. This was a position that drove his rhetoric, empowering young people everywhere, leading to larger movements.

On April 14, 1964, he addressed the Canadian press in Toronto. He opened the speech saying how grateful he was to the Canadian people for the outpouring of support after JFK was killed. "I also have a special relationship toward Canada—I met my wife here about twenty years ago. And that has been an interesting experience." He continued by speaking about what he believed was crucial. "I would like to talk briefly about the importance of the current world-wide contest for the hearts and minds of youth, particularly the youth in undeveloped nations." Kennedy believed that both nations had an interest in this notion. "We approach it from the same traditions of law; the same basis of representative governments." Perhaps the most revealing point was how he linked empowering young people to JFK. "It was the intense personal interest to President Kennedy, who became identified with young people throughout the world to an extent that many did not realize during his lifetime." To compound that notion he emphasized its importance: "It is, I believe, a topic of such transcendent importance that it may powerfully influence the world five, ten or twenty years from now."[1]

This approach to ingratiate the youth of the world was Bobby's attempt to reach out to foreign nations in the same way that the Peace Corps hoped to accomplish. This type of nation building begins with empowering and educating the young people of undeveloped nations. "As you know, we do not live today in a world which will guarantee gradual change. It might happen, but nobody can count on it, and among the developing nations, in particular, the need is felt to race through centuries to the present."[2] Robert Kennedy believed in the power of the youth of the 1960s and saw them as a force of change. This, of course, would have an impact on the United States in the coming years that would reshape American society in much the same way that Bobby hoped it would for undeveloped nations of the world.

He pointed to some of the great moments led by students whom he characterized as "a dynamic force with an importance out of all proportion to their numbers." Staying with the international theme, he spoke of the 1956 Hungarian uprising, which was organized and led by students. "It was a movement that was ultimately repressed by Russian tanks. But before the freedom fighters fell onto the bloodstained cobblestone of Budapest, the world knew them." He saw those students as heroes in the Cold War who gave the ultimate sacrifice. "They rocked the structure of international communism to its very foundation. Because of these students things will never be the same."[3] Kennedy went further with other examples of where young people led the way in world events.

Kennedy believed in the power of "young intellectuals," that they would someday impact the world as future leaders. "We must be concerned with these young people, who they are, where they live, with what they are thinking and saying, and what we are saying to them."[4] Perhaps Kennedy's own youthfulness played a role in recognizing the power of the world's youth. It is clear that he not only understood the strength of how the youth would change things, but he also respected it. He also witnessed the power of that voice when he was attorney general. To be sure this was an important facet of his rhetoric and it empowered people throughout the nation, leading to a movement that reshaped American society.

The nation was at a crossroads where society was moving to challenge social norms. The efforts of the civil rights movement empowered people through the grassroots experience, wherein many groups found a voice that would carry them through the sixties and into subsequent decades. Kennedy was in touch with how the world was changing. "We must recognize the young in many areas of the world today are in the midst of revolution against the status quo," he said. "They are not going to accept platitudes and generalities. Their anger has been turned on the systems which have allowed poverty, illiteracy and oppression to flourish for centuries." Indeed the Students for a Democratic Society was a perfect example of a group that looked to challenge all of these elements that RFK spoke about. America was in the midst of that revolution as well as the rest of the world. "And we must recognize one simple fact; they will prevail. They will achieve their idealistic goals one way or the other." He saw the passion and determination of this generation. "If they have to pull governments tumbling down over their heads, they will do it. But they are going to win their share of a better cleaner world." He understood that they would change the world and he had a responsibility to contribute to that revolution. More importantly, he foresaw the power of these young groups. Later in the decade they would prove not only that they could challenge civil rights violations but also move the nation away from war, questioning leadership to the point that it would create a crisis of confidence.

One of the elements that changed the climate in the nation where Americans accepted the plight of civil rights groups was the fact that the Kennedy brothers were willing to work with these groups and pushed for change. Robert Kennedy and his assistant attorney general, Burke Marshall, were strong supporters of civil rights, and Bobby understood that it was something that should be supported as that struggle continued. "We, in turn, are part of their revolution. At least we should be, and I believe that we must encourage them in their efforts to bring about improvements."[5] He continued his support for these groups as the decade continued.

Robert Kennedy found solace in the Greeks when his brother was killed. He read Edith Hamilton's *The Greek Way*. In addition, he looked to continue his brother's ideals as he moved into his own political career. He pointed out that the future may be perilous, "but it is also exciting." Moving to Hamilton's notions from her book, he said, "It has been said that 'men are made for safe havens.' And if the odds seem long, then as someone once said of Aeschylus, 'to the heroic desperate odds fling a challenge.'" Invoking his brother's inaugural, he said, "We of the western tradition are all heirs of revolution ... our people have achieved the changes that were the felt needs of the time."

Robert Kennedy concluded his speech, saying, "I know these are not easy words. It is hard to prepare for a challenge, maybe harder still to seek out the young from whom the challenges arise.... I want to be certain we make the choice, not for sleep, but for truth."[6] He spoke to the press because they had a unique place in the free world and could do more to affect the perceptions of the youth. Kennedy was still in the throes of getting what he believed was his brother's civil rights bill to President Johnson's desk, and he was determined that he see it through and believed that it would truly have a place in this revolution that he spoke of in his speech.

His rhetoric crafted a vision for the nation and the world. Robert Kennedy paved the way for the ideals of the New Frontier to continue and provided a framework for change. His vision was tied to his brother's ideals, and his speech not only empowered young people but it also empowered Kennedy. His words helped move the nation forward as they came to grips with the loss of his brother and resonated as they were spoken with the same accent and perspective. To be sure, the emotional response from the people and politicians who heard these words played a role in helping legislation and moving the nation to the next phase of the American identity.

II

"We are going to pay for what has gone on in the past."

When President Kennedy met with civil rights leaders, in the weeks just before the March on Washington, he pointed to the low polling numbers since he sent the bill to Congress. "I may lose the next election because of this. I don't care," President Kennedy said.[7] He wanted the bill passed despite the prospect that it could hurt his chances at reelection. In the end, the Kennedy brothers wanted to contribute to this rights revolution. Bobby even commented to John Bartlow Martin in 1964, "If the campaign meant anything, if what Jack Kennedy had always stood for meant anything, it meant doing something in this field." He went on to say that "it was never a question of sitting around thinking, 'well, should we do it or shouldn't we do it,' because it was always quite clear that we *would* do it. And *had* to do it."[8] The Civil Rights Bill and continuing to change the climate in the country was something that JFK and RFK started. Robert Kennedy wanted to see it through to the end. But of course that wasn't the only issue that JFK wanted addressed.

Two days after his speech in Canada, Robert Kennedy participated in a panel discussion at the American Society of Newspaper Editors on April 16, 1964. The theme was "After the Civil Rights Bill, What?" Bobby was clear with his feelings on civil rights. "No matter how one feels on the question of civil rights," he said, "it is a matter that affects all our lives." He had the same points for his brother less than a year earlier. He even went as far as to say, "There are no domestic problems that have greater effect on all of us, whether we be white or negro, than the civil rights problems that are facing the United States at the present time." Kennedy understood the gravity of the issue, and there was no clear, immediate resolution. "I don't think that there is any question that it is a major domestic problem, and I would anticipate that it will be the major domestic problem for a number of years to come," he said, "because the mere passage of the legislation is not going to make these difficulties disappear."[9] Indeed, passing the legislation is the first step, but it would take generations to gain any ground against the racist ideas that have captivated this nation since the first slave ship came over to Jamestown in 1619. Kennedy saw that this, like other issues he was facing, would change the nation, which was why he was so focused on the youth and looking to the future. He realized that legislation would only take people so far. They needed to change the climate. He understood that in some cases this would not be easy and it would take time.

Certainly Kennedy understood that many people in the nation did not see civil rights as an important issue to the nation. "There are those, I think, in the past who have felt that this really hasn't been a national problem, that it has been a problem of the South and the South alone. I think that this feeling really existed until perhaps May, June or July of 1963." He pointed to the issues in Alabama that he and Burke Marshall had navigated at Birmingham and later when Katzenbach and Kennedy had confronted Wallace at the University of Alabama as catalysts of change for the nation. It is also a reference to his brother's civil rights speech in June, which truly began the momentum for the legislation. "So I think that as we face this civil rights legislation, as we consider it in its context, we have to consider it as something that deals with a nationwide problem and not just a sectional problem."[10] That last piece summed up how RFK felt about the Civil Rights Bill and that once it was passed the nation needed to consider where it was going in the aftermath.

Robert Kennedy saw the law as a defining force in American society. "I think, in conclusion, the really major problem that is going to affect all of us is what is going to happen when the legislation is passed." He spoke of the *Brown* decision and how it was challenged in the South. He believed that it was "essential" for America to acknowledge and abide by this legislation.

> I think that if we have learned anything in the Department of Justice over the period of the last three years, it's the heartache, the misery, the pain and the suffering that comes from community leaders telling people of their communities that they don't have to obey the law, that they don't have to follow it.

Kennedy mentioned how leaders in Alabama tried to tell people to resist the court order that desegregated the University of Alabama. "After instructions like that are given to people by the persons who are looked up to as the leaders in the community, I don't see how then we can be surprised to find the result is violence, disorder, or disobedience of the law."[11] Kennedy's comments alluded to the climate that Dr. King and others blamed for JFK's death as well as the racist ideology of southern politicians. The movements that characterized the sixties were as much about changing this climate as they were about challenging segregation and America's role in Vietnam.

Kennedy was at the forefront of that transition, serving as its leader and catalyst for societal change.

A great deal of culpability, according to Kennedy, lay in the truculent rhetoric of leaders who defied the law. Men like George Wallace and Ross Barnett led the way in a segregationist platform that became fossilized by the rights movements of the sixties led by the youth that Kennedy hoped to empower. Of course, Kennedy saw this defiance firsthand. He was afraid that the same thing would happen with the Civil Rights Bill.

> When a governor of a state testifies before a general committee that if this legislation is enacted we are going to have to bring troops back from Berlin in order to enforce it—when such encouragement is given to those who disagree with the legislation—I don't see how we can be surprised when a person puts a bomb under a church or shoots at a Negro.[12]

Kennedy laid the violence at the feet of its leaders, which had its roots in the aftermath of the Civil War and harked back to the "lost cause" that was so pervasive in that society. The problem facing the nation had its roots in a society that fostered a racist status quo. Kennedy saw the importance of leadership to move beyond the norm, the complacent, racist attitudes of Americans when it came to the race issue. His rhetoric was defiant of the old Democratic institution and pointed to his own transformation as well as the nation's journey in those years following the assassination.

Kennedy's feelings on the bill and what it could accomplish spoke to his ability to see the race issue and the role he could play in helping the nation move to the next stage of development.

> It seems to me that the passage of the legislation is not going to make the problem disappear. I don't think anyone involved in the civil rights struggle says that if you pass this law then the difficulties are going to disappear, because they are just not. We are going to have problems in this field for a very long time. We are going to pay for what has gone on in the past.

Kennedy had hope for the nation. He pointed to education as the first step, followed up by poverty legislation that would reform tax law and make jobs available. "Much of the fundamental problem," he said, "stems from the fact that it is true for many Negroes your parents couldn't get a job, you can't get a job and there is no future."[13] He broke the issues down to the basic root of survival. The act had the potential to change some of these circumstances. Education of all Americans equally could make a difference in changing the status of and empowering Americans who were previously powerless.

The disparity in the nation was obvious to Kennedy. Looking at the youth again, he said, "If legislation is not passed, I think that Negroes in many areas of the United States, particularly our younger Negro population who are getting more educated and dissatisfied, are going to say there is no future in this system." He pointed out that people can make speeches on the Fourth of July or Washington's birthday. "We can all make patriotic speeches ... but all these speeches are being made by white people."[14] If African Americans did not see that the federal government was looking to change the status quo, Kennedy implied that they would no longer be invested in the success of that society. He wanted to make opportunities for the young people of the country.

What would become one of Robert Kennedy's strengths was his ability to empathize with other people. It was that aspect of his personality that brought him so far to understanding the plight of African Americans and their struggle for equality. While he was chastised and told differently by many, Robert Kennedy was far beyond many of his generation and would contribute to changing the status quo. "The Negro asks: what is our future? What do you hold out to us? There is a future for a white person, but what is the future for the Negro? I think this is a major question." In this exchange Kennedy translated that empathy so people could see his point. He believed that the nation needed more than action by the federal government. "It is going to have to be action by local citizens; it is going to have to be action by the newspaper; it is going to have to be action by the local political leaders making an effort in their local community to try to do something about the schools, for example." He concluded, "I think the legislation is essential, but I think there has to be something more than that."[15]

In a sweeping point, Kennedy brought together the issue of civil rights and how it related to the growing crisis in Vietnam. He did not speak out against Vietnam until much later in the Senate, as he saw it as part of his brother's legacy. He told the panel that while looking at the casualty list from the war, he noticed some African Americans who were killed—several of them from southern states. "The widow of one of them lives in Alabama," he told the panel. Introspectively Kennedy shared his thoughts on how that relationship between these two defining issues of the sixties impacted each other.

> I was just thinking that if she brought her husband's body back and it was buried in Arlington across the River, and then she had to go back to Alabama, she wouldn't know what hotel she could stop at, she wouldn't know where she could stop at a restaurant, she wouldn't know where she could stop for a restroom. When she gets back to her local community, she can't bring her children to a theatre.

He was able to bring aspects of life that most people take for granted and demonstrate how those aspects of life have been denied to Americans—even those who lost loved ones in war. He said, "And yet her husband had just been killed in Vietnam on behalf of all of us." He finished, saying, "It just doesn't make any sense. It doesn't make any sense to us and it certainly is not going to make any sense to a Negro brought up under that system."[16]

Later that day Robert Kennedy addressed the American Jewish Committee Appeal for Human Relations dinner, where he accepted an award. "For weeks now, almost every night, the light on the top of the dome of the Capitol in Washington has burned late into the evening.... People all over the country know that the debate over the Civil Rights Bill is continuing."[17] He called the discussion a "Great Debate" and characterized the bill as an important piece of legislation that had far implications for the country. "There are a great many wrongs in America to be righted and millions who appreciate, daily and firsthand, that civil rights are more of a goal than a reality."

The bill was the last great effort of his brother and had the potential to make a difference in the daily lives of Americans, Kennedy believed. "The civil rights bill can help ensure equal voting rights," he said. "It can help create fair educational and employment opportunities. It can help remove the insult of segregated accommodations." There was a place in the country, he told his audience, where these laws were so irrational that a store would only allow African Americans to drink Pepsi out of paper cups instead of Coke out of a glass. One of the most important elements of the bill was that it demonstrated strong leadership for civil rights. "More generally," he said, "the civil rights bill can also demonstrate to all of our citizens that the Congress of the United States, like Presidents Kennedy and Johnson and like the Supreme Court, is committed to the pledge of equality on which this country is founded."[18] He was looking to show African Americans that there were people in government who care, who wanted to challenge the status quo, and he was one of them.

The complexity of segregation and the race issue in the nation was not lost on Bobby Kennedy. He said, "Neither this law nor any law can be the solution. The deep social wound of segregation was cut for too long by too many knives of prejudice to be healed by a single poultice." Bobby Kennedy understood that this bill was the first step on the path to solving the race issue in the nation. It was a framework, not, as he said, a "resolution of discord and dispute among men." He believed that the bill could provide guidance to the nation and serve as a "moral precept to the extent that laws are founded on morality and on logic, they can lead men's hearts and minds." Understanding the reality in the nation, he said, "But once again, this aspect of law can have meaning only to the extent that the constituents of the law are moral and rational."[19]

In an effort to demonstrate solidarity not only with the Jewish group but also African Americans, Kennedy said, "We know that systematic exclusion of Irish or Jews or Italians or of any ethnic group has ended not only because law changed, but because men's minds did." This notion was at the heart of Bobby's quest to bring together Americans in those last years of his life. He reinforced the importance "to talk not of the federal enforcement of laws, but of individual obedience to their moral spirit."[20] Kennedy hoped that America and its citizens would be able to make a new journey where they could see the moral implications of the law. His righteous spirit was something that came over time, after witnessing grave injustice in the South in his first few years in office and the death of his brother. Those cathartic experiences opened his eyes to the world around him and emboldened him to push for real change, not token gestures for political gain. He wanted the type of change that would leave an imprint on history and change the way the nation lived.

Kennedy knew that the bill would deconstruct aspects of society that had been there for some time. "For a half century," he said, "the doctrine of 'separate but equal' was perverted by citizens, communities, and local governments into a license not for simple racial segregation, but for racial degradation." His words are in stark contrast to the young campaign manager of the 1960 election. His views had finally evolved to realize that the law could only do so much for societal change. "The lesson is plain. Law is not enough," he said. "Neither sober statutes nor individual responsibility alone are enough; men and their laws much march together.… The cost of defiance touches every aspect of community and national life."[21]

Robert Kennedy was no longer worried about how southern democrats would interpret his words. He wanted to send a message not only for the passage of the bill, nor for the defiant southern politicians that he fought in those early days in office, but also for the historical importance and his brother's legacy, which he was so committed to protect. "The point is that the costs of defiance are beyond measure. They touch generations unborn. They destroy possibilities for progress in the present. They scar our history." He believed that the nation had an opportunity to make up for the past. "Rarely in history are nations presented with a second chance to atone for fundamental failures. I wonder, however, if that isn't exactly the opportunity America has today."[22]

Robert Kennedy finished this speech quoting an excerpt from John Kennedy's speech on civil rights the previous June. "Let us join today not only in his sentiment," he said, "but in his certainty." The passage he chose spoke to the morality and definitive righteousness of the law. Speaking to the Congress on June 19, 1963, in the hopes of getting his bill passed, John F. Kennedy appealed to all lawmakers:

I ask you to look into your hearts—not in search of charity, for the Negro neither wants nor needs condescension—but for the one plain, proud and priceless quality that unites us all as Americans: a sense of justice. In this year of the Emancipation Centennial, justice requires us to ensure the blessings of liberty for all Americans and their posterity—not merely for reasons of economic efficiency, world diplomacy and domestic tranquility—but, above all, because it is right.[23]

Robert Kennedy wanted his brother to matter, and the Civil Rights Bill was something that JFK made very clear was important to him in the months before his death. More importantly, in the wake of his brother's death, Robert Kennedy was searching for answers and where he fit in the world without his brother. The Civil Rights Bill became a lightning rod for Bobby, a link to the New Frontier, and a way to define himself to the world. Moreover, it moved him to take on the plight of the disadvantaged.

III

"They should reach the poor."

There was a direct connection between the poverty programs and the Civil Rights Act. In fact, Lyndon Johnson believed that equality under the law was inevitable. He wanted to devote time to a series of programs to help African Americans. Clay Risen writes that Lyndon Johnson believed "that presidential and congressional energies were better spent on a wide-ranging, deep-pocketed program of material uplift, a second New Deal." The Civil Rights Act, Risen contends, was the "political capital he needed … to shore up his base among the liberals."[24] To that end, Robert Kennedy's efforts to push the War on Poverty had an important goal to support the broad program that had the potential to leave a lasting legacy on the nation and help people. In addition, this program could help the passage of the Civil Rights Act considering that Johnson needed that political capital to push his "second New Deal." With that in mind, Kennedy and King found an ally in Johnson, a Texan who had always been careful with his record on civil rights. It also speaks to the fact that the bill represented political capital to Johnson where it meant something different to the Kennedy brothers.

Continuing to connect with those who were less fortunate, Robert Kennedy went to West Virginia. The unemployment in one place was so bad that children couldn't remember when their fathers went to work. Kennedy half muttered to himself on this trip, "If we can't break this cycle, we've had it…. It will never end."[25] Lyndon Johnson's War on Poverty was an important facet to his legacy. He pushed legislation through Congress and strengthened parts of FDR's New Deal. Indeed, it certainly gave credence to the notion that government could help people. The idea to attack poverty was a New Frontier initiative. Lyndon Johnson gave it life. In April 1964, Robert Kennedy ventured to West Virginia, a place that had been called by then-Senator John Kennedy the "state that refused to die: towns that wouldn't give up and proud men who could not find jobs but kept on looking."[26]

The West Virginia primary made it possible for the 1960 Kennedy campaign to continue. Bobby even compared returning to the state as "coming back to an old home."[27] That experience coupled with what he saw in 1960 opened his eyes to the plight of the disadvantaged and would shape his rhetoric for the rest of his time as attorney general and as senator for New York. Indeed, it would be something that Ted Kennedy would take over in the wake of Robert Kennedy's death. So in some respect Bobby went to Kanawha County not only to push Johnson's War on Poverty, but also to continue in what he saw as his brother's agenda, helping those who needed it.

Kennedy pointed to programs that had helped West Virginia in the last three years to start the speech. He turned very quickly to the issue that had seemed to captivate his thinking since January. Speaking to the Parent and Teacher's Council as well as the Action for Appalachian Youth, he said, "I have become increasingly concerned about the complexities of problems facing our youth, particularly the children of our urban and rural slums."[28] He understood how important these issues were to the members of that community and went through various successes and what government programs had discovered while trying to understand the nation's youth and the problems they face.

Kennedy and Johnson had very little in common; however this was one issue that they seemed to believe was an important element of success for American society. Indeed, this effort had an impact on the program; while LBJ worked to pass the Civil Rights Act, Bobby Kennedy contributed to the Great Society. The fact that they both called for some action to be taken to help the nation's youth and attack impoverished conditions speaks to the growing concern over the disadvantaged. This revitalization of liberalism was something that laid the groundwork for the next forty years and would also polarize the nation politically—almost to the point where there was inaction when the country needed some leadership. Robert Kennedy even went as far as to quote a speech by Lyndon Johnson to Congress regarding the issue of poverty:

> Worst of all, it means hopelessness for the young. The young man or woman who grows up without a decent education, in a broken home, in a hostile and squalid environment, in ill health or in the face of racial injustice—that young man or

woman is often trapped in a life of poverty. He does not have the skills demanded by a complex society. He does not know how to acquire those skills. He faces a mounting sense of despair which drains initiative and ambition and energy.[29]

Interestingly, Robert Kennedy chose an excerpt that not only spoke to the impoverished circumstances, but more specifically how it affected young people. This pointed to his continued theme of empowering America's youth in such a way that many would turn his words into action for the latter part of the decade.

In an effort to continue his fight to help young people, Bobby Kennedy emphasized that juvenile delinquency could be fought with simultaneous programs enhancing education, health and job training to name a few. He also recognized that many cities were not ready for these programs and the government needed to play a role in delivering them to their communities. The initiative was hard and without glory, "but without planning, despite the best intentions, we continue with haphazard, fragmented efforts that waste good intentions, good work, money and, worst of all, the lives of our young people."[30] Robert Kennedy believed the government could work for the people, but it took the effort of many agencies to make the difference. He was talking about a new kind of liberalism that would reinvent government and reshape the role it played in the lives of Americans. They were on the precipice of such programs, and it had the potential to truly make the difference that the New Frontier promised in 1960. What Kennedy, Johnson and even King hoped to do was push these programs through Congress.

This speech spoke to a system that Bobby Kennedy thought would make a difference in the nation. The federal government needed to help the state and local government make a difference. He was at the front line of a new kind of liberalism that was moving America in a different direction, looking to shape society in such a way that it would lay the groundwork for future generations. Kennedy believed that there were important factors that would drive this change. He stressed the quality of the programs and that "they should reach the poor who are the victims of the problem, not the middle class." In addition he wanted "capable professional leadership" coupled with cooperation between local institutions and social agencies. "All of these have a vital role to play," he said. Stressing grassroots leadership, which played a part in the movements of the sixties, he said that he wanted to collaborate with the leaders of these areas. "We must plan with these people, not for them."[31] He believed that those four factors were important, but the fifth one was vital for success. While Kennedy wasn't a grassroots leader, his vision had an effect on leaders who could make change in their communities. That vision became a reality for many groups as the sixties continued to reshape the nation.

Robert Kennedy believed in strong leadership. He had faith in government's ability to solve problems and wanted to see a commitment from "top-level" leaders. "I refer here to elected officials," he said, "and also to the high officials of business, labor and education. I am not talking about lip-service, but a real commitment of time and money and influence."[32] He saw this community as overcoming great odds because they were able to apply those factors. He spoke about his brother's and LBJ's efforts as well, but this speech is another example of Robert Kennedy's evolution to see the issues of other people and want to make it his problem to attack with the power of the government. This version of Robert Kennedy started during the Kennedy administration, but it truly emerged in the wake of his brother's death.

5

"The Clock of Destiny Is Ticking Out"

I

"For him the law is always taking away."

Robert Kennedy continued his positive rhetoric in New Frontier fashion with his May 1, 1964, Law Day address at the University of Chicago Law School. Again, he stressed issues of juvenile delinquency and poverty. "I think the solution to these problems should be a challenge to all of us—and particularly to young people who are now embarking upon professional careers."[1] He believed that the Justice Department should spend more time on juvenile delinquency specifically. Kennedy said, "Youth offenses are not the illness to be dealt with. They are merely symptoms of an illness that go far deeper in our society." He stressed that they don't need more courts. "What is needed are programs which deal directly with the causes of delinquency. These are programs to impart skills, to instill motivation, to create opportunity. These are programs which urge young people to stay in school." Kennedy wanted the efforts of these programs to stress prevention. "We seek to help communities build programs which deal not with law violation but with eliminating its underlying causes." Like Johnson, Kennedy wanted to attack poverty. Indeed, if he could help the impoverished he had a better chance to evoke change—reshaping American society.

In his speech Kennedy stressed the importance of addressing poverty and its implications throughout American society. He said that "poverty is a condition of helplessness—of inability to cope with the conditions of existence in our complex society." He did not see poverty as simply a condition of wanting something. "The inability of a poor, uneducated person to defend himself, unaided by counsel in a court of criminal justice, is both symbolic and symptomatic of his larger helplessness." He went on: "To the poor man, 'legal' has become a synonym simply for technicalities and obstruction, not for that which is to be respected or looked up to. The poor man looks upon the law as an enemy, not as a friend. For him the law is always taking away." Kennedy wanted to contribute to a new dynamic in this country. Instead of a government taking away father and sons from impoverished areas of the nation and sending them to prison, he wanted to see programs that changed their view of government while at the same time giving them an opportunity for success.

At the heart of Kennedy's address was the fact that lawyers and other members of society who were fortunate on a variety of levels had an obligation to those who were less fortunate. He appropriately quoted his brother's speech at Amherst College from October 1963:

> There is inherited wealth in this country and also inherited poverty. And unless the graduates of this college and other colleges like it who are given a running start in life—unless they are willing to put back into our society those talents, the broad sympathy, the understanding, the compassion—unless they are willing to put those qualities back into the service of the Great Republic, then obviously the presuppositions upon which our democracy are based are bound to be fallible.[2]

Bobby stressed to the crowd in his speech to reinforce his brother's ideals from 1963, saying, "All of us have this obligation. We can and we must meet it not only as attorneys, but as individual citizens."[3] To be sure his vision emboldened many Americans and ushered in great change.

America's youth was consistently at the heart of Robert F. Kennedy's rhetoric. Kennedy and Johnson polarized the nation with the vision that hoped to help the unfortunate and gave them new opportunities. This was the revolution where people who struggled and traditionally were from the lower echelons of society found success. Indeed, many American leaders of the late twentieth century and early twenty-first century benefited from these programs. They wanted to empower the youth, and while doing that they shaped the future. Robert Kenned had the ability to reach many people. He was seen as the extension of his brother's legacy.

Robert Kennedy spoke again about the importance of American youth in Philadelphia on May 6. "Under conditions of turbulence, social and political change, the young are often directly involved not in learning about history in the classroom, but in making history themselves." Having seen the impact young people had made in the civil rights movement while he was attorney general, Kennedy understood that there was a new revolution in the nation and it would be led by the young of the new generation that his brother talked about in 1961. "These young people are vitally important to all of us," he said.[4] He believed that this group would play a role in reshaping the United States after his brother's death.

In 1964 they were on the verge of a rights revolution. As the Supreme

Court, led by Earl Warren, continued to redefine individual rights, Johnson and Robert Kennedy pushed the agenda that contributed to that revolution. Beyond the legislation, Kennedy's rhetoric contributed in a way that empowered young people. This role is unquantifiable, but looking at RFK's rhetoric provides insight into his vision of the nation. These words were the foundation of the revolution that followed. Robert Kennedy stressed that President Kennedy was committed to the young people of the world. "He sought them out at every opportunity, and I believe was really able to communicate with them better than almost any other world leader." He contended that JFK "felt that what they thought and what they did would powerfully influence the world of today as well as five, ten, fifteen or twenty-five years from now." He was right. The youth of the sixties led the way into the twenty-first century and still continue to play a vital role at all levels of American society. "The young have significant advantages in influencing affairs, as they are even now proving in country after country."[5] That generation and the people they inspired have reshaped American society, laying the path for other people to enjoy those rights.

It was a similar speech that he gave at the start of the year, but it was clear that Kennedy had done a lot to hone his rhetoric. He stressed that the youth had a significant role to play in developing countries, going through various leaders throughout the world, harking back to the fact that Thomas Jefferson was thirty-three when he wrote the Declaration of Independence and Hamilton and Madison were thirty and thirty-six respectively when they wrote the Federalist Papers. In other words, experience and years were not a mandate to blaze a path of change. Indeed it argues that youth had the potential to bring fresh notions and ideas into sharp focus.

The young people of that generation played an important role in changing American society. Bobby believed that they would play a larger role in the near future. "I mention these young leaders of today only as one important aspect of the youth of the world, for current history suggests that the trend to youth will continue."[6] He said that future leaders will come from these young intellectuals, labor leaders and politicians. He believed in the power of youth because he was also very successful at a young age and was making a difference in his thirties as attorney general. He saw change around him and within him and believed that the world would follow in those footsteps.

Robert Kennedy's belief in the youth was revolutionary at the time. In a period where many people looked to the status quo to lead the way, his vision for the United States involved moving away from the standard and embracing new ideas. Indeed, this generation was about to challenge the status quo, setting in motion a series of events that would alter the state of the nation. Robert Kennedy believed that the nation overlooked "the real significance of young people" and focused on the "established order of the status quo." In addition, he stressed that it was difficult to "look past what we have in the present and to guess for the future."[7] By stressing the importance of the youth in the nation, Kennedy spoke to the larger force that would propel the nation to a new level and inspire the world. Of course, Robert Kennedy was not the only emerging leader who influenced Americans.

II

"It is either nonviolence or nonexistence."

While Robert Kennedy looked to the youth to inspire change, Dr. King looked within, focusing on an innate emotion that had the potential to both heal and inspire the nation. At the American Baptist Convention in Atlantic City, New Jersey, King gave a speech the included some if his most profound ideas. King's speech articulated his message of love, making a connection between that concept and civil rights and poverty. Indeed, he, like Robert Kennedy and Lyndon Johnson, believed that the issues in the nation needed a broad, sweeping program. The speech was titled "Love and Forgiveness" and started with the words of what he termed Jesus's finest hour when he said upon his crucifixion, "Father, forgive them, they know not what they do." The idea of forgiveness and nonviolence are almost interchangeable as King gave his sermon on that day. "Men are slow to forgive," King said. "We live by the philosophy of getting even, of paying back or saving face. And we bow before the altar of retaliation." This speech focused on his philosophies that he stressed in the movement, which were linked to the teachings of Jesus Christ and forgiveness. "Society is even slower to forgive," he said. "It has to have its standards, its norms, its mores."[8]

King's speech focused on how love could play a greater role in the world. He talked about how the past had been governed by its inability to forgive. "And so the oceans of history are made turbulent by the ever-rising tides of revenge. Look down through the fire of retaliation burning through the centuries. An eye for an eye and a tooth for a tooth; a leg for a leg, a life for a life." King cited Christ as an example of how to meet hate, to face the turbulent times that he was a part of. "He decided that He would meet hate with love. And so He gave to history its most supreme example of one who could match words with actions."

At the heart of this message was that good people were ignorant, making poor decisions without realizing the impact of those actions. King gave examples of a "blindness" that plagued good people who committed actions such as crucifying Jesus, forcing Socrates to eat hemlock or the Catholics who threatened Galileo—they were "blind." "They know not what they do," he said. King went on to explain, "This tragic blindness expresses itself in many ominous ways in our contemporary life." Leaders, he stressed, talk about a "balance of terror" or "brinkmanship," but they were not bad people. They just believed in the success of war. "But wisdom born of experience should tell them that war is obsolete." As America built up its arms in Vietnam and the South armed itself against the coming army of civil rights warriors to Mississippi and Alabama, King tried to appeal to the "better Angels of their nature."

King's belief in a zero-sum situation did not leave a nation or a person standing at the end of a war. "It is either nonviolence or nonexistence." King warned that an impending annihilation may be on the horizon for humanity. "We must face the facts today that in so many instances we are moving toward that abyss because there are still all too many individuals who know not what they do."[9] It was through this philosophy that King hoped to challenge society's institutions that had continued to hold back African Americans from achieving full equality under the law. Robert Kennedy used his office while Martin Luther King used his pulpit. Both men empowered individuals to see what was right and wrong, empowering many people on different levels in the hope of inspiring change.

Lyndon Johnson had declared war on poverty, and it was clear that something needed to happen on that issue. Robert Kennedy agreed that poverty had a ripple effect on other aspects of American society. Martin Luther King related the theme of his speech to poverty saying that "poverty is a reality in this world and our nation." He admonished a Republican candidate for the presidency who said that those who were impoverished lacked initiative and were lazy. "He does not realize that many people are poverty-stricken because of the long night of discrimination." He took the issue further in the hopes of bringing the true nature of poverty to the forefront of the discourse in Washington.

> We must come to see that as some of God's children are poverty-stricken we are all insecure because we are all caught in an inescapable network of mutuality, tied in a single garment of destiny and what affects one directly affects all indirectly. For a strange reason I can never be what I ought to be until you are what you ought to be, and you can never be what you ought to be until I am what I ought to be.

Invoking John Donne's philosophy that society was a series of interconnected relationships was something that he did to try and stress the notion that people will only be successful if they are bound to each other's success and survival. It was a consistent topic in his rhetoric and the main precept of his philosophy. Going back to poverty, King said that there were people "smothering in an airtight cage of poverty in the midst of an affluent society because there are too many people who know not what they do."[10] To be sure, King echoed Johnson and Kennedy seeing the societal implications of poverty. His message continued to lay bare the issue of poverty and how it was connected to the growing civil rights struggle in the nation.

Of course King's words were meant to bring down segregation. He saw it as "the Negro's burden and America's shame." He believed that "segregation is a cancer in our body politic which must be removed before our democratic and moral heart can be realized." He concluded, "There can be no justification for segregation." King said that the people who perpetuate segregation are not evil "in the pure sense of the word." They were churchgoers, senators, governors, and teachers. Many people who "perpetuate the system of segregation sincerely believe that segregation is good for themselves, for their children, and for their nation. They know not what they do." King believed that survival of democracy was linked to the demise of segregation. He believed that the world could not afford an "anemic democracy" and the "price that America must pay for the continued oppression of the Negro is the price of its own destruction."[11]

King's speech was about the power of love, forgiveness and solidarity. He wanted America to look in the mirror and begin a new chapter. He was trying to push the passage of the Civil Rights Bill. The law could be the cure that he was talking about. "The hour is late. The clock of destiny is ticking out. And we must act now before it is too late." Prior to his Nobel Peace Prize acceptance speech, this comment was evident of his message that would characterize his vision. He was committed to nonviolence, and in 1964 there were few movements in civil rights that had made as many gains as King's philosophy for protest. Like Kennedy, King understood that the hearts and minds of the people would take time to change.

While Kennedy focused his efforts on the power of the youth in American society, he also made a connection between education and the success of civil rights endeavors. On May 19 Kennedy was given the B'nai B'rith award from the Anti-Defamation League. He accepted the award and praised "the men and women of the Department of Justice, for this tribute to their energy in fulfilling their responsibility in the field of civil rights." He took this opportunity to talk about the race issue in the nation. "There have been, dangerously, too many illustrations to the Negro that law is instead an instrument of indifference. For the Negro to lose faith in the law would be for him to lose substantial faith in this country."[12] It seemed that Bobby had come a long way to make a connection with African Americans. This public demonstration is not only an indication of his evolution as someone who advocated for the disadvantaged; it was also a signal to

African Americans that he was trying to understand their plight and how injustice had been such a part of their lives. Kennedy hoped that legislation could begin to heal this disparity in American society.

The proposed Civil Rights Act was a substantial stride for the nation and would hopefully make a difference to bridge the divide between African Americans and the nation. Kennedy believed that the bill had the potential to reach many Americans and would solidify his brother's legacy, despite the fact that Johnson would sign it into law. "The pending civil rights bill is an attempt to shore up that faith by reasserting fundamental rights whose daily deprivation is a slap in the face," he said. While Kennedy believed the Justice Department needed to play a role in enforcing new laws, he also believed that the path to change lay in something deeper than a new law. In the margins of the draft that Kennedy used to give his speech he wrote to himself in pen, "New laws are not *enough*." He continued his speech saying, "The time of the passage of the Civil Rights Bill will be a time of sober decision for the United States. It is up to all of us, as citizens, but even more so as lawyers, to see that Americans everywhere choose obedience."[13] Of course, what Kennedy was talking about is societal change, and that is something that does not happen easily. Indeed, in 1964 the nation was still dealing with the events from 1865. Nearly one hundred years had passed since the end of the Civil War and the nation was still trying to find a solution for Black America, a problem that Gunnar Myrdal called a "Moral Dilemma."

Kennedy continued his rhetoric on civil rights the next day to the Young Israel of Pelham Parkway. He acknowledged the tenth anniversary of the *Brown* decision and stressed that the race issue in the nation was complex and that "it will require new social attitudes and new laws to solve. The pending civil rights bill alone can not provide the solution, for there is no single solution. But it is an essential step and it will be of great assistance."[14] Kennedy's acknowledgment of this complexity hit his message home; he looked to the past and used his brother's words to make a point about the party that America had to endure to tackle the race issue.

In an effort to highlight that the race issue was not only a problem in the South, Robert Kennedy quoted his brother's remarks at the commencement exercises at San Diego State College on June 6, 1963, days before his famous civil rights speech

> It does no good, as you in California know better than any, to say that that is the business of another State. It is the business of our country, and in addition, these young uneducated boys and girls know no State boundaries and they come West as well as North and East, and they are your citizens as well as citizens of this country.

Had Robert Kennedy quoted a line before this one, he would have hit his point even further as he saw a direct correlation between education and segregation. President Kennedy said, "And we must recognize that segregation and education, and I mean de facto segregation in the North as well as the proclaimed segregation in the South, brings with it serious handicaps to a large proportion of the population."[15] While that was not the line Robert Kennedy quoted, it was the spirit of what both Kennedy brothers were trying to convey to the audience and clearly influenced their ideals regarding the importance of education and its link to the race issue in the nation. The handicaps that JFK referred to in 1963 remained a fierce obstacle as the decade progressed.

Stressing the importance of education in the battle for equality was an important element of Robert Kennedy's message to the nation. He even went as far as to say that governments needed to do more than desegregating the schools. "The larger goal is to see that the education of our youth is not merely desegregated, but that it is excellent. And that the place to start is in the schools which for too long have been separate, or unequal or inadequate." To emphasize his point further, Kennedy brought out the fact that without education, job opportunities were difficult to attain. Since many without education could not attain decent employment, he stressed that this issue was linked to poverty in the county. "In short, a more direct relationship between education and employment exists in modern America than ever before. A very real cycle of ignorance and poverty is at work throughout the country."[16] By linking the anti-poverty legislation to ignorance, Kennedy stressed the need to address the whole system.

Kennedy talked about his trip to what he characterized as the "rural hollow of despair in West Virginia." He said that some children had never known their father to have a job. In addition, he spoke to the point that the dropout rate among children who never knew their fathers to have a job was 95 percent. At the heart of Robert Kennedy's message was that he wanted to create a system that offered equal opportunity for all Americans. He believed that education programs would make the difference. He concluded, "We must do a better job of educating our youth, particularly those with built-in handicaps of race or poverty, or both."[17]

III

"The evil is not what they say about their case, but what they say about their opponents."

Robert Kennedy traveled to Georgia on May 26 to dedicate an interfaith chapel named after his brother at West Georgia College. "His candidacy and election exemplify tolerance," he said. Kennedy talked about history and how Catholics were not allowed in some colonies when the nation took shape in the seventeenth century. "It was in the south, in Virginia, that resentment against these practices flowered into religious freedom."[18] Bobby pointed to the efforts of James Madison and Thomas Jefferson securing religious freedom. His rhetoric was meant to not only show that the South could lead toward tolerance, but also that he belonged to a group that was once discriminated against.

Kennedy spoke about intolerance and how it had led to major issues in U.S. history. He moved from religion and tried to make a connection with the people, saying, "There are those who preach that desegregation of the schools will destroy our society. And there are others who believe that calamity will occur because of the way we may treat our drinking water." This speech points even more to the society Kennedy hoped to achieve, influencing others, while contributing to a larger message that had the potential to change the nation. "What is objectionable, what is dangerous about extremists is not that they are extreme, but that they are intolerant. The evil is not what they say about their case, but what they say about their opponents."[19] What Kennedy wanted the nation to embrace was an evolutionary attitude when it came to race relations. To be sure, this was a message that would resonate into the twenty-first century. People should be able to look beyond strong beliefs and understand that it was not about right or wrong, but rather a society where people acknowledged differences and learned to live with them. That was revolutionary in 1964 and his vision paved the way for the rest of the sixties, despite the fact that he would not live to see the fruits of his labors. This vision was something that contributed to the upcoming years as America was about to deal with some of its most challenging issues.

Kennedy contended that the country would overcome intolerance. "America's answer to the intolerant man is diversity—the very diversity which our heritage of religious freedom has inspired." He even went as far as to link his brother's election to that spirit saying that JFK's election "expanded religious freedom to include the highest office in the land.... It advanced the day when the bars of intolerance against all minority groups will be lifted not only for the Presidency, but for all aspects of our national life."[20] This link to his brother not only shows the belief that America would prevail over intolerance but also that he was personally linked to such a movement. Robert Kennedy was trying to find common language for Americans. Martin Luther King continued to discuss his own thoughts on desegregation that same month.

In a statement on May 7, 1964, Martin Luther King gave his opinion on where school desegregation was ten years after the Supreme Court decision. "The naive might believe that great strides have been made in school desegregation over the past decade, but this is not all true." He called the efforts to desegregate "star tokenism" citing Atlanta and other towns in the South as following through with a policy of "gradualism." On the threshold of Freedom Summer he called Mississippi "the worst of all." It was tragic in the sense that the decision that played such a vital role in the movement had been met with "gradualism" as King had said, "moved only at a creeping pace when it has moved at all."[21] To be sure, the Civil Rights Act would do more to change that.

Later that month King complimented the work of the NAACP defense fund and said that "the struggle for human rights takes place on brightly lighted stages." He brought even further attention to the movement. "This struggle in the United States is in a real sense a part of the world-wide quest for freedom and human dignity." King talked about the opportunity to continue with the legal approach but not at the expense of direct action. "In seeking to bring about a total liquidation of the system of segregation, it is necessary to maintain a creative balance between legal action and direct action," he said. King's approach was not that different from the NAACP. In fact, in the instance of Ole Miss, there was a combination of direct action and legal action. To be sure, in the final analysis, the courts needed to act. Nonviolent action could only take the movement so far.

> Direct action is not a substitute for work in the courts and the halls of government. Bringing about passage of a new and broad law or pleading cases before the courts of the land, does not eliminate the necessity for bringing about the mass dramatization of injustice in front of city hall. Indeed, direct action and legal action complement one another; when skillfully employed, each becomes more effective.[22]

King tried to illuminate how the two groups were connected. Despite King's best efforts, there was a tension in the movement. King and the SCLC, the NAACP and the SNCC all had the same goals, yet they all went about it a little differently. The movement would be crowded further with the coming of Malcolm X, the Black Panthers and the Black Power movement. King, however, remained the great leader of nonviolence. By the end of 1964 the world would recognize his efforts and find both inspiration and a clear strategy to promote societal change.

King's philosophy of direct action played a role in fostering other rights movements outside of African American groups, affecting the way people demonstrated and spoke their minds. He acknowledged the need for civil rights legislation, which was a direct extension of the courts. The main issue that they were confronting was an obstinate Senate that refused to support such legislation. Referring to the act of legislating, King said, "If this ugly process does not end and the Civil Rights Bill is not soon passed without crippling amendments, our nation will drift inevitably toward its moral and political doom. The hour is late. The clock of destiny is ticking out." The Civil Rights Bill was the greatest example of the marriage between direct action and legal action. Indeed every civil rights group wanted to see that bill become a law; despite their differences, they all agreed on that principle. To be sure it was a combination of effects by many groups that inspired John F. Kennedy to propose the bill. Prompted by the acts of the NAACP, the SCLC and SNCC, President Kennedy proposed the bill in June 1963.

The Civil Rights Bill was the result of a myriad of motivators that pushed JFK and RFK to acknowledge the crucial need for such legislation. It was meant not only to change the climate of the 1960s, but also to usher in a wave of progressivism to attack the racist institutions of the United States and bring about the social change that paves the way for a new relationship between African Americans and the government. To some extent it was successful beyond the dreams of John Kennedy, Robert Kennedy or Martin Luther King. In another more complex social way, the racial issues in this country needed more than just an act to govern the relationships of individuals within the society.

The transformation is still going on; King and the Kennedys were killed before they could see the fruits of their labors. On a larger note, the act started the irrevocable process of giving minority people in the nation a voice in government. Those groups were not all related to African Americans. Indeed, African American civil rights leaders should be celebrated not only for the rights that they were able to achieve for African Americans but also for all the Americans who have used the act as a springboard to achieve rights in a changing society that takes its time to accept anyone who is different than what they believe is the norm.

At the heart of the deeper issue of race was poverty. Robert Kennedy and Martin Luther King understood that "the Negro will be pitifully left behind in the World March Towards Human Rights unless his present institutionalized position in the American economy is radically changed," he said. King acknowledged that poverty transcended races and there were also white people who suffered from this issue. However, he cited that African American unemployment was more than twice that of whites and that new technology, which he called "automation," was making it difficult for all people to get jobs. King called for an alliance between whites and African Americans to eliminate poverty. "Only through such an alliance will both the Negro Freedom Movement and the white community ... be able to constructively make a massive assault upon ... the entire culture of poverty."[23]

While Dr. King stressed the importance of government programs to help African Americans, Robert Kennedy gave his vision for how to foster a better society in the words of his commencement speech at Marquette University. Kennedy championed civil rights. His speech pointed to the link between poverty and civil rights, demonstrating that he understood the nature of the problems that African Americans faced every day. After speaking about technology and resources that those college graduates will enjoy given their education and affluent backgrounds, he said, "But less than an hour away in Harlem, people live in squalor and despair more closely resembling the 19th century. A few hundred miles away, in the remote hovels of Appalachia, the life of the people is, if anything, worse than it was a hundred years ago." He pled with the graduates, saying, "Such disparity can not be tolerated in a society which believes in free opportunity, or even in one which only talks about it."[24]

In an effort to empower college students, he said that while it may be an exaggeration to call previous college generations "silly" or "silent," he said, "I think it is fair to describe yours as a generation of unusually genuine and intense concern with social justice and intellectual freedom." He acknowledged not only the times that they lived in, but also the impact that students could have on history. On this occasion Robert Kennedy acknowledged the role that America's youth could play to change the nation. "Political and social involvement have meaning to you and your contemporaries across the country. Thousands of students work on behalf of civil rights, or remedial reading, or community problems," he said. Again, he saw the issue of rights and the role that the youth would play as an important piece of the growing society. Given his experience in the past with students during the sit-in movement or the Freedom Riders, he was cautious in the power he wanted to impart on these students, saying, "Peace marchers or college civil rights demonstrators may not always express their concerns in the wisest most effective manner, but it is clear that those concerns are deeply felt." Nevertheless, Kennedy acknowledged their power and ability to shape society.

The speech demonstrates that Robert Kennedy had an appreciation for the issues that American society had been trying to overcome. He acknowledged that these concerns "stem in part from the intensified concern of our whole society for the problems of social justice." By this time, Bobby had started to consider what was next and how he would start his own legacy while continuing with his brother's ideas. "Let us obliterate the past," he finished, "which is, for so many citizens, the somber present and the hopeless future.... Let us labor to build a future in which all Americans can share, with common prosperity and common pride."[25]

Robert Kennedy was a deep thinker. He wanted to get to the root of all the issues in the nation and find a solution that would help the common person while at the same time bringing prestige to the nation. He was a nationalist, though not in the same way that Theodore Roosevelt was. He believed in America and its ability to help people to succeed. The American dream was reimagined in the sixties, giving people opportunities that they never had. To that end, Kennedy wanted to dig deep and find solutions to these problems that would not only fix the present, but transcend generations, leaving a legacy that would be felt for many years. This was the essence of his own ideals and also the New Frontier. Of course, it would translate, to some extent, into the Great Society, but Kennedy wanted to do more than provide programs that would help people. He wanted to inspire them in a way that would invoke his brother's ideals, using his words and the actions of the government. That was the heart of the change that he wanted for the nation, and it was at the core of his beliefs as he started to venture out on his own.

In a speech titled "The Opening of the Future," Robert Kennedy told the California Institute of Technology that they needed to take an active role in the world beyond the technological achievements that the students from that university were known for. On June 8, 1964, he started his comments by looking back on his own schooling and what it had meant to him. Given his audience, he referred to the power of science. "If you believe, as I do, that our greatest national responsibility is to strengthen and enlarge the opening to the future, then science most obviously will play a central role in this effort." He referred to John Adams's and Thomas Jefferson's recognition that science had the potential to change things. He warned that "the advance of scientific knowledge now confronts our planet with the possibility of disaster far greater than anything Jefferson and Adams could have imagined."[26] What followed was an impassioned plea to the students of Cal Tech to consider science as a way to help, not destroy, humanity with new technology.

Much like his brother, Robert Kennedy understood the power of science and technology and its capacity to render societies powerless. Also, he was in the Cabinet Room when they debated action against Cuba in 1962. "Science depends on what men do with it. And men, as this grim century has reminded us, are capable of unreason and destruction fully as much as they are capable of reason and creation," he said. To hit home with the audience, he quoted Albert Einstein when he said, "It is not enough … that you should understand about applied science in order that your work increase man's blessings…. Concern for man himself and his fate must always form the chief interest of all technical endeavors…." Kennedy said that he came to talk to them as citizens, not scientists, "as some of the best educated, most rational, and most creative citizens of our country." This of course was a constant theme in the United States. One can look no further than Stanley Kubrick's *Dr. Strangelove* and many other popular culture references to the fear of being annihilated by nuclear weapons. Indeed, with the Vietnam War heating up, it was clear that war was a very pervasive issue.

Having been so close to the center of the Cold War, Kennedy understood the dire situation in the world and the potential dangers that the conflict had on the world's people. "There can be no greater concern for each of us, as citizens, than how wisely and how honorably our nation discharges its responsibilities of preserving peace and promoting freedom." Kennedy understood the stakes, had stared down the Soviets in 1961 and 1962, had seen the plans for a nuclear strike when he participated in EXCOMM meetings during the Cuban missile crisis, and understood that the world needed leaders who, like his brother in 1962, could find alternatives to war. "The leaders of the world face no greater task than that of avoiding nuclear war." Instead of the truculent and determined Cold War rhetoric that was associated with the cold warriors of his generation, Bobby Kennedy started to distance himself from that stance. "While preserving the cause of freedom," he said, "we must seek abolition of war through programs of general and complete disarmament."[27]

Détente and finding a way to stop war were at the core of his remarks, blazing a path to a belief that peace and love should be the goal for humanity. Indeed, Robert Kennedy came to embody those qualities. His experience as attorney general and exposure to the potential nuclear exchange tempered his "cold warrior" resolve. It could have also been his determination to keep his brother's ideals, which were so eloquently expressed in his American University speech the year before. In many ways this speech was a sequel to JFK's message which talked about "a strategy of peace."

Kennedy believed in the Nuclear Test Ban Treaty of 1963 as well as other efforts to move toward détente. They were "modest steps. But they are steps forward, steps toward the ultimate goal of effective and reliable international controls over the destructive power of nations." Kennedy saw a future where there would be cooperation and understanding among nations. "The United States must continue to expand its efforts to reach the peoples of other nations—particularly young people." He believed in the ideology of America to inspire young people. His nationalism was not rooted in someone who wanted to fight to expand American interest or lead war because his nation was better and stronger, but one who believed in the principles that made the nation different. To that end he hoped to take those ideas and build on them as the nation moved forward. "Over the years, and understanding of what America really stands for is going to count for more than missiles, aircraft carriers, and supersonic bombers. The big changes of the future will result from this understanding—or lack of it."[28] In his plea to these students, the world catches a glimpse of RFK's vision, what he believed would change the world and have a lasting effect.

Admonishing American foreign policy at the dawn of the tumultuous years of the decade put Kennedy in a different league than other politicians. "Far too often, for narrow tactical reasons, this country has associated itself with tyrannical and unpopular regimes that had no following and no future," he declared.

> Over the past twenty years, we have paid dearly because of the support given to colonial rulers, cruel dictators, or ruling cliques void of social concern. This was one of President Kennedy's gravest concerns. It would be one of his proudest achievements if history records his administration as an era of political friendships made for the United States.

His idealism coupled with his brother's legacy fuel his speech. It led the way to inspire these students and usher in a period where nations tried to avoid war instead of coming to the brink of destroying societies. "Ultimately, Communism must be defeated by progressive political programs which wipe out poverty, misery, and discontent on which it thrives." He wanted to promote these progressive programs in Latin America, Southeast Asia and Africa "and preserve the stability of the world."[29]

Robert Kennedy was looking to move away from the old way of dealing with the Cold War. His vision was different and looked to new avenues to foster change in the nation. "In time, the consensus of good sense which characterizes our political system will digest and discard frozen views and impossible programs." He looked to the future but understood how fear paralyzed the present or "short term," creating a political situation that could "inhibit a president's freedom to take maximum advantage of the openings which the future may present." He knew that there was no way to reason with these elements "for they speak irrationally," and government could not completely stop that momentum. Despite that fact, Bobby had faith and believed in the American people, which was why he was talking to this crowd. He believed, "The answer must come from within the American democracy. It must come from an informed national consensus which can recognize futile fervor and simple solutions for what they are—and reject them quickly." He believed that the young leaders he was addressing had the ability to provide the leadership necessary for that transition.

5: "The Clock of Destiny Is Ticking Out"

After quoting Abraham Lincoln and stressing the urgency of this issue that had the potential to change the world, Robert Kennedy pointed to a speech that his brother was supposed to give on November 22, 1963—the day he was murdered.

> President Kennedy ... wrote that while dissident voices will always be heard in our country, other kinds of voices are being heard today—"voices preaching doctrines," he would have said, "wholly unrelated to reality, wholly unsuited to the sixties, doctrines which apparently assume that words will suffice without weapons, that vituperation is as good as victory and that peace is a sign of weakness.... We cannot expect that everyone, to use the phrase of a decade ago, will 'talk sense to the American people.' But we can hope that fewer people will listen to nonsense. And the notion that this Nation is headed for defeat through deficit, or that strength is but a matter of slogans, is nothing but just plain nonsense."[30]

Using his brother's words not only sharpened Bobby's views for the crowd but also brought back a leader who wanted to find a solution to the problems in the absence caused by his untimely death. To some people it may have seemed that President Kennedy was giving that direction from the grave.

Stressing the strength, courage and fortitude of a nation ready to face the future, Robert Kennedy invoked his brother again who said that the nation was "ready to seize the burden and glory of freedom." Kennedy said that the faith his brother had in the nation was strong. "It is that faith, enlarged by you and by each succeeding class of this great university, which will enable us to meet our responsibilities, be worthy of our strength, and propel the whole world forward toward a new age of decency, justice and peace."[31] The speech was important because Bobby Kennedy's vision is apparent and he is getting ready to make his own move to affect history. While he leaned on his brother's ideals in the months after his murder, this was the first time Bobby goes outside of the status quo and wanted to find peaceful solutions to the issues that the world faced.

John F. Kennedy stressed in a speech of June 1963 at American University many of the ideals of that vision Bobby spoke about, but it was now up to Robert Kennedy to take that "peace speech" and bring those ideals to the forefront of political thought. Indeed, his words would shape a movement within the nation that inspired students and young people not to rebel as much as to question their leadership to look for a peaceful solution to the war in Vietnam and the civil rights struggles that the nation had been facing since Bobby was in office as attorney general. This was a time where the nation was fluid and had the potential to recreate institutions, paving the way for future generations, making it better for every person in the nation. Robert Kennedy's idealism was apparent throughout the speech. It was now up to him to try and bring those ideals to the people and help leaders of the world see what he had envisioned.

IV

"Acts of terrorism."

Robert F. Kennedy remembered in 1965 that Lyndon Johnson was not always a civil rights advocate. When the Kennedy brothers wanted to send legislation to Congress, Johnson "was opposed to the Civil Rights bill. He was opposed to sending up any legislation." In an effort to get Johnson on board when JFK was in office, "Burke Marshall went over and saw him about the legislation he was very, very strongly opposed to," Kennedy recalled.[32] In his final few months as attorney general and before the passage of the Civil Rights Act, Robert Kennedy continued to implore Lyndon Johnson about the dangers of what he termed "acts of terrorism" in the South.

Robert Kennedy was concerned about the efforts of civil rights leaders who planned to go south and work to register African Americans to vote. Freedom Summer would prove to be a vital moment in the movement. On June 5, 1964, Kennedy sent a memo to President Johnson regarding the situation in the South. He sent Burke Marshall to the southwestern part of Mississippi as well as the city of Jackson to "get some first-hand impressions of the possibility for this summer and the future." RFK reported to LBJ,

> There has unquestionably been, as you know, an increase in acts of terrorism in this part of Mississippi. As a result, the tensions are very great not only between whites and Negroes, but among whites. This is not as true in Jackson as in the outlying areas.[33]

Robert Kennedy was trying to get Johnson to see that more had to be done in the South. For Kennedy this was a moral issue, which had largely been ignored, but it was also a major source of concern for the safety of Americans who were asserting their rights. His awakening to the issues in the South came in the early years of the Kennedy administration. He wanted Johnson to see it the same way his brother would and do something using the law. The Civil Rights Act had not been passed yet. "Law enforcement officials, at least outside Jackson, are widely believed to be linked to extremist anti–Negro activity, or at the very least to tolerate it," he wrote. Robert Kennedy saw the struggles that African Americans endured even more clearly in the wake of his brother's death. The memo is evidence that Bobby was trying to understand the injustice and pave the way for further change in how the government addressed the issue.

The fact that law enforcement officials had been entangled in acts of terror against African Americans had been largely ignored by the federal government. Not since the Enforcement Acts of the 1870s had there been strong action from the federal government to stop Klan activity. Kennedy told Johnson, "Groups have been formed under the auspices of the Americans for Preservation of the White Race to act as deputized law enforcement officials in some counties." Bobby went even further to provide data for the president, saying, "A spot check shows that such groups are undergoing a spot of training program in Welthall, Anita, Adams and Leake Counties." He said, "These groups appear to include individuals of the type associated with Klan activities." Kennedy also alluded to a situation in St. Augustine where a "federal judge required the sheriff to list the men deputized by him in connection with a racial conflict ... the list contained a number of persons known to be Klan members."[34]

The memo is an effort to demonstrate to Johnson that there were real racial issues in the South that needed action. It was a warning of the violent nature of a movement that preached nonviolence. Had Johnson and J. Edgar Hoover considered his concerns, it might have avoided a tragedy. Later that month in Neshoba County, Mississippi, three civil rights workers were murdered by the Ku Klux Klan who were law enforcement officials. Bobby went on to say, "The area is characterized by fear based on rumor." In Jackson there were rumors that there would be organized attacks on African Americans. "It seems to me that this situation presents new and quite unprecedented problems of law enforcement." Kennedy saw this as a systemic issue that needed to be dealt with in some way to bring justice back to the South.

Robert Kennedy believed that the federal government could do more to help African Americans in the South. To that end, he proposed some action for Johnson to consider. "As one step," he wrote, "I am directing some of the personnel here in the [Justice] Department who have organized crime experience to make a more detailed survey of the area to substantiate the details concerning the activities of extremist groups." He went further, hoping that Johnson would implore J. Edgar Hoover and the FBI to intervene. Kennedy no longer had the same power over the infamous director he once had when his brother was in office. He suggested that "consideration should be given by the Federal Bureau of Investigation to new procedures for identification of the individuals who may be or have been involved in acts of terrorism, and of the possible participation in such acts by law enforcement officials."[35]

Robert Kennedy saw the issue as an example where the system had failed American citizens.

> The unique difficulty that seems to be presented by the situation in Mississippi (which is duplicated in parts of Alabama and Louisiana at least) is in gathering information on fundamentally lawless activities which have the sanction of local law enforcement agencies, political officials, and a substantial segment of the white population.

The issues in the South went back to the Reconstruction period in American history where the white establishment entrenched itself in power positions in southern society that would systemically keep African Americans away from political power, while at the same time affecting their status as citizens. Kennedy was presiding over a period in American history where the federal government was fighting to alter a system that was engrained in the fabric of southern society. To be sure, it was a difficult fight to take on, but it seems that Bobby was committed to it.

Robert Kennedy wanted the FBI to use similar techniques to those it had used against communist groups as a method to infiltrate the Klan in the South. "If you approve I recommend taking up with the Bureau the possibility of developing a similar effort to meet this new problem." Robert Kennedy concluded to Johnson, "I told you in our meeting yesterday that I consider the situation in Mississippi to be very dangerous. Nothing in the reports I have received since then changes my view on that point."[36]

Bobby Kennedy still believed that much had to be done to fight racial issues in the South. The fact that he needed to press this issue home to Johnson is an indication that there were some in government who did not share that belief and needed evidence to support such a drive into southern society. In the past he would have had an easier time getting the president to see his perspective. It seems that Johnson needed more evidence to qualify action. The death of those three civil rights workers in Mississippi twenty days after RFK wrote this memo to Johnson was glaring proof that the federal government needed to act in some way. Instead of being reactionary to events, Robert Kennedy wanted the administration to be proactive in their pursuit of justice in the South. His time as attorney general had proven to him that it was the only way to fight the racial tension in the country.

The memo on Klan activity in the South points to issues that America will deal with into the twenty-first century. "Acts of terrorism," as he called them, that are racially motivated will not be abolished by one or two generations—the nation needed to go deeper to find a solution. RFK wanted Hoover to attack this. Coming from the young brash Senate lawyer of the

1950s, it seemed very telling that he believed this threat was as great as the communists that he fought so diligently in the 1950s. Robert Kennedy, like the nation, had finally seen not only the injustice but also the danger of racism in America.

V

"We believe that all men are created equal."

On July 2, 1964, Lyndon Johnson signed the Civil Rights Act of 1964 after he received the final version from Congress. The room was bustling with people from the civil rights movement to political leaders. Robert Kennedy and Martin Luther King were among them. They watched Lyndon Johnson deliver an address about the meaning of law. Johnson started the speech saying that the Founders had a vision for the nation. On the cusp of celebrating the Fourth of July, he said, "One hundred and eighty-eight years ago this week a small band of valiant men began a long struggle for freedom." With tension growing in Vietnam he inevitably drifted to the price of freedom and how so many Americans had given their lives to uphold the ideas that galvanized the world in 1776. "From the minutemen at Concord to the soldiers in Viet-Nam, each generation has been equal to that trust," he said. He proclaimed the passage of the bill as a triumph for the nation.

The Civil Rights Act was meant to change the times and begin the transition into a better America—one that embraced people of all races and ethnicities, one that focused on rights instead of privilege. Johnson emphasized the sacrifice of many people throughout history. "Americans of every race and color have died in battle to protect our freedom. Americans of every race and color have worked to build a nation of widening opportunities. Now our generation of Americans has been called on to continue the unending search for justice within our own borders." This was a measure that would bridge that divide and start the healing. It was an acknowledgment that justice had been denied to American citizens. He emphasized that this measure was bringing the nation to a revival of those rights that the Framers had envisioned so many years ago.

> We believe that all men are created equal. Yet many are denied equal treatment. We believe that all men have certain unalienable rights. Yet many Americans do not enjoy those rights. We believe that all men are entitled to the blessings of liberty. Yet millions are being deprived of those blessings—not because of their own failures, but because of the color of their skin.

Following that statement, he said that he may have understood why this situation had perpetuated itself in the years since the framing of the Constitution. "But it cannot continue. Our Constitution, the foundation of our Republic, forbids it. The principles of our freedom forbid it. Morality forbids it. And the law I will sign tonight forbids it."[37]

Robert Kennedy should have been joyous that his brother's bill had been made into a law. Indeed, Johnson gave credit to JFK, saying, "That law is the product of months of the most careful debate and discussion. It was proposed more than one year ago by our late and beloved President John F. Kennedy." He went on to say, "It received the bipartisan support of more than two-thirds of the Members of both the House and the Senate. An overwhelming majority of Republicans as well as Democrats voted for it."[38] This bipartisan acceptance of the bill was a testament not only to Johnson's ability to get it passed through Congress, but also John F. Kennedy's vision of where the nation was going in the early sixties. Robert Kennedy sat in the front row to witness this historic event.[39]

Johnson continued with his speech hoping to inspire others to take heed in the new law and begin the transition of this country to embrace new ideals. "This Civil Rights Act is a challenge to all of us to go to work in our communities and our States, in our homes and in our hearts, to eliminate the last vestiges of injustice in our beloved country," he said. To be sure, he was talking to the southerners who would oppose the adoption of this bill. Indeed, there would be many in the next year that would challenge its authority. Johnson clearly anticipated this outcome.

> My fellow citizens, we have come now to a time of testing. We must not fail.
> Let us close the springs of racial poison. Let us pray for wise and understanding hearts. Let us lay aside irrelevant differences and make our Nation whole. Let us hasten that day when our unmeasured strength and our unbounded spirit will be free to do the great works ordained for this Nation by the just and wise God who is the Father of us all.[40]

His final plea to Americans was rooted in religion and justice. It was given at a time in the nation's history when the institutions that had once been infallible were subject to great ridicule. War was on the horizon, yet the people did not know just how affected they would be by it. They did not understand the nature of the new type of war that would plague this superpower and entrench them in a quagmire in Southeast Asia.

Once the speech was completed, Johnson handed out the ceremonial pens to the people who had played a role in bringing it to life. Martin Luther King had commented to a reporter that the act would bring a great deal of relief to many African Americans, but "it will probably take five years to see the civil rights bill fully implemented in the south."[41] King was among the recipients of pens that Johnson handed out that day. As the crowd of people surrounded Johnson to receive their pens, labor leaders Victor and

Roy Reuther remarked that they saw Robert Kennedy in the back of the room staring at the floor. Victor remembered thinking, "Surely no one had contributed more to this moment than he." His brother Roy took Bobby by the arm and brought him to Johnson, saying, "Mr. President, I know you have reserved a pen for your Attorney General."[42] Johnson gave Bobby a handful of pens. "Give this one to Burke Marshall. Give this one to John Doar," Johnson said listing all the members of Bobby's team. He gave Kennedy one more for good measure.[43] The Rev. Walter Fauntroy, who came with Dr. King, commented, "Our enthusiasm—that of Dr. King and myself—was sort of dampened by the sadness that we saw in Bobby's eyes and the coldness with which the President obviously treated him."[44]

The moment was another example of how Robert Kennedy had been marginalized by Lyndon Johnson. A little over a month after the signing, Bobby would begin his campaign for the Senate position in New York. That campaign continued his movement toward a society that began in 1960. It was his effort to continue passing the torch to the next generation. Kennedy had such a profound impact on his generation that despite the fact that he never completed that six-year term, his words still inspired many and have been a part of the national discourse since his untimely death in 1968.

6

Freedom and the World

I

"That foundation is freedom."

Just before Robert Kennedy was at the civil rights signing, he embarked on a tour of Europe. In some ways he was continuing in his brother's footsteps who took a similar trip in the summer of 1963, which was a huge success. Foreign policy was as much a strength for Bobby as it was for his brother. This trip was not only a way to commemorate his brother's efforts; it was also his way of showing the world that he could be on his own, comment on issues in the world and contribute to the international discourse. He also needed to do this for himself, to demonstrate that he had what it took to be a true leader. The first part of his tour started in a place where President Kennedy believed he had one of the greatest speeches of his presidency.

On June 23, 1964, Robert Kennedy issued a statement saying that he was going to Berlin, at the request of the German leaders, "to participate in ceremonies commemorating President Kennedy's visit to Berlin a year ago." The statement said that many people had contacted him to run for the vacant Senate seat in New York. "I deeply appreciate their loyalty and friendship, and have been heartened by their support," the statement said. "However, in fairness to them and to end speculation, I wish to state that I will not be a candidate for United States Senator from New York."[1] He had, in fact, been contemplating a run for the Senate, which he would ultimately run for in a little over a month. It seemed that he did not want to go to Europe as a candidate but as a government official, the position that his brother appointed him.

When Robert Kennedy arrived in Berlin on June 26, 1964, he said that the "city is a great inspiration to me as it is to men who love freedom throughout the world." He said that he was grateful for all the sympathy regarding his brother's death. It was a very personal trip for Bobby, rooted in a coming of age that he had been experiencing. He returned with his wife and three of his children. Speaking of his children, he said, "I wish to have them, like us, inspired by your courage, and we want them to grow up with the strength which that inspiration gives."[2] The statement was not only meant for its literal implication but also the message of empowering the youth of the world that Robert Kennedy had stressed in the wake of his brother's death. This would be how RFK approached leadership, not just politics. He wanted to inspire youth and drive them to the same activism that peace corps volunteers had been doing around the world. As he implored young students in Tokyo earlier in the year, he wanted students and the youth to participate and contribute and find solutions to world problems.

As part of what was titled "The President John F. Kennedy Lecture," Robert Kennedy spoke at Free University in Berlin the day he arrived in the city. Kennedy started his speech saying that JFK "spoke often of his visit to Berlin. He admired its vitality and its dedication. But most of all, he admired its courage." This speech brought Bobby onto the world stage, to a place where President Kennedy gave one of his most memorable, historic speeches. At this opportunity while the whole world was watching, Robert Kennedy continued to empower students. "Nothing was closer to President Kennedy than the thoughts and feelings of the students of the world ... all those to whom the destiny of our civilization is confided."[3] He spoke to "the young" telling them that they could make a difference. The speech was a rally cry, for people everywhere, to follow his vision, which was linked to his fallen brother.

He wanted to empower the next generation of leaders, to inspire them not only because he believed they were the future, but also because he believed it was what his brother would have done. He set in motion rhetoric that would, in fact, empower young people to act on those ideals, which led to genuine change and redefined American society. Kennedy spoke to them about their responsibility to each other and the world. "We live in the midst of endless revolution—social, technical, intellectual. It reconstructs every aspect of our environment and of our daily lives."[4] Kennedy emphasized that society was moving at a rapid rate, and they had a role to play in it.

Developing nations were slowly coming of age, and people in nations like America were questioning the status quo, demonstrating that the world was in the throes of change. "In my country there has developed in the last three years an accelerating movement of human rights—a revolution which is steadily and surely bringing out Negro citizens to full equality in American society." Kennedy demonstrated his prowess in international affairs—

commenting on issues in Europe and Asia. He said that there was strife in the world. Once again, he moved to empower the crowd. "Thus, we live in a world of exceptional uncertainty and hazard. But we also live in a world which gives us a foundation for the future of exceptional excitement and possibility. That foundation is freedom." His speech went on about freedom, how it could conquer, how it brought the people into the equation. Commenting on the failings of communism and the strength of democracy, Kennedy said, "The future belongs to those who have confidence in it, to free men dedicated to the importance of the individual and the proposition that the state exists for the individual, not the individual for the state." He concluded with certainty: "it is our commitment to freedom which is the mechanism with which to meet and shape the future."[5]

Freedom was a pervasive ideal in the shadow of the Berlin Wall and communist oppression. Kennedy emphasized that freedom needed allies to succeed. The first ally was courage and the second was strength. He saw those characteristics in Berlin. He told the crowd that America had pledged its support to Berlin and that they would always keep an army in Europe to thwart the same aggression that brought the world to war twice in that century. He believed that the third ally to freedom was the capacity for imagination and innovation. "Without it, freedom does not remain a flexible philosophy for the future, but merely a pious fable for our rigidities of the present or the past."[6] Bobby Kennedy used imagination in such a manner that it became a powerful motivator that appealed to a younger generation that believed in the New Frontier rhetoric.

Robert Kennedy wanted to demonstrate that he could be a factor in the relationship between America and the world. Kennedy wanted to strengthen the unity in Europe, thereby strengthening the position of the United States and western ideology. "There is widespread support among the young Europeans for European unity as the best way of assuring peace and progress." In order to continue empowering the youth of the world, Kennedy pointed to the fourth ally of freedom—education. "The university is integral to your freedom, just as education and free inquiry are integral and essential to freedom wherever it exists." He went further later in the speech saying that commitment was "the final and most important ally freedom must have if freedom is to exist, if it is to endure, and if it is to flourish."[7]

The speech was meant to tell the world that Bobby Kennedy was the heir to his brother's vision of the world. More importantly, he was adopting that vision and morphing it into his own, imaginative ideas to foster change in the world. He quoted his brother several times in the speech and even pointed to Jacqueline Kennedy's words. He ended it saying that after traveling through the United States, the Far East and Germany, "I have come to understand that the hope President Kennedy kindled is not dead but alive." He continued, "It is not a memory, but a living force. The torch still burns, and because it does, there remains for all of us, the chance to light up the tomorrows, and to brighten the future."[8] Edwin Guthman wrote how people in Berlin came out to see him in the streets as he passed by. The speech at Free University made Ethel cry.[9] Much like his brother, Bobby Kennedy inspired many people at Berlin. It was the start of his own world tour that would help to define his own message. The outpouring of support for Bobby Kennedy speaks to his presence abroad. The strong showing in Berlin helped his chances to attain another political office.

From Berlin, Bobby went to Poland, despite the fact that the Poles were hesitant to have him there. The people came out to see him, applauding. They threw flowers and overwhelmed the car to the point where it couldn't move. Bobby got out of the car, took Ethel by the hand and stood on top of the car. The crowd went crazy when they appeared atop the car. It got to the point where the driver informed one of Kennedy's advisers, "I say there, would you tell the attorney general that the roof is caving in."[10]

In Poland Kennedy was asked about his brother's assassination by one youth during a question-and-answer session. He responded,

> I believe it was done by a man with the name of Oswald, who was a misfit in society, who lived in the United States and was dissatisfied with our government and our way of life, who took up communism and went to the Soviet Union. He was dissatisfied there. He came back to the United States and was antisocial and felt that the only way to take out his strong feelings against life and society was by killing the President of the United States. There is no question that he did it on his own and by himself. He was not a member of a right wing organization. He was a confessed communist, but even the communists would not have anything to do with him.[11]

His public comments were meant to soothe as well as come to terms with the reality that his brother was gone. It also seemed that, at least publicly, Kennedy believed that Oswald had acted alone and there was no conspiracy.

Kennedy left Poland on July 1, making clear that the chief objective of the United States was to usher in peace and reconciliation between Eastern and Western Europe. This was his last tour abroad before the Senate race. While he had his experience in JFK's cabinet, he wanted to stress to the world that he was still involved in Cold War matters. In a released statement, he pointed to Germany as the root of this division and characterized it as "reinforced by a legacy of old hatreds." The statement was meant to show Poland that the United States would stand with them.

> I believe that now is the time to work earnestly on the problems ahead—the security of Poland and of Eastern Europe; of Germany and Western Europe; of the Soviet Union and the United States. For these problems will not go away by themselves. Unless we move to meet them now they will grow more acute and more unmanageable.[12]

His statement was in line with the usual Cold War rhetoric. In addition he wanted to also make clear that he was committed to finding a solution to the issues that had plagued the continent since the end of the Second World War. "I seek to promote understanding and to foster a determination to meet the challenges that face all of us in Europe." He finished, invoking his brother's inaugural address, "Together I am confident that we can succeed." In allusion to his brother's inaugural, he said, "Let us begin."

The trip to Germany and Poland was meant to spread his rhetoric and demonstrate that Kennedy could hold his own on the world stage. He was, after all, still in his thirties and in that position due to his brother. However, Robert Kennedy had proven himself by this time, and his words and presence made a difference to the people of the world. From Poland he stopped in London, England. He had little to say, but he felt the need to comment on his trip to Germany and Poland. He was realistic but positive at the same time. "First, I am more than convinced that the division of Germany is an unnatural thing." He concluded that as long as it remained, the longer Europe would struggle. However, he reiterated the hope that he spoke of in his Free University speech, saying, "My talks in Poland and Germany led me to believe that there are avenues of thought and action that are worth exploring." He emphasized that he could not go into detail. "It seems to me that we can work out in advance a framework of arrangements that will simultaneously promote the end of the unnatural decision and security of Europe."[13] He believed that they should seize the moment and work toward peace.

II

"I said that we didn't want to fight in Vietnam."

Robert Kennedy had lunch with Anatoly Dobrynin, ambassador to the Soviet Union, on July 7, 1964. They met to exchange a letter from Nikita Khrushchev regarding the Kennedy library. The two men discussed a variety of topics. When Dobrynin asked about Lyndon Johnson, Kennedy said that Johnson "was interested in reaching more accords and more agreements with the Soviet Union, [and] felt that [it] was in the interest of the United States to do so, [Johnson] had groups that were working hard at tasks to try to develop areas in which there could be agreements, that he would, in my judgement, carry out the efforts that had been begun by President Kennedy." They moved on from that point and discussed the situation in Southeast Asia.

"He asked me about Vietnam," Robert Kennedy recalled. "He said as far as Vietnam was concerned, what was our position?" Kennedy went on to articulate the position of the United States as it was under Kennedy. Bobby, as he did with other topics, referred to this issue the way that his brother had when in office, which was the way cold warriors had always dealt with communist aggression overseas.

> I said that we didn't want to fight in Vietnam, if the choice came to attacking North Vietnam or leaving in defeat that we would attack Vietnam, that this was a question of principle to us, that, as he and I had discussed on previous occasions, there were certain matters from which a country could not retreat and that it should be understood by the other powers that one of them as far as the United States was in South Vietnam.[14]

Kennedy was not ready to go against the policy that his brother had championed when he was in office—nor should he. It had been the policy for three presidents and most likely would continue in the face of Cold War polemics. He had to not only consider his brother's previous position, but also that of President Johnson, which at that point he was careful not to cross publicly, as was seen at the start of the meeting with Dobrynin.

The situation in Vietnam in 1964 enjoyed a great deal of support from the American people. Robert Kennedy and many others saw this situation as another front in the Cold War. His view on that war would take time to change and become his own. If he denounced the current policy he would not be denouncing Johnson as much as his brother, and that was out of the question. "We had given our word that we were going to stay there. That word had originally been given by President Eisenhower, then it had been reaffirmed by President Kennedy, and reaffirmed again by President Johnson." The policy in Vietnam had not changed in over ten years. Kennedy did not necessarily want the United States embroiled in war, nor did he know then what the Vietnam War would look like. He did not say he would escalate, but he was clear on the position of the United States. "Our national prestige and position throughout the world was at stake and so we had to remain there." While this was the prevailing feeling among policy makers, he did offer some consternation about that position. "And this was unsatisfactory, I agreed, but we shouldn't be pushed too much because this is a very difficult situation for the United States."[15] He understood the complexity of the matter, and while he showed some empathy for Dobrynin and Ho Chi Minh's position, he also made it clear that the United States would push back.

The meeting between Kennedy and Dobrynin highlighted the tension in the alleged Sino-Soviet alliance. When Kennedy asked about Mao Tse Tung, Dobrynin's response was that Mao was a lot like Stalin, "that he thought he was God, that peasants and farmers were being taught to bow in his direction where ever he might be north, south, or east, or west, it's sort of as if they were bowing to Mecca." Dobrynin commented that Mao said that the "only way to deal with problems, present problems, was to have a nuclear war, that from that nuclear war there would be still two hundred million Chinese and that they would build a world from that." Khrushchev said in response to this, "Well, you'll be building a world on a graveyard." The Polish, according to Dobrynin, said that they would get "destroyed completely." The Chinese said that the Polish did not concern them, according to Dobrynin. He went on to tell Kennedy that the Chinese said "what needed to be done was to have a war and to have a war right away and get it over with." The conversation finished with a short discussion of Cuba. Clearly Kennedy still had a role to play in world affairs. Dobrynin had respected him enough to confide some of the Chinese issues with him as well as some of Khrushchev's concerns regarding Vietnam. Kennedy on the other hand was able to articulate the U.S. position on Southeast Asia.

While Robert Kennedy still enjoyed respect from world leaders, his relationship with Lyndon Johnson was not getting any better, and it was clear that he needed to consider other alternatives and leave the cabinet. After the European trip, it seems that Bobby may have started seriously considering running for the Senate. He gave a summary of his trip to Johnson, and he recalled, "My impression is that he's really not greatly interested by the foreign affairs matters." In this memo Bobby recalled a National Security Council meeting regarding flights over Cuba and "what would happen if an American plane was shot down by the Cubans.... None of the questions were raised that would ordinarily be raised by President Kennedy at these kinds of meetings, searching analytical questions which people would have to come up with answers to." He concluded, "In fact, in my judgement, we don't really get to the heart of the problem."[16]

The day before Kennedy dictated this memo, a *Newsweek* article titled "What Will RFK Do?" written by Ben Bradlee quoted Bobby saying that he was "the last man in the world" that Johnson would want on the ticket for vice president in the 1964 election. He expanded his comment, saying, "because my name is Kennedy, because he wants a Johnson administration with no Kennedys in it, because we travel different paths, because I suppose some businessmen would object, and because I'd cost him a few votes in the south."[17] Bobby concluded later that "Lyndon Johnson was very upset about the *Newsweek* article. I guess he spoke to everybody ... about it, how disturbed he was. Relationship up to that point was improving, but that made it very difficult all the way around." Kennedy lamented, "Ben Bradlee had said that he would clear the quotes and just never did so. But I shouldn't have trusted him anyway."[18]

III

"It is also midnight in our world today."

Freedom Summer, a major civil rights initiative in the South to register African Americans for the vote, had been in full force by July 1964. As students and young leaders looked to confront the racist voting policies of the segregated south, King showed his support in a statement on July 22, 1964. "The Future of the United States of America may well be determined here, in Mississippi," he said in a released statement, "for it is here that Democracy faces its most serious challenge." King posed the question whether the Mississippi government would represent all of the people. "This is the question which must be answered in the affirmative if these United States are to continue to give moral leadership to the Free World." Freedom Summer was something that would captivate the nation and inspire many people. It was led by young people, which both King and Kennedy looked to empower as the sixties continued to confront the status quo.

The tragic loss of three civil rights workers of Freedom Summer remained a constant reminder of the vicious and violent nature of segregation. "But I do not come to Mississippi without reminding us of the three young members of this movement who have been missing and who may have well been murdered here in Mississippi." Indeed, this tragedy demonstrated that in the United States it was a dangerous prospect to confront a system rooted in racism. "Our nation sent out Peace Corps volunteers throughout the underdeveloped nations of the world and none of them experienced the kind of brutality that these voter registration workers have suffered her in Mississippi," King said. Despite the violence, these young leaders stayed determined to make a difference in the state. To be sure, King's determination and support were a piece of moving those embattled workers to a new level. King called on President Johnson to do something about the atrocities in Mississippi, saying that the president has "broad powers to protect citizenship and voting rights."[19] He said that Johnson could appoint marshals, as Kennedy had before, to enforce the 15th Amendment, which forbade any government to take away the right to vote based on race.

The racial tension in the nation was not relegated to the South. In July

1964 riots broke out in New York. In another clear example of the racial strife in the nation, African Americans were rebelling against the white establishment. The *New York Times* reported that people were "shouting at policemen and white people, pulling fire alarms, breaking windows and looting stores." The riots were the result of the people speaking out against the death of fifteen-year-old James Powell, who was shot by Lieutenant Thomas Gilligan, a white police officer. The police sealed off a block in Harlem where over thirty people were arrested and five hundred police officers responded. The *Times* reported, "There was no estimate on the number injured. Scores of persons with bloodied heads were seen throughout the eight-block area ... where most of the rioting occurred." Cars were beaten, glass bottles thrown, landing on civilians and police officers. There was a rumor that the police beat another African American, adding to the violence and racial tension already palpable. The crowds were yelling "killers" at the policemen after the officers went to help a young African American girl who was struck by a hit-and-run driver. The crowd continued yelling, "Killer cops must go. Police brutality must go."[20]

The nation was bleeding. It was going through a revolution aimed at challenging white leadership in the North as well as the South. The press and the leadership in New York implied that the riot was to be blamed on civil rights leaders. King wanted it made clear that he would never advocate violence. "I do not think violence could solve the problem in New York, nor can it solve the problem in Mississippi," he said in a statement. "It creates many more social problems than it solves. The use of violence in our struggle is both impractical and immoral."[21] Of course, King believed that there was a larger, deep-rooted issue in American society that compelled the people in Harlem, and later Brooklyn, to resort to violence. While King advocated for nonviolence, the riots are evidence that people were getting frustrated and expected leaders to do more. It was a prelude to the growing conflict in the movement, which would eventually manifest itself into a movement centered around black militancy and nationalism.

King asked the people in New York to stop rioting and recognize the power of nonviolent resistance. However, he also wanted people to reflect on the causes of such an event. "I must affirm that the important question confronting these communities and our nation as a whole is not merely that there be shallow rhetoric condemning lawlessness, but that there be an honest soul-searching analysis and evaluation of the environmental causes which have spawned the riots." At the heart of the violence was a historic dissatisfaction with society. King went to great lengths to articulate his views.

> The President of the United States, the mayor of New York City, Rochester, the governors and mayors of every state and city throughout our country have the responsibility to see that millions of black Americans acquire an ever-increasing amount of justice in their respective communities. By this I mean the elimination of ghettoized housing, discriminatory barriers to jobs, inferior and segregated schools and discriminatory barriers to the right to vote.[22]

In other words the issue was systemic. He and Robert Kennedy understood that. The riots broke out a little over two weeks after the Civil Rights Act was passed. It was clear from these actions that there needed to be more action on the part of the government to change the hearts and minds of Americans on the race issue. To be sure the hearts and minds of Americans were not easily swayed.

The complex situation in the United States was exacerbated by violent actions of the KKK against voting workers in Mississippi and the growing tension in Vietnam—both of which would embroil the nation and its leaders in 1965. King believed that African American leaders had to confront these issues in New York from two vantage points. "On the one hand we must vigorously condemn the violence and lawlessness of the Negro community. On the other hand we must be equally vigorous in appealing to the white power structure to give us some concrete victories." He concluded that the "Negro sorely needs a sense of somebodiness." King advocated that an "honest and forthright initiation of a massive program to free the Negro from the long night of economic deprivation and social isolation will do much to bring a radiant light into the dark chambers of despair."[23]

Despite the growing violent nature of the racial tension in the nation, King did not waiver on his commitment to nonviolence. On August 9, 1964, King followed up his statement with a sermon titled "A Knock at Midnight." He spoke at the Riverside Church in New York. The sermon used a parable by St. Luke as the basis of his message. The parable is about persistent prayer. King said, "It may also serve as a basis for our thought concerning many contemporary problems and the role of the church in grappling with them." In the story, it is midnight and a friend is looking for loaves of bread. King said, "It is also midnight in our world today and we are experiencing darkness so deep we can hardly see which way to turn." He continued with this notion: "It is midnight within the social order. As we look out on the international horizon we see that nations are engaged in a colossal and bitter contest for supremacy."[24]

Martin Luther King's sermon touched on the history of the nation, reminding people that "within a generation we have fought two world wars and the threat of another hangs ominously low." More related to the civil rights movement, he commented, "The midnight in the social order is nowhere expressed more than the racial crisis confronting our nation. We face the melancholy fact that one hundred years after the Emancipation Proclamation the Negro is still dominated politically, exploited economically, humiliated socially." Speaking to the impoverished conditions in parts of the nation, King said, "Negroes, north and south, still live in segregation—houses in unendurable slums; eat in segregation, pray in segregation, die in segregation."[25] The racial tension and injustice that had been highlighted in several campaigns in the South was not lost on northern citizens. To be sure, the racial divide had many forces, and King's remarks amid the backdrop of the riots that were plaguing the city are evidence that the racial tension in the nation was not specific to the South. Indeed, this issue was pervasive in a great many parts of the nation.

King's sermon spoke not only to the issues in New York City but also to the nature of the movement and how he wanted to protest segregation. He reiterated his earlier statement that the use of violence was wrong, creating more problems in its wake. "But after condemning violence," he said, "we must affirm that the important question facing the nation as a whole is not merely that there be shallow rhetoric condemning lawlessness, but there be an honest soul-searching analysis and evaluation of the environmental causes which have spawned the riots." He concluded, "Non-violence does not exist in a vacuum." It was imperative that the movement confront these issues, but King highlighted the desperation of African Americans brought on by the disparity in society.

> As long as the Negro finds himself on a lonely island of poverty, in the midst of a vast ocean of prosperity, as long as millions of Negroes feel that they are exiles in their own land, to see their plight as a long and desolate corridor with no exit sign, as long as millions of Negroes are forced to accept educational situations that are grossly inadequate, as long as millions of Negroes see life as an endless flight with powerful headwinds of tokenism—token handouts here and there—there will be an ever-present threat of violence and riots.[26]

King's summation of the issues African American's faced in the sixties speaks not only to the system of segregation, but also to the societal structure that had continued to create barriers that separated African Americans and other minorities from enjoying what had been categorized as the American Dream, which was rooted in the notion that every American could achieve success. The denial of basic rights created a situation where the racial tension, like a powder keg, was ready to explode.

The sermon continued with the image of America at midnight and looking for some salvation. "It is one of the ironies of history that in a nation founded on the principle that all men are created equal, men are still arguing about whether the color of a man's skin determines the content of their character. And so our nation faces the dreary and frightening midnight in the social order." He went on to talk about midnight in the "psychological order" and in the "moral order," bringing further the message that this issue was not relegated to the system of segregation. He concluded, "This is the problem modern man confronts, a threefold midnight: midnight in the social order, midnight in the psychological order, midnight in the moral order."[27] Given his multilayered discussion of the issues that plagued the nation, the solution was not something as simple as a Civil Rights Act. While that legislation was a triumph, it needed time to affect Americans' daily life. To be sure, King saw that he could not stop until all of those institutional barriers that have affected so many African Americans were gone.

IV

"This I pledge."

At the World Assembly of Youth, Robert Kennedy, once again, spoke to the young people of the world. Speaking at the University of Massachusetts in Amherst, Massachusetts, Bobby Kennedy talked about how the world was moving at a rapid pace and that it would take groups of people, not individuals, to solve the problems that came with such advances. The developing nations of the world did not enjoy the same advances. "I believe that we recognize now—perhaps for the first time—that the gap between the developing and the developed nations of the world must be closed." He went on about hunger and how there needed to be efforts made to combat that issue in the world. "In the face of shortages, hunger and even starvation, unrest is said to be mounting and the maintenance of law and order difficult."[28]

Emphasizing that education is pivotal for success in developing countries, Kennedy said, "There is an awareness that educational opportunity is the means of individual as well as national advancement." He concluded by empowering the audience, declaring, "If you bring your intelligence and will to bear on these problems, you will be dealing with the central issue of our time…. If we meet this challenge successfully, we shall have carried the torch of freedom to the world of the future." He acknowledged that the effort was staggering. In an effort to inspire the crowd, and maybe even himself, he quoted his brother, who said before the Protestant Council on November 8, 1963, "If we maintain the pace, we shall in due season reap the kind of world we deserve and deserve the kind of world we will have."[29] In a couple of weeks after this speech, Robert Kennedy announced his resignation from the office of attorney general and began his campaign for the Senate seat in New York.

With Ethel at his side, wearing the same black tie he wore to his brother's funeral, Robert Kennedy spoke into a multitude of microphones.[30] "The search for enduring peace and for enduring prosperity begun by President Kennedy and continued by President Johnson has successfully taken our country to many new frontiers," Robert Kennedy said at Gracie Mansion in New York on August 25, 1964.[31] Kennedy told the nation that Democratic leaders had encouraged him to run for the Senate seat in New York. "I have decided to make myself available for the nomination of the Democratic State Convention." He was supposed to be running his brother's campaign, but instead he was the candidate, trying to make sense of this new world, trying to continue his brother's vision for the nation. "I think our country forces a fundamental political choice," he said, qualifying his decision to run. "Our traditional aspirations for peace and prosperity, justice and decency, are being questioned." He went after the opposition, saying, "All that President Kennedy stood for, and all that President Johnson is trying to accomplish, all the progress that has been made, is threatened by a new and dangerous Republican assault."[32]

The election was characterized by Kennedy as a struggle where "no one associated with President Kennedy and with President Johnson ... can sit on the sidelines with so much at stake." Bobby was standing firm on his convictions and his brother's "New Frontier" ideology. To be sure, he knew that there would be some who saw his candidacy as opportunistic, calling him, in fact, a "carpet bagger," an allusion to the Reconstruction era in American history where outsiders tried to take advantage of the defeated south in the aftermath of the Civil War. He acknowledged that, despite the fact that at one point in his life he attended New York schools, his parents owned a home in the state and he, himself, had established residency, his candidacy was not based on those facts. "I base it on the conviction that my experience and my record equip me to understand New York's problems and to do something about them." He emphasized that New York had an important role to play in solving the nation's problems. "And I wish to play a part in that effort." This endeavor was the next step in his evolution as a statesman. He already had extensive experience at the center of power, bearing the cross of his fallen brother, serving as a symbol for the world to look to in his absence. "I shall devote all my effort and whatever talent I possess to the State of New York. This I pledge."[33]

In the days following his announcement, Kennedy prepared to make a speech at the Democratic National Convention in New Jersey. On the day of his speech, the morose Kennedy waited on the platform with a 5 × 7 note card, prepared for him by Ed Guthman, with quotes he wanted to emphasize. On the other side of the typed note card, in Robert Kennedy's own handwriting, was the phrase from a Robert Frost poem: "The woods are lovely, dark and deep, but I have promises to keep." He had memorized the whole speech where he was supposed to introduce a film on President John Kennedy, yet he still nervously glanced at the draft.[34] When they announced his name, the convention hall broke into a standing ovation that would last twenty-two minutes, not letting Kennedy speak as he stood at the podium.

Flashes were going off as cameras took photos of the historic moment, flags were waving in the crowd and Kennedy stood there, holding back tears, nodding to crowd and smiling on occasion, trying to interrupt the crowd, but they wouldn't let him. Finally he was able to speak and started amid the lowering applause, saying, "Mr. Speaker. Mr. Chairman." He started by saying that he appreciated everything that the members of the party had done for his brother. Demonstrating not only his solidarity with the Democratic Party but also its strength, he said, "No matter what talent an individual possesses, what energy he might have, no matter how much integrity and how much honesty he might have, if he is by himself, and particularly a political figure, he can accomplish very little."[35] He emphasized that the party had been there for his brother and that was why he was successful.

Robert Kennedy took this opportunity to tell the world of John F. Kennedy's greatest successes while he was president. He believed that the successes he enjoyed were rooted in the foundation of the Democratic Party going back to James Madison and Thomas Jefferson.

> As president he wanted to do something for the mentally ill and the mentally retarded; for those who were not covered by social security; for those who were not receiving an adequate minimum wage; for those who did not have adequate housing; for our elderly who had difficulty paying their medical bills; for our fellow citizens who are not white and who had difficulty living in this society. To all this he dedicated himself.[36]

It was more than a memorial. Robert Kennedy linked his brother to the War on Poverty and the civil rights revolution.

Bobby spoke about the Cuban missile crisis and his brother's desire to create a better world with the test-ban treaty, saying, "His idea really was that this country, that this world, should be a better place when we turned it over to the next generation than when we inherited it from the last generation." He made a link to his own rhetoric, emphasizing that President Kennedy was invested in the future of the nation, saying, "And that's why he made such an effort and was committed to the young people not only of the United States but to the young people of the world." Kennedy brought out his brother's ideas in the speech, focusing on the success of the New Frontier and the strength and support that John Kennedy enjoyed from the party.

Kennedy nearly stumbled on his words when he tried to express to the crowd what his brother meant to him.

> When I think of President Kennedy, I think of what Shakespeare said in *Romeo and Juliet*: When he shall die take him and cut him out into stars and he shall make the face of heaven so fine that all the world will be in love with night and pay no worship to the garish sun.

As he started the next line of the speech, he was interrupted again by applause. The original draft does not include that famous line. Robert Kennedy inserted it at the last minute. He finished the speech using those Robert Frost lines that he held in his hand, which were also not included in the original speech. "The woods are lovely, dark and deep, but I have promises to keep and miles to go before I sleep, and miles to go before I sleep." After he finished his speech Bobby Kennedy slipped away from the hall, sat on a fire escape and cried.[37]

The speech came on the heels of the announcement that he was going to run for the Senate. He looked like a candidate who was ready to take on a campaign and embody the ideals and strength he spoke of in the speech. In the coming months, Bobby Kennedy would come into his own and commit to a campaign that harked back to the New Frontier while establishing his own voice in the process. That experience launched a new phase in his life, which would ultimately end in his death, but it would provide for the nation something that they needed. Indeed, his words made a difference in the lives of many Americans and even inspired movements that lasted well into the twenty-first century.

V

"We still seek no wider war."

On August 2 and 4, 1964, it was reported to President Johnson that there were attacks by North Vietnamese forces on the naval ships USS *Maddox* and USS *Turner Joy* in the Gulf of Tonkin off the coast of Vietnam. These attacks were met by a show of force from the United States. Johnson felt that the nation needed to reply to the communist aggression building in that area of the world. "That reply is being given as I speak to you tonight," he said on August 4, 1964, from the Fish Room in the White House. "Air action is now in execution against gunboats and certain supporting facilities in North Viet-Nam which have been used in these hostile operations." This was a renewal of sorts in the war against communism. Not since the Korean War had the United States taken such an aggressive act against another nation.

> In the larger sense this new act of aggression, aimed directly at our own forces, again brings home to all of us in the United States the importance of the struggle for peace and security in southeast Asia. Aggression by terror against the peaceful villagers of South Viet-Nam has now been joined by open aggression on the high seas against the United States of America.

Johnson at first did not see a war coming. His Great Society was taking off and he clearly wanted to send money to those programs and not a conflict overseas. He proclaimed, "Yet our response, for the present, will be limited and fitting. We Americans know, although others appear to forget, the risks of spreading conflict. We still seek no wider war."[38] That was early in the conflict. Johnson's leadership would be tested very quickly as the events in Vietnam started to unravel the uneasy armistice in the Cold Car.

Johnson had been advised to act in the wake of this event. Earlier that day, he met with the National Security Council from 6:15 to 6:45pm to discuss the response to the incident. Robert McNamara had recognized that "our efforts to learn the exact situation and protect the Patrol have been complicated by a very low ceiling. One of the two destroyers was fired on by automatic weapons and was lit up by search lights." Dean Rusk, however, saw this incident as a reason to respond. "An immediate and direct reaction by us is necessary. The unprovoked attack on the high seas is an act of war for all practical purposes. We have been trying to get a signal to Hanoi and Peking. Our response to this attack may be that signal." CIA Director John McCone concluded that "the proposed U.S. reprisals will result in a sharp North Vietnamese military reaction, but such actions would not represent a deliberate decision to provoke or accept a major escalation of the Vietnamese war." When asked by Johnson if the North Vietnamese were looking to start a war, McCone responded, "No." However, he continued with mixed analysis to the president's question, saying, "They are responding out of pride and on the basis of defense considerations. The attack is a signal to us that the North Vietnamese have the will and determination to continue the war. They are raising the ante."[39] The meeting demonstrates that there were varied opinions on the attack and what it meant. Further, if they could not accurately assess the meaning of the attack, then the response was flawed.

President Johnson continued meeting with congressional leadership to discuss his course of action. Dean Rusk outlined what he believed were the stakes in the situation.

> We would make it clear as we can that we are not going to run out of South East Asia, but that we have no national ambitions nor either in a war to the north. They made the choice themselves. They will have some doubts there if it comes to choice, but if we go back in a limited fashion, there would still be a showing that we want to limit the escalation. We have not had time to consult our Allies.

At the beginning Johnson did not want a "wider war." On the other hand, Rusk seemed hawkish in this meeting and the one prior. He made it clear to the leadership: "We are trying to get across two points: (1) leave your neighbors alone and (2) If you don't, we will have to get busy."[40]

Johnson, however, seemed resolute and at ease with his decision to escalate the situation in Vietnam. He said to congressional leadership,

> We thought there were two decisions to make after we were attacked yesterday and today and nine torpedoes were shot at our destroyers 40 miles on the high seas. We had to answer that attack. There are four bases. There have been many discussions and recommendations by people in the country that we go into the northern area and not allow them to murder us from bases of safety. These boats came from these bases and have been shooting at American ships. I think I know what the reaction would be if we tucked our tails.[41]

Johnson's answers to the attack and subsequent attacks brought the Vietnam War to a new phase and ushered in a period in American history that would have war permeate the daily lives of Americans.

There are some historians who question whether JFK would have responded in the same manner. Some say that the same advisers were present at Cuba as well as the Gulf of Tonkin. That said, Robert Kennedy, who was an enormous asset to President Kennedy during the Cuban missile crisis was not at the table. To be sure, only one member, Defense Secretary McNamara, had urged President Kennedy to issue a quarantine of the island. Indeed, the ghosts of the Cuban missile crisis certainly lingered at the meeting. Senator Bourke Hickenlooper asked, "May I ask if there is a comparison between Cuba and this? Cuba was a bold and dangerous operation as far as Washington is concerned. No one knows what would have happened had we not reacted." He went further to ask, "Is it possible this follows the same route? If we don't react, what kind of position does it put us in with the North VietNamese?" Rusk responded, "What the Russians learned in Cuba could have an influence on the entire world." Johnson made it clear, "We want them to know we are not going to take it lying down, but we are not going to destroy their cities. We hope we can prepare them for the course we will follow."[42]

The dubious resolution that would give President Johnson so much power was also discussed at this meeting. Johnson brought the leadership into his decision making, which Kennedy did not do in Cuba, saying, "I wanted the advice of each of you and wanted to consult with you." He continued, "We felt we should move with the action recommended by the Joint Chiefs, but I wanted to get the Congressional concurrence. I think it would be very damaging to ask for it and not get it." Kennedy did not have the support of congressional leadership when he decided to quarantine Cuba. Of course that action was against military advice, which illuminated even further just how different LBJ and JFK were when confronting these issues. This group, however, wanted to demonstrate a firm commitment behind Johnson. Speaker of the House John McCormack said, "I think Congress has a responsibility and should show a united front to the world." With that in mind Johnson believed that there should be some action from Congress, not just his office. "I would hope we could pretty well work out a resolution which is good with a minimum of doctoring. I wanted to see if you felt it was the wise thing to do." Hickenlooper responded, "I think the resolution is appropriate and proper."[43] There was overwhelming support around the table for action in North Vietnam. This conflict had a shared burden, which Johnson has carried as a legacy of his presidency. Congressional leaders supported and even, to some extent, helped define the resolution that would pave the way for action in that region.

The situation continued to escalate as Johnson took his resolution to the floor of Congress on the evening of August 5, 1964. "After consultation with the leaders of both parties in the Congress, I further announced a decision to ask the Congress for a Resolution expressing the unity and determination of the United States in supporting freedom and in protecting peace in Southeast Asia," he started. His response was meant to be quick and decisive. Indeed, he discussed the nature of the war and how it played in the grand scheme of world events. "These latest actions of the North Vietnamese regime have given a new and grave turn to the already serious situation in Southeast Asia. Our commitments in that area are well known to the Congress."

Johnson went on to list four aspects of U.S. policy in that region: "1. America keeps her word. Here as elsewhere, we must and shall honor our commitments. 2. The issue is the future of Southeast Asia as a whole. A threat to any nation in that region is a threat to all, and a threat to us." The second one is an allusion to the "domino theory." He believed that this action was a peaceful one, meant to stop the escalation and honor U.S. commitments to nations in that region, maintaining the prestige of the United States. "3. Our purpose is peace. We have no military, political or territorial ambitions in the area." Johnson took his rhetoric to another level with his fourth and final point in Cold War fashion "4. This is not just a jungle war, but a struggle for freedom on every front of human activity.

Our military and economic assistance to South Vietnam and Laos in particular has the purpose of helping these countries to repel aggression and strengthen their independence."[44] This speech outlined his intentions in the region, his motivation and panned response to what he termed a "struggle for freedom."

His speech was clear and even reiterated what he had said the day before about escalation of the conflict. "As President of the United States I have concluded that I should now ask the Congress, on its part, to join in affirming the national determination that all such attacks will be met, and that the U.S. will continue in its basic policy of assisting the free nations of the area to defend their freedom." He highlighted to Congress and the people, once again, "As I have repeatedly made clear, the United States intends no rashness, and seeks no wider war." Yet he followed up that statement with a clear, Cold War response: "We must make it clear to all that the United States is united in its determination to bring about the end of Communist subversion and aggression in the area." In this moment, Congress and the president had acted together. Between the consultation with congressional leadership as well as President Johnson's advisers, this moment had a myriad of culpability. Nothing is more glaring than the decisive vote that took place five days later, giving Johnson the resolution that he wanted.

In the midst of this Cold War rhetoric, Nikita Khrushchev sent Johnson a letter outlining his concerns over the growing tension in North Vietnam. Khrushchev acknowledged "the seriousness of these developments—indeed, it is impossible to rule out that they may mushroom into such proportions and turn in such a way that it will be difficult to say where they will stop." Khrushchev went through what he knew about the incident and then gave Johnson his own analysis, which included a critique of the South Vietnamese government.

> With all frankness I must say that if these actions of American warships and air forces pursue the aim of strengthening somehow the position of the corrupt and rotten South Vietnamese regime which exists—and this is no secret to anyone—only because of the foreign support, then such actions will not achieve the given aim. But to increase the danger of a serious military conflict—they can.

Unlike Johnson, Khrushchev saw the potential for a wider war. In Khrushchev-like fashion, he used a mixed metaphor to consider the potential of these actions in Vietnam, saying,

> A question arises before me: have not clouds been deliberately darkened around the developments in the Gulf of Tonkin? Is not the influence felt here by those quarters and persons who do not conceal their desire to inflame the passions, to pour oil on the flame and whose militant frame of mind one should regard with great caution and restraint?

He went on to ask the important question to Johnson, "But if this influence is indeed real and if it has an ear, then another, more serious question arises—where the present developments can lead to?"[45] Khrushchev had learned from the lessons of the 1962 missile crisis and knew when to tone down the rhetoric and action in cases like this. Johnson, in all his experience as a politician, did not have that same perspective. This was the first time he had to commit such a large military force. Johnson did not blink when it came to sending a message to the world as well as to communist nations. Unlike Kennedy he agreed with the aggressive action of keeping communist Vietnam in check with a commitment of U.S. forces.

Khrushchev recognized that he did not have all the information, but he still made sure that he condemned U.S. action in the region. "I would not like here to give play to feelings although this, in all appearance, is justified by the situation," he wrote. "Because of lack of reliable information I confine myself to expressing those thoughts which follow from the main and undeniable fact, namely, that the warships and air forces of the United States have taken military action in the Gulf of Tonkin area." He finished his letter saying, "I would like to hope that on your part there will be shown necessary composure and restraint in order to remove the military tension and stop defiant actions of the American armed forces in the Gulf of Tonkin area which may lead to an appropriate response from the other side."[46] Khrushchev understood that some action "may" have been justified; however, he could only speak to what he knew. Perhaps the most telling aspect of this letter is Khrushchev's plea for "composure and restraint." He learned with President Kennedy that leaders have to be ready to embrace avenues other than war.

Johnson replied to that letter on August 7, 1964. He started saying, "I share the concern expressed in your message of August fifth concerning the incidents in the Gulf of Tonkin." He continued in an effort to demonstrate to Khrushchev that he understood the burden that these two leaders had in maintaining peace: "I also fully share your view of the heavy responsibility which we both bear for keeping the peace and for preventing incidents anywhere in the world from starting a chain of dangerous and irreversible developments." Johnson, however, emphasized that the response from the United States was measured. "It was for this reason that we took only the minimum defensive action in response to the first attack upon the American destroyer in the Gulf of Tonkin.... Our action was carefully measured to fit the circumstances, and we have no wish at all to see this matter go further." Again, Johnson's intention was not to escalate the incident into a war. He had said so on several occasions and continued to reiterate this to Khrushchev. He said again in the letter, "I have made it clear, publicly, that we ourselves do not wish an escalation of this situation." He concluded his letter asserting the position of the United States and maintaining the same Cold War rhetoric: "My country will always be prompt and firm in its positive reply to acts of aggression, and our power is equal to any such test. But the mission of that power is peace."[47]

Johnson met again with his advisers on August 10, 1964, the day that he signed the joint resolution in the East Room of the White House. At the meeting, which took place in the Cabinet Room, Dean Rusk "emphasized, as he has repeatedly before and since, the importance from his point of view of keeping the responsibility for escalation on the other side." In response to that, McNamara "indicated that our side was well prepared for a response to any likely form of escalation." It seems that these men were expecting the incident to escalate. Johnson "expressed his basic satisfaction with what had been accomplished in the last week. He said the reaction from Congress was good, and also from the people, judging by the polls."[48]

According to the memo of the meeting, Johnson "warned, however, that if we should fail in the second challenge, or if we should do nothing further, we could find ourselves even worse off than before this last set of events." Perhaps the greatest indicator that Johnson saw this situation giving way to the "wider war" that he publicly wanted to avoid were his remarks at the end of the meeting: "The President did not wish to escalate just because the public liked what happened last week. We would have to pick our own ground; nonetheless, instead of letting the other side have the ball, we should be prepared to take it." This strategy was different from what some advisers said about staying away from escalation. "[Johnson] asked for prompt study and recommendations as to ways this might be done with maximum results and minimum danger. He did not believe that the existing situation would last very long."[49] President Johnson went into the Gulf of Tonkin Resolution thinking that there would not be an escalation—or at least believing that the "existing situation" would not last and did not have the potential to produce the "wider war" that Johnson had claimed he was trying to avoid.

When Johnson signed the resolution, he said, "The cause of peace clearly required that we respond with a prompt and unmistakable reply." Demonstrating strong resolve in Cold War fashion, Johnson said, "As Commander in Chief the responsibility was mine—and mine alone. I gave the orders for that reply, and it has been given." He stated that he went to the congressional leadership to find solutions to the threat to peace. It passed overwhelmingly in the House, with only two people dissenting, and unanimously in the Senate. "The unanimity of the Congress reflects the unanimity of the country," he said, arguing that the American people were behind these actions in Southeast Asia. As if he was professing American doctrine regarding attacks on our ships, he said,

> The resolution is short. It is straightforward. I hope that it will be read around the world. The position of the United States is stated plainly. To any armed attack upon our forces, we shall reply. To any in southeast Asia who ask our help in defending their freedom, we shall give it.

Just before signing the resolution, he said, "This resolution confirms and reinforces powers of the Presidency. I pledge to all Americans to use those powers with all the wisdom and judgment God grants to me." Then he went on to justify the actions, emphasizing that it was done with measured restraint.

> It is everlastingly right that we should be resolute in reply to aggression and steadfast in support of our friends. But it is everlastingly necessary that our actions should be careful and should be measured. We are the most powerful of all nations—we must strive also to be the most responsible of nations.[50]

On that day, with his signature, the Vietnam War was born. More than any other issue, that conflict reshaped the American identity, thrusting American soldiers to the front line of a war that they struggled to understand.

7

New Awakenings

I

"I'd like to serve."

Upon learning that Robert Kennedy had resigned his position as attorney general, Lyndon Johnson, in his acceptance of that resignation, wrote, "You have played a very vital role in the conduct of public affairs." Indeed Robert Kennedy was an important piece of President Kennedy's administration as well as the start of the Johnson years. "Both President Kennedy and I sought your counsel on a wide range of matters going far beyond the usual concerns of the Department of Justice." Johnson even went as far as to say that Kennedy's contributions on national security, in particular, "have been significant."[1]

It was not a given that Robert Kennedy was going to serve in the Senate for New York State. Ed Guthman remembered Kennedy contemplating running for the office. "But if I were elected to the Senate," Kennedy told him, "I'd have some impact along with other younger senators.... As a group, we could have some effect. [Johnson] would have to listen to us."[2] As Kennedy considered New York as a possible spot to run, his younger brother, Ted, was in a plane crash breaking his back and killing two others. "How much more do they have to take?" he said of his mother and father. "I think I should just get out of it all. Somebody up there doesn't like us."[3] At that point Kennedy was also in contention for the vice presidency. He even made a statement saying that he would not seek a seat for the Senate in New York.

In 1964 Robert Kennedy ran for the Senate seat of New York against Kenneth Keating, the Republican senator from New York, who was described as "a silver haired, pink faced gentlemen of sixty-four" by Arthur Schlesinger. Keating claimed that the youthful Kennedy, who wanted the seat for himself, as a "carpet bagger" and had no right to run for the office. In fact, Robert Kennedy had lived in New York but had always voted in Hyannis Port and attended school in Massachusetts.[4] Kennedy's Senate run laid a foundation to highlight his own ideals and hopes for the coming years. He relied, however, on what he helped to sow with his brother four years earlier. While it was good to point to his successes in the Kennedy White House, that strategy may have hampered the early days of his campaign.

The *New York Times* was very critical of Robert Kennedy and instead endorsed Keating for the office. "At least they can never say I got my job though *The New York Times*," RFK would say.[5] He welcomed large crowds of children and people from all walks of life. By running on his brother's record and talking about the New Frontier, people naturally saw him as a successor to his brother. Kennedy knew that many were there to see the person who looked and sounded like the man they had lost almost a year prior to the election. "They're for him. They're for him," Kennedy said to Guthman.[6] Paul Corbin, who was a part of the campaign, saw that Bobby had failed to show the crowds what he stood for. "Get out of this mysticism. Get out of your daze," he said. "Bob, be yourself. Get hold of yourself. You're real. Your brother's dead."[7] To be sure, this had been an issue since JFK's murder the previous year. The Senate seat was Kennedy's opportunity to continue with New Frontier ideas, but also to leave his own imprint on history. It was difficult for him to come to the realization that his brother would not play a role in shaping that legacy. The election was not easy, and he would eventually have to turn to the man who occupied the Oval Office.

Keating attacked Bobby Kennedy on his civil rights record. While speaking at the NAACP convention on October 2, he claimed that Kennedy had "abandoned his post at the Department of Justice with an unfinished task before him." At the same convention, on the same day, Charles Evers, brother of the slain civil rights leader Medgar Evers, addressed the convention. The New York NAACP president wrote Evers a note prior to the speech, saying, "I know Bobby's your man, but not here." Evers did not appreciate the sentiment, and when it was time for him to speak, he said, "You're fortunate to have a man of Kennedy's caliber even visit the state of New York, much less running for Senator." Then addressing Keating directly, he said, "Bobby Kennedy means more to us in Mississippi than any white man I know, including yourself, Senator."[8]

Civil rights was an issue that continued to stymie lawmakers throughout the nation. Evers's support draws attention to Kennedy's efforts as attorney general to make a difference for African Americans throughout the nation. Evers continued, "We don't need someone who will talk civil rights and go along, we've had that. We need action. We need young blood and he is the one man who has cared."[9] The NAACP found themselves as neutrals in the race and released a statement saying that Keating had a "long and excellent record of support of civil rights." They also said that Kennedy "was the best Attorney General on civil rights in the whole history of the United States."[10]

Keating went even further and hoped to gain ground with the Italian and Jewish votes in New York. Keating claimed that Kennedy went after an Italian, Joe Malachi, when he was attorney general to distract the nation from the Bobby Baker case, who was a close associate of Lyndon Johnson. In addition to that, he claimed that Kennedy had made a deal with a "huge Nazi cartel." Kennedy had settled a case involving the General Aniline and Film Corporation in 1963, a group that allegedly had ties to the Nazi government. This maneuver backfired on Keating as it was seen in the record that he had supported the deal, which was a case dating back to 1942. Bobby had a few things to say about this:

> The charge that I made a deal with Nazis can't help but have an adverse effect on how Jewish people feel about me.... If this kind of charge were true, I wouldn't deserve to be elected to any public office. The charge isn't true.... I lost my brother and brother-in-law to the Germans. The idea that I would turn over money to the Nazis is ridiculous.

Kennedy couldn't believe that the campaign had taken such a turn. "I just didn't expect it would be as bad as that," he said later. The silver lining was that the reluctant candidate who did not want a smear campaign suddenly had a reason to fight back. "If he hadn't attacked me, I would have had a hell of a time."[11]

Robert Kennedy went on the offensive hoping to gain ground on Keating. He started to become a campaigner. Instead of running the campaign, which he was so used to, Bobby started to show his strength as a leader, a politician. On occasion he visited his father, who was incapacitated from a stroke a couple of years prior. "I'll make changes, Dad. You know I'll make changes. Millions of people need help. My God they need help."[12] What followed was a decisive media barrage that helped him define his voice for the next generation.

In an effort to connect with the people, Kennedy took questions at the Columbia/Barnard Democratic Club. The event was filmed and used in the campaign videos that aired on TV across the state. It has been lauded by scholars as one of his strongest televised showings. Schlesinger remarked that "he was forceful and persuasive dealing with questions" as the campaign continued and that the TV spot was his "strongest."[13] His demeanor and ability to relate with people came out in this venue. Indeed, Robert Kennedy turned a corner. The journey he had started when his brother was murdered seemed apparent. Empathy and concern for others was the dominant feature of the event. He looked relaxed and ready to confront issues.

Exuding confidence and not shying away from tough questions, Robert Kennedy took each question in stride. When asked why he chose to run for the state of New York and not another state, he resounded, "If the election's going to be decided based on my accent or where I have other associations, I think that then people are going to vote for my opponent." He stressed that the election should be decided on whether "my opponent or myself can do more for the state of New York and make the greatest amount of difference for this state and for the country over the period of the next six years."[14] Kennedy knew that Keating's claim of his being a carpetbagger was hurting him in the polls. Shrewdly, Kennedy wanted to make the election about the issues, which was something that was getting lost with the political rancor and rhetoric that was being said to discredit him.

Kennedy stressed education, which mirrored some of his speeches he had made in the last few months as attorney general. He invigorated the crowd by raising "the question of domestic matters, the problem of what we're going to do about our young people, what we're going to do about education, what we're going to do about unemployment, what we're going to do about housing." In a manner that was characteristic of the Kennedys, he laid out the issues in machine-gun fashion for the people listening. He followed up with, "All of these matters, again, are questions about which I have strong opinions and in which I've been involved, over the period of the last three and a half years, and in which we made an effort to do something about." He gestured like his brother, taking time to respond and crafting a message, without notes. "I don't say that we made these problems disappear. But I was involved in them, and we accomplished something." He stressed that they passed bills on housing, education, crime and civil rights. "We did something about it. I think that's what a United States Senator should do."[15]

Kennedy was pressed on why he chose New York to make is claim for the Senate. He demonstrated a level of humor that was characteristic of a style that he would embrace in the next four years, saying that he had "really two choices over the period of the last ten months. I could have stayed in— I could have retired." The crowd laughed, embraced him, understood that not being involved was never an option for Kennedy. He even took it a step further, saying, "My father has done very well and I could have lived off him," to which the crowd applauded. He said he wanted to work for the government. "I mean that's my major interest and it's been the major interest of my family." Kennedy wanted to stress service and that his chief motivator to run was that he wanted to make a difference. "I'd like to just be a good United States Senator. I'd like to serve."[16] The crowd applauded.

He was endearing and sincere. He exemplified everything that his brother represented. The nation was finally seeing what Robert Kennedy stood for, and they liked it. Robert Kennedy inspired the leaders from that generation who would lead on the greatest rights revolutions in the history of the United States. Robert Kennedy was different from his brother. Frank Sinatra was not singing his campaign song, and he was not seen with Hollywood stars. Despite his wealthy background, he was able to relate with most people and inspired them to lead.

Of all the issues he dealt with as attorney general, nothing defined him more than his civil rights record. When asked what was his "moral commitment to civil rights," he paused for a moment, taking in the question, and then responded thoughtfully: "Well I've been involved in this struggle now for three and half years, and I think I have indicated how I feel about it all over the country in the efforts I have made, and I think a good deal more could be done elsewhere."[17] Kennedy's civil rights record has been marginalized by many historians. His off-the-cuff characterization of the movement as a "struggle" demonstrated the empathy he tried to communicate to civil rights leaders across the nation. It was also indicative of how he viewed the movement to which he has been attached by historians. He was committed to civil rights more than any other attorney general up to that point in U.S. history. He also understood that the key to success in this field lay not only in the desegregation laws that Congress passed but also other tangible aspects of society that the government could control. "In my judgment, the answer, as far as the state of New York is concerned, now rests with education and it rests with employment and it rests with decent housing and it rests with proper recreation facilities and it rests basically in giving our young people some hope."[18]

II

"I don't have an easy solution."

Hope was a theme that Robert Kennedy saw as a tangible game-changing motivator for people. Kennedy used that notion in many of his public addresses, and in many ways he came to symbolize the hope he wanted to instill in others. His talk with students was inspirational, showing that he could relate to people and that he had ideas to affect issues that were relevant not only in New York but in the nation at large. Indeed, his vision for the nation did not end with New York, and this discussion gives historians a preview of the main issues that Kennedy and the nation would confront as the decade continued. No issues came to symbolize the sixties more than the Vietnam War. Robert Kennedy was not in the Senate when the vote came after the Gulf of Tonkin incident, but he was there to pick up the pieces in the aftermath of a conflict that would take over 58,000 American lives.

Kennedy's response to a question on Vietnam demonstrated that his position on the topic was not that much different from his brother's when he was in office. It is evidence that the young candidate may not have seen it as the quagmire that it became, but then again, few people did in 1964. "Well I think we should continue the effort," he said. "I think it's a very difficult problem." By signaling that the United States should continue the effort, Kennedy made clear that his position on the war was not different from Johnson's. However he was also commenting on the policy as it had been fought, not in terms of the escalation that took place in the early days of 1965. He did make a distinction, however, on how he believed the war could be won. "In my judgment, the war has to be won in South Vietnam." While his words were that of a cold warrior, he acknowledged the complexity of the solution. "But in the last analysis that war is going to be won when the people are convinced that this is an effort that is going to be successful and that it's in their interest to make that kind of effort."[19] In late 1964, Robert Kennedy, like his brother, understood that the only way for the United States to be successful was if they had the support of the Vietnamese people.

Robert Kennedy saw the obstacles that the French had to deal with when they were in the region firsthand when he visited Vietnam in 1951. He saw what were called the "best troops" of the French army. He declared that "they didn't win because they didn't have the support of the people. And we're not going to win unless we have the support of the people. That, in my judgement, is the key to success in Vietnam."[20] On the heels of the Gulf of Tonkin incident, the nation was coming to grips with the role that America would play in Vietnam. No longer a part of the cabinet, Bobby Kennedy had no voice in where the Johnson administration planned to take the nation.

Kennedy went even further at this event to characterize the conflict as "different wars." He quoted his brother, who said, "They're ancient in heritage ... but they're new in intensity." This use of the term "ancient" to describe the conflict adds to the complex nature of it. "I am in favor of continuing the effort there, as long as people support the effort, and as long as we have a hope of success." Kennedy saw Vietnam as multilayered, encompassing more than just a military solution. Unlike others in government, he saw that there was not an easy solution and just sending in the military was not the final solution to this problem. After all, the French were not successful with that strategy. "I don't have an easy solution. I think that as we continue our military effort, that our political effort to do things for the villages and the people who live in the city, is really going to be key."[21] At the heart of his plan was counterinsurgency, which was something he advocated for with his brother in the early sixties. Given that the war was about to dramatically change in the next year, it is interesting hat Bobby knew in 1964 that the way to be successful lay not in the military might of the United States, but in the people of Vietnam. It was important that they were a part of the solution. The war, however, would be fought differently.

Robert Kennedy eloquently articulated why he wanted to run for the Senate. He quoted JFK, Sophocles, Pericles and Dante. He believed in the notion that he was among the greatest generation and that they would live up to President Kennedy's ideals, calling them "the best generation in the history of mankind." He stressed how education was an integral part of that effort. "I think, really, it's going to rest with those who are educated, those people who are trained." He emphasized that people who were educated "have a special and particular responsibility." He quoted JFK's favorite quote from Dante, saying, "The hottest places in Hell are reserved for those who in time of moral crisis preserve their neutrality." At the heart of his philosophy was that the true solution to these issues was how communities would work together.

"So it's all of us," he proclaimed, "whether it's in the field of civil rights or housing or whether it's in Vietnam or whatever it is." Kennedy stressed the same community relationship that Dr. King did when he preached nonviolence and how communities could make a difference. Bobby was nothing like his brother. He was an idealist trying to find his voice in a world where his brother's type of rhetoric was the accepted form of communication. He believed in people and their ability to overcome adversity, and he would eventually find his voice. "And we have a special—not only responsibility—but a special opportunity to make a difference in the world, and make a difference for this country."[22]

His words went beyond the usual political rhetoric and offered a unique way to approach the problems that many people faced. His new voice in the late sixties would pave the path to a new way of dealing with problems, and through that voice he would share his vision of the world. He quoted Archimedes: "Show me where I can stand and I can move the world." He stressed, "And I think we can. I think that we started three and half years ago and I think that we can continue it. And I don't think it's just a question of political belief. I think that we can make a difference." His idealism and passion drove his words, conveying a sense of sincerity not common in politicians. He spoke to the students humbly, not looking for their approval, but rather trying to ingratiate them to his cause which he saw as the cause for the world, not only New York. In that exchange with students, a group that Kennedy saw as the key to provoking change, he gave the nation a preview of the issues that would captivate the nation for the remainder of the decade and beyond. His vision drove those same students, and many others, to question authority and strive for a new world.

III

"This is ma boy."

Despite his success at Columbia University, Robert Kennedy was still behind in the polls. Lyndon Johnson, however, was enjoying a great deal of support from the American people. Robert Kennedy would have to look to this campaign master for help in his own election. "You don't often find a man who has the understanding, the heart and the compassion that Bobby Kennedy has," Lyndon Johnson said. While Kennedy and Johnson had a myriad of issues between them, it was understood that the young candidate needed help from the veteran politician. It must have bothered Kennedy to rely on Johnson, but it was very effective and arguably could have made the difference in a tight election. Johnson went on stage, draped his arm around Kennedy and said to the crowd, "This is ma boy. I want you to elect ma boy."[23]

Lyndon Johnson had proven very effective for Bobby in the campaign. "Of all the things in life, this is what I enjoy the most," Johnson told Kennedy after campaigning in New York. Later Kennedy told Arthur Schlesinger, "Imagine saying that, of all the things in life, this is what you like most."[24] The exchange points to the major difference in these two men who would have such an important impact on the times they lived in. Bobby was not a politician, yet there he was trying to get elected to the Senate, out of his comfort zone—pushing the limit. Johnson, on the other hand, was a political animal, the consummate campaigner and would be on the trail every day if he could. They both needed a little bit of each other in order to be successful, yet they could not bring themselves to see it. Of the two, Bobby created his own type of politicking and, to some extent, would leave a deeper mark on the American consciousness as a result.

The election came to a sudden crossroads when Keating, who wanted to debate Kennedy on live TV, tried to embarrass Kennedy, who declined the invitation, by debating an empty chair. When Keating went on the air, Bobby decided to join him in the studio. His attempt was met with studio guards who would not let him in. The media recorded the exchange and even went as far as taking a picture of Bobby looking at a sign that said "please keep out" while Keating debated an empty chair instead of Kennedy, who was just outside. Ed Guthman remembered the incident in his book *We Band of Brothers*. Bobby met the guard at the studio and said, "I'm here to debate—Senator Keating has invited me to debate." The guard responded by saying, "I'm sorry. I can't let you in."[25] Bobby was relentless and said, "Senator Keating said he would have an empty chair for me. I'm here and I want to go in." With news cameras watching the exchange, the guard told Kennedy that Keating had bought the air time, and Kennedy was not allowed to go into the studio. Robert Kennedy responded, "Then kindly inform Senator Keating that I'm here and ready to go on the air." Kennedy asked him, "Why were you waiting for me?" To that, the guard responded, "We wanted to see you in your proper place." Kennedy shot back, "This is my proper place." The news crews were filming and documenting the exchange while Keating was debating the empty chair in the studio. Kennedy asked the CBS guard to go into the studio and tell Keating he was there. As the guard did that, Kennedy waited with the news crew.[26]

The man came back with a lawyer and told Kennedy that this was a "paid political broadcast" and he would not be let in. "Then kindly remove the empty seat from the stage and ask Senator Keating to withdraw his remark about my not showing up." The lawyer said, "I can not." Bobby walked away from the studio saying, "You are obviously being unfair. This is dishonest."[27] The episode became an example where Bobby had been able to distinguish himself, giving him distance from his brother and helping him win the election. It was a political tactic, but it worked and did much to show that he was willing to talk about the issues. Indeed, it helped his campaign while also showcasing his ability to prevail. "There was Javits and Keating on television really giving it to this empty chair," Bobby said later that night. "They kicked that chair all over the room. And there was I outside trying to get in."[28]

Robert Kennedy became a senator for New York State by 719,613 votes. He was helped by a landslide Johnson victory. In his victory speech, Kennedy failed to mention Johnson. "I wonder why he doesn't mention me," LBJ asked. For Bobby it was a surreal experience. "If my brother was alive I wouldn't be here. I'd rather have it that way," he said that night. The road ahead had a great deal of potential. He tried to capture that sentiment by quoting Tennyson, saying to the crowd, "Come my friends, 'tis not too late to seek a newer world."[29]

Of course the decade ahead had many obstacles and Robert Kennedy would do what he could to make a difference. It was his time to find solutions and carry on New Frontier ideals. He was not alone in this endeavor. Martin Luther King came along, as well as many other people that would pave the way and paint the nation in a new light, truly shaping the "newer world" that Kennedy invited his supporters to join him in on this quest. He said in his speech that his election "was a mandate to continue what we started four years ago."[30]

IV

"This is but a beginning of a long journey."

On September 13, 1964, Martin Luther King attended the Berlin Freedom Festival in Berlin, West Germany. At this event he reflected on John Kennedy's leadership and influence throughout the world. "There were two basic elements in President Kennedy's political philosophy which made him a major figure of history at one of its climactic turning points," he said. "First he grasped the fact that we live in an era in which human rights have become the central world issue."[31] King commented that many people observe that the world has become smaller with new innovations of communication and transportation. "In fact, however, the world has become larger as millions of people left out of the mainstream of civilization for centuries have crowded their way into modern society. They can not identify with the miracles of the space age from their mud hovels amid grinding poverty." Again, King reiterated the need to address poverty in the world, which had the potential to destroy progress.

King saw this as a world movement. People around the globe were challenging the status quo and forcing governments to acknowledge their place. "President Kennedy realized that the struggle for Negroes in his own nation was a component of this world movement." King alluded to Kennedy's speech that launched the Civil Rights Act, calling it a "forthright declaration of total war on inequality. No other American president had written with such compassion and resolution to make clear that our nation's destiny was unfulfilled so long as the scar of racial prejudice disfigured it." King saw Kennedy as a leader who did more than promise action or grant token measures, "for words alone had become insufficient to achieve human rights," King declared. President Kennedy "committed the federal government to action on a series of fronts. He saw that the struggle was essentially between right and wrong, and that no democratic sovereignty belongs in the middle."[32] King characterized Kennedy's actions in office as something that helped the movement, contributing to the rights revolution that came in the wake of his death.

King said that every administration after Kennedy would "have to grapple with the issue now emerging sharply" and decide what role federal power would play in state and local matters. King looked to history to make his point, saying, "This issue had tormented President Lincoln in the Civil War and during its aftermath. It was not resolved then." King believed that history had now brought into sharp focus the question of federal power over these matters. "One hundred years later a cold civil war afflicts the United States." Federal power, King believed, would have to play a role in solving this issue that has plagued the nation. "Sooner or later it will act in this direction as Lincoln had to act out of necessity.... What was left unaccomplished in the Civil War will have to be finished today because human rights are no longer a simple, exclusively domestic issue but have become a world concern."[33]

When Kennedy proposed the Civil Rights Bill it was an affirmation of federal power, King said. The new Civil Rights Act will "be both a living and lasting testament to him." King understood that the act was a start of federal intervention. "It is but a beginning on a long journey, but it took courage to offer it at a moment and in the manner he did." He emphasized, "It illustrated a special difference which made John Kennedy unique." King said that JFK responded to the demands of mass protest because he believed it was right. "This is the secret of the deep affection he evoked. He was responsive, sensitive, humble before the people, and bold on their behalf." Of course, King was very critical of Kennedy when he was alive. To be sure, his death gave Johnson the political capital necessary to pass the act. However, that was not the only thing that Kennedy left for Johnson. The Kennedy brothers did a great deal to change the climate in this nation where there was broad acceptance for civil rights issues. King's speech is a testament to his belief that Kennedy was effective in fostering that climate and ushering in change.

King reflected not only on Kennedy's action in the civil rights movement, but he also applauded his work on foreign policy saying that the Nuclear Test Ban Treaty was an example of Kennedy's ability to relate with people. Kennedy "believed that there could be, and should be, a world of diversity. He believed that different societies, different political systems and different races could exist in some small planet. He believed in the conscience of man," King said. Dr. King's words illuminate how he viewed the Kennedy years and what obstacles lay ahead for the struggle. He also acknowledged the visionary rhetoric that Kennedy used to articulate how he saw the world. To be sure, those speeches as well as the actions of the Justice Department made a difference for the civil rights movement.

The assassination of Kennedy, according to King, had a profound impact on the American people. "We went through a period of profound soul searching. We acknowledged that we were all involved in the death of John Kennedy. We had tolerated hate; we had tolerated the sick stimulation of violence in all walks of life." King continued, "And we tolerated the differential application of law, which said that a man's life was sacred only if we agree with his views." King believed that the very climate of hate had killed Kennedy. He also said that his death created a great deal of guilt for not working toward a climate that tolerated different beliefs. In fact, President Kennedy and Martin Luther King's efforts had done a great deal to move the nation toward greater tolerance, and even acceptance, of differences.

King believed that the climate that killed Kennedy was still very much a problem in America. "There are storm clouds forming on the American political horizon which indicate that the root of violence and extremism are still very deep in some parts of our country." King no longer only spoke for Montgomery or Atlanta or even the civil rights movement; he was a world figure, whose views were seen as revolutionary, crafting a message that had the potential to change not only the segregationist south, but the world. "It is my conviction," he said, "that ultimately the forces of goodwill will prevail."

In this document, King added some other thoughts in his own handwriting. King invoked not only the meaning of JFK, but how his brother, Robert Kennedy, expressed it at the Democratic National Convention, using the same quote from Romeo and Juliet. "John F. Kennedy was a dream," he wrote. What followed was a summation of his "I Have a Dream" speech, linking JFK to that dream he had for the nation. He continued, saying that JFK "dreamed of a day when poverty would be eliminated from the face of the south.... He dreamed of a day when there would be 'peace on earth and goodwill toward man.'" He concluded, "We are the glad heirs of this dream."

His words highlighted what John F. Kennedy meant to King, the movement and ultimately the world. John F. Kennedy had the potential to affect many people. This speech was clear evidence that King believed JFK could bring his own dream closer to reality. It seemed that he continued to look for that same leadership in Johnson. On a larger note, King's speech is an example that he had moved beyond the United States and had become a world figure. To be sure, that honor would become very clear when not long after his speech he learned that he had won the Nobel Peace Prize.

V

"We are through with racial segregation now, henceforth and forever more."

King received the Nobel Peace Prize on December 10, 1964. At the ceremony he told the world about the injustices of the South that he had experienced from the vicious, pernicious tactics of Bull Connor in Birmingham to the Ku Klux Klan that killed three Freedom Summer volunteers in Philadelphia, Mississippi. He also acknowledged that poverty "afflicts my people and chains them to the lowest rung of the economic ladder." He asked openly why, given the "beleaguered" nature of the movement, he was awarded this prize. "After contemplation, I conclude that the award, which I receive on behalf of that movement is a profound recognition that non-violence is the answer to the crucial political and moral question of our time—the need for man to overcome oppression and violence without resorting to violence and oppression." King believed that "sooner or later all the people in the world will have to discover a way to live together in peace, and thereby transform this cosmic elegy into a creative psalm of brotherhood."[34] King's dream resonated to the world that still struggled with the Cold War. His philosophy of nonviolence, rooted in India, was a way to bring nations, religions, and ethnicities together. While it was altruistic at times, it had the potential to unite a world once divided by world war for over thirty years at the start of the century. King's words represented the hope of the future.

King believed in the power of the civil rights movement, saying that he accepted the award "with an abiding faith in America and an audacious faith in the future of mankind." He went further, saying he refused to accept that humankind was incapable of overcoming the issues that plagued society, "the view that mankind is so tragically bound to the starless midnight of racism and war that the bright daybreak of peace and brotherhood can never become a reality." He had faith in the people's ability to vanquish evil and prevent a thermonuclear war. He declared, "I believe that unarmed truth and unconditional love will have the final word in reality. This is why a right temporarily defeated is stronger than evil triumphant." His prose was majestic, getting to the core of his beliefs, invigorating the movement, demonstrating to the world that there was hope and his vision would lead the way. As a testament to the power of this message, President Barack Obama alluded to this speech in his final State of the Union address in 2016—fifty-two years later.

King brought the message of peace and brotherhood back to the United States on December 18, 1964, in New York City, saying, "I return here more convinced than ever that segregation is evil, I return here more convinced than ever that segregation is nothing but a new form of slavery." He emphasized in his statement that he was determined to rid the nation of that evil. "We must make it clear all over this land that we are through with racial segregation now, henceforth and forever more."[35] Upon King's return to the United States, he embarked on a grand effort to continue what the Freedom Summer had started earlier that year. He and the SCLC chose Selma, Alabama, to make that stand.

PART III. MARCHING ON AND HITTING FULL STRIDE, 1965-1966

8

Selma

I

"A symbol of bitter-end resistance to the civil rights movement in the deep south."

On January 4, 1965, Robert Kennedy took his seat in the Senate. Bobby started his time there ranked 98th in seniority and sitting in the back row. The *New York Times* reported that President Kennedy also spent his time as a "backbencher" when he was in the Senate. With his brother Ted, it marked the first time that two brothers took the oath of office together. When Bobby was asked if he liked his new seat in government, he smiled and quipped, "Well at least I got inside the building."[1] Joseph Palermo argues that this new role as senator took some getting used to. RFK was used to being in charge, or at least of having a great deal of authority. He always watched the Senate from a distance as an investigator on the Rackets Committee, a campaign manager or a close adviser to the president. Whenever he gave speeches, the press filled the room, which was uncommon for freshmen senators. RFK did not want to attack Johnson's Vietnam policy at first because he thought it would be like attacking JFK.[2]

Edwin Guthman argued that in mid-January 1965, Bobby Kennedy felt strongly about not abandoning South Vietnam. "However," Guthman wrote, "he was just as strongly opposed to escalation of the war and thought counterinsurgency still had a chance to force a reasonably satisfactory solution."[3] After the Vietcong attack at Pleiku on February 7, 1965, Johnson struck back with an extensive bombing campaign of the North. According to Guthman, "The bombing deeply troubled Bob." In response, Kennedy drafted a piece to include in a speech that read,

> We must understand that while bombing targets in North Vietnam may induce more caution in Hanoi, they will not bring peace to South Vietnam. In the last analysis, the way to defeat the terrorists is to increase the capability to fight their kind of war.

Guthman said that Bobby chose not to express these concerns as he was a freshman senator, just three weeks in office at the time of the bombing, and it would seem that he was fighting Johnson in public.[4] Robert Kennedy wanted to see South Vietnam develop politically. He wanted to avoid military conflict. It seemed that RFK and LBJ were apart on the issue of Vietnam. Ultimately Bobby wanted to see more peace overtures and less fighting, but there were many policy makers who believed in the war. In 1965 it was still too early politically to side with the peace protests. The peace movement was not fully mature and did not factor into many discussions in the White House.[5]

As Dr. King approached 1965, he told close aids that he planned demonstrations in Alabama and Mississippi to confront the injustices in voting practices. Once he was done there, he planned to go north and make progress for African Americans in the inner cities.[6] In the wake of the Nobel Peace Prize, King found himself as the outright leader of the movement for civil rights in the nation. His vision of nonviolence, as articulated at Oslo in December, had captivated the world, and, like a great politician, he planned to use that capital to foster change.

Just after the 1964 election, the SCLC strategized on the best place to bring awareness to the nation of voting atrocities in the South.[7] Like Bull Connor in Birmingham, Sheriff Jim Clark of Selma had a similar style of confrontation that would showcase to the nation, indeed the world, the pernicious violent nature of segregation. King and the SCLC decided to start this protest at a January 2, 1965, kickoff rally in Selma. He spoke at Brown Chapel African Methodist Episcopal Church telling people what he planned to do to force the issue with Jim Clark.

King stood at the podium, galvanizing the people of Selma, telling them that he planned to bring the vote to that city, and from that effort gain the support of President Johnson and the American people. It was a brilliantly orchestrated demonstration that started with strong, soaring rhetoric from King. "If they refuse to register us we will appeal to Governor Wallace. If he doesn't listen, we will appeal to the legislature." He went further, saying, "If the legislature doesn't listen, we will seek to arouse the federal government by marching by the thousands by the places of registration." Asserting the nonviolent philosophy, he declared, "We must be willing to go to jail by the thousands. We are not asking, we are demanding the ballot." King proclaimed at the rally that this was a serious test of whether American democracy "can exist for her 22 million black children."[8]

The right to vote was a precious power of a democracy and had been denied to African American voters since the passage of the Fifteenth Amendment through literacy tests and poll taxes among other methods.

This system of oppression was a sad vestige of the Civil War that had not finished its revolution for freed slaves and created a multitiered system of discrimination in southern society since the late nineteenth century. Alluding to Governor Wallace's interposition at the doorway of the University of Alabama in 1963, King said,

> When we get the right to vote we will send to the State House not men who will stand in the doorways of universities to keep Negroes out but men who will uphold the cause of justice, and we will send to Congress men who will sign not a manifesto for segregation but a manifesto of justice.[9]

King's proclamation energized the movement, bringing the full weight of his worldwide notoriety to the movement. This speech started a series of events that led President Lyndon Johnson to embrace legislation to protect the right to vote for all Americans. King wanted to get the attention of Congress and Johnson with this protest. He believed that Selma was "a symbol of bitter-end resistance to the civil rights movement in the deep south."[10]

King and Kennedy stood at the precipice of change when 1965 began. They were both in roles of power and influence. King would begin the year with the campaign in Selma. That effort would not only move the nation to embrace civil rights, but it also solidified King's role as the leader of the movement. Kennedy, meanwhile, struggled to find his place in the Senate. However, by the end of the year, he would find his voice on some major issues, especially civil rights and Vietnam. With those issues he would make a considerable break with Johnson publicly.

Lyndon Johnson declared in his January 4, 1965, State of the Union address that a part of his national agenda was to "eliminate every remaining obstacle to the right and the opportunity to vote." Johnson may have been influenced by the Freedom Summer initiative the previous year or even by King's declaration in Selma. Despite what the 2015 movie *Selma* portrayed, Johnson wanted to pass legislation that protected African Americans' right to vote. The State of the Union was evidence to this point of his intention to pass legislation. He emphasized that point again later in the speech, saying that he wanted to open the "opportunity to all our people" and, specifically stated, "to Negro Americans, through enforcement of the Civil Rights law and elimination of barriers to the right to vote." To be sure, Johnson looked at the year ahead, expecting the vote to be a major issue, and even part of the Great Society that he hoped to create as a part of his legacy.[11]

King returned to Selma on January 18, 1965. He marched with John Lewis of the SNCC and 400 citizens on the county courthouse. They were met by Sheriff Jim Clark who told the group that they could wait in the nearby alleyway and attempt to register one at a time. None of them were allowed to register to vote. From there, King and others in his party registered at the Albert Hotel as the first African American guests, breaking another segregationist barrier. In the process of registering, King was attacked by James Robinson, a Nazi. He punched King in the face twice before John Lewis was able to get him off of King. King spoke later that night at a rally and prepared to continue the demonstrations the next day.[12]

The day after his encounter with Robinson at the Albert Hotel, King led a group of demonstrators to the county courthouse once again. This time the group refused to wait in the alleyway, forcing Jim Clark to use another, more violent tactic of forcibly removing people from the sidewalk. John Herbers of the *New York Times* reported that Clark took one protestor, Amelia Boynton, "grabbed her by the back of her collar and pushed her roughly and swiftly for half a block into a patrol car." Dr. King, who was across the street witnessing the act, went straight into the courthouse to file an injunction against Clark. King proclaimed, "It was one of the most brutal and unlawful acts I have seen an officer commit." The protestors who refused to go into the alley were arrested for unlawful assembly. The leaders of the protest were arrested for criminal provocation. King left Selma that night saying he would return by the end of the week.[13]

Dr. King's efforts were brilliantly orchestrated to expose not only the reality that Americans were denied the right to vote but also the police brutality that was so much a part of the white leadership's reaction to these protests. The Selma campaign, like Birmingham, was meant to invoke emotion through the images and descriptions of the event. Newspapers were there to witness the speeches as well as the violent response. To be sure, King used the media effectively, pushing Johnson to take a stand on the issue. This went beyond the usual rhetoric, invoking a passionate plea from the movement to the leaders of country. It would not fall on deaf ears.

II

"Because of what we believe."

On Inauguration Day, January 20, 1965, the freshman senator from New York stopped at his brother's gravesite in Arlington National Cemetery before and after Johnson's inaugural address. On a snow-topped hillside overlooking the Potomac, the eternal flame stood as a reminder of both the nation's and his own loss. His brother was supposed to be getting ready to initiate his second term. Instead, Bobby stood beside the flame, bowed his head and prayed silently. After he attended the inauguration, sitting near his brother Ted, he returned to JFK's side, where it all began four years prior, bowing his head once again. He picked up a piece of snow with his left hand, crushed it in his palm and walked down the hill.[14]

From the steps of the Capitol, Lyndon Johnson gave his only inaugural address to the nation. Taking over in the wake of the tragic loss of JFK tied the first part of his presidency to the fallen leader. His vision for the nation was something that drove his presidency moving forward. He started, saying, "For every generation there is a destiny. For some, history decides. For this generation the choice must be our own." In many ways the statement was not only for the nation but also for him as he embarked to define what his presidency would look like to the nation and the world. Johnson wanted to stress his vision for the nation, and it was tied to his Great Society and the War on Poverty that he championed in the previous year as well as in the election. "In a land of great wealth, families must not live in hopeless poverty," he said. "In a land rich in harvest, children just must not go hungry. In a land of healing miracles, neighbors must not suffer and die untended. In a great land of learning and scholars, young people must be taught to read and write."[15] To be sure, he hoped to create a society that made it possible for every person to have a chance to achieve the American dream. Both Robert Kennedy and Martin Luther King wanted to build on that idea as they continued to attack the issues that America faced in the sixties.

Johnson addressed the growing racial tension indirectly in saying, "Justice requires us to remember: when any citizen denies his fellow, saying: 'His color is not mine or his beliefs are strange and different,' in that moment he betrays America, though his forebears created this Nation." It was more than what Kennedy had said four years prior, and it specifically addressed "color" in the statement. His themes were liberty, world issues, the Union and "the American Belief." In a similar way he addressed the growing tension in Vietnam indirectly.

> Change has brought new meaning to that old mission. We can never again stand aside, prideful in isolation. Terrific dangers and troubles that we once called "foreign" now constantly live among us. If American lives must end, and American treasure be spilled, in countries that we barely know, then that is the price that change has demanded of conviction and of our enduring covenant.[16]

Johnson linked the role that America played in the world to a "covenant" that had been forged at the founding of the American spirit, alluding to the first colonies in America. He saw that plight continued with his own presidency. Whether it was in Vietnam or Selma, Alabama, Johnson was maintaining that spirit and vision for the nation.

Johnson had plans for his administration to create a nation that would do wonderful things for its people. He believed that this endeavor, not any foreign wars, was his greatest legacy. He said, "I do not believe that the

Great Society is the ordered, changeless, and sterile battalion of the ants. It is the excitement of becoming—always becoming, trying, probing, falling, resting, and trying again—but always trying and always gaining." To be sure, LBJ saw his vision as something that was flexible and adapted to the needs of the people, ever moving and ready to take on the issues that confronted the nation. Touching on emotion and hope, he said, "If we succeed it will not be because of what we have, but it will be because of what we are; not because of what we own, but rather because of what we believe."[17] His endearing belief in the American people and his own dream drove his actions in those days and stressed the tenacious nature of the American spirit, not the affluence and material things that they possessed.

Robert Kennedy and Lyndon Johnson left that day with a vision for their future. For Bobby, it was tied inexorably to his brother, which was why he felt the need to see him on that day. To be sure, Kennedy had every intention to forge his own path, but it was not something that came natural for him. He was still his brother's keeper and looked to that vision for guidance in his new role. Johnson, on the other hand, was forever in the long shadow of JFK. His intention was to take this moment to assert his vision for the nation. His speech set the tone for the coming months, and he would wage that war against poverty that he hoped. However, that vision was hampered by a growing war in Southeast Asia and racial tension in Selma, Alabama.

A week later on January 27, 1965, Martin Luther King gave a speech in Atlanta at his Nobel Peace Prize recognition dinner. King continued to take any opportunity to give his vision of the nation. "Anyone sensitive to the present moods, morals, and trends in our nation must know that the time for racial justice has come," he said.

> The issue is no longer whether segregation and discrimination will be eliminated, but how they will pass from the American scene. The deep rumbling of discontent that we hear today is the thunder from the disinherited masses, rising from dungeons of oppression to the bright hills of freedom.[18]

In the midst of a major movement in Selma, King's vision was something that looked to a future where America was a "Great Society" in a different way than LBJ. His version of this dream had opportunity for African Americans and a promise that oppression would be obliterated.

King told a story at the start of the speech about a time when he was waiting for a flight and there was a delay due to a mechanical failure. He said that a ground crew came out and fixed the issues, getting the plane in the air, allowing the pilot to fly them to their destination. His story illuminated to the audience that it took every person to make the next step to racial integration. He commented on the people further, demonstrating the strength of the movement, saying, "Oppressed people cannot remain oppressed forever. The yearning for freedom eventually manifests itself." He continued, "Something within has reminded the Negro of his birthright of freedom, and something without has reminded him that it can be gained." King called the *Brown* decision a "beacon light of hope to millions of disinherited people" laying the groundwork for the freedom that he was fighting for, empowering the movement, leading to the eventual Civil Rights Bill in 1964.

While King was hopeful in his comments, he did not want the audience to believe that there was not more work to do in the movement. "We still have a long, long way to go before racial justice is a reality for the Negro." King implored the people of southern states to work together to "stand up for justice" and "remove the yoke of segregation from its own body." He asserted his beliefs once more that nonviolence was the only method to defeat segregation and discrimination. He proclaimed that "non-violence is the most potent weapon available to oppressed people in their struggle for freedom and justice." This was King's dream—an equal society obtained through the use of methods that did no harm to the people.

> As a race we must work unrelentingly for first class citizenship, but we must never use second-class methods to gain it. We must never succumb to the temptation of using violence in the struggle, for if this happens, unborn generations will be the recipients of a long and desolate night of bitterness and our chief legacy to the future will be an endless reign of meaningless chaos.[19]

This was the core of King's vision of the nation; it was rooted in love and brotherhood, not hate and disdain for fellow human beings. This was the future he hoped to forge not only for African American, but for all Americans as they moved further into the decade and confronted the issue of Vietnam and further racial tension.

King concluded the speech talking about how his experience of winning the peace prize had brought him to the mountaintop, but he felt that the time had come to return to the valley below. "So I must return to the valley," he said, "a valley filled with misguided bloodthirsty mobs." With the impending confrontation in Alabama and the past Freedom Summer in Mississippi, King said, "I must return to the valley—a valley filled with literally thousands of Negroes in Alabama and Mississippi who are brutalized intimidated and sometimes killed when they seek to register and vote."[20] King's speech stood on the threshold of his work in Selma, hoping to force Johnson to include voting rights in his Great Society. To be sure, Johnson had every intention of giving African Americans more power at the polls. While the Fifteenth Amendment ensured the right for everyone in the nation, the white southern leadership worked to deny that right. King's efforts to rid the nation of discrimination at the polls was about to become a major moment in the struggle.

III

"Why do they go to Selma? Why not to 125th Street?"

In an effort to realize Johnson's Great Society, Robert Kennedy gave his maiden speech on the floor of the Senate on February 1, 1965, to support a measure that would bring economic aid to Appalachia. Kennedy asked to include thirteen New York counties in the bill, which passed the Senate. Robert Kennedy called out Governor Rockefeller as "short-sighted" for not including the state in Johnson's program. Kennedy was supported by Republican senator Jacob K. Javits in this endeavor. He released a statement later that stressed the need for development along the Appalachia region, which had been riddled with poverty.[21] Bobby was still feeling his way around the Senate. Supporting a bill for a Great Society program was good for the party as well as the vision that he had for the nation. While he may have differed with Johnson on many things, they both agreed that poverty was the greatest issue that the nation had to deal with as they moved into the next decade. Kennedy was not only supporting Johnson but also his brother's vision for the nation. LBJ may have been the politician to get the bill passed, but the measures were the brainchild of the New Frontier.

It was still early for Kennedy to make his mark in the Senate, and he was feeling his way around the room before he believed he could make major waves. Evan Thomas writes, "In time, Kennedy did use the Senate effectively as a bully pulpit, as a platform to float new ideas, especially about ways to fight poverty." Robert Kennedy, Thomas argues, "was far more passionate about the poor" than his brother had been. While JFK acknowledged that there needed to be a program to help the impoverished, he also wanted to help the middle class.[22] John F. Kennedy was the pragmatic politician, looking to address as many issues as he could and help as many groups as possible with his legislation. While Bobby felt the same way, it is clear that he had an activist side to his politics, and that was realized in that first year of the Senate.

When King was gathering momentum in Selma and asked for people to come to the Selma march, Kennedy questioned the logic, saying, "Why do they go to Selma? Why not to 125th Street?"[23] Kennedy saw the next battle for racial tension in northern cities. He wanted to see people doing more in the North. King's movements in the South captivated many people to go there and bring freedom to a group of people that had suffered oppression, but there was also a war in the North against poverty that was just as important to the success of the nation, and Kennedy believed that he was on the forefront of that fight. With the impoverished conditions of the North also came an oppressive discrimination. Kennedy hoped to make that his fight as he moved forward in the Senate and his own endeavors. To be sure, he supported King's efforts but still was concerned about the nation as a whole.

The Selma campaign was in full force by the start of February. Jim Clark had received help from the Alabama State Troopers, and they started to arrest demonstrators. It had been decided that Martin Luther King would get arrested in Selma on February 1. Before he led his group of 250 demonstrators to the courthouse, he said, "If Negroes could vote," King told them, "there would be no Jim Clarks, there would be no oppressive poverty directed against Negroes, our children would not be crippled by segregated schools, and the whole community might live together in harmony."[24] While Robert Kennedy made his maiden speech on the floor of the Senate, Martin Luther King led a group back to the courthouse only to be intercepted and arrested.

Once in jail, King refused to be released and even commented to a news reporter, "I must confess this is a deliberate attempt to dramatize conditions in this city, state and community." While he was in jail King continued to lead the movement, giving Andrew Young, executive director for the SCLC, detailed instructions to keep attention on the Selma campaign. King wanted him to keep calling politicians and get a congressional delegation to Selma. He wanted Young to call President Johnson "urging him to intervene in some way." He made it clear to "keep some activity alive every day this week." He outlined twelve points for Young to follow up on.[25] King was the spearhead, the core of this movement in Selma. The marches continued for the remainder of the week, leading to more arrests and media attention.

Andrew Young had contacted Lee C. White, an adviser to President Johnson and asked him to intervene. He wanted Johnson to send someone to Selma to evaluate the situation and make a statement regarding voting rights and start the process for legislation.[26] Meanwhile the protests continued, leading to the arrest of many other people, including schoolchildren, on that Wednesday. By Thursday, February 4, 1965, two major events helped the movement. District Court judge Daniel H. Thomas issued an injunction instructing the registrar to stop using a difficult process to register voters. Following that move, Johnson issued a statement that afternoon.

At a press conference that day at the White House, Lyndon Johnson made a statement that supported the movement in Selma. He started, saying, "I should like to say that all Americans should be indignant when one American is denied the right to vote. The loss of that right to a single citizen undermines the freedom of every citizen." He asserted in his statement, "This is why all of us should be concerned with the efforts of our fellow Americans to register to vote in Alabama." Johnson went further to clarify his remarks:

> The basic problem in Selma is the slow pace of voting registration for Negroes who are qualified to vote. We are using the tools of the Civil Rights Act of 1964 in an effort to secure their right to vote. One of those tools of course is legal action to guarantee a citizen his right.... I hope that all Americans will join with me in expressing their concern over the loss of any American's right to vote. Nothing is more fundamental to American citizenship and to our freedom as a nation and as a people. I intend to see that that right is secured for all of our citizens.[27]

Johnson's remarks were a welcome boost to the movement. They are also evidence that he publicly supported legislation to secure the right to vote for all Americans. However, King continued to push for more protests.

In the hopes of bringing in the power of the Birmingham struggle, on Friday February 5, as the protests continued, the *New York Times* carried an advertisement by Dr. King from "a Selma, Alabama Jail." King started the letter saying, "When the King of Norway participated in awarding the Nobel Peace Prize to me he surely did not think that in less than sixty days I would be in jail. He, and almost all world opinion will be shocked because they are little aware of the unfinished business in the South." He continued with his statement:

> By jailing hundreds of Negroes, the city of Selma, Alabama, has revealed the persisting ugliness of segregation to the nation and the world. When the Civil Rights Act of 1964 was passed many decent Americans were lulled into complacency because they thought the day of difficult struggle was over. Why are we in jail? Have you ever been required to answer 100 questions on government, some abstruse even to a political science specialist, merely to vote? Have you ever stood in line with over a hundred others and after waiting an entire day seen less than ten given the qualifying test?

His statement went on to bring into sharp focus the issues, which was larger than only voting rights, though that was the main thrust for the movement. He emphasized the "ugliness" of the system that continued to take away the rights of American citizens.

> But apart from voting rights, merely to be a person in Selma is not easy. When reporters asked Sheriff Clark if a woman defendant was married, he replied, "She's a nigger woman and she hasn't got a Miss or Mrs. in front of her name." This is the U.S.A. in 1965. We are in jail simply because we cannot tolerate these conditions for ourselves or our nation.[28]

To be sure, King's words had an effect on the national movement, not only in Selma, Alabama. However, while King was in jail, there was another civil rights leader who came to Selma.

In the midst of the protests, Malcolm X had made an appearance in Selma with the message that the right to vote should be guaranteed to all people by any means necessary. To be sure, his appearance was something that the SCLC did not plan. Coretta Scott King and Juanita Abernathy were sent to meet with Malcolm X. Malcolm said to an audience at Brown Chapel, "I'm not intending to try and stir you up and make you do something that you wouldn't have done anyway.... I pray that God will bless you in everything that you do. I pray that you will grow intellectually, so that you can understand the problems of the world and where you fit into that world picture." He also said, "And I pray that all the fear that has even been in your heart will be taken out." After his speech, Malcolm told Coretta Scott King that he had wanted to tell her husband that he meant to help his cause in Selma and not make it worse, but he had to be at a conference in London.[29]

The contrast of Malcolm X and Martin Luther King at the same protest speaks to the complications within the national movement for equality. Dr. King's nonviolent philosophy was seen as a better solution to these issues by many people in the government. King's philosophy was meant to shape a generation for peaceful protest. Malcolm X, who had a militant philosophy, may have given King the leverage he needed for Johnson to embrace King's movement. There were some promising results for the Selma campaign. King was able to get Johnson to make a statement for voting rights on three occasions following the start of the Selma campaign. The next months would affect the nation and lead not only to legislation on voting rights, but also a strong voice from both King and Robert Kennedy, paving the way for further discourse on not only civil rights, but also the conflict in Vietnam.

9

Bloody Sunday and the Aftermath

I

"One has to conquer the fear of death."

Martin Luther King needed rest. After he came home from jail, he fell ill and was in bed with a fever for two days before he took the podium again at Brown Chapel on February 17, 1965. On the previous day, civil rights leader the Rev. C.T. Vivian had been beaten by Jim Clark. Vivian led a group of protesters to the courthouse steps, compared Clark to Hitler and dared him to hit him. Despite the effort of his deputies, Clark punched Vivian in the mouth, sending him down the steps of the courthouse.[1] The act seemed to lead to a boost in media attention. One SCLC staff member commented to John Herbers of the *New York Times*, "Every time it appears that the movement is dying out, Sheriff Clark comes to our rescue."[2] In the wake of that attack, King looked to bring things in Selma to a head as he went in front of the people the next night to begin a series of marches.

After being in bed for two days, King asked the people in Selma to adopt a stronger campaign against Jim Clark. He stressed the need for night campaigns and "broader forms of civil disobedience." John Herbers of the *New York Times* wrote, "It was the strongest speech that Dr. King has delivered to a Negro rally since the campaign to speed Negro voting opened almost five weeks ago." After meeting with leaders in a strategy session, King said to his audience, "We concluded in that meeting that Selma still is not right. Far from letting up our efforts in Selma and Dallas County, we're going to broaden our activities here." He stressed to the people there, "We aren't going to let up until Negroes can go down and register without a single stumbling block." He made a clear connection between the issues in Selma and Sheriff Jim Clark when he said, "Until Sheriff Clark is removed the evils of Selma will not be removed." King wanted the people to challenge the power structure in Selma.

> It is time for us to say to the businessmen, the Mayor and white power structure that they must take the responsibility for what Jim Clark does. It is time for us to say to those men "If you don't do something about it we will engage in broader forms of civil disobedience." We might have to march out of this church tonight and stand at the courthouse all night long.

Prior to the speech, the people attending the meeting voted to boycott downtown businesses. This was something that King wanted them to do as he saw local businessmen linked to Sheriff Clark and his staff.[3]

C.T. Vivian addressed a crowd at Zion's Chapel Methodist Church in Marion, Alabama, a town just twenty-three miles away from Selma. After the address, Vivian led four hundred marchers on a nighttime march to protest the arrest of James Orange, a civil rights worker. They were met by a group of fifty state troopers. The troopers announced to the group, "This is an unlawful assembly. You are hereby ordered to disperse. Go home or go back in the church." The group refused to move. The streetlights, which were lighting the march, went out, and the troopers attacked the group with their nightsticks. What followed was a brief riot in the darkness with the protesters at the mercy of the state troopers. In the melee a reporter and two photographers were beaten, and Jimmy Lee Jackson, a twenty-six-year-old African American, was shot in the stomach by a trooper.[4] John Lewis recalled in his memoir, "It was mayhem. The marchers broke ranks and tried fleeing through the darkness to the church. There was screaming and blood on the pavement from head wounds."[5]

The *New York Times* reported the next day that the incident was being investigated by the FBI and state officials. Governor George Wallace went on record saying, "I regret the incident that happened in Marion. I am conducting a full investigation." He went on to blame what he termed "career agitators," referring to the SCLC and the SNCC, who had been in Selma longer than the SCLC. "I don't want to jump to conclusions of what happened in the still of the night in a small community. I will take proper actions," he said. Attorney General Nicholas Katzenbach also said that he was conducting a full investigation into the events.[6] These events of the movement not only brought further tension to the situation but also shined the national spotlight on Selma and Dr. King. The civil rights movement had come a long way since those early days in Montgomery, Alabama, when Dr. King had led a group to boycott the buses. Days after this incident in Marion, another violent episode would affect King and the movement.

On February 21, 1965, Malcolm X was shot to death by three assassins in New York City. King issued a statement saying, "I am deeply saddened and appalled to learn of the brutal assassination of Malcolm X. This evil act must be strongly condemned by all people of goodwill." While King and Malcolm X had not gotten along philosophically, this was another stark reminder that this nonviolent movement had taken too many turns to violence. King spoke about the climate of the nation, in the same way that he did when he articulated his feelings on JFK's assassination. "We must face the tragic fact that Malcolm X was murdered by a morally inclement climate. It reveals that our society is still sick enough to express dissent through murder." King's message harked back to the notion that America needed to embrace a climate where people can disagree without resorting to violence. "We have not learned to disagree without being violently disagreeable. The viscous assassination should cause our whole society to see that violence and hatred are evil forces that must be cast into the unending limbo."[7]

In the aftermath of that assassination, Attorney General Katzenbach called King and warned him against any night marches. He said that he had authentic reports that there were two men who intended to kill him. They had tried the previous Monday when King was in Marion, Alabama, but could not get a clear shot.[8] When asked about the threats by reporters, King responded, "I get threats quite often. This is almost a daily and weekly occurrence." He went on to say, "I have learned now to take them rather philosophically." He concluded, "One has to conquer the fear of death if he is going to do anything constructive in life and take a stand against evil." David Garrow writes, "Malcolm's death reminded King again that black liberation in America would require much more than a civil rights act or voting bill."[9]

II

"We must work passionately and unrelentingly to make the American dream a reality."

On Wednesday March 3, 1965, King was in Marion, Alabama, to attend Jimmy Lee Jackson's funeral. "He was murdered by the indifference of every white minister of the gospel who has remained silent behind the safe security of his stained glass windows," King said. "He was murdered by the irresponsibility of every politician from governors on down who has fed his constituents the stale bread of hatred and the spoiled meat of racism." King made reference to the growing crisis in Southeast Asia through the complicity of the federal government in the murder. "He was murdered by the timidity of a Federal Government that is willing to spend millions of dollars a day to defend freedom in Vietnam but cannot protect the rights of its citizens at home." King pointed to Jim Clark, Bull Connor and anyone who stood idly by to accept segregation as responsible. "He was murdered by the brutality of every sheriff who practices lawlessness in the name of the law. And he was murdered by the cowardice of every Negro who passively accepts the evil of segregation and stands on the sidelines in the struggle for justice."[10] King's sermon was an extension of his insistence that the climate in the nation had contributed to the violence of the movement.

King's plea to African Americans who were not a part of the movement was evidence that he believed more people should be involved in the struggle and each tragedy lay on the shoulders of those who were not committed to equality. Indeed, this was an extension of his philosophy that the nation was all connected and needed to commit to the movement for there to be change. John Lewis also spoke, saying, "We just recognize the fact that the evil climate created by men like Governor Wallace and Sheriff Jim Clark was responsible for the death of Jimmie Jackson."[11]

King's oration spoke of Jackson's sacrifice for the movement and that they needed to continue in the wake of this tragedy. "Jimmie Lee Jackson is speaking to us from the casket and he is saying to us that we must substitute courage for caution," King said. "His death says to us that we must work passionately and unrelentingly to make the American dream a reality. His death must prove that unmerited suffering does not go unredempted." In an effort to promote his strategy of nonviolence, he declared, "We must not be bitter and we must not harbor ideas of retaliating with violence. We must not lose faith in our white brothers." The Rev. Ralph Abernathy, King's closest adviser, said at the funeral, "Jimmie Jackson has joined the ranks of many martyrs who have fallen along the way in the building of this great nation and in bringing us to this hour."[12]

When Dr. King had announced that the movement was going to march from Selma to Montgomery in protest, he said, "We hope to have our forces mobilized to have carloads of people from all over the state to march on the capital." He went on to say, "We will be going there to tell Governor Wallace we aren't going to take it anymore."[13] The SCLC and SNCC decided that the protest would take place on Sunday, March 7. King decided not to attend the march and to stay in Atlanta. There were various reasons for this decision ranging from Sunday obligations to a fear of being killed to SCLC members telling him to stay away from it.[14]

SNCC was not happy with the situation in Selma and on March 7 sent a letter to King and the SCLC expressing their concerns. They started the letter saying that they had been in Selma for some time prior to the SCLC. "After numerous meetings with key SCLC staff ... it was agreed that there would be organizational autonomy.... We believe that this relationship has not existed, because of a lack of effort, and a serious unwillingness on the part of key SCLC staff ... to deal honestly with SNCC." The letter was sent directly to King "because we understand that you are central to the final solution of these problems." The letter said that the SNCC wanted to reconcile with SCLC and "was willing to accept some degree of responsibility." The letter said that there was some disagreement over the protest march on March 7. "No serious consideration was ever given to the fact that the Alabama SNCC staff basically disagreed with the march.... We strongly believe that the objectives of the march do not justify the danger and the resources involved." The letter asked for a meeting "to discuss the issues raised in the letter." It was signed by John Lewis, chairman of the SNCC, and Silas Norman, Jr., project director in Alabama.[15]

The letter is evidence not only of the tense relationship between the SNCC and the SCLC but also of the growing division within the civil rights movement. The rise and death of Malcolm X demonstrates that African Americans in the 1960s were looking for something to change the status quo. The people were growing impatient and wanted change. Indeed, King's methods had done a great deal to make a difference in the movement. While it seemed clear that those methods and the efforts of many others had a lasting effect on the movement and brought about the Civil Rights Act of 1964, the philosophy of nonviolent protest was being questioned. After all, both Kennedy and King believed that it would take more than legislation to confront the racial tension in the nation. With that in mind it is fair to say that people wanted a type of protest that had an immediate effect on the movement. King and the SNCC both believed in the strategy of nonviolent protest, so the division in their ranks was especially troubling to King who was trying to keep it all together. After all, he inspired them to organize, and now they were confronting him on his own strategy. The events that followed the letter would only add to the tense relationship.

On early Sunday afternoon, on March 7, the group, led by the SNCC's John Lewis and the SCLC's Hosea Williams, left from Brown Chapel in a double-file column to Edmund Pettus Bridge. They were told by State Police Major John Cloud, who was surrounded by white-helmeted state troopers, "This is an unlawful assembly. Your march is not conducive to the public safety. You are ordered to disperse and go back to your church or to your homes." Behind the troopers were men on horseback. Knowing that the situation looked dire and that people would get hurt, Williams asked, "May we have a word with the major?" "There is no word to be had," Cloud responded. Williams and Lewis tried to get the attention of the troopers again, but it was in vain. "You have two minutes to turn around and go back to your church," Cloud said. The group did not move. Cloud's response to them was, "Troopers, advance."[16] To the side of the confrontation were newspeople.

Roy Reed of the *New York Times* reported that the state troopers "tore through a column of Negro demonstrators with tear gas, nightsticks and whips here today to enforce Gov. George C. Wallace's order against a protest march from Selma to Montgomery." He wrote, "The troopers rushed forward, their blue uniforms and white helmets blurring into a flying wedge as they moved. The wedge moved with such force that it seems almost to pass over the waiting column instead of through it." From the South side of the highway, spectators cheered as the troopers moved through the crowd, taking down the protesters, blazing a path over the bridge with tear gas, violence and brutality. Some of the troopers were on horseback, hitting and slashing at the protesters.[17] After the carnage, the protesters retreated back to the church turned into a hospital. Roy Reed wrote, "Negroes lay on the floors and chairs, many weeping and moaning.... Doctors and nurses threaded feverishly through the crowd administering first aid and daubing a solution of water and baking soda on the eyes of those who had been in the worst of the gas."[18]

That night, ABC news interrupted a broadcast of *Judgement at Nuremberg* to broadcast a report that showed the violence on Edmund Pettus Bridge.[19] King made a statement immediately following the attack on the protesters saying that he planned to begin another march on Tuesday. In his statement, he said that he was "calling on religious leaders from all over the nation to join us on Tuesday in our peaceful, non-violent march for freedom." King went on to say,

> I am shocked at the terrible reign of terror that took place in Alabama today. Negro citizens engaged in a peaceful and orderly march to protest racial injustice were beaten, brutalized and harassed by state troopers, and Alabama revealed its law enforcement agents have no respect for the democracy nor the rights of its Negro citizens.

King responded to the fact that he was not at the march and had trusted Williams to represent him in his stead. "I must confess that I had no idea that the kind of brutality and tragic expression of man's inhumanity to man as existed today would take place." King had said that he planned to lead the next march with Ralph Abernathy, "in an attempt to arouse a deeper concern of this nation over the ills that are perpetrated against Negro citizens of Alabama."[20]

The Selma campaign was an example where King had started to use his new world-renowned influence to foster change in the United States. The Nobel Peace Prize as well as his success in 1963 were poignant reminders for the nation, indeed the world, that this man was the leader of the movement. While there was some tension in the movement, King had the ability and political prowess to bring in other leaders from across the nation to support the movement. The effort to gain so much support in such a short amount of time is representative of his impact on the period not only in the United States but in the world at large.

On another level Selma represents the pinnacle of the movement, demonstrating to the world the violence so pervasive in the segregationist south. The tactics of Jim Clark and the members of the state police, with the direction and implied leadership of George Wallace, are the desperate efforts of a white society on the brink of a major shift in the culture of the South. To be sure, the southern culture of the 1950s and 1960s was not much different from that of the 1850s and 1860s. Then the southern elite prior to the Civil War were trying to hold back the forward movement of the northern intellectuals and newly formed Republican Party.

King was making headway to change the status quo in the Deep South. He had supporters not only in the government but in leadership throughout the nation and the world. The South was running out of allies, and King knew it. The main issue that King had in continuing the march on Tuesday was that Federal Judge Frank Johnson refused to grant an injunction against state interference by the troopers without a hearing, which was scheduled for Thursday. The judge wanted the march called off until the hearing. Members of the SCLC and the SNCC debated whether to take Judge Johnson's offer to have a hearing on the trooper's right to interfere with the march. The leadership met to decide what the group would do about the march on Tuesday. James Forman writes later, "It was clear that the consensus was to accept Judge Johnson's offer; Hosea Williams was the only SCLC leader pushing for the march. [James] Farmer stated that, while he had come down to march and emotionally understood the position of Hosea, rationally he had to agree with waiting until Thursday." Eventually King "decided to accept the judge's condition. The march would be postponed."[21]

The Johnson administration had sent John Doar, a representative from the Justice Department, as well as members of the Community Relations Services (CRS) to Selma. They wanted to avoid another "Bloody Sunday," which was what many were calling the confrontation at Edmund Pettus Bridge. Johnson did not want to hastily send troops into the South. He believed that action could "destroy whatever possibilities existed for the passage of voting rights legislation" and also that "such action would play into the hands of those looking for a states' rights martyr in Governor Wallace."[22] John Doar was on the ground in Selma and believed that the SCLC and SNCC had made a decision to postpone the Tuesday march.

The night before the proposed march, people came to Selma at the behest of King, filed into the church, and prepared themselves to listen to King's words. It was almost midnight when he finally spoke. Much to the surprise of Forman, King stood up in Brown Chapel that Monday night and told the crowd that the march would take place early the next morning. After the rally the SNCC, SCLC and members of the Justice Department met at the home of Dr. Sullivan Jackson to reconsider the march. Doar was present at this meeting. In the early morning hours, sitting across a kitchen table, the two men talked about the potential march. In addition to Doar, LBJ summoned CRS director LeRoy Collins to Selma in an effort to intervene and avoid another bloody standoff. Doar had assured King that Judge Johnson would let them march to Montgomery if they called off the Tuesday march. King was at a crossroads and not sure what to do. He had the pressure of SNCC and SCLC leadership to contend with in addition to all the people who responded to his plea for help in Selma. To make matters even more difficult, it seemed that Judge Johnson would ban the march regardless of what King decided.[23]

Attorney General Nicholas Katzenbach called King that night to talk with him personally. Katzenbach reportedly kept repeating, "Dr. King, you promised you would not," referring to the earlier decision, before the rally, to not march on Tuesday. King responded, "But Mr. Attorney General, you have not been a black man in America for three hundred years." When they got off the phone, it was believed that the march was going to take place.[24] Katzenbach recalled later, "King's march at Selma and all that great public pressure on this and focus on it really required a legislative solution."[25] To be sure, King wanted to do what was right for the movement. In addition to all this pressure, there were reports that there would be an attempt on his life.

After King had gotten some sleep, Doar and Collins had found him in his pajamas to plead with him to postpone the march. King told them that his "conscience commanded that he go forward" and that SNCC members would most likely go through with it despite what he had to say. Since King was so determined to go forward with the march, Collins and Doar had come up with an alternative. They recommended that the march go forward, over the bridge and then turn around in the face of the troopers and walk back to Selma. "I don't believe you can get those people not to charge into us even if we do stop." Collins wanted to try and work out this deal. "I cannot agree to do anything because I don't know what I can get my people to do, but if you will get Sheriff Clark and [public safety director Colonel Al] Lingo to agree to something like that, I will try." Collins took that assurance and went to find Clark and Lingo to make the deal.[26]

Collins was able to get the troopers to agree to the conditions and raced back over the bridge to find King as he gathered the people to make the march over the bridge again. Surrounded by dignitaries and the "people of goodwill" that he had asked to come to Selma, King was taken aside by Collins and told that the troopers and Clark's men would not charge the crowd. Collins was given a hand-drawn map from Clark and asked that King follow that path back into Selma. There were many forces at work in this movement and King said that he would try to accommodate Collins and President Johnson. "I'll do my best to turn them back. I won't promise you, but I'll do my best."[27] What happened as a result of this agreement contributed to a further schism between the SCLC and SNCC.

King was at the head of the column with politicians and other dignitaries. As the group approached the barricade of troopers and Clark's men, U.S. Marshal H. Stanley Fountain read Judge Johnson's order to King, banning any march to Montgomery from Selma. King said nothing and continued toward the troopers once Fountain moved out of the way. John Doar was on the phone with the attorney general. Within fifty yards of the blockade, King stopped. He asked the column to kneel and pray. Ralph Abernathy and others led the group in prayer while King remained on his knee. After singing "We Shall Overcome," King and the people behind him turned around and led the column back over the bridge. As the column turned around, in what seemed like an unplanned move, the troopers moved to the side to make way for the march. They were reportedly told to move out of the way by Governor Wallace after the column decided to turn around.[28]

In what would be called "Turnaround Tuesday," Martin Luther King was under a great deal of scrutiny. The media asked if he did not want to defy the court order, while civil rights groups questioned his leadership. James Forman of the SNCC reportedly said of King's decision that it was "a classic example of trickery against the people." The movement in Selma, which had the support of many other people besides the SCLC and the SNCC after King's call to "people of goodwill" seemed to be in question. "We knew we would not get to Montgomery," King told the media. "We knew we would not get past troopers ... we agreed that we would not break the lines."[29] In what had seemed to be such a promising turn of events prior to the march with the outpouring of support from people across the nation, King was now trying to bring it all back together and keep the movement alive.

After the march on Tuesday, President Lyndon Johnson released a statement about the violence from Bloody Sunday. He said that since that event "the administration has been in close touch with the situation and has made every effort to prevent a repetition." He emphasized, "I am certain Americans everywhere join in deploring the brutality with which a number of Negro citizens of Alabama were treated when they sought to dramatize their deep and sincere interest in attaining the precious right to vote." In another public comment regarding voting rights legislation, Johnson said,

> The best legal talent in the Federal Government is engaged in preparing legislation which will secure that right for every American. I expect to complete work on my recommendations by this weekend and shall dispatch a special message to Congress as soon as the drafting of the legislation is finished.

To support the movement in Selma, LBJ said, "Federal officials have been sent to Selma and are supplying up-to-the-minute reports on developments there." In addition to telling the public that the administration was working on legislation, he also made a comment on the hearings to allow the march from Selma to Montgomery.

> The Federal District Court in Alabama has before it a request to enjoin State officials from interfering with the right of Alabama citizens to walk from Selma to Montgomery in order to focus attention on their efforts to secure the right to register and vote. I have directed the Justice Department to enter the case as a "friend of the court" so that it can present its recommendations and otherwise assist the court in every manner in resolving the legal issues involved in the case.

In this statement it was clear that Johnson wanted to make a difference in the movement. He was following Kennedy's lead in using the courts to determine the legality of the protest. In addition, he was working on the legislation to bring this matter to a close in the same way that Kennedy did in the wake of Birmingham. In a final plea Johnson said, "We will continue our efforts to work with the individuals involved to relieve tensions and to make it possible for every citizen to vote." Further he asked for help from anyone "in positions of leadership and capable of influencing the conduct of others to approach this tense situation with calmness, reasonableness, and respect for law and order."[30] Unfortunately, that night, more blood was shed in Selma over voting rights.

Tuesday night three men who came to Selma to support the movement were beaten. Among the men attacked, the Rev. James J. Reeb of Boston suffered serious injuries to the head. The authorities waited several hours before they transported him to the hospital. He died on Thursday.[31] King released a statement to the press, saying, "This murder, like so many others, is the direct consensus of the height of terror in some parts of our nation. This unprovoked attack on the streets of an Alabama city cannot be considered an isolated incident in a smooth sea of tolerance and understanding." Once again, he pointed to the climate of the nation and how that had made the violence and oppression possible in the South. He emphasized his message that "it is a result of a malignant sickness in our society that comes from tolerance of organized hatred and violence." He said that Reeb was "murdered by a morally inclement climate—a climate filled with torrents of hatred and jostling winds of violence."[32]

The climate that King was referring to in his statement was the same climate that he believed had killed John F. Kennedy and Malcolm X. It was the very same climate that would kill him and only two months later Robert Kennedy. "He was murdered by an atmosphere of inhumanity in Alabama that tolerated the vicious murder of Jimmy Lee Jackson ... and the brutal beatings of Sunday in Selma." King went even further to specifically point to the law enforcement officials who went after the marchers. "Had policemen not brutally beaten unarmed, non-violent persons desiring the right to vote on Sunday, it is doubtful whether this act of murder by other Alabamans would have taken place on Tuesday." He concluded, saying, "This is additional proof that segregation knows no color line in attempts to control the movement and mind of white persons as well as Negroes."[33]

This was a message that King had been bringing to the forefront of his rhetoric since his speech about JFK in Germany. To be sure, it was rooted in the notion that the climate in the nation needed to change before there could be any true movement for civil rights. While legislation was a step in the right direction, the true goal of the civil rights movement was to address a climate that plagued American society and contributed to violent acts throughout history. The climate that had contributed to the death of Jimmy Lee Jackson and James Reeb also contributed to the deaths and continued violence in the South in the ten years since King led the boycott at Montgomery. King's statement laid the blame for this atmosphere not only at the feet the southern leadership or the politicians in Washington but also on the people who lived in the communities that sat idly by and allowed this climate to continue in their communities. The movement in Selma was an example for the world to see not only what racism and segregation could do, but also what intolerance, capitulation and silence could do in instances where there were moral issues that had the potential to change if people got involved. This was where his message took the movement, and it was also where, in the wake of this event, it would continue to move people as the civil rights movement changed.

III

"What happened in Selma was an American tragedy."

Speaking from the Rose Garden on the afternoon on Sunday, March 13, President Johnson had a news conference to address the death of Reeb in Selma saying that the event had "brought a very deep and painful challenge to the unending search for American freedom." He said that the challenge was still not over and that "every resource of this Government will be directed to insuring justice for all men of all races, in Alabama and everywhere in this land." Johnson declared that since Bloody Sunday the U.S. government had "acted effectively to protect the constitutional rights of the citizens of Selma, and to prevent further violence and lawlessness in this country wherever it occurred." In the strongest support for the voting rights movement, Johnson declared that he intended to move forward with legislation:

> The events of last Sunday cannot and will not be repeated, but the demonstrations in Selma have a much larger meaning, They are a protest against a deep and very unjust flaw in American democracy itself. Ninety-five years ago our Constitution was amended to require that no American be denied the right to vote because of race or color. Almost a century later, many Americans are kept from voting simply because they are Negroes. Therefore, this Monday I will send to the Congress a request for legislation to carry out the amendment of the Constitution.

Johnson looked to enact legislation that would make a difference in voting irregularities in the South. "Wherever there is discrimination, this law will strike down all restrictions used to deny the people the right to vote. It will establish a simple, uniform standard which cannot be used, however ingenuous the effort, to flaunt our Constitution." He even went as far as to say, "If State officials refuse to cooperate, then citizens will be registered by Federal officials."[34]

Johnson was clearly looking for a way to address this issue. It was clear that Martin Luther King, the SCLC and SNCC had done a great deal to bring this oppression to light. Johnson said, "What happened in Selma was an American tragedy. The blows that were received, the blood that was shed, the life of the good man that was lost, must strengthen the determination of each of us to bring full and equal and exact justice to all of our people." Johnson's solidarity with the movement is yet another example where he had every intention to support them. It was, however, on his own timetable. He said to the press, "Over the past few weeks, I have determined that we would have a voting rights law this year on about November 15th, and so informed certain Members of the Congress and certain Governors of the States." He went further to say that this issue was originally a part of the Civil Rights Act of 1964.

> As you know, President Kennedy in the Kennedy-Johnson administration in 1963, in the civil rights measure that I counseled on and worked on and approved, submitted to the Congress a voting rights section that provided, however, for voting only in Federal elections. That section was deleted in the legislation that finally

came to me and, as a result of that deletion, I have felt that we should again approach that subject, but to extend it from Federal elections to both State and local elections.³⁵

To be sure, this was a welcome turn of events for King and the others who had spent so much time in Selma, Alabama, in 1965 and Mississippi the previous summer in 1964.

In response to the events in Selma as well as Johnson's press conference, the *New York Times* wrote in an editorial on March 14, saying, "The past week in Alabama has been a time of dangerous competition between the forces of racism and reason, of violence and law, of the defeated past and the struggling future." The editorial contended that Johnson's intention to do something about the situation "has improved the prospect for a peaceful and prompt triumph of reason on this crucial battleground." It characterized Wallace and Clark as symbols of a "reactionary racist cause that is already defeated and dying. In its final stage it has nothing to fall back upon except the desperate tactic of brutal force." On the other side of the struggle they said that King "symbolizes the cause of the Southern Negro who, at the beginning of the second century of emancipation, is struggling to achieve his rights by legal, peaceful means." The *Times* editorial is significant in seeing just how polarizing the struggle was in the South. It does, however, declare that the nation as whole was not as conflicted. "By law and by moral commitment, the overwhelming majority of Americans have taken their stand in this contest."³⁶

The *Times* pointed to Martin Luther King and others who advocated nonviolence as an important facet to this struggle in the nation. "The United States has been extremely fortunate that the struggle for Negro rights has remained up to now under the mature responsible leadership which always seeks peaceful solution by legal and political means." The editorial concluded, "If that leadership is to be vindicated, then those means must be seen to be working." The movement was experiencing a radical shift in 1965. The death of Malcolm X coupled with the emergence of the Black Panther organization and later the Black Power movement challenged the nonviolent tactic as too slow. The *Times* was concerned that the "young Negro hotheads thirsting for a dramatic showdown for its own sake will be encouraged, and the white demagogues and their police henchmen will be emboldened to new acts of violence and repression." The *Times* had faith in Johnson, saying, "Law and political leadership will master this crisis—effectively and quickly."³⁷ The *New York Times* editorial board would not have to wait too much longer for Johnson to make a move on this issue.

The nation had indeed embraced the actions by King. The injustice of the situation had inspired people to speak out. Francis B. Sayre, who was dean of the National Cathedral, said, "By defying the federal court's injunction against marching, Martin Luther King bore witness to a higher law than any man's." Sayre, however, believed that King's decision to turn around, which was criticized by the SNCC and others in the movement, was just as important. "But yet, when he met the wall of police, King turned back, and in this he acknowledged the precious importance of law to human society." Sayre was speaking from the National Cathedral in Washington, D.C. "Thus we saw enacted in the tense drama of this week the position of every Christian whose first allegiance is to the higher law of God, but who nevertheless must ever strive to embed true justice in the laws and customs of life."[38]

In the case of Selma, King brilliantly used not only his words, which continued to define the goals and direction of the movement, but also his actions. Sayre's comments highlighted something that many of King's contemporaries had not been able to acknowledge. While King wanted to march and believed that he was right, he understood the political atmosphere better than most African Americans who were his contemporaries. The goal of the movement, as it was in Birmingham and other places, was to get the support of not only the White House, but the people in the nation. King clearly demonstrated that while the march was morally just and needed to happen in the wake of Bloody Sunday, he respected the need for law and order in society. As result of that action, he strengthened not only his own position but the entire movement.

IV

"And we shall overcome."

Martin Luther King was under a great deal of scrutiny after his decision to turn around the column on Tuesday, March 9. He had told Judge Johnson in a hearing that he had no intention to lead the protesters in that Tuesday march from Selma to Montgomery. King pointed to the agreements that he had with federal officials as the main reason why he did not complete the march. King's testimony did not help his situation with the other rights leaders. Some said that they felt "betrayed" by his decision to work with federal officials. King made it clear that he was conflicted over what to do, given that Judge Johnson had issued a temporary injunction over any protest marches. King characterized it as an "unjust order" and went on to say, "I was very upset. I felt like it was condemning the robbed man for being robbed. I was disturbed."[39]

King felt a great deal of responsibility not only to the people he had been working with but also the people who came to his aid at his request. "Thousands of people who came to Selma to march were deeply aroused by the brutality of Sunday. I felt if I had not done it [led the march], pent up emotions could have developed into an uncontrollable situation." He went on to call Clark's behavior on Bloody Sunday "harsh, vitriolic, brutal behavior ... brutal language and physical brutalization and intimidation" of the African Americans in Selma. King contended that he led the march as far he did "to give them an outlet. Maybe there will be some blood let in the state of Alabama before we get through, but it will be our blood and not the blood of our white brothers." King was asked directly by Judge Johnson if it was correct to say that "when you started across the bridge, you knew at that time that you did not intend to march to Montgomery," referring to the agreement that King brokered with Collins. King responded, "Yes it is. There was a tacit agreement at the bridge that we would go no further." There was some discussion that the troopers' movement to withdraw was meant to embarrass King given that they were also aware of the agreement to withdraw.[40]

Six days later on Monday, March 15, King came out for the first time in public in Selma to pay tribute to the fallen Rev. James Reeb. On March 15 a march was organized from Brown Chapel to the Dallas County courthouse as a memorial service for Reeb. "Why must a good man die for doing good?" King asked the crowd, which included dignitaries and politicians. "His death may cause the white south to come to terms with its conscience." The march was agreed to by Clark's office and King stood on the steps of the courthouse, held a floral wreath and said, "We are here to reaffirm our commitment that racial segregation is evil and the nation will never rise to its maturity until we get rid of it. This witness will help transform dark yesterdays into bright tomorrows."[41] King's words went a long way to begin the healing that was needed for the movement to continue in Selma. With Judge Johnson's decision looming and the fact that many in the nation were upset over the events from the previous Sunday, Sheriff Clark and his office worked with the SCLC to have this march. To be sure, it helped that there were politicians and others present for the service. That also speaks to King's ability to bring them all together and shed light on the brutality of the movement.

March 15, 1965, proved to be a pivotal day for the movement in Selma. Not only did King publicly come out and speak, but President Lyndon Johnson addressed a joint session of Congress to lay out his plans for the Voting Rights Act. "I speak tonight for the dignity of man and the destiny of democracy," Johnson started. He used history as a way to commemorate the moment: "At times history and fate meet at a single time in a single place to shape a turning point in man's unending search for freedom. So it was at Lexington and Concord. So it was a century ago at Appomattox. So it was last week in Selma, Alabama." Using those momentous historic events as way to demonstrate the importance of the Selma movement is evidence that Johnson understood the gravity of the situation. Johnson wanted solidarity on this matter. He spoke for the movement and recognized the brutality and sacrifice thus far.

> There, long-suffering men and women peacefully protested the denial of their rights as Americans. Many were brutally assaulted. One good man, a man of God, was killed. There is no cause for pride in what has happened in Selma. There is no cause for self-satisfaction in the long denial of equal rights of millions of Americans. But there is cause for hope and for faith in our democracy in what is happening here tonight.[42]

Johnson's historic speech was similar to John F. Kennedy's speech from June 11, 1963. Johnson, like Kennedy, was speaking out and affirming the goals of the movement.

This speech laid out Johnson's intentions to intervene and secure the right to vote for all Americans, as the Fifteenth Amendment guarantees. "There is no Negro problem. There is no Southern problem. There is no Northern problem. There is only an American problem," Johnson declared. "And we are met here tonight as Americans—not as Democrats or Republicans—we are met here as Americans to solve that problem." He told the world that he intended to "send to Congress a law designed to eliminate illegal barriers to the right to vote." Like Kennedy did in 1963, Johnson stressed the morality of the issue. "There is no moral issue. It is wrong—deadly wrong—to deny any of your fellow Americans the right to vote in this country. There is no issue of States rights or national rights. There is only the struggle for human rights." Johnson, like Kennedy, wanted to be on the right side of history in this long struggle for equal rights in the nation. His speech was contributed to that legacy.

In what perhaps was the greatest example of solidarity with the movement, Johnson used the same words that had driven so many African Americans to protest for their rights. He understood that legislation could only do so much and the true struggle was to win the hearts and minds of Americans. "But even if we pass this bill, the battle will not be over. What happened in Selma is part of a far larger movement which reaches into every section and State of America." Resolute in his task, Johnson wanted to empower not only African Americans but also the rest of the nation. To be sure, Johnson was also hoping to gain solidarity within the ranks of the people in the room. "Their cause must be our cause too. Because it is not just Negroes, but really it is all of us, who must overcome the crippling legacy of bigotry and injustice. And we shall overcome."[43]

Martin Luther King was invited to attend the speech by Johnson, but he chose to stay in Selma. John Lewis was with him. "I was deeply moved," Lewis recalled in his memoirs.

> Lyndon Johnson was no politician that night. He was a man who spoke from his heart. His were the words of a statesman and more; they were the words of a poet. Dr King must have agreed. He wiped away a tear at the point where Johnson said the words "We shall overcome."[44]

Johnson wanted to have that effect on the moment. While he was preparing for the speech he told aides that he "wanted to use every ounce of moral persuasion the Presidency held. I wanted no hedging, no equivocation. And I wanted to talk from my own heart, from my own experience."[45]

V

"Our bodies are tired, our feet are somewhat sore."

Martin Luther King publicly praised Johnson's speech the next day. "President Johnson made one of the most eloquent, unequivocal and passionate pleas for human rights ever made by a President of the United States. He revealed great and amazing understanding of the depth and dimension of the problem of racial injustice." King went on to say, "His tone and delivery were disarmingly sincere. His power of persuasion has nowhere been more forcefully set forth. We are happy to know that our struggle in Selma, Alabama has brought the whole issue of the right to vote to the forefront of the conscience of the nation." Despite his praise of the bill, King also wanted to keep demonstrating until the bill became a law. "We must keep this issue alive and the urgency of it before the nation," he said.[46]

Johnson's speech was a major success and demonstrated to the nation that he supported the protests in Selma and would put the full force of the presidency behind the Voting Rights Bill. Later that week, Judge Johnson ruled in favor of the march from Selma to Montgomery. The SCLC and SNCC made arrangements to make the march with one eventful finish in Montgomery, where King planned to give a major speech. To be sure, the symbolism of King's triumphant return to Montgomery ten years after the bus boycott that started the modern-day movement was not lost on the occasion. John Lewis recalled later, "When we made it across the Alabama River into the city of Montgomery, it was almost like crossing our own Red Sea, our own River of Jordan. We made it to the steps of the state capitol on Thursday, March 25, 1965, and yet people said we would never get there."[47]

King's speech on the steps of the capital building in Montgomery paid homage to the sacrifice of everyone who contributed to the movement in Selma. It was strong rhetoric that not only marked the occasion but also brought home the ideals of the movement while the nation, indeed the world, was watching. "We have walked through desolate valleys and across trying hills. We have walked on meandering highways and rested our bodies on rocky byways.... Our bodies are tired, our feet are somewhat sore."[48] He continued to empower the people who marched with him to Montgomery, who marched with John Lewis and Josea Williams on Bloody Sunday, who sacrificed their lives for an ideal that he represented. "And in a real sense this afternoon, we can say that our feet are tired, but our souls are rested." King pointed to the notion that providence shined down on the movement.

Marking the momentous occasion of the march while at the same time pointing to the reality that they were in the same city that started the movement, King said it was "not an accident" that the march ended up in Montgomery. "Just ten years ago, in this very city, a new philosophy was born of the Negro struggle." He said,

> Montgomery was the first city in the South in which the entire Negro community united and squarely faced its age-old oppressors. Out of this struggle, more than bus desegregation was won; a new idea, more powerful than guns or clubs was born. Negroes took it and carried it across the South in epic battles that electrified the nation and the world.[49]

King's vision had indeed come full circle, and they stood in the city that began the struggle for equality. However, he could not ignore the fact that the movement needed more than one victory to shed the vestiges of the Civil War.

Recognizing that the movement was multilayered and that victories built on each other, King acknowledged the importance of the Birmingham campaign in 1963, saying that "not until the colossus of segregation was challenged in Birmingham did the conscience of America begin to bleed. White America was profoundly aroused by Birmingham because it witnessed the whole community of Negroes facing terror and brutality with majestic scorn and heroic courage."[50] King said that the Civil Rights Act was another such victory, but "without the vote it was dignity without strength." With that in mind, King pointed to the greatest weapon that had given the most encouragement and victories to African American since the civil rights struggle had started.

No tactic, speech or strategy had such an impact on the civil rights movement as nonviolent direct action. From this approach King and others had been able to force Washington to legislate on the issue of racism and discrimination. There was nothing like it in American history. While the

American Revolution of the eighteenth century had momentous protest, they were far from nonviolent. King's philosophy started a revolution that continued into the twenty-first century. From that point of strength he proclaimed that it was the defining moment of the Selma movement. "Once more the method of non-violent resistance was unsheathed from its scabbard, and once again the entire community was mobilized to confront the adversary. And again the brutality of a dying order shrieks across the land." The march was more than just a journey from Selma to Montgomery, King said. It was a moment in history where "Selma became a shining moment in the conscience of man."[51]

The march was something that transcended race and ethnicity; it served as a bridge for politicians, musicians, actors and the common person. It created a moment where people from everywhere saw themselves as one, marching for freedom and equality, for liberty that had been denied to a group of Americans that had paved the way for America's greatness from as far back as 1619 in Jamestown. "There never was a moment in American history more honorable and more inspiring than the pilgrimage of clergymen and laymen of every race and faith pouring into Selma to face danger at the side of embattled Negroes."[52] He praised the community of Selma and President Johnson for taking a stand against the voting atrocities that were taking place in the South.

King's speech continued, empowering the movement and sending a message that the struggle would continue and that they would attain equality. He proclaimed that he wanted to tell the state of Alabama, the nation and the world, "We are not about to turn around. We are on the move now."[53] Indeed, it was that progression that not only signified the occasion but also sent a clear message that he would continue until there was full equality under the law.

> Yes, we are on the move and no wave of racism can stop us. We are on the move now. The burning of our churches will not deter us. The bombing of our homes will not dissuade us. We are on the move now. The beating and killing of our clergymen and young people will not divert us. We are on the move now. The wanton release of their known murderers will not discourage us. We are on the move now. Like an idea whose time has come, not even the marching of mighty armies can halt us. We are moving to the land of freedom.

King effectively utilized the same phrase to make his point, driving home the idea that the struggle, indeed his nonviolent action, was on the move. In an effort to continue that theme he declared to the audience that they needed to continue that march they just completed on Montgomery, but in a different way.

In the same manner that King was able to eloquently express the passion and determination of the movement, he was also able to empower the crowd through rhetoric that continued to inspire generations of Americans. He used the phrase "Let us march" and attacked poverty and the vote as a way to show that people could make a difference. For example, he said, "Let us march on poverty, until no American parent has to skip a meal so that their children may eat." In the same vein he considered the vote as a way to make a difference and change the conditions of many people. "Let us march on ballot boxes until the salient misdeeds of bloodthirsty mobs will be transformed into the calculated good deeds of orderly citizens."[54] His use of that imagery brought home his message and transformed the steps of the capitol in Montgomery into an oasis of soaring rhetoric that cut to the heart of the atrocities of segregation and oppression in the South. It was finally a moment where an oppressed group could rise up and make a difference.

In the jubilation of the day, King acknowledged that there was still a long way to go before the journey for full equality was complete. With the onslaught of militant groups knocking on the door of the movement, hoping to achieve equality sooner than King's tactics could guarantee, King pled with the crowd to hold true to the philosophy that had achieved so much in the last ten years. "The battle is on our hands. And we can answer with creative non-violence," he said. "In the glow of the lamplight on my desk a few nights ago, I gazed upon a wondrous sign of our times, full of hope and promise of the future."[55]

King wanted to mark this moment not only for the Selma movement, but also for the philosophy of nonviolence. "And so as we go away this afternoon, let us go away more committed to non-violence.... If we go on with the faith that non-violence and its power can transform dark yesterdays into bright tomorrows, we will be able to change all these conditions." He finished the speech using Julia Ward Howe's "Battle Hymn of the Republic" in a stirring rendition that moved the crowd and brought home the efforts of the march from Selma to Montgomery.

The Voting Rights Bill was still before Congress and had a long road ahead before it would be signed into law later that year. Selma had rippling effects on the nation and demonstrated that nonviolence was one effective tool in combating racism and segregation. As the nation moved forward and continued to redefine the American experience, the civil rights movement continued to evolve and expose the racial tension in the nation. To be sure this was an important aspect of the new identity that was such a crucial part of American society. While this civil rights struggle continued, America was about to face another momentous, nation-changing struggle in Southeast Asia that had a similar impact on the American identity.

This moment did more than just solidify King's place in civil rights history. In many ways it was the culmination of events that started ten years before. It was also a moment that brought a great deal of credibility to the tactic of nonviolent protest. King's influence was at its height. His message from that point on focused on poverty and Vietnam, two important issues. But no issue is more sacred to the success of the republic than the right to vote. This was a victory for generations of African Americans. To be sure, this march in 1965 contributed to Barack Obama's march to the White House in November 2008.

10

"The Crises of the Moment"

I

"Heading toward a disastrous U.S. defeat."

While the issues in Selma were captivating the nation, Johnson and his advisers were trying to deal with an increase in activity in Vietnam. After an attack on Americans at the Pleiku air base early in February 1965, Johnson and his cabinet decided to step up efforts to "pacify" North Vietnam's aggressive actions against the South. The Vietnam War was just as impactful to the United States as civil rights. In a special intelligence report, McGeorge Bundy wrote that the administration planned to lay out for the American people a new program to stop the forward movement of the Vietcong, saying that he wanted to make it "clear that the US means to go beyond specific reprisals for individual major Viet Cong actions and to continue air attacks until the threat to South Vietnam has been reduced to levels which the US regards as tolerable." He went further in his estimate, saying, "We consider in this estimate present Communist attitudes and Communist reactions, particularly Soviet reactions, in the period before and during continuing air attacks, and during any period when these attacks are suspended."[1]

The decision to escalate the war in Vietnam had not been taken lightly by Johnson and his advisers. In a memo to Johnson, Bundy went further, saying, "Rightly or wrongly, those of us who favor continuing military action against the North do see it as a major watershed decision." He said that this action to increase U.S. involvement was not like the retaliatory response in August, after the Gulf of Tonkin incident.

> And it is not the same as a policy of episodic retaliation for particular attacks against large numbers of Americans. It is very different indeed, and the difference is just what we are counting on as the one possible means of turning around a desperate situation which has been heading toward a disastrous U.S. defeat.

Bundy understood that this was a pivotal, no-turning-back moment in this conflict. Complicating the issues, however, was Johnson's reluctance to make this new change in policy known publicly. Bundy wrote that another issue to the situation "is that you do not want to give a loud public signal of a major change in policy right now. This is a position which makes a lot of sense on a lot of grounds." Bundy summed up at the end of the memo, "What I think we need is internal clarity about the importance and scope of the decisions you are taking, and as much public calm and coolness as possible."[2] Of course in the wake of Vietnam, this policy had been disastrous not only for the Johnson administration but for the future presidencies that followed.

In his personal notes from a meeting with Johnson, Bundy recorded his response to the potential strikes that they were planning. "We have done it in less spectacular ways. Killing 16,000, in less spectacular ways. But bombers—I'm just hoping out of hope they'll draw people in Saigon together," Johnson is reported to have said. "But bombers won't bring 'em to their knees—unless we do something we wouldn't do. We'll be called warmongers—elsewhere & here in the U.S. that'll be more pronounced—peacemakers'll be after us."[3] His comments point to the notion that there had to be something more than dropping bombs on North Vietnam. Indeed, he was thinking, if not already planning out, troops on the ground. He knew that the war would not begin and end with only air strikes.

By March 6, 1965, Bundy saw the action in Vietnam as successful to the point where he even said to Johnson in a memo that "it will be your personal achievement. You alone—against your noisiest advisers—made the basic decision to present these actions within the framework of a continuing policy and a continuing purpose, and not as major new departures." However, the memo was also clear that there needed to be an escalation in order to completely "pacify" the communists. Bundy contended, "The air actions have lifted morale, but it is not clear how much, and there is no evidence yet that the new government has the necessary will, skill and human resources which a turn-around will require." Further, he acknowledged, "Our own basic framework for the support of the pacification program leaves a great deal to be desired." He felt, with regard to diplomacy, that "we can always get to the conference table when we need to, and that there is no great hurry about it right now."[4] The real question was whether or not the United States should escalate their role in the region and what that entailed.

In his memorandum to Johnson, Bundy intimated and even pointed to the need for ground forces. He contemplated in one part "whether it would be useful right now to get a substantial allied ground force in place in the central and northern part of Vietnam." He went on, saying that Maxwell Taylor was "doubtful about this, but in the heat of discussion last night Rusk, McNamara and I all thought it worth serious further exploration." Further he said that such contingency thinking "should be done—but very, very privately." In Fact, Bundy said to Johnson, "Our current plan is that there should be no paper work on this subject at all, but simply some intensive discussion limited completely to the three of us and one subordinate each. There will be no papers, and this mission will not exist anywhere except in this memorandum."[5] This memo was the start of a new policy in Vietnam. In the midst of the turmoil in Selma, Alabama, Lyndon Johnson embarked on his contribution to the Vietnam War, and it would have rippling effects for his and subsequent administrations. On March 8, 1965, at approximately 8:00pm (Eastern Standard Time) two marine battalions landed at Danang.

II

"Tomorrow's will be harder still."

Robert F. Kennedy had spent the beginning of 1965 getting used to his new role in the Senate. In early March, Kennedy started to champion different issues. He wanted to see better education for Puerto Ricans in New York, saying on one occasion, "We have to see that the next generation of Puerto Ricans in New York City is not a lost generation."[6] He got involved in local issues such as the New Haven railroad from New York to Connecticut and scenic areas along the Hudson—both measures he worked on with Senator Javits in the Senate.[7] In addition to that, Kennedy was involved in controversy over whether he had planted a story in *Life* magazine about Jimmy Hoffa while he was attorney general. No stranger to controversy, Kennedy defended himself, saying, "There was an implication across the nation that I had acted improperly and I resent it."[8]

During his time in the Senate, Kennedy continued to evolve on issues of race, and he saw the blatant injustice in the nation from a new perspective. He was no longer the young, impetuous campaign manager from 1960. This man considered how the race issue had plagued the nation, but he looked further and deeper than the South. Speaking in Chicago to the National Council of Christians and Jews, Kennedy said, "The unfinished business at hand is the most difficult and dangerous that we have ever faced. Today's problems of intolerance are harder than yesterday's; tomorrow's will be harder still."[9] Kennedy continued, talking about the harsh reality of being African American in the nation.

Kennedy's time as attorney general had awakened his moral spirit, and he saw the plight of the disadvantaged more clearly than ever. He told the group that their children, being Jewish and Catholic, could play together and they would not know the difference between them. "But if a Negro walks down a quiet suburban street, or Negro children attend a school, all know it immediately. Simply by being more visible, the Negro is more vulnerable to prejudice." Kennedy acknowledged the importance of Selma, saying, "The brutalities of Selma, and its denial of elementary rights of citizenship, were condemned throughout the North; and thousands of Northerners went there to march to Montgomery."[10] The racial divide in the nation was larger than Selma, as Kennedy saw it. He expected more from the people and hoped to shed some light on other racial divides that were not relegated to the South.

The issues in American urban centers were at the heart of a struggle that plagued American society according to Kennedy. "The many brutalities of the north receive no such attention," he said, referring again to Selma. "I have been in tenements in Harlem in the past several weeks where the smell of rats was so strong that it was difficult to stay there for five minutes, and where children slept with lights turned on their feet to discourage attacks." He acknowledged that the lives of people who live in these conditions were "tragically insecure." Kennedy saw that the nation needed to do more than pass legislation. "It is not enough, in these circumstances, to preach for fair employment, or even pass a fair employment law." Kennedy's awakening was something that drove him in those years after he was elected to the Senate. Visiting the impoverished places of New York brought him to a point where he recognized that it was time to go further and draw some attention to those issues. Dr. King was exposing the racism and oppression of the South while Robert Kennedy looked to shed light on the oppressive societal issues in northern cities that were just as destructive to American society as the segregationist policies in the South.

Kennedy started to see the plight of the African Americans in the nation as it existed in the urban centers of America. He considered education a vital way to bring about equality. "If we wish to achieve peaceful desegregation of the schools—if we wish to improve the quality of education afforded Negro children—we must improve the quality of education throughout our schools, and assure every qualified child the chance of higher education." Kennedy wanted to go further than legislation, than goodwill. He said, "We must now act to bring about changes in the conditions which breed intolerance and discrimination." Bobby wanted to find an alternative to the issues that many African Americans faced.

When John Kennedy came to office in 1961, the New Frontier looked to help people who needed a voice, and Robert Kennedy reinvigorated that effort as he started his time in the Senate. "If we are to meet our responsibilities—to them, to ourselves, to all our children—we must address ourselves to the difficult and dangerous problems of the urban North," he said. To be sure, Kennedy believed that it was the responsibility of the government to not only craft the proper legislation but also to foster a better environment to help those ideals grow. He believed that the country could find solutions to these problems and stressed that they needed to go further; however it was "not enough to teach brotherhood in schools; we must assure that they educate each child to the limit of his capacity." He concluded, "These are not easy things to do. But the fulfillment of American ideals has never been easy, if only because they are so high."[11]

Kennedy's rhetoric was something that people could use as a measurement of where society needed to go in order to achieve greatness. His ideals and tone echoed the New Frontier of the early 1960s, something that he helped craft and certainly wanted to see withstand the tests of time. Robert Kennedy was reshaping American society, and with his vision came a new identity that would thrive into the next generation. He understood the stakes and was committed to bringing the same ideals that embodied the civil rights movement in the South to the urban centers in the North.

III

"This would be a deep and terrible decision."

In addition to sending troops into Vietnam, Johnson had continued his bombing of North Vietnam in the wake of the attack at Pleiku on February 7, 1965. Kennedy struggled with the Vietnam issue in those early days in the Senate. He did not want to speak out against Johnson. He saw Vietnam as an extension of his brother's policies in the region. Johnson had requested more money for the war, and Kennedy had an opportunity to make his views on the war public. On May 6, 1965, he stood on the Senate floor and gave a speech regarding this new development in the war.

Kennedy's speech on the Vietnam War was in support of Johnson's bill to gain more money. He did not, however, see it as a blank check. As in the past, Kennedy saw this bill as an extension of his brother's philosophy on how to fight the Cold War. He said that there were three possible scenarios in Vietnam: withdrawal, enlargement or negotiation. He contended that withdrawal would "involve a repudiation of commitments undertaken and confirmed by three administrations. It would imply the acquiescence in communist domination of South Asia—a domination unacceptable to the peoples of the area struggling to control and master their own destiny."[12] He even went as far as to characterize such action as an "explicit gross betrayal" of the Vietnamese who opposed the growth of communism in the region. It was a public statement as much about his brother as it was about Johnson.

While Kennedy was supporting the bill, he was not advocating for enlarging the war. He said, "Let us not deceive ourselves; this would be a deep and terrible decision." In the first hint that he was breaking with Johnson's plan, he said, "We cannot hope to win a victory over Hanoi by such remote and antiseptic means as sending bombers off aircraft carriers." In almost prophetic words, Kennedy saw the struggles that would tangle American forces in Vietnam as the decade progressed.

> The course of enlarging the war would mean the commitment to Vietnam of hundreds of thousands of American troops. It would tie our forces down in a terrain more difficult than Korea with lines of communication and supply far longer and more vulnerable.

He stressed that the relationship between the Chinese and the Soviet Union would be affected. He even went as far as to argue that enlarging the war would "lead to heavy pressures on our own government by thoughtless people for the use of nuclear weapons, and it might easily lead to nuclear warfare and the third world war."[13] To be sure, Kennedy saw this moment in U.S. foreign policy as dire and as one that should be approached with caution.

Robert Kennedy's experience in 1962 with the Cuban missile crisis as well as other foreign policy issues while his brother was in office shaped his vision for possible outcomes in the Vietnam conflict. He said that withdrawal and enlargement of the war "are contrary to the interests of the United States and to humanity's hope for peace." He saw a policy of "honorable negotiation" as the third and best alternative. He also believed that by supporting this bill he was promoting that course of action. Negotiation was at the core of JFK's response to Khrushchev and the growing threat of nuclear war while he was in office. Robert Kennedy hoped to pose a similar option to the people and the Congress.

Kennedy wanted to "create an atmosphere for negotiation" by demonstrating to Hanoi that the United States was prepared to meet its commitments with military action. "But I believe that our efforts for peace should continue with the same intensity as our efforts in the military field." He went further with this notion, saying that the United States had "erred for some time in regarding Vietnam as purely a military problem when in its essential aspects it is also a political and diplomatic problem."[14] He wished that the request for more money had also included "programs to better the lives of the people in South Vietnam." Success, he believed, was only possible if the United States not only protected the people from aggression but also gave them hope for a better life.

While he supported the measure for Vietnam, Kennedy broke with the Johnson administration and condemned the administration's actions in the Dominican Republic, characterizing the action as "tragic events." For many years the policy of the United States was to confront communist aggression wherever they saw it. This "containment policy" was something that harked back to the Truman administration. Robert Kennedy, however, was showing signs that his vision was evolving. The previous statement to focus on negotiations in the war in Vietnam was consistent with JFK's visions for détente.

With regard to the actions of the U.S. military in the Dominican Republic, Kennedy said that the nation should not act unilaterally "without regard to our friends and allies in the Organization of American States." He emphasized, "We are all involved in the struggle for free government in the hemisphere together." In stark contrast to Johnson's actions in Latin America as well as a tacit reproach for any further enlargement of the war in Vietnam, Kennedy made it clear that unilateral action was not only ill advised but contrary to our ideals as a nation.

> Moreover, since we believe in rule of law, we must always take care to respect the sovereignty of other nations; to proceed on the basis of our obligations to each other; and to make sure that every action reinforces the structure of law in our hemisphere. Of course unilateral action is easier than collective action; but we are much stronger when we act in concert with the rest of the hemisphere than when we act alone; and consultation is the price we must pay for the extra strength our alliances give us.[15]

Kennedy's comment spoke to the unilateral actions of U.S. foreign policy. He did not agree with that policy. Kennedy's vision not only played a role in the Dominican Republic, but it also was clearly linked to the war in Vietnam. "My only concern," Kennedy said in the speech, "is that we emerge from these crises in an honorable position to continue our leadership in the world at large."[16] The next day in the *New York Times*, the headline read, "Kennedy Critical of Johnson Move."

Kennedy told the *Times* that his brother had the support of the OAS when he opposed the Soviet Union in Cuba in 1962. "I think there should have been consultation prior to any action we would take in the Dominican situation," Kennedy said. Perhaps upon further review of his stand on the Vietnam War and other military action by the United States, he recognized that the decision to send troops may have set a dangerous precedent. "I don't think we addressed ourselves to the implications of what we did in the Dominican Republic." Kennedy saw this action as undermining friendly governments in Latin America. He even went as far as to say that this action was evidence for enemies of the United States "of our misuse of power."[17]

To be sure Kennedy's remarks struck a chord with some in the foreign policy establishment. The speech demonstrated that he was able to articulate his own position on foreign policy matters and make headlines in the process. Moreover, he was also willing to break with Johnson if he believed that he was wrong in his approach in any policy, especially foreign affairs. While this speech was the first time he broke with Johnson publicly, it was not enough to clearly state that RFK did not support LBJ. However, it was representative of the first movement to that position. As the year continued, Bobby built on his own ideals while trying to address the issues that confronted America in the sixties.

IV

"That we must stand, not for the status quo, but for progress."

Robert Kennedy believed that the youth in the nation had the potential to foster the change that the New Frontier had promised the nation in the 1960 election. He saw in the youth a "revolutionary spirit" that had captured the nation, indeed the world. In a commencement address at Queens College on June 15, 1965, Kennedy stressed to the graduating students their role in the ever-changing world. He stressed the movements that were taking place in third-world countries. America, he believed was the example they needed to strive for a better life. "A revolution is now in progress," Kennedy told his audience. "It is a revolution for self-sufficiency, in societies which have been forced to rely on more fortunate nations ... in societies where 40 percent of all children die before reaching the age of five."[18]

Kennedy saw the divergence in the societies. He was in the final stages of finding his voice that shaped his rhetoric. He also articulated for the graduates the stark differences in American society and these other nations and how that pitted them against each other, creating a dynamic that would play a role in the twenty-first century.

> This revolution is directed against us—against the one third of the world that diets while the others starve; against a nation that buys eight million new cars a year while most of the world goes without shoes; against developed nations which spend over one hundred billion dollars on armaments while the poor countries cannot obtain the ten to fifteen billion dollars of investment capital they need just to keep pace with their expanding populations.[19]

Kennedy said that this revolution was not just about economics—it was also "for social reform and political freedom, for internal justice and international independence." He pointed to the power of these ideals and something that had sustained the nation throughout its history.

In this speech Kennedy invoked his brother by hanging on a notion that was so prevalent in his inaugural address. He said, "We are the heirs of a revolution that lit the imagination of all those who seek a better life for themselves and their children; that we must seize the chance to lead this continuing revolution, not block its path; that we must stand, not for the status quo, but for progress." In his remarks, Kennedy inspired in the way that his brother did in 1961, but it was his voice now, his vision for the world and he wanted to bring the young people with him in this endeavor. He knew that there was power in this generation and it would be from that effort that his ideals would shine through and he could someday recapture the presidency.

Kennedy believed, indeed encouraged, these young people to interact and participate in the democratic process and argued that it was a vital aspect of a free society. He pointed to the American Revolution and its generation saying that they defined freedom through their actions and, quoting Jefferson, that it was something that they did every day, not just in elections.

> But the sit-ins and the teach-ins, the summer projects, the civil rights vigils and civil liberties protest, organizing the poor and marching on Washington—all these may be helping to return us to a politics of public participation—where individual citizens, without holding political office, may still contribute to the public dialogue—where they do something more than write letters to the newspaper or answer yes or no on a public opinion poll.[20]

This public praise for the civil rights movement and encouragement for the young people of the generation to take part in similar movements was meant to empower these groups so they could continue their own pursuit to improve American society.

Kennedy stressed the importance of the education that they received at the university and the role that it played in this process. He wanted them to use that experience and approach the problems they faced responsibly. He even went as far as to praise the Free Speech Movement. "The Berkeley students of the Free Speech movement made a contribution to academic freedom, and help also to remind universities all over the country that schools are for teaching." Kennedy was careful, however, and said that any irresponsible protest against the Vietnam War was not something he was advocating. Vietnam was a complicated situation and there was not an easy solution, he told the crowd. However, he followed that by saying, "But the complexity and difficulty of any question should not keep you from speech or action."[21] Kennedy's words both inspired and empowered the future generation that would play such a major role in defining the new American identity in the midst of Vietnam and civil rights. Kennedy had the potential to reignite New Frontier ideals and bring it further. As the decade moved forward, people were starting to see it.

On June 23, 1965, Robert Kennedy took another major step in becoming the heir to his brother's legacy. In what would be his formal maiden speech on the floor of the Senate, Kennedy spoke about the threat posed by nuclear weapons. To be sure, Kennedy's experience in the Cuban missile crisis had awakened him to the dangers of nuclear weapons. This speech was as much his vision as it was JFK's. Looking back at the American University speech, from June 1963 President Kennedy wanted to usher in an era of peace and cooperation.

Kennedy started his speech by saying that nuclear proliferation was something that was in the headlines in places like Vietnam and the Dominican Republic, yet he saw it as a "mounting threat." He went into the different nations that had the ability to use nuclear weapons and the threat that they posed to world peace. He said that it was easy to develop these bombs. "Within a very few years, an investment of a few million dollars ... will produce nuclear weapons." He believed that "nuclear capability, then will soon lie within the grasp of many."[22] Indeed, the proliferation of these weapons would bring the world closer to a nuclear exchange.

Like his brother before, RFK understood that once nuclear weapons were deployed in war, it would be difficult to stop the progression into a larger conflict. "Once nuclear war were to start, even between small remote countries, it would be exceedingly difficult to stop a step-by-step progression of local war into a general conflagration," he said. He was concerned that hundreds of millions of people would die as a result of this exchange within twenty-four hours. He declared that "the proliferation of nuclear weapons immensely increases the chances that the world might stumble into catastrophe."

Kennedy paraphrased his brother's 1963 stance on this issue when he said, "If nuclear weapons spread, they may be thus set off—for it is far more difficult and expensive to construct an adequate system of control and custody than to develop the weapons themselves." His greatest fear was that if a nuclear weapon were deployed and a nation could not ascertain its origin, then there would be chaos while the nation and its leaders looked to strike back against the enemy. "And what can be the response—what but a reprisal grounded on suspicion, leading to ever widening circles to the utter destruction of the world we know." He declared to the Senate, "The need to halt the spread of nuclear weapons must be a central priority of American policy."²³

Kennedy linked the growing concern with the role that nuclear weapons played in the world to the growing issues that America had been confronting in other parts of the world.

> The need to be strong—to meet aggression in far-off places—to work closely with allies all over the world—all these needs must be met. And the crises of the moment often pose urgent questions, of grave importance for national security.... Should nuclear weapons become generally available to the world, however, each crisis of the moment might well become the last crisis for all mankind.²⁴

The growing crisis in Vietnam as well as America's policy to continue its Cold War policies in parts of the world, to halt the spread of aggression and communism, were the battlegrounds that Kennedy spoke about. To be sure, in October 1962 as attorney general Kennedy witnessed how a small island in the Caribbean had the potential to start a nuclear war.

Kennedy lauded the efforts of his brother and President Johnson as committed to the Nuclear Test Ban Treaty of 1963. However, he believed that the world needed to go beyond that treaty. "If we are to leave our children a planet in which to live safely, to fulfill the bright promise of their lives, we must resume the journey toward peace." In a clear referral to Vietnam and the Dominican Republic, Kennedy said, "And at the outset of this journey, we cannot allow the demands of day-to-day policy to obstruct our efforts to solve the problem of nuclear spread." He went on to say that the nation could not wait for peace in Southeast Asia or a peace agreement in Europe. "We can not wait until all nations learn to behave—for bad behavior armed with nuclear weapons is the danger we must try to prevent."²⁵ Kennedy wanted the people of the world to move as quickly as possible to meet this issue. In a step that mirrored his brother's efforts, Kennedy outlined his vision for the world.

Kennedy believed that the United States should immediately start to negotiate with the Soviet Union toward a nonproliferation treaty. He believed, as he said later in the speech, that this effort was "in the interest of every nation." In addition to a treaty, Kennedy wanted to explore the notion of nuclear free zones in the world. Thirdly, Kennedy wanted to extend the Nuclear Test Ban Treaty to include underground tests. In addition to that, he wanted to stop the growth of nuclear arms in the United States, support and empower the International Atomic Energy Agency and lessen the United States' reliance on nuclear weapons.²⁶ Kennedy's program was a concerted effort to bring the world away from the brink of war and embrace a peaceful coexistence. Like King's vision for the nation, Kennedy was looking to affect the world. In that endeavor, he was asking that America lead the charge for peace as it had in times of war. This was a revolutionary idea that flew in the face of the cold warrior attitudes of the period.

While Kennedy was idealistic and hopeful that this was something that the nation could explore, he was realistic as well and saw China as a major barrier between peace and the world on the brink of war. To make matters worse, America's involvement in Vietnam complicated that relationship further. He declared that despite the differences between the United States and the Chinese government, "at an appropriate time and manner, therefore, we should vigorously pursue negotiations on this subject with China." Understanding the role and the power of the United States, Kennedy said, "We are stronger—and therefore have more responsibility—than any nation on earth; we should make the first effort—the greatest effort—to control nuclear weapons. We can and must begin immediately."[27]

It could have been that the growing conflict in the world gave Robert Kennedy pause as he stepped into a realm where his voice would be heard and linked to this brother's vision. Referring to his brother, he concluded that peace was a process. "It is only as we devote our every effort to the solution of these problems that we are at peace; it's only if we succeed that there will be peace for our children."[28] His message of peace was something that many groups in the 1960s embraced. That rhetoric laid a foundation for people who were trying to stop the fighting in Vietnam as well as the inequality in the South and the cities in the North. Kennedy had moved into his own, and it was clear that many people in the nation saw him taking on those leadership reins.

The *New York Times* published an editorial praising Robert Kennedy for his speech saying that Kennedy "addressed himself to the most important issue confronting not only the Government of the United States but all of mankind." The *Times* said that Kennedy's plan "to prevent proliferation reflects the best thinking that has developed on this problem both within the Disarmament Agency and among outside experts." The editorial went further saying that Kennedy was "making a useful contribution in his general discussion of foreign affairs." Further, the *Times* acknowledged Kennedy's comments from the previous weeks on Latin America and Vietnam. "His observations flow naturally out of his experience in the Cabinet and as a close adviser to his brother, President Kennedy. The nation and the Administration can benefit from this kind of informed criticism."[29]

Robert and Ted Kennedy were coming into their own and demonstrating to the nation and the Johnson administration that they were independent and sharing their own voice in the nation. According to the *New York Times*, Robert Kennedy's speech on nuclear proliferation was "another cautious step today in the emergence of the brothers Kennedy as powerfully independent figures within the Democratic Party." Reporter Tom Wicker said that Robert Kennedy's speech implied that Johnson had not done enough to halt the proliferation of nuclear weapons—"or as much as President Kennedy had planned to do." The speech was the latest in what Wicker saw as clear breaks with the Johnson administration. He also referenced Kennedy's opposition to Johnson's actions in the Dominican Republic and Vietnam. In addition to those speeches, Ted and Robert Kennedy had led a movement in the Senate to include a ban on the poll tax in the voting rights legislation. While they lost that fight, they came within three votes of adding it to the bill.[30] These events served as a springboard to a larger statement where Robert Kennedy distinguished himself further from the Johnson administration. In that process, he emboldened not only democrats, but also Americans who believed that Johnson's plan had flaws.

V

"The inadequacy of military action is that it can give no hope."

Following up with his strong rhetoric, Robert Kennedy gave a speech to the International Police Academy in Washington, D.C., on July 9, 1965, that opposed the Johnson administration's foreign policy in Southeast Asia. His speech was critical of Johnson's strategy to militarily defeat the Vietcong. The original text was released to news agencies the day before he gave the speech and was met with questions from journalists if Kennedy was breaking with Johnson on Vietnam. As a result of that reaction, Kennedy changed the language of his address. Despite Kennedy's efforts to tone down the rhetoric, newspapers published the original version.[31]

To set the tone and show that his brother would not support the type of war that had developed in Vietnam, Kennedy quoted President Kennedy's West Point Address from 1962. Johnson was trying to win the war with conventional tactics. However, in the nuclear age, that type of warfare was on the verge of extinction. Robert Kennedy believed in counterinsurgency. He quoted President John F. Kennedy's address from 1962.

> This is another type of war, new in its intensity, ancient in its origin—war by guerrillas, subversives, insurgents, assassins, war by ambush instead of by combat; by infiltration, instead of aggression, seeking victory by eroding and exhausting the enemy instead of engaging him.

Robert Kennedy could have also quoted the next line in the speech that brought into sharp focus the type of war that he was advocating in 1965.

JFK said, "It is a form of warfare uniquely adapted to what has been strangely called 'wars of liberation,' to undermine the efforts of new and poor countries to maintain the freedom that they have finally achieved."[32]

Robert Kennedy understood that one of the nation's largest issues was Vietnam. He emphasized that Vietnam had become "more and more an open military conflict." The United States needed to commit more resources so the South Vietnamese government would succeed. "What I say today is in the hope that the lessons of the last twenty years will be applied to other places, so that we are able to win these wars before they reach the stage of all-out military conflict now apparent in South Vietnam."[33] Kennedy not only advocated for a different approach to the conflict in Vietnam, but also in future foreign policy initiatives that were coming from the Johnson administration. At the heart of the war in Vietnam was effective government, Kennedy said.

His message on that day was that the United States should not rely on a strong military response in Vietnam.

> In the 1960s, it should not be necessary to repeat that the great struggle of the coming decades is one for the hearts and minds of men. But too often, of late, we have instead the language of gadgets—of force ratios and oil blots, techniques and technology, of bombs or grenades which explode with special violence, of guns which shoot around corners, of new uses for helicopters and special vehicles.

In laying out the military options and advanced technology of the United States, Robert Kennedy said that a strategy that relied on these techniques was flawed and had a great chance of failure. He concluded, "Men's allegiance, however, and this kind of war, are not won by superior force, by the might of numbers, or by the sophistication of technology."[34] The heart of the issue in Vietnam, as it would be for future wars, was truly a story of people, not governments or ideology.

From Kennedy's perspective the great technology that the United States was trying to use to overwhelm the North was not the answer. "Guns and bombs cannot build," he said, "cannot fill empty stomachs or educate children, cannot build homes or heal the sick. But these are the ends for which men establish and obey governments; they will give their allegiance only to government which meet these needs." Kennedy wanted to create a situation where a government that addressed the growing needs of the people was enough to compel them to create a democratic government. His view was logical, but also compassionate. He said, "The inadequacy of military action is that it can give no hope."[35] It was also a clear indication that Kennedy was becoming an advocate for peace and not the usual "cold warrior" that he was associated with.

Kennedy believed that counterinsurgency should be the policy of the

United States, not a costly and open-ended military action in Vietnam. He believed that this policy would gradually change the situation. He stressed, "I think the history of the last twenty years demonstrates beyond doubt that our approach to revolutionary war must be political—political first, political last, political always." In addition to counterinsurgency and political action, the United States needed to give the people of Vietnam something else to believe in. "Most important, we must impart hope—hope for progress, fulfilled as quickly as circumstances permit."[36] In the end, he told the group that a police force, not the military, was vital to maintain law and order.

The *New York Times* reported the next day that people who listened to Kennedy's speech believed that he was "criticizing the foreign policy of the Johnson Administration, particularly as it has been applied in South Vietnam." The article reported that Kennedy tried to edit his speech from the original prepared text. The *Times* reported that one statement in the prepared text read, "Victory in a revolutionary war is won not by escalation but by de-escalation." The article also reported another piece deleted from the original text, which said, "If all a government can promise its people, in response to insurgent activity, is 10 years of napalm and heavy artillery, it will not be a government for long." Kennedy cut the sentences because he was afraid that reporters would use the language out of context to show that he was criticizing the Johnson administration. When Kennedy spoke to the press after the speech, he said that he had been involved in some of the policy decisions for the last twenty years when he served for his brother as attorney general. He said, "We can all do better."[37]

As 1965 continued, Robert Kennedy found his voice, and it was clear that it was in his own direction, not that of the sitting president. By questioning Johnson's intentions and considering other alternatives than sending more money and troops to Vietnam and Latin America, Kennedy started to show the nation where he stood on important issues that shaped the 1960s. He wanted a solution that did not commit American soldiers. Joseph Palermo contends that RFK's early criticism of the war had a lasting effect on the peace movement. Given the lack of structure in the early peace movement, Kennedy's comments at that stage were very important and served as a foundation for some movements as well as legitimacy. The fact that a former attorney general was advocating for others to speak out made a difference.[38] Palermo also said that Kennedy evolved with his foreign policy—much like civil rights—rejecting counterinsurgency and a buildup of military forces to win in Southeast Asia.[39]

Robert Kennedy was slowly taking the position in the government that he believed was his own, as it was passed down to him by his brother. He continued with his evolution as the year continued. While he established his own voice in some major speeches to start the year, he moved forward to address the growing concerns in urban areas of the nation. Martin Luther King, Jr., was also on a path to come to the North and start a movement that would consider the nature of the racial divide in that same arena. The two men were once again coming together in their rhetoric and vision for the nation. Their direction would prove to empower many others and blaze a path to a new awakening in the nation.

11

Urban Crisis, Voting Rights and Watts

I

*"The consequence of ancient brutality,
past injustice, and present prejudice."*

After his famous march from Selma to Montgomery, Martin Luther King was interviewed on NBC's *Meet the Press* later in March. Lawrence Spivak asked King if he agreed with former president Harry Truman's comment calling the march "silly." King responded, "I think it was the most powerful and dramatic civil rights protest that has ever taken place in the South, and I think it well justified the cost we put in it." When asked if the protest was meant for the Voting Rights Act, King said that it was, but it represented something much larger than that as well, saying, "We must recognize that there are other very tragic conditions existing in the State of Alabama which are humiliating, as degrading and as unjust as the detail of the right to vote, namely police brutality." King went on, saying that the violence in the South has killed many people, creating a culture of violence and oppression for the African Americans who lived there. "There have been untold bombings of homes and churches. Again nothing has been done about this on the whole. We were marching there to protest these brutalities, these murders and all of the things that go along with them, as much as to gain the right to vote." He finished saying that the march was twofold: "aimed at trying to rectify the conditions of Alabama and expose the evils that are deeply engulfed in that state."[1]

King believed that the only way to address the issues in the South was through the acts of protest. He believed that there were people of goodwill across the South and it was up to him to expose the oppressive tendencies of these governments. He told Spivak that the protests would continue as long as rights were denied to African Americans. He said that first "there must be an agreement on the part of the political power structure of the South to guarantee the unhampered right to vote. This must be done with zeal and it must be done with good faith." He concluded that in order to achieve this goal it meant "removing every obstacle including the poll tax." After the issue of the vote had been addressed, King looked to tackle the issue of police brutality. He said, "We feel that before demonstrations can cease, something must be done to end this kind of unnecessary abuse of police power and what we see as outright police brutality." Finally, King saw another need beyond the vote and the brutality. This was something that he shared with both Robert Kennedy and Lyndon Johnson.

The issue of poverty in the nation had been a focus not only within the African American community but throughout the nation, touching a myriad of races, ethnicities and groups. King said that in order for the demonstrations in the South to stop "there must be some equality in terms of grappling with the problem of poverty." King declared that "Negroes must be brought into the very central structure of the whole poverty program." At the heart of his comments was that African Americans were being left out of programs that had the potential to help them. He planned to continue protests in Alabama until these issues were addressed. One issue that came up, which would become a source of concern with not only King but also other leaders of the sixties, was how the nature of the civil rights movement was on the cusp of moving away from nonviolence.

As the movement continued and many African American were frustrated with the gradualistic nature not only of King's tactics but also how the government responded to these issues, King was concerned with the fact that violence seemed to be on the horizon. "I feel that we have to continue to have a non-violent movement," he said. King believed that most African Americans were committed to that tactic. However, he understood

> when there is justice and the pursuit of justice, violence appears, and where there is injustice and frustration, the potentialities for violence are greater, and I would like to strongly stress the point that the more we can achieve victories through non-violence, the more it will be possible to keep the non-violent discipline at the center of the movement.[2]

King stressed that frustration, disappointment and despair contributed to the violent nature of some of the other movements and that as long as there was a failure to change the conditions, "the more it will be possible for the apostles of violence to interfere."[3]

King made his case for nonviolent protest again in May when he spoke in front of the American Jewish Committee. Also in attendance was Vice President Humphrey. King said that nonviolent protest had its roots as far back as the American Revolution's Boston Tea Party, the women's suffrage movement and unions who utilized the sit-down strike. The idea had its roots not in the civil rights movement of the 1950s, but in the history of the United States. "When the Quakers refused to return runaway slaves, they were defying the Supreme Court and the Dred Scott decision. When Thoreau refused to pay taxes in protest against the Mexican War, he was breaking a fundamental legislative enactment and opposing the declaration of war of the Congress."[4] In the case of the civil rights movement, however, African Americans were not protesting the Constitution or acts of Congress; they are marching to uphold those rights.

King's argument hoped to bridge the divide between people who saw his actions as unnecessary and futile. African Americans "may be violating local municipal ordinances or state laws but it is these laws which contradict basic national law; Negroes by their direct action, are exposing the contradiction." He concluded that the "civil disobedience in this situation, resting on unjust foundations, is that of the segregationist."[5] King's perspective harks back to the truculent southern culture that refused to move forward and accept the demise of slavery just prior to the Civil War. Indeed, this moment in history was similar. Instead of accepting the notion that segregation was wrong and no longer acceptable in the nation, indeed the world, southerners chose to challenge that idea.

The movement was meant to help more than African Americans. "It is the axiom of non-violent action and democracy that when any group struggles properly and justly to achieve its own rights it enlarges the rights of all. This element is what makes both democracy and non-violent action self-renewing and creative."[6] The civil rights movement had an effect on other movements as the sixties continued to challenge the status quo in the nation. To be sure, many of the leaders of other movements felt empowered by King's tactics and success. They used this model to bring about change, to challenging not only social norms but the power structure of the United States. A few days later, President Johnson gave a commencement address that showed solidarity with the movement. In a phone call to Johnson, King told him that it was "the greatest speech that any President has made on the question of civil rights."[7]

As the year progressed Martin Luther King articulated his position on the Vietnam War saying on July 2 in a speech at the Virginia branch of the SCLC, "I'm not going to sit by and see war escalated without saying anything about it." He declared that the war "must be stopped" and said that he was considering joining the sit-ins and teach-ins that had been gaining momentum across the nation. King said that the nation must look to peace. "It must be a negotiated settlement. We must even negotiate with the Vietcong." King's position was more about his peace activism than it was about his ability to understand Cold War polemics. However, he did comment on that issue, saying, "We're not going to defeat Communism with bombs and guns and gasses." He went on to say, "We can never accept Communism. We must work this out in a framework of our democracy."[8]

King was one of the first civil rights leaders to speak out against the war in Vietnam. Two days after his speech, the *New York Times* published an article highlighting how African Americans were coming out against the war. In that same speech in Virginia, King went even further, saying, "The long night of war must be stopped," using the same imagery that he had attached to the struggle for equality under the law. The *Times* went on, saying that Roy Wilkins of the NAACP had said, "We have enough Vietnam in Alabama." Wilkins wanted to see African Americans involved in other parts of the government.[9]

II

"But freedom is not enough."

As the war in Vietnam continued to grow in the summer of 1965 and the nation was still dealing with the growing racial tension, Lyndon Johnson gave the commencement address at Howard University titled "To Fulfill These Rights" on June 4, 1965. The speech was Johnson's civil rights doctrine and demonstrated his resolve to address the racial divide in the nation. After talking to the students about the revolutions of the world and the impact they would have in history, he said, "But nothing in any country touches us more profoundly, and nothing is more freighted with meaning for our own destiny than the revolution of the Negro American." The waves of change were hitting the nation, and Johnson saw the impact that it was having. "In far too many ways American Negroes have been another nation: deprived of freedom, crippled by hatred, the doors of opportunity closed to hope," he said.[10] What followed was as an elegant and masterful declaration of what his administration hoped to do to fulfill the rights of all Americans.

Johnson advocated, indeed praised, the efforts of men like King and John Lewis who practiced nonviolent protest. "The American Negro, acting with impressive restraint, has peacefully protested and marched, entered the courtrooms and the seats of government, demanding a justice that has long been denied," Johnson said. He continued with the speech, saying, "The voice of the Negro was the call to action. But it is a tribute to America that, once aroused, the courts and the Congress, the President and most of the people, have been the allies of progress." Johnson praised the nation's ability to pass civil rights legislation and emphasized that he was ready to pass another act that would secure voting rights for all Americans. "No act of my entire administration will give me greater satisfaction than the day when my signature makes this bill, too, the law of this land," he said.

The speech was rooted in the notion that more needed to be done for all Americans, but especially African Americans who had been denied basic rights guaranteed by the Constitution. Johnson spoke of this freedom and how that was an important piece of American culture. "But freedom is not enough," he declared. "You do not wipe away the scars of centuries by saying: Now you are free to go where you want, and do as you desire, and choose the leaders you please." As Kennedy and King had articulated in previous speeches for nearly two years, it was important to consider not only legislation but the hearts and minds of people. "You do not take a person who, for years, has been hobbled by chains and liberate him, bring him up to the starting line of a race and then say, 'you are free to compete with all the others,' and still justly believe that you have been completely fair." Johnson acknowledged, "Thus it is not enough just to open the gates of opportunity. All our citizens must have the ability to walk through those gates."[11]

The speech articulated not only the fact that justice had been denied to African Americans, but also that more needed to be done in order for there to be true change in the nation. At the heart of the speech, and the movement, was that all Americans should be given the same opportunities. "For the task is to give 20 million Negroes the same chance as every other American to learn and grow, to work and share in society, to develop their abilities—physical, mental and spiritual, and to pursue their individual happiness," Johnson said. It was revolutionary and inspired by the efforts of King, Lewis and many others who risked their life for the struggle of all African Americans to attain the same rights as every American in the nation. The struggle for many African Americans lay not in the lack of legislation. Many of them needed opportunity to fight against the impoverished circumstances that they had to endure.

The civil rights movement was linked to the War on Poverty, and Johnson hoped that by addressing one of them, he was helping the other. In his speech, he acknowledged that poverty was as much an enemy for African Americans as segregation.

> But for the great majority of Negro Americans—the poor, the unemployed, the uprooted, and the dispossessed—there is a much grimmer story. They still, as we meet here tonight, are another nation. Despite the court orders and the laws, despite the legislative victories and the speeches, for them the walls are rising and the gulf is widening.

This "widening gulf" was something that needed the same attention as the right to vote or to be served in the same restaurants as other Americans. To be sure, this was an issue within the urban centers of the nation as well as the South. Johnson, Kennedy and King were waging war against the growing divide within the nation against the segregationist policies of the South.

Johnson articulated that these problems are complicated and had an enormous impact on African Americans. "Negroes are trapped—as many whites are trapped—in inherited, gate-less poverty. They lack training and skills. They are shut in, in slums, without decent medical care. Private and public poverty combine to cripple their capacities." He said that the government worked hard to address these issues with poverty programs, trying to stop the tide of oppression that had made it so difficult for many Americans to succeed. "But there is a second cause," he said, "much more difficult to explain, more deeply grounded, more desperate in its force. It is the devastating heritage of long years of slavery; and a century of oppression, hatred, and injustice." Johnson was among an elite group of presidents to acknowledge how the vestige of slavery had impacted the growing the racial tension in the nation.

Despite the fact that slavery had been outlawed in 1865, Johnson made it clear that impoverished African Americans had a different cross to bear when it came to what they had to overcome to become part of the "American dream."

> These differences are not racial differences. They are solely and simply the consequence of ancient brutality, past injustice, and present prejudice. They are anguishing to observe. For the Negro they are a constant reminder of oppression. For the white they are a constant reminder of guilt. But they must be faced and they must be dealt with and they must be overcome, if we are ever to reach the time when the only difference between Negroes and whites is the color of their skin.[12]

Johnson acknowledged to the leaders of the movement that their efforts were not in vain. They were at the precipice of change for the nation, but it would take time to change the hearts and minds of people in the nation. The fact that Johnson was willing to make a speech that acknowledged this disparity in the nation and emphasize the efforts of the government to bridge that divide shows that the country was moving in a new, profound direction that had the potential to challenge institutions that were so pervasive in the American identity. In short, change was on the horizon. To be sure, King and Kennedy would play a role in the efforts that Johnson highlighted to the nation.

Dr. King continued to redefine the aims of his movement as he journeyed to the northern cities in an effort to confront the issue of poverty in

America's inner cities. He chose Chicago as the place to begin this quest in the North. King went to Chicago early in July but then returned to lead a series of rallies throughout the city on July 23. He gave twenty speeches in less than two days. After this hectic schedule he was rushed to a doctor's office for an emergency checkup.[13] King's goal was to make a three-day sweep through the city, creating support for a march on city hall. The main goal of these marches was to expose the horrid conditions of Chicago's urban areas that were predominantly African American. These impoverished conditions were as much a part of the plight for equality as the efforts of King's southern campaign. In addition to this, the education system was segregated to the point that students in urban areas did not have the same opportunities as those in the suburbs. King used this moment to highlight this disparity as well as to bring his movement to the North.

King said at a rally in the suburb of Winnetka that he was there to add to the efforts by local groups who had been exposing "injustice that exists in this area." King spoke in several parks in the area.[14] The march on city hall was scheduled for the next day and King wanted to get as much support for the rally as he could. In what was called by the *New York Times* "the biggest civil rights demonstration in Chicago's history," King led approximately 30,000 people in a march on Chicago's city hall. One of the main targets for the march, Mayor Richard Daley, was not at city hall. King, who spoke to the crowd from the back of a blue truck, wanted to begin the campaign in Chicago because he believed it was one of "the most rigidly segregated cities in the country." At the heart of this rally was to get Mayor Daley to replace School Superintendent Benjamin Willis who was accused of using segregation tactics in his management of the school system. King stressed that the nation was entering a technological society and students needed specific training to compete in this new market. "The chances of the schools of Chicago producing such men and women are extremely limited," he said. "Presently, Chicago spends just a little more than half as much per child on education as does New York. Ninety per cent of the Negro children are in segregated, overcrowded classrooms. The Negro youth are crippled educationally," King told the crowd.[15]

Much to the dismay of some of the local leaders, King went on to address issues in Philadelphia. Cecil B. Moore, a leader of the local chapter of the NAACP, said that he did not want King in the city and felt that it had the potential to divide African Americans. Moore, who had a militant philosophy on how to confront civil rights issues, said that "the NAACP should have been consulted before a visitor of his stature" came to the city. He went on to say, "There is nothing wrong with Philadelphia that southern bigots, Communists, and egghead subversive, alleged white liberals can cure. The imported Gandhi philosophy of nonviolence that still exists in the south will not be accepted in Philadelphia, where we believe in self-help and self-defense." King planned on going to Girard College, a boarding school in Philadelphia, where there was a "white-only" admission policy, where the NAACP had been demonstrating since May 1. The school had a charter that stipulated admission to the school was limited to "poor while male orphans."[16]

On August 3, King led a rally of 5,000 people on Girard College. Singing and chanting the group challenged the segregation policy of the college. Standing in the back of a truck at the main gate of the boarding school, King used the ten-foot-high stone wall that surrounded the school as a symbol of oppression. "At this stage of the 20th century in the city that has been known as the cradle of liberty, the Girard College wall is like the Berlin wall," King said. "This wall, this school, is symbolic of a cancer in the body politic that must be removed before there will be freedom and democracy in this country." King stood with the militant Cecil B. Moore. He emphasized his commitment to nonviolence saying, "I have seen too much violence. I am tired of it." In addition to confronting the issue of segregation in Philadelphia he addressed the growing conflict in Vietnam reiterating some of his earlier statements on the subject: "War is obsolete. No nation today can win a war. It is no longer a choice between violence and nonviolence. It is a choice between violence and nonexistence." He would go further in his comments during this northern city tour stressing the need for a negotiated peace in Vietnam and acknowledging that he was "not prepared to say that either side is wholly right or wholly wrong."[17]

King's trip extended the movement for civil rights to include not only the segregation-ridden states of the South, but also the poverty-stricken cities of the North. It was unprecedented for King to reach out in these communities and address racial issues at such a national level. This effort did a great deal to highlight to the nation that racial issues did not begin and end with segregation. These issues hid covertly beneath layers of tacit acceptance of the racial attitudes in America. King's efforts did a lot to bring all of that to the surface. To be sure, these trips were not on a grand scale, and to some extent King was trying to ascertain just how bad these areas were before he committed his time and resources to one of them for a long period. Nevertheless, it demonstrated his ability to reach out to communities both in the North and the South. After King left Philadelphia, the birthplace of the nation, he went to Washington, D.C., and visited the impoverished areas of that city.

Bomb threats and Nazis picketing outside the venue where Martin Luther King was scheduled to speak did not deter the leader from continuing his tour of major northern cities. King said that economic freedom was the new issue for the civil rights movement, which had been so successful at attacking the major issues of African Americans in the sixties. "What good does it do to be able to eat at a lunch counter if you can't buy a hamburger? What good is it to live in integrated housing if you can't afford to take your family on vacation? Why be able to stay in hotels and restaurants if you don't have the money to take your wife out to dinner?" King was attacking the core of the racial issues in the nation. "The Negro is not free in the United States of America, North or South," King proclaimed. The next day King had an appointment with President Johnson.[18]

King had come to Washington not only to bring his campaign to northern cities but also to attend the signing of the Voting Rights Act, which he had lobbied for. After meeting with Johnson for one hour on August 5, King said that he planned to send Johnson a series of proposals to end "increasing segregation" in northern states. "In the suggestions and recommendations I will submit, I will draw on the experiences and the studies we have made in Northern communities that we have toured." King went on to say, "I see segregation on the increase in the North rather than on the decline." He also concluded that impoverished "ghetto" areas were "more intensified than dispersed."[19]

III

"They came in darkness and they came in chains."

"Today is a triumph for freedom as huge as any victory that has ever been won on any battlefield. Yet to seize the meaning of this day, we must recall darker times," Lyndon Johnson proclaimed in the rotunda of the United States Capitol on August 6, 1965. "Three and a half centuries ago the first Negroes arrived at Jamestown," Johnson said. "They came in darkness and they came in chains."[20] President Johnson addressed the people in attendance on the passage of the Voting Rights Act of 1965. Born from the ashes of the Civil War with the Fifteenth Amendment, African Americans would have unfettered access to the polls in the South. It was a momentous, historic occasion that finally ended one hundred years of legal discrimination against African Americans at the voting booths.

Johnson understood the historic nature of the signing and was eloquent with his words to mark the occasion, saying, "It was only at Appomattox, a century ago, that an American victory was also a Negro victory. And the two rivers—one shining with promise, the other dark-stained with oppression—began to move toward one another." Johnson made it clear to the people of the United States that the act was meant to rectify the injustice that had been so pervasive in the South in the years after the Civil War. "This act flows from a clear and simple wrong. Its only purpose is to right that wrong. Millions of Americans are denied the right to vote because of their color. This law will ensure them the right to vote," he said. "The wrong is one which no American, in his heart, can justify. The right is one which no American, true to our principles, can deny."[21] The Voting Rights Act of 1965 was also born from the efforts of Martin Luther King, Jr., and the movement in Selma, Alabama, to start the year. From the rotunda Johnson went to the President's Room in the Capitol, just off the Senate Chamber, to officially sign the bill. The room was allegedly a place where Lincoln had freed some slaves when he was in office. Martin Luther King and other civil rights leaders were in attendance.[22]

The Voting Rights Act hoped to attack the poll tax in addition to the literacy tests that had plagued African Americans' quest for the vote since the end of the Civil War. Johnson had instructed the Justice Department to sue Alabama, Texas and Virginia regarding their use of the poll tax.[23] The act was another measure in a series of legislation that looked to secure rights for African Americans. Many of the people in the room and elsewhere within the United States believed that the racial tension would ease in the wake of this momentous occasion. However, as King and others tried to shed light on these hypocritical elements of American democracy, it was clear that this was a complex issue that had a myriad of injustices going back to the institution of slavery and the racist culture that had been born from the Civil War.

Five days after the historic signing of the Voting Rights Act, one of the worst race riots in American history erupted in the Watts section of Los Angeles. The cause of the rioting in the immediate aftermath was unknown, and some pointed to a drunken driving arrest. Most of the riot pointed to police brutality as the main cause of the discontent at the start of the riots, which would continue for days. The riots engulfed a twenty-block radius, which would eventually be closed by the police.[24] The National Guard would eventually have to enter the city and confront the rioters with machine guns with plans to "hit them and make them stop." The crowds started chanting, "White devils what are you doing here?"[25] The riots continued for six days. Thirty-four people would be killed and more than one thousand injured.[26] Despite the initiatives of the government to attack the civil rights issue in the nation, it seemed that there were deeper issues that had not been addressed in the sixties. Hoping for solutions, Robert Kennedy and Martin Luther King confronted those issues in their statements that followed the riots.

IV
"But the main issue is economic."

Robert Kennedy spoke about the Watts riots in Spring Valley, New York, on August 18, 1965. He started by saying that he wanted to talk about the "dead and the orphans of the rioting in Los Angeles; about the sick and the distressed of all our urban ghettos; about the hatred and the fear and the brutality we saw in Los Angeles; and about what we can and must do if this cancer is not to spread beyond control." His speech emphasized a complex reason for the violence that had the potential to get better through government intervention. He declared that the riots were "no isolated phenomenon, no unlucky chance." He went on to talk about the reasons for the riots in Watts, Harlem and the South Side of Chicago, saying, "In all these places ... are riots waiting to happen."[27]

At the heart of the matter, Kennedy argued, was the fact that all of these places had been experiencing tremendous poverty. "Our society—all our values, our views of each other, and our own self-esteem; the contribution we can make to ourselves, our families and the community around us; all these things are built on the work we do," Kennedy told the audience. "But too many of the inhabitants of these areas are without the purpose, the satisfaction or the dignity that we find in our work." Kennedy went on to say that the people who came from the rural south expecting a new beginning in the North were especially stricken by these unfortunate circumstances. "Their disappointment is all the keener because of the prosperity and the affluence all around them." Kennedy went even further to address this growing disparity saying that America's youth is told to stay in school and work hard in order to be successful, "but a Negro youth who finishes high school is more likely to be unemployed than a white youth who drops out of school—and is more likely to find menial work at lower pay."[28] Kennedy even made a connection between the American Revolution and the plight of African Americans in the 1960s.

Americans take pride in the fact that the nation was founded by a group of individuals who overthrew an oppressive force. "I think there is no doubt that if Washington or Jefferson or Adams were Negroes in a Northern city today, they would be in the forefront of the effort to change the conditions under which Negroes live in our society." Kennedy recalled his time in the wake of the Birmingham crisis in 1963 saying that many in the North did not believe that this would ever be an issue in northern cities. "But as we are learning now, it is one thing to assure a man the legal right to eat in a restaurant; it is another thing to assure that he can earn the money to eat there," Kennedy said, echoing King's comments from earlier in the month. Kennedy lauded the leaders of the southern movement saying that their tactic of nonviolence was in the forefront. "Northern problems are the problems of everyday living, in jobs and housing and education," Kennedy said. "They affect too many people, too directly, for involvement to be restricted to those with the patience, the discipline, and the inclination to practice nonviolence."

The problems for African Americans were complex, and Kennedy believed that in order to do something about these issues they needed to consider a new way of dealing with them. Many Americans considered this a "racial issue." Kennedy thought differently, saying, "The difficulties these people face are far greater because of the color of their skin; but the problems themselves are as various as ours are." These problems must be brought into the political process. "Only when these problems are being dealt with in the political process can we expect to channel people's frustration and resentment and insecurity into constructive action programs," Kennedy said. He went on to say that there were no true solutions to these problems. "There should be no illusions, however, that any or all of these steps will usher in the millennium. Poor people and Negro leaders will make mistakes; there will be graft and waste."[29] Kennedy was trying to provide leadership in the wake of the riots. If these problems were addressed by strong civil rights leaders in the North as they had been in the South, then they had a higher chance of success. Martin Luther King may have heard Kennedy's message as he was preparing his response to the Watts riots.

Martin Luther King's initial reaction to the people in Watts emphasized his doctrine of nonviolence. "I'm gonna tell you one very important thing, if we're gonna win the victory … we can't fight against each other," King said. He went further to help stop the violence, saying, "While we have legitimate gripes, while we have legitimate discontent, we must not hate all white people." He reminded the people that it was a white woman who supported the Selma campaign who was killed by the KKK. "We want to know what we can do to create right here in Los Angeles a better city, a beloved community. So speak out of your hearts and speak frankly."[30]

King followed up with a formal statement on the riots and what he saw as the main reasons for the crisis: "What we are witnessing here is the beginning of a stirring of those people in our society who have been bypassed by the progress of the past decade." King wanted to stress the economic, not racial, reasons for the riots saying that "these were the rumblings of discontent from the 'have nots' within the midst of an affluent society." King had visited the scenes of the riots and talked with the people. He believed that "these riots grew out of the depths of despair which afflict a people who see no way out of their economic dilemma." In addition to the issue of poverty, King pointed to the growing leadership role that African Americans had been playing in American society as another issue. "There is also a growing disillusionment and resentment toward the Negro middle class and the leadership which it has produced," King said. "This ever widening breach is a serious factor which leads to the feeling that they are alone in their struggle and must resort to any method to gain attention to their plight. The non-violent movement of the South has meant little to them since we have been fighting for rights which theoretically are already theirs."[31]

King's reasons were deeper and more societally driven than the fact that they were black and living in a nation that had a deepening racial divide. To be sure the issues of the day were complicated, and trying to make it as simple as racial tension demeaned the true nature of the problems in American society. "Their fight is for dignity and work," King said. He stressed that police brutality was a "deprivation of the dignity" which they were lacking. "But the main issue is economic," King concluded. "Unless some work can be found for the un-employed and the underemployed we continually face the possibility of this kind of outbreak at every encounter with police brutality." King said that this issue was not unique to Los Angeles. "It is a national problem. At a time when the Negro's aspirations are at a peak, his actual conditions of employment, education and housing are worsening." King concluded that the "paramount problem is one of economic stability for this sector of our society."[32] King understood that this growing disparity threatened not only northern and southern cities, but also the success of the nonviolent movement.

The discontent among African Americans led to a division in the civil rights movement. The Black Panthers as well as the Black Power movement were rooted in militancy that used Black Nationalism as a tool to empower African Americans. Violence was often the outcome of these tactics. King saw these riots as a

> crisis for the non-violent movement. I am trying desperately to maintain a non-violent atmosphere in which our nation can under go the tremendous period of social change which confronts us, but this is dependent on progress and victories if those of us who counsel reason and love are to maintain our leadership.[33]

King's movement was in a state of crisis. In order for him to gain the momentum back in his favor he needed to continue his movements in the North and address the growing issue of poverty among African Americans. To be sure the Great Society programs had only started to make a difference while the Vietnam War hampered its ability to be fully effective.

V

"What exploded in Watts is what lies beneath the surface."

By October 1965 King returned to Chicago to continue his movement in northern cities. "Chicago represents all the problems that you can find in the major urban areas of our country.... If we can break the system in Chicago, it can be broken anywhere in the country," King said. "The movement in Chicago will be different from that in the South," King acknowledged. "There will be fewer overt acts to aid us here ... naive targets such as the Jim Clarks and George Wallace's will be harder to find and use as symbols." King told newspeople, "Reforms will require political power. Direct action in and of itself will not get what we want—but it will point out the need."[34] King was on the precipice of taking his movement into the North—an effort that he took very seriously and would eventually embrace completely given the success of his efforts to get the Civil Rights Act of 1964 and the Voting Rights Act of 1965 passed. In addition to his efforts, Robert Kennedy took the opportunity to outline his vision and start to offer the "political power" that King referred to.

Doing something about the impoverished conditions in American cities was something that Robert Kennedy had always wanted to confront. He had toured and visited impoverished parts of the city to get a better idea of what the issues were as he considered legislation. On one of those occasions he was visiting an apartment in Brooklyn and saw a child with a mangled face. Kennedy asked the child's mother, "What happened to her?" The mother explained that rats had bitten her face when she was a baby. Kennedy was outraged and couldn't understand how something like that could "happen in the richest city on earth."[35] At the beginning of 1966 Kennedy gave a series of speeches that looked to address this growing "urban crisis."

In the summer of 1965 Kennedy and a group of his aides met at Kennedy's home in Virginia to discuss the growing conflict in American cities and what could be done. Sitting around his pool and discussing the best way to address these issues, the group came to a conclusion that they needed an education and ecumenical reform to start. In November 1965, Kennedy and his aide Peter Edelman, who was at the poolside discussion, toured Watts. Edelman recalled, "It was like seeing a war-torn area in one's own country for the first time." Edelman would eventually work with Burke Marshall, Kennedy's former assistant attorney general, who was no longer working with the Justice Department and was in private practice, to draft a memo for Bobby about programs to address these issues.[36] The result was a series of three speeches that addressed education, housing and employment. When Marshall read the speeches at Kennedy's request, he commented, "Well, it's very radical. But then the challenges are radical."[37]

Kennedy's speeches were a big part of his vision for where America needed to go. Indeed, they played a role in defining his campaign for the presidency in 1968. Kennedy gave these three speeches in January 1966. He started the speeches on January 20, saying that he did not want to diminish the issues in the South. He wanted to "emphasize the magnitude of the problem in the North." Kennedy acknowledged that cities have changed in the "course of the last generation." He told the audience, "Millions of Negros, impelled by hopes of job opportunities and a better life, have poured into the cities of the north and the west." Of course, Kennedy was referring to the "Great Migration" that led many African Americans to come north to find a better life for their families in the early decades of the twentieth century. "Their arrival and the simultaneous flight of millions of whites to the suburbs, has created a situation of segregation unparalleled in our country's history." Kennedy said that while the segregation of these areas was tragic, "the worst part is that the ghetto is also a slum."

These speeches are evidence that Kennedy was seeing the racial divide in the nation and how it affected the lives of Americans, especially in the North. Like King, he understood that poverty played a role in the racial disparity in the nation. He acknowledged that African Americans did not have the same opportunities as other Americans and wanted to do something to change that situation. "For three hundred years the Negro has been a nation apart, a people governed by a repression that has been softened to the point where it is now only a massive indifference," he said. Kennedy understood that this repression of African American rights had created a climate in the nation that had major ramifications.

> The Watts riots were as much a revolt against official indifference, an explosion of frustration at the inability to communicate and participate, as they were an uprising about inferior jobs and education and housing. What exploded in Watts is what lies beneath the surface.... We can expect continuing explosions like Watts, continuing crises in the management of our cities, and, worst of all, a continuing second-class status for a large group of American citizens. Clearly the present pace is unsatisfactory.[38]

Kennedy's acknowledgment of these issues was not unique, but the fact that he wanted to stress this as a major initiative brought the power of the Kennedy legacy to bear down on these issues. As a senator from New York it was an issue that became a part of his duty to his constituents.

Kennedy wanted to find "racial balance" in the hopes of attacking these issues. He wanted to improve living conditions and rebuild African American neighborhoods, "giving their residents new job skills and jobs to go with them, to improving the education of their children, to providing new cultural interests for those who live there." Kennedy's awakening to these issues illuminated the issues in impoverished areas of the nation in the hopes of finding a way to give African Americans in the North the same hope that King inspired for southern African Americans. To that end, Kennedy wanted to evaluate housing programs and work toward desegregation of those areas, use federal power to break down those barriers, strengthen efforts in those neighborhoods to complement housing initiatives and establish a well-publicized federal assistance program in those areas. "Our ultimate purpose is to assure that every American comes to know the full meaning of the truths that we held to be self evident for the rest of America almost 190 years ago."[39]

That first speech was not as successful as Kennedy would have hoped. Edelman called the speech an "utter bomb" and recalled that Kennedy was "very irritated with me afterwards."[40] Despite the failure of the speech to the audience, it was clear from the rhetoric that Kennedy was trying to redefine the role that the government played in inner-city America. His speech the next day focused on addressing the disparity in the education of African Americans, saying that the most important problem in Harlem "is education of every kind." He contended that "fathers must learn job skills, and mothers how to buy food economically; students must learn to read, and little children how to speak; teachers must learn how to teach and employers how to hire." Kennedy said that the better schools do not always produce good students. The issues were deeper, more complex than that. "For perhaps the greatest barrier to education in Harlem is simply a lack of hope, a lack of belief that education is meaningful to a Negro in the city of New York." This was the essence of Kennedy's message. He wanted to instill hope in the lives of Americans. Hope is something that is not easily measured, but it was clearly Kennedy's goal in 1966, as he led up to his speech in South Africa, to inspire people and give them hope as they dealt with major racial issues. Indeed, the rhetoric inspired many to believe that the problems they faced in the sixties had solutions and he was working hard to find them.

While Kennedy was proposing new legislation, he could not promise that all of it would get done. What was the most pervasive element of his speeches was the fact that he was paying attention to the issues in these communities. With that attention and time came a newfound hope for people who were looking for leadership in these areas. Kennedy offered a nine-part program that was rooted in education programs to stimulate jobs in urban areas. This initiative was meant to upend the status quo and create a new culture in those urban areas, leading to the hope that Kennedy referred to. He even said that the "greatest returns of the program I have outlined would be returns in human spirit: in lessened dependency, in lower delinquency and crime, in more beautified cities, and children stronger and healthier in every way; and these returns are beyond our capacity to measure."[41] He finished this speech in similar fashion as he did on the first day, referring to the formation of the nation. "The dream of liberty and equality set out in our Constitution 190 years ago [was] never completely fulfilled, yet [is] always alive, still asserting itself with ever-growing intensity."[42] Kennedy wanted to bring that dream closer for all Americans.

Kennedy gave his last speech in this series on January 22. In this speech he wanted to go even further in his vision of anti-poverty legislation efforts and address "all Americans." He acknowledged that there were workers who needed to learn new skills in order to contribute to a new economy. Kennedy proposed an effort that led to an "upgrade" of the workforce. His program focused on giving people the ability to educate themselves further, creating better proficiency and opportunities. His program looked to enjoin local, state and federal offices to offer training. This initiative was the final piece of his vision to better prepare the people for the challenges ahead while at the same time creating a better life for many working-class Americans. "Let us now prepare the minds of all our people," he said, "and the tides of chance and change will favor us all." Kennedy met with his advisers after this speech and said, "Now listen. I don't just want to talk about this; I want to do something about it.... Now we've got to do it."[43]

12

"Ripples of Hope"

I

"Money by itself is no answer."

Kennedy and King continued to address the growing racial concerns that impacted the nation. Both leaders, however, turned their attention to South Africa and the issue of apartheid, bringing their activism onto the world stage. King commented on apartheid in December 1965 while Robert Kennedy gave what is considered by many historians one of his greatest speeches of all time in South Africa in June 1966. By 1966 these leaders were established as voices of their generation. By the end of the year many people were looking to Robert Kennedy as a future president. His legacy was solidified by the rhetoric and legislation that he championed in an effort to empower the disadvantaged and create opportunities for the impoverished. Martin Luther King continued his campaign in northern cities, attacking the poverty that plagued African Americans while at the same time staving off the growing discontent among African Americans to violently fight back instead of embracing the notion of nonviolence.

Kennedy and King were both daring in their approach to the problems of the 1960s. King went as far as to move into a slum in Chicago while the privileged Kennedy toured the poor sections of Brooklyn in the hopes of passing legislation to help that part of New York. Both men spoke against the nation's Vietnam policy, and both men advocated for a better response to the racial issues in the nation and the world. They blazed a path for people to follow—moving in a direction to redefine American ideals for the rest of the 1960s and beyond.

In December 1965, Dr. King commented on the racist policy of apartheid. King started by saying that for years people who lived in South Africa had been depicted as "black cannibals and ignorant primitives." He said that the stereotype has persisted for more than a century in books, movies and other mediums. "Africa does have spectacular savages and brutes to-day, but they are not black," he said. "They are the sophisticated white rulers of South Africa who profess to be cultured, religious and civilized, but whose conduct and philosophy stamp them unmistakably as modern day barbarians." King went on to talk about the violations of human rights that had been occurring in South Africa, saying that all opposition to the white government was characterized as communism, due process was nonexistent and free speech and press were suppressed. Speaking of the slave trade King characterized it as "one of the blackest pages of our history." He continued, "There are few parallels in human history of the period in which Africans were seized and branded like animals, packed into ships' holds like cargo and transported into chattel slavery."[1]

King emphasized the economic relationship of the major nations and South Africa. King wanted to initiate a "massive international boycott" against the repressive regime in South Africa. "Civilization has come a long way," King said. "It has far still to go and it cannot afford to [be] set back by resolute wicked men." Hoping to unite African Americans and white Americans, King said,

> The powerful unity of Negro with Negro and white with Negro is stronger than the most potent and entrenched racism. The whole human race will benefit when it ends the abomination that has diminished the stature of man for too long. This is the task to which we are called by the suffering in South Africa and our response should be swift and unstinting. Out of this struggle will come the generous reality of the family of man.[2]

King wanted the United States to use its capital and use it as a weapon to defeat racism in South Africa. To be sure, this method was not much different than what he did in Montgomery in 1955. King wanted to defeat racism with nonviolence at home and abroad.

After his comments on apartheid, King started 1966 with a new maneuver that would characterize his campaign in the North to attack racism. On January 7 he announced a "full-scale assault" against the impoverished conditions in Chicago. Looking to make gains in education and housing for African Americans, King planned to lead the SCLC in a series of various "boycotts." Speaking to reporters, King said, "I don't subscribe to the philosophy that the day of demonstrations is over" and called for the SCLC's "first sustained northern movement" in Chicago.[3]

King's "Chicago Plan" said that "the problems of Chicago, indeed the problems of the northern city, demand something new. In our work in the south, two principles have emerged. One, the crystallization of issues, and two, the concentration of action." In the same spirit with which he confronted the segregation laws of the South, King made it clear that the energy of the SCLC was committed to confronting the issues in Chicago. "Their work has been concerned with strengthening community organizations and recruiting new forces to join in the nonviolent movement, but they have also given a great deal of thought to the crystallization and definition of the problem in Chicago in terms which can be communicated to the man on the street, who is most affected." King's "Chicago Plan" was multilayered, designed to attack issues in education, housing, the welfare system, the courts, police and the political infrastructure of the city. The statement said that he planned to create a "full understanding" of the issues in the first couple of months of the campaign. King made it clear that phases 2 and 3 would come soon after his work to expose the issues in the impoverished parts of Chicago. His statement made note of the fact that the Selma movement the previous year was done in similar fashion and that this would be as successful.[4] King went even further to demonstrate his commitment later that month, showing solidarity with the people in an impoverished area of the city by renting an apartment on the West Side of Chicago.

King's efforts to bring his movement into the North demonstrate his resolve to not only address the racial tension in the nation but also his commitment to use nonviolence as a means to bring about that change. People cheered as King made his entrance into the four-room flat in a neighborhood that African Americans called "Slumdale." Sharing the apartment with Andrew Young, King planned to use it as a "command center" to implement his "Chicago Plan." The Rev. James Bevel was appointed as the director for this effort.[5] The next day, King met with city officials in an effort to keep them informed of his actions in the city. The police superintendent invited King to discuss his efforts. King believed that the same conditions that led to the Watts riots were as pervasive in Chicago as they were in Los Angeles. "This was no threat—the same problems are here and if something isn't done in a hurry we can see a darker night of social disruption," King said. He went on to say that police action in the South had created a dynamic where they were viewed as enemies.[6] King's daring movement in Chicago shined a light on the disparity for African Americans in the North. While it was not as overt as the segregation tactics of Bull Connor or Jim Clark, it was just as oppressive and in many ways more tragic than the circumstances in the South. King was showing the nation, indeed the world, that racism was pervasive in American society whether it be the South or the North. While King wanted to confront the South African government and expose the racial divide in Chicago, Robert Kennedy believed that the U.S. government could do more to help Americans.

At the start of 1966, Senator Robert Kennedy toured the Bedford-Stuyvesant neighborhood in Brooklyn, New York, to assess the issues in that area. Many of the people whom he visited were fed up, dealing with everyday issues that beleaguered their lives. "We've been studied to death," one person said of the visit. "I am weary of study, Senator, very weary," Civil Court Judge Thomas Jones said. "The Negro people are angry, Senator, and judge that I am, I'm angry too," he said. One five-year-old boy answered the door to Kennedy's knock. When Kennedy asked why he wasn't in school, the five-year-old replied, "I went," and slammed the door in his face. Kennedy stressed that more direction and leadership from the city would make a difference in that area.[7] Not long after this visit, Kennedy gave a speech on how the government could make a difference in these impoverished situations.

In a revitalization of liberalism, Robert Kennedy spoke out on how government could help people as they struggled. Like King in Chicago, Kennedy was trying to reexamine the strategies that have been employed and find better solutions to the problems that confronted the nation. Kennedy declared in February, "We stand at a new crossroads to an uncertain future. The way ahead is not charted. We know only that it will be filled with difficulty and danger." While he believed that the ideals of the New Deal had been upheld by the Great Society, Kennedy wanted to see more done. "There is not a problem for which there is not a program. There is not a problem for which money is not being spent." He asked, "But does this represent a solution to our problems? Manifestly it does not." Kennedy envisioned a different world and believed that Americans could do more to create that reality.

> We have spent ever-increasing amounts on our schools. Yet far too many children still graduate totally unequipped to contribute to themselves, their families, or the communities in which they live.... We have spent unprecedented sums on buildings of all kinds. Yet our communities seem less beautiful and sensible every year. We have spent billions on agricultural price supports. Yet the rural economy continues to decline.... We have spent billions on armaments and on foreign aid. Yet the world is still unsafe, and our position more precarious and painful as time goes by.

Kennedy asked, "Why is this so?" The answer speaks to the notion that the solution to problems is deeper than legislation. "Money by itself is no answer," he said. "There are things more important than spending. Their names are imagination, courage and determination." He furthered his notions by stating that "candor" was the fourth and gave his opinion on the programs that the nation was employing to help others.[8]

Kennedy criticized the welfare system saying that the more important way to help people was to help them attain "decent, dignified jobs." He also said that schools needed to revamp their systems. "If our present educational methods cannot do better, then they must be changed to fit the student, just as doctors change a treatment which fails to cure a sick patient. We must now regard a student's failure as the school's failure, and as our failure—and hold ourselves responsible for our children's shortcomings." Kennedy, like King, believed that society was connected, that in order to achieve success everyone has to contribute to the solutions. "There is no question which does not require the same new thinking, the same willingness to dare," he said.

Kennedy finished his speech saying, "It is not easy, in the middle of one's life or political career, to say that the old horizons are too limited, that our education must begin again, that new visions must replace the old if our vitality is to remain and be renewed." He concluded that "surely we must be determined to do this."[9] Kennedy's vision for the future meant examining the old ways of doing things, stretching his mind and attacking these problems with new innovative solutions. Kennedy not only found his voice as 1966 continued, but he also offered people hope that there would be solutions for the problems that plagued their lives and that was more valuable than all the money committed to new programs.

II

"To walk the final mile toward peace."

While the issues in northern cities were something that both Kennedy and King were confronting, the war in Vietnam was something else that they believed needed to be reexamined. In December 1965, Kennedy commented at a party at Hickory Hill, "We're in a stalemate [in Vietnam]." He was reported to have said, "I'd like to speak out more on Vietnam. I have talked again and again on my desire for negotiations. But if I broke with the administration it might be disastrous for the country."[10] Kennedy made good on that comment and rose on the floor of the Senate on January 31 to say

> If we regard bombing as the answer in Vietnam we are headed straight for disaster. In the past, bombing has not proved a decisive weapon against a rural economy—or against a guerrilla army. And the temptation will now be to argue that if limited bombing does not produce a solution, that further bombing, more extended military action, is the answer. The danger is that the decision to resume may become the first in a series of steps on a road from which there is no turning back—a road which leads to catastrophe for all mankind.[11]

Kennedy was testing the waters to make a greater statement on his position in Vietnam. Kennedy had already articulated in public comments that he wanted to see a different approach to the war in Vietnam.

On February 19 Kennedy issued a press release that outlined his strategy for the war in Vietnam. At the heart of the statement was the notion that the nation needed to invite leaders of the Vietcong to the negotiation table for peace. "Democracy is no easy form of government," Kennedy expressed in the statement. He went on to say that debate was essential for the success of a democracy. "Men must seek acceptance of their views through reason, and not through intimidation; through argument and not through accusation," he said. "We are all patriots here.... We are all Americans." Kennedy wrote that attacking the motives of people who spoke out against the Vietnam War "is to strike at the foundations of the democratic process which our fellow citizens, even today, are dying in order to protect."[12] The beginning of this statement was an impassioned argument about the foundation of the democratic process and the importance in maintaining a discussion of ideas. It was meant to inspire as well as to awaken people to the fact that there are other ways to approach the problems that the nation confronts every day.

Kennedy's statement went on to directly deal with the Vietnam War. "All of us are concerned, as the American people are concerned, about the progress of the struggle in Vietnam," he wrote. Kennedy went on to list the different concerns of what was foremost on his mind. "We are concerned at the casualties, the death and suffering of our young men in Vietnam." He went further and questioned the tactics of the Johnson administration and the effects it had on the people of Vietnam, saying, "We are concerned over the effect of some of our military action on the people of South Vietnam—whether more cannot be done to lessen the death and destruction of the innocent that comes with war. For a military victory at the cost of a completely destroyed South Vietnam would be a defeat for our larger purposes." Kennedy and King were some of the first major public figures to speak about the effect that the war was having on the people who lived in Vietnam. While Kennedy was not saying that the United States had to withdraw, he was suggesting an approach that was not the usual Cold War rhetoric, which points to the change in the times and how he was a leader of it.

Robert Kennedy had always advocated for an approach that gave the South Vietnamese a different, better government than the one that Ho Chi Minh was offering. "We are concerned whether the people of South Vietnam are being offered something positive to live and fight for—something beyond negative anticommunism." He went on to speak about the turmoil that the war had created at home, "which could split our society irrevocably" and that "the war perpetuates discrimination—for the poor and less fortunate serve in Vietnam."[13] Those comments alone were enough to strike at the core of Johnson's approach to the Vietnam War. He went further, offering a solution that few people considered.

Kennedy stressed the need for a "negotiated settlement." Kennedy went on to talk about the major differences on both sides of the war and that neither side was willing to compromise. "It may be that negotiation is not possible in this war because our political aims are irreconcilable; because one side, or both sides, are not willing to accept anything less than the fruits of victory." Going back to the heart of his message, which he expressed at the start of the statement, "If that is so, then we must reluctantly let slip the hope of reasoned discussion and proceed to the uncertain, uncharted course of war."[14] Kennedy offered what he called a "middle way" to achieve success in this conflict for both sides.

Kennedy believed that in order to be successful in a negotiated settlement, the United States had to recognize the National Liberation Front (NLF) as a party at the table for peace. He stressed that "to admit to a share of the power and responsibility—is at the heart of the hope for a negotiated settlement." While Kennedy stated that this process needed international guarantee, it could result in a compromise that neither side wanted, and "such a settlement would not end our burden or our vigilance in Vietnam." He concluded by talking about how the United States needed to adapt its methods in order to be successful, and if the nation could accomplish this with little force, "then there is hope that [these objectives] may be achieved without prohibitive costs to ourselves, to the people of Vietnam, or to the peace of the world." His acknowledgment of other methods to achieve peace is another example of his evolution from a "cold warrior" to someone who advocated for peace rather than force. He stated that if they tried to follow this course then at least the nation was realistic and reasonable in their approach. "And we will have worked to meet our responsibilities to our posterity—to walk the final mile toward peace, not so much for ourselves, but for those who come after."[15]

The day after Kennedy's statement, the *New York Times* reported that Kennedy's "suggestion is almost certain to have far reaching repercussions. It marks a dramatic policy break with the administration as well as with two former Cabinet colleagues—Secretary of State Dean Rusk and Secretary of Defense Robert S. McNamara—who were appointed by his brother, President Kennedy." The *Times* went on to report that General Maxwell Taylor, an adviser to President Johnson and a close friend to Robert Kennedy, opposed the compromise and said to the Senate Foreign Relations Committee that "the objective of the United States was to apply enough military power to force the Communists to accept an independent and non–Communist South Vietnam." The *Times* article also reported that Kennedy had learned important lessons from the Cuban missile crisis and believed that some of that thinking applied to this circumstance. "If our objective had been much greater than it was there would have been war," Kennedy was reported to have said of the crisis. "It is always necessary to realize what an opponent can accept and what he cannot retreat from."[16]

George Ball and McGeorge Bundy, who were both appointed by President Kennedy, appeared on *Meet the Press* that Sunday and said that they opposed Robert Kennedy's proposal. In his book *Robert F. Kennedy and His Times*, Arthur Schlesinger quoted a letter that Bobby wrote to Bundy but later deleted the passage: "I would have obviously appreciated a call before you dealt with [my position] and me on Sunday afternoon. Perhaps a call would not have taken any more time than for someone to look up the quote of President Kennedy to use against my position." Instead of the letter, Kennedy called Bundy. Bundy responded by saying that a call would have been nice from him as well.[17] Robert Kennedy appeared on *Face the Nation* a week later and said, "that we will never deal with assassins or murderers makes it difficult for [the other side] to believe that they are being asked to come to the negotiating table for anything other than to surrender." Vice President Hubert Humphrey responded saying that the Vietcong "engage in assassination, murder, pillage, conquest, and I can't for the life of me see why the United States of America would want to propose that such an outfit be made part of any government."[18]

While Kennedy's plea to bring the NLF to the table angered some in the Democratic Party and the nation, there were other Democratic leaders who welcomed the statement. According to the *Times*, "some self-described liberals who formerly regarded him as a ruthless, cold-blooded and even unprincipled political operator now look to him increasingly as the symbol and exponent of their dissatisfactions with the Johnson administration." One politician said that Kennedy was "the only one with the strength and independence to stand up to Johnson." According to David Broder, the reporter who wrote the article, many in the left wing of the Democratic Party believed that Kennedy's statement was a major gain to "escalate the Vietnam debate in intraparty politics."[19] Kennedy continued his argument for a negotiated settlement with little success. "I made some mistakes in handling it.... I think it was unpopular politically. But I would do it all over again if I had to," Kennedy said later.[20]

Kennedy's opposition to the Johnson administration's handling of the Vietnam War is another example of his evolution as a leader. He came into his own and was trying to tell the government that the current policy would not be successful. It was from his comments that Martin Luther King sent Kennedy a note saying that Kennedy had "expressed a political philosophy for an era."[21] Kennedy's commitment to peace and negotiation were prevailing elements of his plea to the people of the United States. To be sure, his comments on the Senate floor opposing the bombing were at the heart of this political statement. Kennedy wanted to end the bloodshed but also keep American prestige. Indeed, the United States was at a crossroads in Vietnam in 1966. If the Johnson administration had followed Kennedy's advice, the war might have ended differently.

III

"We ourselves must change in order to master change."

Besides Vietnam, the racial tension and impoverished conditions in the urban centers of the nation continued to be something that both King and Kennedy commented on. Martin Luther King continued his efforts in Chicago. King embraced the slogan "End Slums" hoping to gain the support of volunteers in the city and from elsewhere. However, it seemed that by March, the movement was still trying to find a program that would confront these issues directly. "We haven't gotten things under control. The strategy hasn't emerged yet, but now we know what we are dealing with and eventually we'll come up with the answers," Andrew Young said.[22] King had plans to go to Europe, but before he left he made stops in Hartford, Bridgeport, Detroit and Dallas to raise funds for his program. He commented at one of these events, "Slums with hundreds of thousands of living units are not as easily eradicated as lunch counters or buses are integrated." To be sure his movement spoke to the pervasive issues of poverty that had plagued American society. He also said, "A stage has been reached in which the reality of equality will require extensive adjustments in the way of life of some of the white majority."[23] King's movement looked to upend the white establishment, and it would be a difficult road to accomplish such a feat in a short period of time. By March he had only been in Chicago for three months.

On March 31, King made remarks in Stockholm, Sweden. He said that he was "deeply moved by this magnificent demonstration of good will and support for the cause of racial justice in America. Never before has an entire nation come forth with such total commitment to our cause." He referred to John Donne's poem "For Whom the Bell Tolls," as he did on other occasions, to demonstrate the solidarity of mankind. King acknowledged the success in the South with trepidation, saying, "We have come a long way, but still have a long way to go." He referred to his "I Have a Dream" speech and what he had hoped for African Americans in the nation whom he spoke to.

> Since that time several tragic events have turned that dream into a nightmare, for I watched millions of my black brothers slowly perishing on an island of poverty in the midst of a sea of affluence. I watched in horror as Ku Klux Klan violence reared its ugly head and streaming death upon four innocent little girls as they sat in Sunday school and brutally murdering unarmed, non-violent civil rights workers in Mississippi and Alabama.

King's recollection of those tragedies brought into sharp focus just how much the movement had to endure in order to bring about the change that would define the nation for the sixties and into the twenty-first century. He went further talking about the Watts riots and the issues that African Americans had to endure every day. Despite these challenges and tragedies, King said, "I awaken from these nightmares of chaos and hostility and begin to fashion a new reality of love and brotherhood amid the rubble of hatred and bitterness, for I still have a dream."[24]

King told the audience about the dream that he still had for America. He said, "I still have a dream that one day all men will have food and material necessities for their bodies, education and culture for their minds, freedom and dignity for their spirits." He echoed the issues of poverty that he was confronting in Chicago saying that he hoped that "one day we will no longer walk the streets in search of jobs that do not exist and return at night to houses filled with rats, roaches and fallen plaster." He believed that one day integration would be possible and seen as "an opportunity to participate in the beauty of diversity." He stressed that his vision for the world was inclusive of everyone.

> I still have a dream that one day black men and brown men, yellow men and white men, Protestant, Catholic and Jew, Believer and atheist will coexist in a world where men are judged only by the content of their character rather than the color of their skin or the nature of heritage. And where brotherhood is more than just a meaningless word at the end of a prayer, but the first order of business on every legislative agenda.

He concluded saying that he hoped war would be eradicated and justice would rule the day.[25] His vision was something that endured in the wake of the tragedy that he spoke of in the beginning of his remarks. It was an example of his steadfast, determined and visionary approach to the problems that plagued the United States and the world.

King had hoped to give lectures in South Africa on his trip overseas, but he was denied a visa from that government. The South African government maintained its state-sanctioned segregation even with foreigners. "This is an expression of the continuing policies of totalitarianism in South

Africa," King said. "It is an expression that democracy is not alive at all in that country."²⁶ Robert Kennedy would not have the same luck, and a couple of months later, he would express the message to the South African people that King had hoped to bring. Before that, however, Robert Kennedy would return to a place where he made enemies when he was attorney general—Mississippi.

Despite the fact that there were threats to Robert Kennedy's life, he decided to accept an invitation to speak at the University of Mississippi Law School in March 1966. When he got off the plane there were about 150 people who welcomed him. Among those people was a person who called out above the noise, "James Meredith," and then repeated it. When Kennedy heard the person, he stopped, looked squarely at the man and glared at him for a long moment. Over five thousand people came out to see Robert Kennedy speak at the school. The day before, a state legislator rose in debate in Jackson and denounced the visit. He said the senator could potentially be harmed if he went to Mississippi. Kennedy was guarded by the police and FBI agents for the four hours that he spent at Ole Miss.²⁷

Kennedy wanted to impart a message of responsibility to this student group on what it could do to bridge the divide between the North and South. "Your generation—South and North, white and black—is the first with the chance not only to remedy the mistakes which all of us have made in the past, but to transcend them," he said. Kennedy believed that the generation he was speaking to was the future of the nation and they had an opportunity to change it. He emphasized that they needed to "create a society in which Negroes will be as free as other Americans—free to vote, and to earn their way, and to share in the decisions of government which shape their lives." He went on to talk about the impoverished conditions in cities, the modernization of society and how the world had become complicated. "In such a challenging world—such a fantastic and dangerous world—we will not find answers in old dogmas, by repeating outworn slogans, or fighting on ancient battlegrounds against fading enemies long after the real struggle has moved on."²⁸

Kennedy believed, like other great thinkers and leaders, that true change must being within each other. "We ourselves must change in order to master change," he declared. Indeed, Kennedy was at the pinnacle of the evolution that started nearly three years before that moment. Certainly he had come a long way in understanding the great racial dilemma since he was attorney general in 1962 when he had a major standoff with the Mississippi government over the admission of James Meredith to the school. "We must rethink our old ideas and beliefs before they capture and before they destroy us. For those answers America must look to its young people, the children of this time of change." Looking to set the tone for this journey, Kennedy said, "For the answers we seek must be found in the light of reason—by fact and logic and careful thought, unsustained by violent prejudices or by myths."[29]

Kennedy's speech continued his rhetoric that was meant to shape the age, contributing to solutions for the problems that he outlined at the start of the speech and since his brother was assassinated in 1963. "The future will be shaped in the arena of human activity, but those willing to commit their minds and their bodies to the task." The reflective Kennedy invoked Ralph Waldo Emerson and even quoted him, saying, "God gives each of us the choice between truth and repose. Take which you please. You cannot have both." Kennedy empowered the group, giving them a cause to change the world, saying, "You will go as ambassadors of the twentieth century to a past struggling toward the possibilities of the modern world. And in doing so you will serve not only man, but the cause of national growth and of national independence, which is the foundation of a peaceful world order."[30] Kennedy embodied where the nation was headed as they confronted the issues of the twentieth century. The fact that students accepted Kennedy's remarks, given his history with the university, in itself is evidence that his influence continued to affect the period in a myriad of ways. His words were meant to not only empower this group, but to help them see that the North and South were connected as Americans and despite the differences that these two sections may have, they all shared a common ideal implicit within the American experience.

Kennedy emphasized to the students that it would be difficult to usher such change into American society:

> It is more comfortable to sit content in the easy approval of friends and of neighbors than to risk the friction and the controversy that comes with public affairs. It is easier to fall in step with slogans of others than to march to the beat of the internal drummer—to make a stand on judgements of your own. And it is far easier to accept and to stand on the past than to fight for the answers of the future.

Kennedy stressed to the students that the future of the nation was their responsibility. "And each of us will ultimately be judged—and will ultimately judge himself—on the extent to which he personally contributed to the life of this nation and to world society of the kind we are trying to build."[31]

Kennedy brought the speech back to Boston saying that when Jefferson Davis went there he addressed the audience as "countrymen, brethren, Democrats." Referring to the Civil War, he said, "Rivers of blood and years of darkness divide that day from this." He went on, saying, "Those words echo down into this hall, bringing the lesson that only as countrymen and as brothers can we hope to master and subdue to the service of mankind the enormous forces which rage across the world in which all of us live." He concluded, "And only in this way can we pursue our personal talents to the limits of our possibility—not as Northerners or Southerners, black or white—but as men and women in the service of the American dream." Kennedy finished the speech to enormous applause from the students and teachers who attended.[32]

The success of Kennedy's speech speaks to his appeal among students. Indeed, his message was something that would not have been cheered four years prior when he was a part of the effort to admit James Meredith to the school. The reaction from the students is another example of how Kennedy and other civil rights leaders had been able to bridge the racial divide in some circumstances. Those historic victories led to a change in the political climate, which Kennedy continued to promote in the wake of his brother's death. Arthur Schlesinger wrote, "The trip confirmed [Kennedy's] conviction that the next battle for racial justice lay in the northern city." Robert Kennedy acknowledged that there were many in the nation who "hate my guts" because of his record on civil rights. He also acknowledged that the victories in the South to secure equal rights in public accommodations and the vote were "an easy job compared to what we face in the North."[33]

IV

"Only those who dare to fail greatly, can ever achieve greatly."

The greatest example of Robert Kennedy's ability to understand the plight of others and that he had achieved his own vision for the nation, indeed the world, was outlined in what has been termed his "Day of Affirmation" speech that he gave in South Africa. The speech brought together all of the ideas that drove him in the days following his brother's death, entwining his and Martin Luther King's vision as they moved into the final act of their lives, enjoining fundamental ideals that shaped the nation in the wake of their deaths, inspiring others to continue that message. His vision was palpable and rooted in the historic struggles of Americans as well as his own plight to create a legacy while at the same time building on his brother's ideals. It was the greatest speech of his life.

Ian Robertson, a young medical student and president of the National Union of South African Students (NUSAS), extended an invitation to Robert Kennedy to speak at the annual Day of Reaffirmation of Academic and Human Freedom at the University of Cape Town. After some delay, Kennedy's visa was granted in March 1966. He could come to speak, but the visit could only last four days. In addition, it had to be in June and not May, which he had originally requested. Robertson was subsequently "banned" for five years for inviting Kennedy and was not able to be present at the speech. Kennedy took time to read and acquaint himself with the issues that were pervasive in South Africa. He especially wanted to address racism. He asked one group in London, where he stopped briefly on his way to Africa, for advice. He acknowledged that this was a difficult situation and he needed to tread lightly. Kennedy said, "It's easy to make speeches that would win votes in New York, but that won't help the Africans—it might even be harmful. What can I say that will really be useful to them?"[34]

Robert and Ethel Kennedy came off the plane into Johannesburg on June 4, 1966. The crowd screamed in approval as he walked off the plane. As the crowd came toward him, they got so close that they tore off his cuff links. "We are, like you, a people of diverse origins," he said to the crowd. "And we too have a problem, though less difficult than yours, of learning to live together, regardless of origins, in mutual respect for the rights and well being of all our people." He expressed to the crowd that he was there to "exchange views" and wanted to work with them to "meet the challenges of our time." He concluded saying that he hoped "above all, to learn; and I thank you for giving me the opportunity to do so."[35]

Before Kennedy gave his first major address he met with Ian Robertson and gave him a copy of *Profiles of Courage*, which he and Jacqueline Kennedy had autographed for him. Kennedy chose Cape Town University's Jameson Hall to give his speech. He went to the hall on June 6, 1966. The people crowded the path for Senator Kennedy, and it took a half hour before it was cleared. The venue was sold out. As Kennedy made his way to the stage, there was an empty chair there in honor of Robertson, who was not allowed to come to the speech.[36] Kennedy's words were meant to inspire and help the people of South Africa who were battling a vicious, racist government. In addition to that, Kennedy demonstrated to the world that he was able to stand up to a government that took away the rights of the people with his words, not the military, which was a big part of his brother's legacy.

In an effort to demonstrate the connection between South Africa and the United States, Kennedy started his speech speaking of his "deep interest and affection" for a nation that had ties to the Dutch and was once taken over by the British only to gain independence. He went on, describing

> a land in which the native inhabitants were at first subdued, but relations with whom remain a problem to this day; a land which defined itself on a hostile frontier; a land which has tamed rich natural resources through the energetic application of modern technology; a land which was once the importer of slaves, and now must struggle to wipe out the last traces of that former bondage.[37]

He then told the crowd that he was referring to the United States of America. The roaring applause from the audience demonstrated how successful he was at capturing the essence of the struggle that plagued both the United States and South Africa. His ability to connect with the people was astounding and set the stage for a meaningful dialogue.

Kennedy went as far as to say, "I am making an effort to meet and exchange views with people of all walks of life, and all segments of South African opinion—including those who represent the views of the government." While he was clearly speaking out against the policy of that government, Kennedy understood the need for diplomacy and that there were many stakeholders at the table when trying to bring about meaningful change. When he acknowledged Ian Robertson, there was more applause. "I wish to thank him for his kindness to me in inviting me. I am very sorry that he can not be with us here this evening." By doing that Kennedy made it clear that he supported Robertson but also understood that he was an outsider to this country. What followed was a discussion about liberty and the rights of individual people.

"This is a Day of Affirmation—a celebration of liberty. We stand here in the name of freedom," Kennedy said. He went on to define that the heart of freedom and democracy "is the belief that the individual man, the child of God, is the touchstone of value, and all society, all groups, and states, exist for that person's benefit." With that in mind he turned to the concept of liberty and its importance to society. "Therefore the enlargement of liberty for individual human beings must be the supreme goal and the abiding practice of any western society."[38] To be sure, liberty was at the heart of America's history and foundation. While he acknowledged at the start of the speech that America struggled with similar race issues, he also stressed that at the heart of the struggle for equality and human rights was the concept of liberty, which had been defined by the founders of the United States for America.

Kennedy went on to speak about the elements of liberty within society. He stated that freedom of speech was an important element of the individual liberty that he was talking about.

> The right to express and communicate ideas, to set oneself apart from the dumb beasts of field and forest; the right to recall governments to their duties and obligations; above all, the right to affirm one's membership and allegiance to the body politic—to society—to the men with whom we share our land, our heritage and our children's future.

For Kennedy freedom of speech brought with it the power to be heard by the government and even the world. The people could share in the power of the government through freedom of speech. With that power came the ability for the people to secure its freedom to worship, to be secure in one's home or from arbitrary punishment. Kennedy stressed, "Therefore, the essential humanity of man can be protected and preserved only where the government must answer—not just to the wealthy; not just to those of a particular religion, not just to those of a particular race; but to all of the people."[39]

Stressing the power of the government to uphold rights and not take them away, Kennedy went into the power of the Constitution saying that the government "must be limited in its power to act against its people ... so that each man may become all that he is capable of becoming." He stressed that "these are the sacred rights of western society. These were the essential differences between us and Nazi Germany as they were between Athens and Persia." He went further and talked about communism, his opposition and how it took away the individual liberty and freedom that he believed was important for a society to succeed. Speaking directly to the South African government, he said, "The way of opposition to communism, however, is not to imitate its dictatorship, but to enlarge individual human freedom."[40] The room burst into thunderous applause.

Considering the path that the United States had been on with its own racial tension, Kennedy stressed that freedom was something that is hard to attain. However, the United States was moving in the right direction. "And—with painful slowness—we in the United States have extended and enlarged the meaning and the practice of freedom to all of our people," Kennedy said. He continued to offer how his own ancestors were also mistreated. "For two centuries, my own country has struggled to overcome the self-imposed handicap of prejudice and discrimination based on nationality, on social class or race," he said, "discrimination profoundly repugnant to the theory and to the command of our Constitution. Even as my father grew up in Boston, Massachusetts, signs told him that 'No Irish Need Apply.'" This was something that he had consistently gone back to in order to attain some solidarity with the people he was talking to. But the real essence of the comment spoke to the notion that Americans were moving in a direction to give opportunities to people.

Alluding to the impoverished conditions and the opportunities for African Americans, Kennedy made a plea to the people saying that the United States had come a long way but still had much to do to secure rights for all races in the nation.

> For there are millions of Negroes untrained for the simplest of jobs, and thousands every day denied their full and equal rights under the law; and the violence of the disinherited, the insulted and the injured, looms over the streets of Harlem and of Watts and Southside Chicago.[41]

He went on to say, however, that there were jobs ranging from being an astronaut to serving on the courts. This was his way to demonstrate to the people of South Africa that with individual liberty and freedom came opportunity for all to succeed, despite the road that the nation still had to travel.

Kennedy directly referenced Dr. King and his efforts as an example of how African Americans were making a difference in the nation and the world. "Dr. Martin Luther King is the second man of African descent to win the Nobel Peace Prize for his non-violent efforts for social justice between all of the races," he said. Going further with King's philosophy of nonviolence, he stressed, "So the road toward equality of freedom is not easy, and great cost and danger march alongside all of us. We are committed to peaceful and non-violent change and that is important for all to understand—though change is unsettling." He concluded that this needed to happen because it was the right thing to do and he was committed to this type of change.

Nations took different paths to bringing about change, and Kennedy stressed that the United States was not any different in its pursuit of justice. In soaring rhetoric and taking his time with each word, Kennedy stressed that while a nation may take time to come to terms with freedom for its people, he believed that "what is important however is that all nations must march toward increasing freedom; toward justice for all; toward a society strong and flexible enough to meet the demands of all of its people, whatever their race, and the demands of a world of immense and dizzying change that face us all." In an effort to demonstrate solidarity with the people and the world, Kennedy talked about his trip on the plane from the United States. From that bird's-eye view, he said, "We could see no national boundaries, no vast gulfs or high walls dividing people from people; only nature and the works of man—homes and factories and farms—everywhere reflecting man's common effort to enrich his life."[42]

Technology and innovative methods to communicate had made the world smaller. This technology was something that transcended societies, opening new perspectives for all people throughout the world. In a similar way that Dr. King used John Donne's poetry, Kennedy said, "The concerns of one inevitably become the concerns of all." To further this notion that the world was connected and that focusing on differences led to further problems with society, he said, "And our new closeness is stripping away the false masks, the illusion of differences which is at the root of injustice and hate and war." He concluded, "Only earthbound man still clings to the dark and poisoning superstition that his world is bounded by the nearest hill, his universe ends at the river's shore, his common humanity is enclosed in the tight circle of those who share his town or his views and the color of his skin." This was his vision for the nation, indeed the world. He wanted people to see each other for who they were and the talents that they could offer, not the color of one's skin or their socioeconomic level. He envisioned a world where humanity confronted evil together, not as separate entities.

The speech went into some detail on apartheid, communist Russia and other instances in the world where people's rights were taken from them by the government. "They reflect the imperfections of human justice, the inadequacy of human compassion, the defectiveness of our sensibility toward the sufferings of our fellows; they mark the limit of our ability to use knowledge for the well-being of our fellow human beings throughout the world." While he was clearly outlining his views of justice and how they relate to liberty and freedom, Kennedy was also making it clear to the world that the new doctrine of justice and equal treatment under the law was a fundamental piece of society. To be sure he was speaking not only to the South African government, but also communist Russia, the racist politicians in the United States and other groups around the world that continuously took away the rights of the minority in an effort to strengthen the positions of the majority. His vision is something that the world continues to strive for in the twenty-first century.

Kennedy spoke about independent nations and a world that had an "international community" that respected "basic human freedoms." He wanted South Africa to play a role in that world, providing leadership and knowledge. However, he acknowledged that it would be difficult for the United States and South Africa to provide that leadership if both countries continued to "deny individual integrity, human dignity, and the common humanity of man." As he had brought up in the past, Kennedy believed that the young people of the world had a special role to play in this leadership role

> Our answer is the world's hope; it is to rely on youth. The cruelties and the obstacles of this swiftly changing planet will not yield to obsolete dogmas and outworn slogans. It cannot be moved by those who cling to a present which is already dying, who prefer the illusion of security to the excitement and danger which comes with even the most peaceful progress.

He said that young people had certain qualities that could lead this transition and start the path to a new world. "This world demands the qualities of youth: not a time of life but a state of mind, a temper of the will, a quality of imagination, a predominance of courage over timidity, of the appetite for adventure over the life of ease." Indeed, this speech was a culmination of Kennedy's rhetoric from the last three years and embodied much of what he hoped for the world. He wanted to be a part of that change and inspire others to follow. From this point, Kennedy outlined what he believed were the most effective ways to bring about the change and the leadership that the world needed to succeed.

After acknowledging that such change in the status quo was wrought with danger, Kennedy laid out what he believed would be the biggest problems that young people would have to confront as they ushered in this change. The first of these dangers was "futility; the belief there is nothing one man or one woman can do against the enormous array of the world's ills—against misery, against ignorance, or injustice and violence." However, he pointed out that many of the greatest movements started with a single person. He cited Martin Luther, Christopher Columbus and Thomas Jefferson. They moved the world, he said, and so could they. "Few will have the greatness to bend history; but each of us can work to change a small portion of the events, and in the total of all these acts will be written the history of this generation." This was the essence of his message—change the world in small moments and all of them would contribute to a larger outcome.

Kennedy went further with the concept that each person had to contribute to change, saying, "It is from numberless diverse acts of courage such as these that the belief that human history is thus shaped." Adding to the imagery that the acts of one person could have an effect on many, he said,

> Each time a man stands up for an ideal, or acts to improve the lot of others, or strikes out against injustice, he sends forth a tiny ripple of hope, and crossing each other from a million different centers of energy and daring those ripples build a current which can sweep down the mightiest walls of oppression and resistance.

These "ripples" were something that Kennedy would be known for. This is one of his most quoted lines from the speech because it speaks to the essence of what he was trying to accomplish in the wake of his brother's death. To be sure, it captured the nature of how one person can make a difference, which was a message that his brother had as well.

The second danger Kennedy pointed out was one of "expediency; of those who say that hopes and beliefs must bend before immediate necessities. Of course if we must act effectively we must deal with the world as it is. We must get things done." He said that if President Kennedy stood for something that spoke to young people in the world,

> it was the belief that idealism, high aspiration and deep convictions are not incompatible with the most practical and efficient of programs—that there is no basic inconsistency between ideals and realistic possibilities—no separation between the deepest desires of heart and of mind and the rational application of human effort to human problems.

There was no easy way to approach the problems that plagued the world. It took time to confront these issues if there was going to change that lasted generations. He believed that this was the challenge of this generation. "But we also know that only those who dare to fail greatly, can ever achieve greatly," he stressed.

The third danger was timidity. "Few men are willing to brave the disapproval of their fellows, the censure of their colleagues, the wrath of their society. Moral courage is a rarer commodity than bravery in battle or great intelligence." Kennedy proclaimed that it would take someone who was willing to stand up for ideals. The "moral courage" that Kennedy defined was an essential "vital quality for those who seek to change the world which yields most painfully to change." In the style of Theodore Roosevelt, Kennedy encouraged people to contribute to solutions. "I believe that in this generation those with the courage to enter the conflict will find themselves with companions in every corner of the world."

The final and fourth danger was one of "comfort; the temptation to follow the easy and familiar path of personal ambition and financial success so grandly spread before those who have the privilege of an education." Kennedy told the audience, "But that is not the road history has marked out for us." The times, according to Kennedy, were interesting and it would take people who were willing to confront issues to make a difference. "They are times of danger and uncertainty; but they are also the most creative of any time in the history of mankind," he said. "And everyone here will ultimately be judged—will ultimately judge himself—on the effort he has contributed to building a new world society and the extent to which his ideals and goals have shaped that effort."

Kennedy finished the speech saying they both went back to the work in their respective countries. "We are—if a man of forty can claim the privilege—fellow members of the world's largest younger generation. Each of us have our own work to do." He went on to foster solidarity with the group. "I know at times you must feel very alone with your problems and with your difficulties," he said.

> But I want to say how impressed I am with what you stand for and for the effort you are making; and I say this not just for myself, but men and women all over the world. And I hope you will often take heart from the knowledge that you are joined with your fellow young people in every land, they struggling with their problems and you with yours, but all joined in a common purpose; that, like the young people of my own country and of every country that I have visited, you are all in many ways more closely united to the brothers of your time than to the older generation in any of these nations; you are determined to build a better future.[43]

This appeal to the young and fostering a shared brotherhood was how he wanted to conclude this speech in the hopes of empowering them to continue the work to confront injustice. He finished with a quote from his brother's inaugural address and thanked them. They applauded him as he left the stage.

The Day of Affirmation speech is an example of Robert Kennedy's evolution as a crusader of the disadvantaged. In this case, there is no doubt that he is committed to vanquishing racism and discrimination. The *New York Times* applauded the speech, and President Johnson issued a similar statement regarding the apartheid policy. The *New York Times* declared that the statements of these two men are evidence that "the United States is now committed irrevocably to building a nonracial society."[44] Kennedy continued his tour through Africa, making statements with the same message as he had in the Day of Affirmation speech. On one stop after a speech, he stood on top of car and sang "We Shall Overcome" with the crowd, a song that the South African government did not approve of.[45]

PART IV. VISIONS OF AMERICA, 1967-1968

13

"A Coalition of Conscience"

I

"When I die I'm going to die for something."

On the same day that Kennedy gave his Day of Affirmation speech, James Meredith was on his way from Tennessee to Mississippi on his "March against Fear." When he reached Hernando, Mississippi, Aubrey Norvell shouted, as he moved the reporters and people around Meredith aside, "I only want James Meredith!" He raised his sixteen-gauge shotgun and fired into Meredith three times. He surrendered and appeared to be intoxicated. The news reported Meredith's death at 6:33pm only to make a correction saying that Meredith was in surgery at 7:08pm.[1] People arrived to continue what would be called the Meredith March. It would be a moment in the movement that contributed to the division between nonviolent and violent protest.

Robert Kennedy, who was still in Africa, heard about the shooting and commented to the *New York Times* that he was "shocked and saddened" by it. Of course, Kennedy was attorney general when Meredith challenged the Ole Miss systems of segregation. He also said that he hoped that Meredith would recover quickly from his wounds.[2] As Robert Kennedy made his way through Africa, Martin Luther King, Jr., continued his own trek through the urban areas of the North in the hopes of making the same difference he did in the South. In the wake of the Meredith shooting in June, and as a part of the continued march, King took his message to Yazoo City, Mississippi. He called Mississippi a "terrible state" and said the "Negro in Mississippi is totally poverty stricken." He said that this was true all over the state. In addition to that, "Mississippi will kill people," he said. He brought in Emmett Till, Medgar Evers and the three Freedom Summer civil rights workers. "They shot James Meredith on Highway Fifty-One of this state. And so in Mississippi murder is a popular pasttime," King said. He asked the crowd, "What are you going to do about it? What are you going to do about these terrible injustices engulfing this total state?"[3]

King challenged the group by saying that some people have just accepted this situation in Mississippi and not challenged it. "Some of them have become Uncle Toms and Nervous Nellies," he said. Some, he said, see it as an insurmountable obstacle that could never be changed. King said that it was not right for people to accept this situation and do nothing. "Because if you allow your brother to engage in evil acts you allow him to oppress you, to segregate you, to beat you and kill you and then you go around making him think that you are satisfied with it," King said. He went on to say, "Then you are just as much involved in the perpetuation of the evil as the man who commits the evil." King wanted people to stand up to the racist policies of Mississippi. "We are our brother's keeper," he said.

In this speech, King emphasized that in order to secure equal rights they were going to need the help of many people. He stressed that people needed to work together.

> We are ten percent of the population of this nation, and it would be foolish for me to stand up and tell you we are going to get our freedom by ourselves. There's going to have to be a coalition of conscience, as we aren't going to be free here in Mississippi and anywhere in the United States until there is committed empathy on the part of the white man of this country, and he comes to see along with us that segregation degenerates him as much as it does the Negro.

In addition to seeking a coalition of conscience, King made it clear that violence was not the way to gain these rights. "I would be misleading you if I made you feel that we could win a violent campaign. It's impractical to even think about it," King said. People would be killed unnecessarily, he said to the crowd. "When I die I'm going to die for something, and at that moment, I guess, it will be necessary ... we have a power, we can't win violently."[4]

King focused on the use of nonviolent protest and highlighted its success in places like Birmingham. "We are going to win," he told the audience to applause. "We are going to win right here in Mississippi." He wanted to keep the movement as a nonviolent one. "Don't worry about getting your guns tonight. Don't worry about your molotov cocktails tonight. You have something more powerful and if you work with it, morning will come." The speech came at a time when Stokely Carmichael, in the wake of the shooting, started to invoke "Black Power," which was something that Martin Luther King did not agree with. When the two leaders were asked about the meaning of the phrase by the press, Carmichael said, "I mean that the only way that black people in Mississippi will create an attitude where they will not be shot down like pigs, where they will not be shot down like dogs, is when they get the power where they constitute a majority in counties to institute justice." King commented in the same interview, "I feel, however, that while believing firmly that power is necessary, that it would be difficult for me to use the phrase black power because of the connotative meaning that it has for many people."⁵

The Meredith March turned bloody very quickly, and from its ashes the Black Power and Black Nationalist movements gained momentum. People wanted to see action from someone. The Highway Patrol told the marchers that they could not set up tents on the roadside. King spoke to the marchers from the flatbed of a pickup truck. "I don't know what they have planned for us, but we aren't going to fight any state troopers." Carmichael took the microphone and said, "The time for running has come to an end! You tell them white folks in Mississippi that all the scared niggers are dead!" Just after the speeches, there were loud pops of tear gas in the air. "Nobody leave," King yelled. "Nobody fight back. We're going to stand our ground." What happened has been compared to the Selma beatings. The tear gas blanketed the area and people were clubbed and kicked and the tents were confiscated. King was questioned later whether his ideals of nonviolence still applied to the movement. He held firm. "I still feel that we've got to be nonviolent."⁶

Gene Roberts of the *New York Times* wrote that the Black Power movement "grew out of six years of cumulative anger on the part of student committee members." He went on to write that the "anger was given fuel by incident after incident, disappointment after disappointment, in the drive for civil rights." This new slogan was something that the Student Nonviolent Coordinating Committee had adopted in the wake of the tragedies that had befallen so many civil rights advocates in such a short time. This new "black consciousness" was a philosophy that had "Malcolm X as its prophet but its own war cry, 'black power,' and a new slogan directed at whites: 'Move on over, or we'll move on over you.'"⁷ This new approach to the movement was something that continued to stymie the efforts of Dr. King and others to keep the movement a nonviolent one.

II

"We need each other."

After the "Meredith March," King focused his efforts on his program in Chicago, which led to a greater understanding of the issues that many in the inner city had to deal with on a daily basis. Speaking at Soldier Field in 98 degree heat on July 10, King looked to challenge the administration of Mayor Richard Daley. The SCLC believed that there were forty-five thousand people in attendance, while the police believed that there were thirty thousand. King and Congress of Racial Equality (CORE) leader Floyd McKissick spoke not only about the issues that they planned to confront in Chicago, but also about the growing schism in the movement between militancy and nonviolence.[8]

"We are here today because we are tired. We are tired of being seared in the flames of withering injustice. We are tired of living in rat-infested slums," King started his speech. He also emphasized that there was a sense of urgency to addressing these problems in the inner city. "Now is the time to open the door of opportunity to all of God's children. Now is the time to end the long and desolate night of slumism." He continued his belief that they needed to act soon and used rhetoric that was successful in his southern campaigns. "Freedom is never voluntarily granted by the oppressor," he said. "It must be demanded by the oppressed." He told the people that they should not wait for President Johnson, the Supreme Court or Mayor Daley to give them freedom. "These forces will only respond when they realize that we have a powerful determination to be free.... So, we must go out with grim and bold determination to free ourselves." King's message was meant to empower the people but also to affirm that nonviolence was the way to confront the problems that they faced.

King understood that violence would only further divide the people of the nation, making it difficult to gain the coalition that he strived for to bring about lasting social change. "We must work passionately and unrelentingly for first class citizenship, but we must never use second class citizenship to get it," he told the crowd. "I understand our impatience. We have been victims of so many broken promises and deferred dreams." He went on to address the "discontent" and "nagging frustrations," saying, "We are the victims of a crisis of disappointment." To be sure, King was there for many of those disappointments and understood the issues as well as any black man from the sixties. Despite that, he wanted to maintain his philosophy. "But I must reaffirm that I do not see the answer to our problems in violence. Our movement's adherence to nonviolence has been a major factor in the creation of a moral climate that has made progress possible." King believed that the climate that he worked so hard to create was at risk and addressed the militant rhetoric of Carmichael and others. "This climate may well be dissipated not only by acts of violence but by the threats of it verbalized by those who equate it with militancy."[9] King struggled to maintain his own philosophy in light of the growing discontent that the nation was enduring at the time.

King's message was struggling to survive in an era where people wanted action and justice for the frequent abuses of power. He said that the power of the movement was not in violence. "Our power is in our unity, the force of our souls, and the determination of our bodies." He concluded, "This is a force that no army can overcome, for there is nothing more powerful in all the world than the surge of unarmed truth." He said that he had watched the power of this philosophy make a difference in the movement. "I watched it crush the sagging walls of bus segregation on Montgomery, Alabama. I watched it stand before violent dogs and powerful water hoses in Birmingham, Alabama with a strength and endurance that forced the nation to write a revolutionary civil rights bill."[10] King's message was important as the nation moved in a vital period in its awakening since the Kennedy assassination.

The violence of the 1960s had the potential to irrevocably alter the fabric of American society. To be sure, this violence challenged notions of democracy and free speech as groups pushed forward to craft a new society that included everyone and challenged the government's role in Vietnam. King wanted people to approach this challenge peacefully. "Nonviolence does not mean doing nothing," he said. "It does not mean passively accepting evil. It means standing up so strongly with your body and soul that you can not stoop to the low places of violence and hatred." King's words were for the people of Chicago, but they had reverberations throughout a movement that was struggling to agree on a method to challenge the racial tension in the nation. King looked for cooperation and even advocated in this speech working with white people as they tried to solve these issues. "So, let us all, white and black alike, see that we are tied to a single garment of destiny. We need each other," he said.[11] After the speech King ceremoniously taped his list of fourteen demands to the door of a locked city hall, which was an homage to his namesake, Martin Luther, who nailed his 95 theses to a church door in 1517.[12]

King met with Daley on July 11 and left the meeting saying that the mayor did not make any commitments and was forcing King the racial disparity in Chicago. King said that he was "demanding" changes "not requesting" them. Mayor Daley responded, "They have no solutions. It isn't any single problem that can be solved by one person."[13] As the SCLC looked to expand the protest, a series of incidents led to violence. In the midst of the sweltering heat, the city turned off the gushing fire hydrants, which was something that helped cool off the people. Many in that part of the city reacted with violence as three blocks away, in the Italian section, the hydrants continued to gush water for the people. King was losing his ability to keep the demonstrations nonviolent as people walked away from one of his speeches. Gang members continued the violence, which would eventually slow down, until July 13.[14]

Four hundred policemen moved in to stop the violence on the West

Side of Chicago on July 13. It started when the city decided to turn off the fire hydrants once again. Daley was reluctant to call the discord "riots." People were throwing rocks and pieces of asphalt into the street. Policemen formed thirty-two-person wedges, moving up and down the streets saying through a bullhorn, "Get into your houses and stay there or we will arrest you."[15] By July 16 the violence had gotten to levels where Governor Otto Kerner asked for help from the National Guard. The violence culminated, after three nights of rioting, with an exchange of gunfire between police and rioters. Two African Americans were killed, six policemen were wounded, and fifty-one others were injured in the melee that ensued. Dr. King got Mayor Daley to put sprinklers on fire hydrants to cool the people who lived in those neighborhoods. Eight hundred police and 1,500 guardsmen patrolled the streets. Daley blamed some of the SCLC staff for the violence, saying that they came to the city a year prior and told people how to use violent tactics. King said to the press that his statement was "absolutely untrue."[16]

King made a statement on July 17 regarding the violent events of the previous week. He was grateful to the people who worked hard to bring peace to the area, but he did not want to ignore the reasons for the violence in the first place. "I cannot in good conscience praise those whose insensitivity and callousness toward the social ills which plague Negro residents on the west side made it necessary to send military might into the community." King stressed, "It must be remembered that genuine peace is not the absence of tension, but the presence of justice. And at this very moment, justice is not present on Chicago's west side, or for that matter in other slum communities in Chicago." King blamed the city officials for the violence. "Chicago's west side remains an island of despair in one of the most affluent cities of this nation." King said that he pledged "all of the nonviolent resources at my command to work toward the elimination of slum conditions." He went even further saying that he believed that if he had gotten a better response from city hall the previous Sunday, the rioting could have been prevented. "These demands dealt with deprivation in housing, education, job opportunities and welfare, and even at this late hour it is not too late for Chicago's leadership to recognize the aspirations of a despairing people and give them a hand in acquiring them."[17]

King's efforts and the growing racial tension in the nation is evidence of the times and how his peaceful voice was needed in order to keep demonstrations from becoming violent expressions of African Americans who were fed up with impoverished conditions and racist tendencies. He was still looking for that "coalition of conscience" using nonviolent rhetoric to drive his message home not only to the city leaders, but also to African

Americans who were struggling to embrace the notion of peaceful nonviolent direct action. King was hampered by this growing discontent that plagued the movement. As the summer went on, the nation grappled with the growing war in Vietnam and the continuing racial tension.

III

"We need striped power—black and white together."

In October, Kennedy gave a speech about American foreign policy at the Columbus Day dinner at the Waldorf Astoria in New York City. Building on his Day of Affirmation speech, Kennedy showed a great deal of maturity in his vision for the world. "For the first time in five centuries since Columbus," he said, "we have the chance, the power, and the obligation not only to build a great nation for ourselves, but to be powerful, shaping forces in that world from which he came, and in obscure continents we barely know." In what was a very profound observation, Kennedy asked the crowd to suppose that they were from another planet and traversed continents. They would see technological feats, extraordinary cities basked in knowledge and other scientific achievements. "Yet he would also observe that most of mankind was living in misery and hunger, that some of the inhabitants of this tiny, crowded globe were killing others, and that a few patches of land were pointing large instruments of death and war at others." It was a realization that in the midst of celebrating the arrival of the Renaissance to America with the passage of Columbus there was also an aspect of society that was as deadly as the most beautiful art from the Renaissance period. "Since what he was seeing proved our intelligence, he could only wonder at our sanity," Kennedy said.[18]

It was uncommon for a politician during the Cold War to publicly imply that the use of the military against our enemies was insane. Robert Kennedy's vision was not a world where nations fought each other, but one where there was a common understanding and a commitment to peace. "This monstrous absurdity—that in the midst of such possibility, men should hate and kill and oppress one another—that must be the target of the modern American Revolution." America needed to think bigger than being the richest or the strongest nation in the world. "An America piled high with gold, and clothed in impenetrable armor, yet living among desperate and poor nations in a chaotic world, could neither guarantee its own security nor pursue the dream of civilization devoted to the fulfillment of man."[19] Kennedy was a product of World War II and always believed that America was meant to be the strongest superpower in the world. It is clear that as he watched world events while he was attorney general and then senator, he became more in touch with the fact that at its core, the world was connected.

He wanted to see the fortunate members of society help others who were not so fortunate. "It is not permissible to allow most of mankind to live in poverty, stricken by disease, threatened by hunger, and doomed to an early death after a life of painful labor." To be sure the nation had come a long way since the end of the nineteenth century where this hard life was a reality for many Americans. Kennedy believed in America's ability to provide a better life for all of its citizens and he wanted to be a part of the process to make that happen. In a condemnation of the attitude that people can help themselves and find a way on their own, Kennedy said that it was easy for people to say that. "The fact is that the fortunate fraction of mankind now has the technology and the knowledge to improve all of these afflictions, and we must seek huge leaps of imagination and effort to shatter the frustrating and resistant barriers between human capacity and human need." Kennedy's compassion for the "afflicted," as he called them, was something that defined him in those years after the assassination. Indeed, it was a big part of his rhetoric as he moved forward and certainly had a lasting effect on his legacy.

Kennedy invoked ideals that Dr. King had been stressing throughout the civil rights movement, and that is the concept that we are all connected. He said that the nation must find a way to help "dissolve the attitudes which permit men to indulge those passions and ambitions which keep the world in constant conflict, and which threaten the survival of us." He believed that the world needed to understand that in order for there to be true peace, everyone needed to work together. He went on to say that the peace he envisioned was "simply the absence of armed conflict or hostile division. It is the creation among nations of a web of unity, woven from the strands of economic interdependence, political cooperation, and a mounting flow of people and ideas."[20]

Kennedy saw America as the future of the world. "We must, if we seek not merely to lead, but to lead greatly, act consistently with our belief in human freedom and equality. Those are the seminal values of our entire history," he said. The notion of liberty and freedom was something that other nations struggled to define. While he believed that the nation should not "compel other nations to adopt our principles," he stressed that those ideals should be a major piece of U.S. foreign policy. "Yet there should be no doubt that we stand—in Africa, Asia or in Latin America, and in the United States itself, on the side of equality and increasing freedom; never yielding that position to the demands of temporary expediency to short-run realism." He concluded, "If we allow immediate considerations, one by one, to chip away proclaimed ideals and values, then we soon stand for nothing at all, except ourselves." He went further, saying, "Nor should our own success and good fortune allow us to treat with scorn and condescension or lack of understanding those who are struggling to build nations under the crushing weight of instability, desperate economies, and fragile society."[21]

Kennedy's vision for the world was entwined with Dr. King's vision for the nation. It also seemed that Kennedy had embraced not only a world where nations were joined in a common purpose, but that he wanted to foster that attitude at home. This was beyond the usual Cold War rhetoric and signified not only a change in Kennedy's rhetoric but also the attitude of the nation. To be sure, the notion that we are all connected was something that had come out of the nation's struggle to understand the war in Vietnam as well as a growing rights movement that included groups beyond African Americans. America was in the midst of a revolution, and Kennedy's voice complemented King's rhetoric that people needed to work together to find solutions to the problems that plagued American society.

In the same month that Kennedy outlined his vision for American foreign policy, King continued to articulate his own vision for the civil rights movement and how violence was not the answer for greater change in the nation. The constant turmoil and violence that took shape in Chicago during his campaign to expose the impoverished conditions bothered King. He called these developments "very depressing." He went further in an address at the annual conference of the Radio and Television News Directors Association, saying, "We confront desolate days ahead." In a further affirmation of his philosophy, he said, "I'm more convinced than ever that nonviolence is the most effective weapon available to the Negro." He said that he had "not lost faith in the future" and wanted to see a combined effort. In an allusion to "Black Power," he said, "We need striped power — black and white together."[22]

According to an article published by the *New York Times*, King contemplated repudiating Black Power altogether and met with his advisers to decide if they were going to move forward on such a statement. This was a major move for King, as CORE and the SNCC had been embracing the Black Power ideal in the wake of the Meredith March. this that he was isolating two civil rights organizations that he had worked with in the early years of the movement. King was asked if this meant that he would consider starting a campaign in opposition to the SNCC and CORE if they all decide that their ideology did not work with the SCLC, and King responded, "Yes it does."[23] In addition to the article, King was asked to join an advertisement in the *New York Times*, led by Roy Wilkins and A. Philip Randolph, that denounced Black Power. It was titled "Crisis and Commitment." Notably, King did not sign the statement.[24]

After some scrutiny in the press and other groups, Martin Luther King released a statement that supported "Crisis and Commitment" on October 14. King told news reporters that the meeting he was having with advisers of the SCLC to discuss their support had just concluded. King made it clear that he intended to unite the civil rights movement under a "banner of nonviolence." In addition to the issue of Black Power, King and the SCLC were discussing the effects of the Vietnam War.[25] King's statement acknowledged that "the Negro is powerless and it is absolutely necessary for him to amass political and economic power to reach his legitimate goals." He made it clear in the opening lines of the statement that "connotations of violence and separatism attached to the Black Power slogan must be resolutely opposed by the Southern Christian Leadership Conference."[26]

The statement emphasized the power of nonviolence and that the SCLC was founded on that principle and "Negro unity with all people of good will." he emphasized its success at Birmingham, Selma, Montgomery and Chicago. "The nonviolent movement has never resorted to violence or separatism. We are justified, therefore, in reaffirming adherence to our founding principles on both moral and practical grounds." King wanted to stop the division in the movement and focus on nonviolence as the only tactic to combat the racial issues in the nation. "Surrounded by historic prosperity in the white society, taunted by empty promises, humiliated and deprived by the filth and decay of his ghetto home, the manhood of the Negro compels him to demand far reaching immediate changes."[27]

King's acknowledgment of the "anger" that African Americans had been experiencing is representative of the times and the struggle that he was trying to lead. King said that this anger had driven many African Americans to "passive cynicism toward society, for others it has exploded in violence." He went on further to state that it was a "false assumption that the so-called white backlash is caused by the slogan 'Black Power.' Actually the Black Power slogan has been exploited by the decision makers to justify resistance to change."[28] King's role in the movement as an ambassador between the white leadership and civil rights groups is highlighted in this statement. Despite setbacks and growing opposition to his philosophy, he maintained that the only way to achieve equal status was through the use of nonviolence. To help people see that he was committed he went on to outline the major projects of the SCLC.

The programs of the SCLC were meant to empower African Americans through nonviolence. King said that they were looking to "organize the poor in a crusade to reform society in order to realize economic and social justice." He said that he was working with many community organizations to make this happen. In addition to local community organizations, King said he would work with international trade unions, colleges, universities and civil rights groups. He went as far as to endorse A. Philip Randolph's "Freedom Budget," which was a statement to secure income for African Americans. In addition to that, King was committed to "a reconstruction of youth through meaningful training and education." In this case, he was in line with Robert Kennedy, who believed that the youth of the nation were the future and needed to be empowered to help shape the nation as it moved forward.

King also stressed the "political reformation of the south." Interestingly in this statement King said that in the South "political racism is ascendant, and in the north it is merely thinly disguised." King spent some time on the nature of racism and how it comes from the South and its institutions. However, at the heart of this statement was one of power. "The question of power is not as complex and ominous as it has been made to appear," King stated. "The vast majority of Negroes seek only to share power in order to bring about a community in which neither power nor dignity will be black or white."[29] It was a difficult position that King was confronted with while trying to work with different civil rights groups in Chicago and maintain some semblance of unity with other civil rights groups.

Two days later, King clarified his statement further saying that the SCLC was in support of four basic tenets of the "Crisis and Commitment" statement: "nonviolence, democratic process, integration and Negro-white collaboration." He went on to say that he would continue to be critical of the slogan "Black Power."

> Some consider certain civil rights groups conclusively and irrevocably committed to error and wish them barred from the movement. I cannot agree with this approach because it involves an acceptance of the interpretation of enemies of civil rights and bases polices on their distortion. Actually, much thinking, particularly by young Negroes is in a state of flux.

King's comment is another example of how he had been trying to find common ground with those groups that were looking for an approach other than nonviolence. King reiterated what he said in his statement from October 14 that African Americans were "outraged and dismayed" and that "in frustration and despair they are groping for new approaches." Focusing on unity and finding common ground, King said, "Negro unity and Negro white unity, both of which are decisive, can only be harmed by a precipitated effort to excommunicate any group even if silencing or isolating some groups is unintended."[30]

King's efforts to unify the movement were consistent with his goals from when he entered in the 1950s. His message is something that has endured and continues to shape the national discourse when it comes to addressing race relations. That said, his back-and-forth in the media may have caused some confusion in where the leader stood on the issue of Black Power, which may have stymied King's efforts with other organizations as well as the Chicago movement. Some historians see his statements as setbacks to his usual consistency to make sure he considered all perspectives when issuing major statements for the SCLC.[31] By the end of the month, King had moved his attention to the Chicago campaign, which would occupy much of his time for the remainder of the year.

IV

"Here is the seat of tragedy for black and white alike."

In an effort to find new solutions to problems in impoverished sections of the city, Robert Kennedy worked to combine the efforts of private industry and government. He was a vital voice in creating the Bedford-Stuyvesant Community Development Corporation, which was a private, nonprofit firm that combined the efforts of community leaders and private businessmen. "The basic purpose of the program is to create jobs," Kennedy told reporters. "There isn't enough government money to solve the problems of the ghettos. Private enterprise must be brought into this area."[32] Kennedy's effort is an example of how he hoped to approach problems in the nation with different resources. By combining private business and government, his approach hoped to give the efforts of community leaders more capital. It is also evidence of a different type of liberalism that combined the efforts of private business and government intervention.

While the venture in Brooklyn continued to take shape, Robert Kennedy went out and campaigned for other Democrats in the 1966 congressional elections. He went to Oregon, Connecticut and California to name a few places. When he was in California, Kennedy addressed students at the University of California at Berkeley campus—the birthplace of the 1964 Free Speech Movement. He spoke at the outdoor Greek Theatre, which was filled to capacity as he rose to the podium.[33] Speaking of the Free Speech Movement, Kennedy said, "You are the first college to become a major political issue since George III attacked Harvard for being the center of political rebellion and subversion. And he was right." Kennedy found solidarity with the students, saying that he was "glad" to be there, "For I am sympathetic, and I welcome the passionate concern with the condition and future of the American nation which can be found on this campus."[34]

Kennedy's emphasis on the power in the nation's youth was something that gave him credit to the crowd. He told them that the future of the nation did not belong to people who were "apathetic toward common problems and man alike, timid and fearful in the face of new ideas and bold projects." Emphasizing the power of the Free Speech Movement, Kennedy said that the future belonged to "those who can blend passion, reason and courage in a personal commitment to the ideals and great enterprises of American society." What followed was an impassioned to plea for what students should expect from American society.

> We dissent from the fact that millions are trapped in poverty while the nation grows rich. We dissent from the conditions and hatreds which deny a full life to our fellow citizen because of the color of their skin. We dissent from the monstrous absurdity of a world where nations stand poised to destroy one another, and men must kill their fellow men. We dissent from the sight of most of mankind living in poverty, stricken by disease, threatened by hunger and doomed to an early death after a life of unremitting labor. We dissent from cities which blunt our senses and turn the ordinary acts of daily life into struggle. We dissent from the willful, heedless destruction of natural pleasure and beauty.[35]

Kennedy's vision had never been expressed in such deep, poignant ideas. To be sure, this speech is evidence that Kennedy was ready to embark upon a new quest to bring that vision to the nation. This was something that he was not able to do even when his brother was alive, because his vision was entwined with John F. Kennedy's police prowess. Instead, Bobby Kennedy's moralist vision for the nation was something that defined him and continued to fuel the movement to change American society in the sixties.

Kennedy also emphasized that to dissent for the sake of it and not with any way to contribute to the solutions of these problems was "merely self-indulgence." He believed that America continued to change and that it was important to acknowledge how they could make a difference in those changes. "That revolution has now entered a new stage, one that is at once more hopeful and more difficult, more important and more painful. It is the effort to enforce newly won rights and give them content." Kennedy's vision for the nation went deeper than words and grandstanding speeches. He wanted to create opportunities for all Americans, and this played into his rhetoric as he finished 1966 and looked toward the future. "It is to give every Negro the same opportunity as every white man to educate his children, provide for his family, live in a decent house, and win human acceptance as well as ecumenic achievement in the society of his fellows," he said.[36]

In this speech Kennedy stressed the growing civil rights issues and wanted to find solutions for African Americans. He spoke to the comments of people who claimed that Black Americans should be "satisfied and patient" with the progress of civil rights. Alluding to his brother's famous civil rights speech from 1963, which he was an integral part of, he said, "But if any man claims that the Negro should be content or satisfied, let him say he would willingly change the color of his skin and go to live in the Negro section of a large city. Then, and only then, has he the right to such a claim." Like King, Kennedy wanted to see a movement in the nation that addressed these issues peacefully, not violently, saying that "the violence of a few demands condemnation and action." In addition, Kennedy also saw the danger in the violent rhetoric of some groups. "Still far more disturbing than the chaotic, self-destructive violence of Watts or Oakland are the statements of a very few Negro spokesmen—those who have called for hatred to fight prejudice, racism to meet racism, violence to destroy oppression. Here is the seat of tragedy for black and white alike."[37]

There was no point in the parallel lives of these two men where Kennedy and King were more linked in their philosophy than at the end of 1966.

> But the course of violence would be terribly, awfully wrong: Not just because hatred and violence are self-defeating—though they are self-defeating, for they strike at the heart of obedience to law, peaceful process and political cooperation which are man's last, best hopes for a decent world. We must oppose violence not just because of what violence does to the possibility of cooperation between whites and blacks; not just because it hampers the passage of civil rights bills, or poverty legislation, or open-occupancy laws.[38]

Kennedy's comments condemning "hatred and violence" as self-defeating was an example of his commitment to peaceful acts to address the problems that Americans confronted in the sixties. Violence would only make it more difficult to find peaceful cooperation. Kennedy, like King, hoped to sow the seeds of peaceful cooperation, or as King called it, a "coalition of conscience."

Kennedy understood the growing dissent among civil rights leaders and how that had the potential to stymie any effort to bring real, societal change. "It would be a national disaster to permit resentment or fear at the actions of a few to drive increasing numbers of white and black Americans into opposing camps of distrust and enmity," Robert Kennedy told students. He affirmed, "We must continue to enforce the command of the Constitution against the racial discrimination, and the many laws passed to carry out that command. We can never move too fast by giving men the liberty they were guaranteed a century ago." The issue of racial equality was something that Kennedy was committed to and went back to his time as attorney general. The issues that he painted in the speech for the students led him to see this moment as an important step in the profession of American ideals.

Robert Kennedy and Martin Luther King were speaking to Americans at a crucial period in the development of a nation that hoped to live up to the ideals set forth in the Constitution. "This is one of the many crossroads at which American life now stands. In the world and at home you have the opportunity and the responsibility to help make the choices that will determine the greatness of this nation," he said. "You are a generation which is coming of age at one of the rarest moments in history—a time when all around us the old order of things is crumbling a new world society is painfully struggling to take shape." Kennedy stressed to the crowd that they had a responsibility to the world and the nation. In one of his more poignant expressions of the power that young people had, he said, "In your hands, not with Presidents or leaders, is the future of your world and the fulfillment of the best qualities of your own spirit."[39]

Vice President Hubert Humphrey praised Kennedy's speech saying it was "courageous, just and timely." During the question-and-answer period, one student asked for him to publicly disassociate himself from Lyndon Johnson regarding the Vietnam War. Kennedy responded, "No. I'd be glad to tell you what I think about that, but not on those terms." He went on to speak at three other campuses in California. In Sacramento there were signs saying, "Kennedy for President!" Jokingly, after the applause, he said, "I'm very pleased to come here and accept your nomination." However, later in the question-and-answer period he was asked if he planned to run for president. "Well, I just quite frankly don't know what the future brings. I think that one cannot plan that far in advance. I'm going to continue as long as I am around on this globe, I'm going to continue in public life in some way," he said. "I don't know where the man way up there is going to take me. That's not a very satisfactory answer, but it's the best I can do."[40]

V

"The bombs in Vietnam explode at home."

By December 1966, Kennedy and King had turned their efforts to the programs that they were pursuing in Brooklyn and Chicago. King's Chicago Freedom Movement hoped to empower the people there by stressing political power in elections. "Politics is one of the new directions of the civil rights movement itself," King told reporters.

> We are political in the sense that we feel the community and all registered voters should be aware of the issues facing the community. At the same time, we do not endorse candidates. We feel the people will be intelligent enough to vote for the right candidate when they know the issues.

King told the press that he planned to lead the program in a similar way the he drove voting registration in the South.[41]

In a prepared statement, King went further to outline his political approach to the program. "Chicago is a political city and to a great degree the moral and social fabric of this great urban center is woven by individuals and institutions who pull political threads," it read. "The ultimate goal of this drive is to add substantially to the voter registration rolls, while mobilizing, stimulating and motivating the entire Negro community to participate in the political process."[42] King would ultimately go before the Senate Subcommittee on Urban Reorganization later that month to testify on what he saw as the great needs of inner-city Americans.

In his testimony before the Senate, King said that evil in America was not systematic or even overt acts of a group. Evil was "in the sense of the destruction of hope, after the raising of expectations, the forced separation of the poor, whether black or white, from the rest of society, the confinement to poverty and squalor of millions of Americans." King emphasized that there needed to be a larger commitment to education and finding solutions to poverty. "No such fervor nor exhilaration attends the war on poverty. There is impatience with its problems, indifference toward its progress, and pronounced hostility toward its errors." King alluded to the fact that money was being spent on other things. Criticizing other initiatives, he said, "With the continuation of these strange values in a few years we can be assured that we will set a man on the moon and with an adequate telescope he will be able to see the slums on earth with their intensified congestion, decay, and turbulence. On what scales of values is this a program of progress?"[43]

King went even further to admonish the Johnson administration for spending money on the war in Vietnam instead of poverty programs at home. "The security we profess to seek in foreign adventures we will lose in our decaying cities. The bombs in Vietnam explode at home; they destroy the hopes and possibilities for a decent America."[44] King's eloquent plea before the Senate is a testament to his diligence to find solutions to the issue of poverty. King's testimony was the last one. Senator Abraham Ribicoff of Connecticut was instrumental in bringing these issues to light. "The problems of urban America are as important as Vietnam," Ribicoff told the press. "We will always have foreign problems."[45]

Just before the hearings, King told the press that he intended to take a two-month leave of absence to focus on a book. "There is an uneasy feeling in the rights movement that we may have lost our sense of direction, and that forces of goodwill are in disarray. I feel the need to examine the course of our movement and to suggest new ideas and programs." The tentative title of the book was *Where Do We Go from Here?* "Our traditional allies are now in search of a new purpose and meaning, and I hope the book will help in this quest," King said.[46]

While King was testifying before the Senate and preparing to write another book, Robert Kennedy announced his initiative in the Bedford-Stuyvesant neighborhood in Brooklyn. "The plight of the cities—the physical decay and human despair that pervades them—is the great internal problem of the American nation, a challenge which must be met," Kennedy said to a group of one thousand people gathered at Public School 305 in Bedford-Stuyvesant. "The peculiar genius of America has been its ability, in the face of such challenges, to summon all our resources of mind and body, to focus these resources, and our attention and effort, in whatever amount is necessary to solve the deepest and most resistant problems."[47] Kennedy's effort to combine government assistance and private industry was the genius that he refers to in the above passage. When all the other ideas did not work, Kennedy looked beyond to find solutions.

The biggest issue in this plight against poverty was trying to get people jobs to stimulate growth. To that end Kennedy emphasized to the group how this initiative planned to achieve that goal through three threads:

> cooperation with the private business community in self sustaining economically viable enterprises; integration of programs for education, employment and community development under a coordinated overall plan; and impetus and direction to be given in these efforts by the united strength of the community, working with private foundations, labor unions, and universities, in Community Development Corporations organized for this purpose.

Kennedy formally announced the creation of the Bedford-Stuyvesant Renewal and Rehabilitation Corporation, a board comprised of people from the community, to facilitate this effort. In addition, he announced the creation of the Bedford-Stuyvesant Development and Services Corporation to work to work with the Bedford-Stuyvesant Renewal and Rehabilitation Corporation. "This corporation will involve, and draw on the talents and energies and knowledge of some of the foremost members of the American business community."[48] Kennedy's approach, like his rhetoric that had developed since the death of his brother, was an innovative approach to the problems that the inner city suffered.

Kennedy's initiative acknowledged that the issues from the inner cities of the nation were complicated. "It is a beginning," he said. "Bedford-Stuyvesant is on its way. That way, as I will stress again and again, is not easy. It is complex and complicated and fraught with difficulty." By utilizing private business and government, Kennedy was instituting a new kind of liberalism that looked to bridge the divide between Democrats and Republicans. "To turn promise into performance, plan into reality ... we must combine the best of community action with the best of the private enterprise system. Neither by itself is enough; but in their combination lies our hope for the future."[49] Kennedy acknowledged to the press that he "sounded like a Republican" by utilizing private business. However, Kennedy stressed that "the power to act is the power to command resources, of money and minds and skill: to build housing, create the social and educational services, and buy the goods which this community wants and needs and deserves."[50] Kennedy's initiative capped off one of the most successful years of his political life. As he and King approached the next year, they both further defined their visions publicly while the nation continued to struggle with the growing conflict in Vietnam and the racial tension that plagued the nation.

14

"Beyond Vietnam"

I

*"I don't think we're going to end
the war by military action."*

As the war in Vietnam continued to escalate, Lyndon Johnson, Robert Kennedy and Martin Luther King found themselves at odds over the United States' involvement in that region. At the start of the new year, Kennedy went on a European tour, giving speeches in England, France and Italy. He commented on the war and the impact that it was having on U.S. prestige. When he arrived at Oxford University there were protestors against the Vietnam War. One sign read, "Not bad in South Africa Bobby—how about Vietnam." After being greeted with a two-minute standing ovation, Kennedy told the students that he was not breaking with the Johnson administration. He said that the Johnson administration wanted a peaceful solution to the war so the people had the opportunity "to choose any kind of government they want." Kennedy told the students that he believed that the next three or four weeks were "critical and crucial" toward this endeavor for peace. He stressed that there were "secret talks" that could not be made public.[1]

Kennedy went to France to continue discussions on the state of the war with European leaders. White House officials told the media that they were unclear what Kennedy was referring to in his comments about the next few weeks being "crucial and critical." George Christian, White House press secretary, said he did not know what Kennedy was referring to in his comments at Oxford but that the Johnson administration continued to seek a peaceful solution to the war in Vietnam. Kennedy said in France that the nation had a "vital and significant role" to play in the peace efforts in Vietnam.[2] When he met with de Gaulle, the French president said, "As I told your brother the United States is involved in the wrong course in Vietnam." De Gaulle said that there would be no peace without a cessation of bombing.

"South Vietnam would not permit the North ... to run their country. Ho Chi Minh realizes this and would not attempt it." De Gaulle emphasized that America had always demonstrated high ideals to the world. "All of this is being destroyed by your role in Vietnam.... History is a force at work in Vietnam, and the United States will not prevail against it," de Gaulle said. The French president went on to compliment Kennedy saying that he had a "brilliant political future." He urged him not to become involved in the issues in Vietnam. In the wake of this war, it was up to Kennedy to "help your country regain its proper course."[3]

In addition to de Gaulle, Kennedy met with the French director of Far Eastern Affairs, Étienne Manac'h. He was accompanied by John Gunther Dean from the American embassy, who translated for Kennedy. At the end of the conversation, Kennedy understood that peace would only come if the United States stopped bombing North Vietnam. Speaking only in French with Dean interpreting, Manac'h stressed that there was distrust between the United States and the North Vietnamese, but that he believed that the North was interested in peace. Manac'h's interpretation of the North Vietnamese position was a new important concession in the negations toward peace. Dean took the matter seriously and cabled the State Department after he confirmed its contents with Manac'h.[4] Kennedy moved on to Germany and Italy where he again commented on foreign policy and had a meeting with the pope.

In Bonn, Germany, Chancellor Kiesinger said, "The majority of the people do not understand what and why the United States is doing in Vietnam." In Italy, Kennedy received the same reaction, which led him to determine that the United States was losing its prestige abroad as a result of the Vietnam War. The pope said that there was in fact a change in the North Vietnamese attitude and they were willing to negotiate for peace. All of the leaders expressed a disdain toward the bombing campaign of the United States and how it hurt peace negotiations.[5]

"We are dealing with different kinds of problems and the answers of the nineteen-forties and nineteen-fifties are not automatically those of today," Kennedy said in Rome. To be sure, Kennedy was referring to the Cold War attitudes that both the United States and its allies had stressed since the end of the Second World War. In his visits with European leaders, it was clear that Kennedy had a voice and allies of his own overseas. People came to see him talk, and there was a warm reception. He said again that the next few weeks would be crucial to finding a peaceful solution to the war in Vietnam.[6] When he returned to the United States, Kennedy had something to say about how the United States was seen abroad.

Speaking at an "improvised" press conference, Kennedy spoke to reporters about how some influential leaders saw the war in Vietnam. "Prime Minister Wilson, President de Gaulle and the Pope all wanted to discuss Vietnam," he said. He went as far as to say that as a result of the United States' policy in Vietnam, the relations of European nations "to each other and the United States are quite different than they were three years ago." He went on to say, "We must realize that the situation is not what it was in the past and that our influence is diminishing." He reiterated the crucial nature of the next few weeks and with a strained relationship with North Vietnam, "Hanoi is now more receptive to negotiations." When he was asked about comments from the White House that said there were no indications that Hanoi wanted to negotiate, Kennedy responded, "I'm not certain exactly what President Johnson said on that; all I can report is the feeling in other capitals." When the reporters asked if he was going to the White House to meet with President Johnson, he said, "I just got back." After Kennedy was questioned whether his meetings in Europe were counter to Johnson's efforts in Vietnam, he said, "I think we are all interested in learning the facts" and that the conflict in Vietnam is "important to all of us."[7]

Newsweek had a story that said Robert Kennedy was approached with "peace feelers" on his trip to Europe. A spokesperson for Kennedy would not comment on the article when the *New York Times* approached him about the report and went as far as to say that Kennedy needed to confer "with the Executive Branch of Government." According to the *Times* article, there would be a three-phase halt to the war that would begin with an end to the bombings.[8] When Johnson and Dean Rusk, who had been chasing peace opportunities in the State Department, heard about the Kennedy article, they were "outraged." Johnson believed that there was no such thing as a peace "feeler" and that Kennedy was trying to embarrass to White House.[9] This story contributed to the already tense relationship between President Johnson and Kennedy. Johnson was aggravated that Kennedy, a senator from New York, was traveling Europe and meeting with heads of state to discuss Vietnam, but he also felt that Kennedy was trying to force his hand in the negotiations. The president believed that Kennedy leaked the story to the press. Kennedy and Johnson did not know that Dean had sent a cable to the State Department outlining the conversation that Kennedy had with Manac'h.[10] A *Newsweek* reporter had been at the State Department and given the cable from Manac'h. That was the source of the article, not Kennedy, whom Johnson blamed.[11]

The trip to Europe and the *Newsweek* article prompted a Kennedy and Johnson meeting. On February 6, Kennedy called the White House to arrange a meeting. Instead of Johnson, Kennedy's friend Nicholas Katzenbach, who was now undersecretary of state, called back and arranged a lunch at Kennedy's office. "I'm working for President Johnson and I treat him just as you would have had me treat President Kennedy," Katzenbach said. "Of course," Kennedy replied. While he disagreed with some of Johnson's policy in Vietnam, Kennedy assured Katzenbach that he would never fabricate a story to embarrass the president. Katzenbach wanted Kennedy to deny the story, but before they could come to terms on that, the meeting was interrupted with a call from the White House. Johnson was ready to meet with Kennedy.[12]

Katzenbach remarked later, "It wasn't a very pleasant meeting.... And the President was quite harsh in terms of things that he said to Senator Kennedy." He remembered that Kennedy "was quite angry; both men, though they didn't raise their voices, were quite angry."[13] Johnson started the meeting by accusing Kennedy of a leak. Kennedy said that he did not do it and that it probably came "from your State Department," which was the truth. Johnson's response to that comment was, "It's not my State Department, goddamnit, it's your State Department." Johnson went on to talk about the progress of the war, warning Kennedy that further talk of peace would lead to political calamity for the senator and others who supported that position. "I'll destroy you and every one of your dove friends. You'll be dead politically in six months."[14] Kennedy kept his composure and insisted that the bombing campaign stop; that was what the leaders in Europe had emphasized to him. He wanted Johnson to follow through with measures to remove U.S. troops from Vietnam. "There just isn't a chance in hell that I will do that. Not the slightest chance," Johnson responded. He went further in his attack on Kennedy saying his actions had emboldened the enemy and that he had American blood on his hands. "I don't have to take that from you," Kennedy responded, getting up to leave. Katzenbach and Walt Rostow, who were also present, intervened. They came to an agreement that Kennedy would talk to the press about the story.[15]

"I did not bring home any peace feelers," Kennedy said in the lobby of the White House after the meeting with Johnson. The *Times* reported that Kennedy and Johnson had "been at odds" over the war in Vietnam. It went on to say that the quickly arranged meeting was meant to correct "any impression that Senator Kennedy might have succeeded where the administration had failed in arranging negotiations."[16] The meeting, however, most likely played a role in Kennedy's decision to speak out against the administration the following month on the floor of the Senate. When he returned to his office he was somewhat shaken. "You know ... what I've been through is just unbelievable," Kennedy commented to an aide in his office after the meeting. "What does he mean, my State Department," he asked Frank Mankiewicz privately.[17] "He was shouting and seemed very unstable," Kennedy commented to a friend regarding the meeting with Johnson. "I kept thinking that if he exploded like that with me, how could he ever negotiate with Hanoi," Kennedy said.[18]

The meeting with Johnson was the final event that pushed Robert Kennedy to a point where he felt that he should speak out against the war. He started with a speech on China in Chicago. "If the lives of thousands of Americans are lost and billions of dollars committed on the theory that Vietnam is essential to us," he said at Chicago University's Center of Policy Studies, "how can we refuse to assist others on the border of China whose demands may be less but whose strategic importance and whose vulnerability to external and internal Communist dominion may be greater?" He criticized U.S. policy, saying, "We have striven to isolate China from the world and treated it with unremitting hostility.... That, however, is not a policy. It is an attitude founded upon fear and passion and wishful hopes." He characterized this policy as "empty rhetoric."[19]

Kennedy went further in the speech admonishing Dean Rusk and his statements on Vietnam who said that the United States must "keep our commitments." Kennedy said, "Of course we must keep our commitments and obligations.... But by what standards and toward what ends are those commitments made? How deeply do they extend and what means will be used to fulfill them?"[20] The speech was more about the attempt by the administration to view the Vietnam War as inspired by the Chinese.[21] Kennedy's words were a prelude to a speech that he was planning to give on Vietnam. By attacking Johnson's policy on China he was showing the world that he had his own voice and was willing to break with the administration on matters of foreign policy. Indeed, his direct mention of the Vietnam War is a clear indicator that he intended to go further with his criticism of the administration.

Johnson resumed the bombing campaign of North Vietnam a few days after Kennedy made the speech on China. "I deeply regret that the bombing in North Vietnam has resumed," Kennedy told the press. "Beyond that, it is most unfortunate that the truce period has gone by without greater progress being made by all of us on both sides toward a peaceful ending of this tragic war."[22] By February 17 Kennedy had made it clear that he planned to make a major address on the war. Speaking to a high school in Long Island, Kennedy said, "I have serious reservations about the effectiveness of military bombing in North Vietnam."[23]

Kennedy did more to lay the groundwork for his speech when he spoke at a dinner of Americans for Democratic Action in Philadelphia on February 25. He said that the "elders" in the nation should not ignore how the youth of the nation were questioning the war. He said that the young people of the sixties were "the children not of the cold war, but of the thaw," in an allusion to détente. He said that Vietnam was "surrounded by rhetoric they do not understand or accept." He went further to make a distinction

> They see the world as one in which Communist states can be each other's deadliest enemies or even friends of the West; in which Communism is certainly no better, but perhaps no worse, than many other evil and repressive dictatorships all around the world—with which we conclude alliances when that is felt to be in our interest.

He took it further saying that regardless of how the "elder" people of the nation viewed the war, "they see it as one in which the largest and most powerful nation on earth is killing children ... in a remote and insignificant land."[24]

In addition to speaking engagements about the Vietnam War, Kennedy consulted people in the administration as well as those who were against the conflict in an attempt to gain a deeper understanding. He got in touch with Robert McNamara, Maxwell Taylor and Averell Harriman for the administration's point of view. In the end Richard Goodwin and Kennedy drafted most of what would become Kennedy's comment on the war.[25]

On the morning of March 2, Kennedy allowed journalists into his office just before the speech. "The President makes the charge that speeches like this do a disservice to our boys," one of them said to Kennedy. After thinking for a moment he responded, "You have to balance that against what you think does the greatest amount of good. I don't think we're going to end the war by military action." By 3:40pm Kennedy was on the floor of the Senate giving his address that he hoped would clarify his position on the Vietnam War.[26]

Speaking to a packed gallery, Kennedy proposed a three-step plan that he hoped would set the stage for peace. "Ten thousand miles from this chamber we are engaged n a violent conflict that has engulfed the land in Vietnam. I discuss this war knowing that its tangled and resistant complexities make judgement difficult and uncertain," he started. He acknowledged that the president bore a burden for this war and that Johnson was not the only one who had made decisions leading to this point. "Three Presidents have taken action in Vietnam. As one who was involved in many of those decisions, I can testify that if fault is to be found or responsibility assessed, there is enough to go round for all—including myself." He stressed that the United States, "the most powerful country the world has known now turns its strength and will upon a small primitive land. And still there is no peace." Kennedy wanted the nation to consider every option in its quest to find peace. "For if this war was not our doing, and is not our fault, still it is partly our responsibility."[27]

Kennedy pointed out the responsibility of the people in the room. "All we say and all we do must be informed by our awareness that this horror is partly our responsibility; not just a nation's responsibility but yours and mine." He went on to say, "It is we who live in abundance and send our young men out to die. It is our chemicals that scorch and our bombs that level the villages. We are all participants." Kennedy believed that the nation had an opportunity to achieve peace. "We are now at a critical turning point of our stated limited objectives; balanced between the rising prospects of peace and surely rising war, between the promised negotiations and the perils of a spreading conflict." The heart of Kennedy's proposal was a three-step plan that started with a cessation of the bombing campaign. He told the group, "The steps I am suggesting are intimately related."[28]

Kennedy emphasized that the first step was for the administration to stop the bombing campaign in the North. With that action Kennedy believed that they were sending a sign to the North that "we are ready to negotiate within a week." Once all the parties were at the negotiating table, then there should be a group to "inspect the borders and ports of the country to report any further escalation." Finally, Kennedy proposed a United Nations force "with an international presence gradually replacing American forces," which would move the war toward a final settlement. "These are the three stages toward a final resolution of the war in Vietnam: beginning negotiations, continuing those discussions without increasing conflict, and final settlement which liberated the people of South Vietnam to govern their own future," Kennedy concluded.

It was a major break from the administration, and Kennedy was willing to lead the way for others to follow. Kennedy's suggestion was not a "fixed or frozen formula." He wanted to start a new direction for American policy in Vietnam. These solutions were "suggestions to be refined and revised by a critical examination of other minds; enhanced by the imagination of the thoughtful and concerned; molded and reworked by shifting events," Kennedy said. He concluded that if they pursue this program they could take some solace in knowing that they did everything they could to find a solution, "that we have let neither pride nor fear deter us in the quest for peace."[29] Kennedy's proposal was the first time that he strongly admonished the Johnson administration over the Vietnam War.

Secretary of State Dean Rusk immediately responded to Kennedy's plan saying that the administration had explored these options "without result." Rusk went further, saying, "The President has consistently made clear that the door to peace is and will remain open and we are prepared at any time to go more than halfway to meet any equitable overture from the other side." President Johnson said in a letter to Senator Henry Jackson with regard to halting the bombing campaign, "The bombing in the North is an action undertaken by your Government only after the most careful reflection. It is a response to a serious and systemic and protracted violation of international agreements."[30]

Many senators on the floor commended the speech by Kennedy. Mike Mansfield of Montana said that the ultimate responsibility to decide if the north was signaling for peace lay with President Johnson. He also commented that Kennedy's speech was "free of rancor."[31] Barry Goldwater said that Kennedy had "stuck his foot in his mouth" with the call for a halt in bombing. "And if he doesn't stop," Goldwater said, "he's going to have an orthopedic mouth."[32]

The *New York Times* said in an editorial the next day that Kennedy's speech "comes at what is clearly a crucial moment either for peace negotiations or for an escalated war." The editorial said that Kennedy joined the likes of "world statesmen, the Pope and the Secretary General of the United Nations." The *Times* went on to say that Kennedy's speech "was a carefully calculated move that will have great impact despite some cloudy language and disclaimers of any intention to blame President Johnson for the current situation."[33] The reaction to his speech demonstrated both solidarity and criticism of his ideas. The speech was a turning point for Kennedy. As he approached what would be the last year of his life, he made decisions that would shape not only his but also his brother's legacy. His stand against the administration empowered many Democrats as well as the peace movement that was gaining momentum in the nation. To be sure, Kennedy's position on the war was even closer to Martin Luther King, Jr's, who also continued to shape the civil rights movement.

II

"But we must speak."

While Kennedy took a stand against the administration's policy in Vietnam, Dr. King continued his quest against poverty in Chicago but also took time to find his own voice on Vietnam. King was in the midst of crafting the voice of the movement in a book that he was writing. By the end of February he joined other leaders and spoke out on Vietnam. King believed that involvement in the war both violated the United Nations Charter's principle of self-determination and "crippled" the anti-poverty movement in the United States. King spoke at a conference titled "National Priority No. 1: Redirecting American Power" held by *The Nation* magazine and attended by Senators Eugene McCarthy and George McGovern among others. King said that after the French were forced to leave, "United States Government officials began to brainwash the American public. We supported Ngo Dinh Diem in his betrayal of the Geneva accord," which left the United States "in an untenable position morally and politically."[34]

King believed that the efforts in Vietnam had done a great deal to undermine the efforts of Johnson's domestic program to fight poverty. "The promises of the Great Society have been shot down on the battlefield of Vietnam." King went on to say that the "pursuit of this widened war has narrowed domestic welfare programs, making the poor white and Negro bear the heaviest burdens both at the front and at home."[35] To be sure, King's perspective was multilayered in that it looked to attack not only the act of war and its violation of international treaties but also the fact that there was a racist aspect in the pursuit of this war that affected African Americans.

King articulated his position further with rhetoric that pointed to the cost of the war on the American economy and society, saying, "The 10-billion mis-estimate of the war budget alone is more than five times the amount committed to anti-poverty programs. The security we profess to seek in foreign adventures we will lose in our decaying cities." In addition, he emphasized the inequality at home. "We are willing to make the Negro 100 per cent of a citizen in warfare, but reduce him to 50 per cent of a citizen on American soil.... There were twice as many Negroes in combat in Vietnam at the beginning of 1967 and twice as many died in action—20.6 per cent—in proportion to their numbers in the population as whites."[36] The glaring disparity between white and black America was even more pronounced as the numbers of American dead were reported at home.

In a preview of what would become King's message on the war he spoke to the "conscience" of the American people. "We are presently moving down a dead-end road that can lead to national disaster. It is time for all people of conscience to call upon America to return to her true home of brotherhood and peaceful pursuits." He concluded his remarks, saying, "There is an element of urgency in our redirecting or American power. We still have a choice: nonviolent co-existence or violent co-annihilation."[37] King was not far from Kennedy's position, which would be presented before the Senate not long after this speech. It is clear that they were both advocating for an end to the war; however, King's position was rooted not only in the violation of international accord, but also the devastating effects that he believed the war had on American society.

In March, King went even further to articulate his position on the Vietnam War. In an interview with the *New York Times* he said that he planned to take "a much stronger stand against the war." He reiterated that the war was hurting domestic programs and that it took away attention and resources form the civil rights movement. King stressed that the economic struggles of the nation could lead to violence and rioting. He said, "Nothing much has been done. And this only intensifies the feelings in the slums." King believed that all of this led to an "atmosphere of turmoil" and proposed a series of demonstrations in Chicago to shed light on these issues. In addition to that, King planned a nationwide program called "Operation Breadbasket" that involved working with businesses in the hiring and promotion of African Americans. When asked by the *Times* if the civil rights movement was "dead," he responded, "I think it is more alive than ever."[38]

On March 25, King led his first antiwar rally in Chicago. "Our nation which initiated so much of the revolutionary spirit of the modern world is now cast in the mold of being an arch antirevolutionary," King told the crowd that day. "Certainly this stream of events is not contributing to freedom and democracy abroad. It leaves us in the weakest posture of world stature since our birth as a nation." There were signs in the crowd that said "No More War" and "Education, Not Escalation." American Nazi Party members shouted "Treason!" to the crowd and took some of the signs and threw them into the river. "We are committing atrocities equal to any perpetrated by the Vietcong," King continued. "We are left standing before a world glutted by our own barbarity. We are engaged in a war that seeks to turn the clock of history back and perpetuate white colonialism."

King continued to link the war to the failure of poverty programs in the United States. "The bombs in Vietnam explode at home—they destroy the dream and possibility for a decent America." He spoke of American foreign policy, saying, "We often arrogantly feel that we have some divine messianic mission to police the whole world; we are arrogant in not allowing young nations to go through the same growing pains, turbulence and revolution that characterized our history. Our arrogance can be our doom." He believed that the administration was leading the country "down a dead-end road which can lead to national disaster." King emphasized that the nation should be focused on moral goals instead of being "an inhumane power unleashed against defenseless people."[39]

In a resolution on March 30, the SCLC went even further to condemn the war, making it a part of their national policy. The board, which had anywhere from sixty to seventy members, characterized the war as "morally and politically" unjust. There was a problem, they argued, for leaders of the movement to preach "nonviolence at home while our nation is practicing the very essence of violence abroad." The board made it clear that there were racial issues within the war saying that there was a "frustration of a people asked to fight with all their life at stake for a nation which grants them only partial life at home." They concluded, "Rather than have the American dream slain in the jungles and swamps of Vietnam, we pledge our selves to do everything in our power to end that war."[40]

Dr. King's statements and the resolution by the SCLC made it clear to the nation that King was going to come out with a major position on the Vietnam War. On April 4, 1967, King spoke at Riverside Church in New York City. In front of three thousand people, which gave him a standing ovation at the beginning and end of his speech, King articulated his position on the war.[41] The "Clergy and Laymen Concerned about Vietnam" asked King to speak at the church. He started the speech commenting on a statement from that group that read, "A time comes when silence is betrayal." King responded to it, saying, "And that time has come for us in relation to Vietnam." He reflected on that "truth" as he saw it and emphasized to the people that this was not an easy position to take. "Even when pressed by the demands of inner truth, men do not easily assume the task of opposing their government's policy, especially in time of war."[42]

King made it clear that it was important for people to speak out, despite the fact that it may be difficult for them. "And some of us who have already begun to break the silence of the night have found that the calling to speak is often a vocation of agony, but we must speak," he said.

> We must speak with all the humility that is appropriate to our limited vision, but we must speak. And we must rejoice as well, for surely this is the first time in our nation's history that a significant number of its religious leaders have chosen to move beyond the prophesying of smooth patriotism to the high grounds of a firm dissent based upon the mandates of conscience and the reading of history. Perhaps a new spirit is rising among us.[43]

King's call for people to speak out on the war empowered African Americans and gave a new thread to the movement. While this was more in line with King's commitment to nonviolence, he was very skillful in his previous public comments to make a connection to the injustice that the war had on African Americans.

King talked about his own journey to come to the conclusion that he needed to condemn the war. He appealed to the crowed, referring to "the past two years, as I have moved to break the betrayal of my own silences and to speak from the burnings of my own heart, as I have called for radical departures from the destruction of Vietnam." There were people who told him that he was wrong to speak out against the government and that it hurt the cause for civil rights. King was steadfast in his appeal, believing that the nature of the movement was inextricably tied to the dissolution of the war in Vietnam. Instead, King looked to the issues of the movement as a reason to end the war. King saw the poverty programs of the Great Society as a "shining moment in that struggle."

> It seemed as if there was a real promise of hope for the poor—both black and white—through the poverty program. There were experiments, hopes, new beginnings. Then came the buildup in Vietnam, and I watched this program broken and eviscerated, as if it were some idle political plaything of a society gone mad on war, and I knew that America would never invest the necessary funds or energies in rehabilitation of its poor so long as adventures like Vietnam continued to draw men and skills and money like some demonic destructive suction tube. So, I was increasingly compelled to see the war as an enemy of the poor and to attack it as such.[44]

His commitment to the poor in America led his conscience to question the war. It was clear that the movement was affected by the vast amount of resources that went toward the war effort and not to people at home. This above all linked his opposition of the war to the strengthening of the civil rights movement. The war did even more harm to African Americans.

King made the link between the war and the growing numbers of African Americans who went overseas to fight in it. "It was sending their sons and their brothers and their husbands to fight and to die in extraordinarily high proportions relative to the rest of the population," he said. "We were taking the black young men who had been crippled by our society and sending them eight thousand miles away to guarantee liberties in Southeast Asia which they had not found in southwest Georgia and East Harlem." He called the white and black soldiers who fought and died together as a "cruel irony." He went on, "And so we watch them in brutal solidarity burning the huts of a poor village, but we realize that they would hardly live on the same block in Chicago. I could not be silent in the face of such cruel manipulation of the poor."[45]

King's third reason for speaking out on the war was his commitment to nonviolence in America's cities as people spoke out for their tights. "As I have walked among the desperate, rejected, and angry young men, I have told them that Molotov cocktails and rifles would not solve their problems," King said. The people in those cities would ask King, "What about Vietnam?" This question perplexed King. "Their questions hit home," King said, "and I knew that I could never again raise my voice against the violence of the oppressed in the ghettos without having first spoken clearly to the greatest purveyor of violence in the world today—my own government." He concluded, "For the sake of those boys, for the sake of this government, for the sake of the hundreds of thousands trembling under our violence, I cannot be silent."[46]

The final reason why King was speaking against the war went back to his relationship with God and his commitment to the teachings of Jesus Christ. "To me the relationship of this ministry to the making of peace is so obvious that I sometimes marvel at those who ask me why I'm speaking against the war," he said.

> I must be true to my conviction that I share with all men the calling to be a son of the living God. Beyond the calling of race or nation or creed is this vocation of sonship and brotherhood, and because I believe that the Father is deeply concerned especially for his suffering and helpless and outcast children, I come tonight to speak for them.

King's faith and his commitment to nonviolence were at the heart of his reasoning for making this stand on the war. In addition to that, however, he went further and talked about how American actions caused damage to the everyday life of the Vietnamese and how that deteriorated the societal structure while at the same time destroying U.S. prestige.

King commented on the damage that the United States was doing to the people living in Vietnam. "They watch as we poison their water, as we kill a million acres of their crops. They must weep as the bulldozers roar through their areas preparing to destroy the precious trees. They wander into the hospitals with at least twenty casualties from American firepower for one Vietcong-inflicted injury," King told the audience. Going further with the imagery, he went into the number of casualties and who was affected by U.S. actions in the region.

> So far we may have killed a million of them, mostly children. They wander into the towns and see thousands of the children, homeless, without clothes, running in packs on the streets like animals. They see the children degraded by our soldiers as they beg for food. They see the children selling their sisters to our soldiers, soliciting for their mothers.

King's use of Vietnamese children suffering was his way to bring his rhetoric to new levels, looking not only for the logic and reason of the people listening, but also the emotion and sentimentality that came with moving people to action. To be sure, the sheer number of people, nearly a million he said, should be enough. In order to get his point across to the people, he meant to leave them with an image of a family suffering from U.S. actions.

King implored the people to put themselves in the place of the Vietcong and try to see how they felt about the United States getting involved in their country. "Here is the true meaning and value of compassion and nonviolence, when it helps us to see the enemy's point of view, to hear his questions, to know his assessment of ourselves," King said. "For from his view we may indeed see the basic weaknesses of our own condition, and if we are mature, we may learn and grow and profit from the wisdom of the brothers who are called the opposition." This empathetic approach was another way that King was able to bring people together and infuse the tactics of the civil rights movement. It was his way of attacking the violence of war through the teachings of Christ. "Somehow this madness must cease. We must stop now," King said. "I speak as a child of God and brother to the suffering poor of Vietnam. I speak for those whose land is being laid waste, whose homes are being destroyed, whose culture is being subverted."

After his eloquent plea to consider the war from the point of view of the Vietnamese, King outlined what he called "five concrete things" that the U.S. government should do immediately in Vietnam:

> Number one: End all bombing in North and South Vietnam. Number two: Declare a unilateral cease-fire in the hope that such action will create the atmosphere for negotiation. Three: Take immediate steps to prevent other battlegrounds in Southeast Asia by curtailing our military buildup in Thailand and our interference in Laos. Four: Realistically accept the fact that the National Liberation Front has substantial support in South Vietnam and must thereby play a role in any meaningful negotiations and any future Vietnam government. Five: Set a date that we will remove all foreign troops from Vietnam in accordance with the 1954 Geneva Agreement.[47]

King's ideas were not that dissimilar to Robert Kennedy's speech a month prior. Indeed, it is evidence that the two men shared a common goal in Vietnam and wanted to see the war take a new direction that advocated for peace and cooperation, not the bloodshed that had plagued the effort. Certainly numbers 1 and 2 are exactly what Kennedy wanted Johnson to do. In addition, Kennedy and King agreed on the NLF playing a role in a peace agreement.

King believed that Vietnam was something that they needed to confront immediately or else it would plague future generations of Americans. "The war in Vietnam is but a symptom of a far deeper malady within the American spirit," he said, "and so, such thoughts take us beyond Vietnam, but not beyond our calling as sons of the living God." He quoted President John F. Kennedy to make his point: "Five years ago he said, 'Those who make peaceful revolution impossible will make violent revolution inevitable.'" King continued, saying, "Increasingly, by choice or by accident, this is the role our nation has taken, the role of those who make peaceful revolution impossible by refusing to give up the privileges and the pleasures that come from the immense profits of overseas investments."[48]

Prophetically King talked about how America would eventually question its role in parts of the world. He said that a "true revolution of values will soon cause us to question the fairness and justice of many of our past and present policies ... will soon look uneasily on the glaring contrast of poverty and wealth ... will lay hand on the world order and say of war, 'This way of settling differences is not just.'" He concluded that America could play a role in leading the world in a different direction. "America, the richest and most powerful nation in the world, can well lead the way in this revolution of values. There is nothing except a tragic death wish to prevent us from reordering our priorities so that the pursuit of peace will take precedence over the pursuit of war," he concluded.[49]

King acknowledged that they were living in interesting times that had the potential to remake the world. "These are revolutionary times," he said. "All over the globe men are revolting against old systems of exploitation and oppression, and out of the wounds of a frail world, new systems of justice and equality are being born. The shirtless and barefoot people of the land are rising up as never before." He believed, however, that America was not playing the role that they should. The Cold War and fear of communism had changed the nation. "It is a sad fact that because of comfort, complacency, a morbid fear of communism, and our proneness to adjust to injustice, the Western nations that initiated so much of the revolutionary spirit of the modern world have now become the arch antirevolutionaries."[50]

King brought his ideas to together toward the end of his speech. He demonstrated his commitment to nonviolence, while at the same time saying,

> We still have a choice today: nonviolent coexistence or violent coannihilation. We must move past indecision to action. We must find new ways to speak for peace in Vietnam and justice throughout the developing world, a world that borders on our doors. If we do not act, we shall surely be dragged down the long, dark, and shameful corridors of time reserved for those who possess power without compassion, might without morality, and strength without sight.[51]

His words, ideals and vision were forever emblazoned on the American conscience with this speech. To be sure, it embodied the essence of his nonviolent movement, bringing together that strategy to highlight the issue of war and how it was the antithesis of progress in society. It was the doctrine of nonviolence, which went beyond the civil rights movement, attempted to influence international affairs, and led the nation to question the morality of American action overseas, that came to embody American society in the sixties.

King implored the group, indeed the nation, to look inside themselves and find a way to affect the war. By doing that, he argued, they would be setting in motion a powerful movement for peace. "Now let us begin. Now let us rededicate ourselves to the long and bitter, but beautiful, struggle for a new world," he said. "The choice is ours," he concluded, "and though we might prefer it otherwise, we must choose in this crucial moment of human history."[52] King concluded the speech stressing that the choice was theirs to make and that it could have rippling effects in its wake that would change the nation and the world as a result.

This speech was as powerful as Robert Kennedy's speech before the Senate and set the tone for King's position on the Vietnam War. King's vision for peace complemented Kennedy's in many ways. His five "concrete things" were similar to Kennedy's. While Kennedy took the point of view of the government, King went further and made it about the philosophy of nonviolence. Indeed, that was a pervasive idea that had the potential to shape the discussion on Vietnam. To be sure, King and Kennedy played a decisive role in changing attitudes on the war. In addition, their opposition may have played a role in empowering other groups to make a similar stand, thus having an impact that lasted beyond their own deaths, which was exactly one year later for King in Memphis, Tennessee.

15

"A Newer World"

I

"I ain't going to study war no more."

The war in Vietnam was in the forefront of the American experience for the remainder of 1967. Robert Kennedy and Martin Luther King, Jr., were vocal about their views on the war. Those views led to significant debate from the people of the nation as well as government officials for the remainder of the year. Robert Kennedy was lauded by many for his position, indeed his stand on the war, while King, on the other hand, was criticized a great deal in the press for linking the civil rights movement to the war in Vietnam.

The *New York Times* wrote that King was wrong to make a connection between the war and the movement. "This is fusing two public problems that are distinct and separate," the *Times* editorial entitled "Dr. King's Error" read. "By drawing them together, Dr. King has done a disservice to both. The moral issues in Vietnam are less clear-cut than he suggests; the political strategy of uniting the peace movement and the civil rights movement could very well be disastrous for both causes." The piece went on to say that the civil rights movement had entered a stage where jobs and housing were the main thrust for action, not the war. "Dr. King makes too facile a connection between the speeding up of the war in Vietnam and the slowing down of the war against poverty." The editorial admonished King, saying that he had a responsibility to guide the civil rights movement in the right direction. "Linking these hard, complex problems will lead not to solutions but to deeper confusion."[1]

The *Times* was not the only group who did not like the connection between the war and the movement. The NAACP came out and called King's April 4 speech a "serious tactical mistake." In a resolution that they made public, they said that to fuse the two movements "will serve the cause neither of civil rights nor of peace." The organization said, "Civil rights battles will have to be fought and won on their own merits, irrespective of the state of war or peace in the world." It went on to say, "We are not a peace organization nor a foreign policy organization. We are a civil rights organization."[2]

Not everyone felt the same way about King's stand on the war. In a letter to the *Times*, James Bevel made it clear that Dr, King was justified in his position on the war. A longtime friend and supporter of King, it is no surprise that he felt that way. "The New York Times has rendered a great disservice to the peace and civil rights movements in this country by making a futile attempt to disassociate the two," Bevel wrote. "The American Government seems, in fact, to be embarked upon a program of systematic genocide in Vietnam and it is for this reason, perhaps more than any other, that colored peoples everywhere must speak out and act courageously."[3] Bevel was not the only high-profile person to support King's efforts.

Dr. Benjamin Spock spoke out in a letter to the *Times* where he disagreed with the editorial. "Our mistreatment of Negroes and our lawlessness in Vietnam are both manifestations of the same self-deceptive kinds of thinking. And they require similar solutions," he concluded. Spock continued, "I believe that the civil rights and peace movements should cooperate closely in their educational and organization work. Their common aim is to save the world—literally—by fostering the brotherhood of man."[4] In addition to Bevel and Spock, the Social Justice Department of the National Council of Churches supported Dr. King. They said that King "has once again focused our attention on the relationship between a growing commitment to military expansion and the daily deterioration of economic development at home and abroad." They also said, "Dr. King has raised these issues in an acute form, and we must not allow attacks upon him to divert attention from the necessity of facing these issues."[5]

While the public debate over Vietnam continued, there was the largest antiwar demonstration in New York City since the war began. In a march from Central Park to the United Nations on April 16, King, Spock and Harry Belafonte linked arms and led a parade of people dedicated to peace in Vietnam. Draft cards were burned and people threw eggs at the parade. Some of the younger people chanted, "Hell no, we won't go" and "Hey, hey, LBJ, how many kids did you kill today?" King addressed the crowd calling on the United States to honor its commitment to stop the bombing campaign in the North. "I would like to urge students from colleges all over the nation to use this summer and coming summers educating and organizing communities across the nation against war." Prior to his speech, King and others presented a note to undersecretary for special political affairs for the United Nations, Dr. Ralph Bunche, which read, "We rally at the United

Nations in order to affirm support of the principles of peace, universality, equal rights and self determination of peoples embodied in the Charter and acclaimed by mankind, but violated by the United States."[6]

King's antiwar stand was gaining momentum and having an effect on both movements. He followed up the rally at the United Nations with a nationwide peace effort called "Vietnam Summer." King and Dr. Spock made it an initiative that they supported. King said that the war had "increased the possibilities of nuclear war to destroy mankind." In addition to that, King believed that there needed to be a national discussion on this matter. "There comes a time when silence is betrayal," he said, "and today we are involved in one of the most bloody and cruel wars in history. It is poisoning the soul of our nation and has isolated our nation morally and politically." In a reference to the African American population, he continued his position that the war had "damaged the movement to aid the disinherited people of our nation." Further, he said, "It has diverted civil rights aims and fighting the slums…. So we feel the need to take a stand on the war."[7]

In an effort to stop the growing dissent at home regarding the Vietnam War, President Johnson had General William Westmoreland address a joint session of Congress on April 28, 1967. Westmoreland was the commander of U.S. forces in Vietnam and wanted to assure the American people that the war was going well and he had a plan. He said that the only way to defeat the enemy was a strategy of "unrelenting but discriminating military, political and psychological pressure on his whole structure and at all levels." In a veiled comment to the growing antiwar movement at home, Westmoreland said, "In evaluating the enemy strategy, it is evident to me that he believes our Achilles' heel is our resolve." Once done with his speech, Westmorland turned to Vice President Humphrey and Speaker of the House John McCormack and saluted. Then he turned and saluted the audience. Senator Robert Kennedy and other "peace Democrats" were seated in the front row for the speech. It was noted that their applause was not as enthusiastic as the rest of the chamber.[8]

Westmoreland was invited to a luncheon to address the governors of the states at 2:55 p.m. in the East Room of the White House. In his introduction of Westmorland, Johnson said, "The war in Vietnam reaches deep into every State and into every community and into every home in our land. And thus I think it concerns each of us very deeply as Americans and as executives of the States and the Nation." Johnson told the group that he wanted them there first for their opinion. "As long as the fighting continues in Vietnam, we have not achieved our goal—the goal of a just and honorable and workable peace. And I hope that your counsel will help us to find the way to peace." In addition to that, he said he wanted the governors to understand the issues so they could talk to their constituents about the war.⁹

King saw this speech as a maneuver by the Johnson administration to stop the growing antiwar movement in the nation. Given the nature of the speech, King believed that the Westmorland speech was meant to gain support for an escalation of the war. Calling the United States "the greatest purveyor of violence in the world today," he asked young people around the nation who were against the war to file as conscientious objectors. From this pulpit in Atlanta, he went further to talk about the attack on the antiwar movement. "There is a very dangerous development in the nation now to equate dissent with disloyalty," King said. He went further saying that Westmoreland was brought back to the United States "to develop a sentiment and consensus for the further escalation of the war to further silence dissent." King continued his position that the United States was on the wrong side of a revolutionary movement He was interrupted by applause twice and given a standing ovation at the end. Stokely Carmichael of the Black Power movement was in attendance. "I don't know about you, but I ain't going to study war no more," King said to the group.¹⁰

Beyond the speech in Atlanta, King continued to publicly respond to his critics on how the antiwar movement and the civil rights movement were connected. He said in an address to five hundred people at a joint luncheon of the Hungry Club and the Alpha Phi Alpha organizations in Atlanta that it would be "absurd to be concerned about integrated schools without being concerned about the survival of the world in which to integrate." King remarked that the "two issues are tied together and I'm going to keep them together." King went on to say that his opposition also stemmed from his belief that Vietnam might cause a larger war with China.¹¹ King's feelings on the war were part of a nationwide movement that involved not only the civil rights leader, but also members of the Senate.

II

*"I think that what we are doing
at the present time in Vietnam is a mistake."*

Robert Kennedy appeared on CBS television and on the radio on May 15, 1967. On that broadcast he and Governor Ronald Reagan discussed the Vietnam War. It was part of the *Town Meeting of the World*, where people asked questions from the BBC studio in London. Kennedy was asked whether he agreed with Dean Rusk's assertion that the demonstrations in the United States were prolonging the war. "The war is going on in Vietnam, being extended in Vietnam, really because of the determination of those who are our adversaries, the North Vietnamese, the Vietcong, National Liberation Front," he responded. "I don't think a particular action takes place … because of the protests here in the United States. I think that if all the protests were ended, and even if all of the objections to the war came to an end here in this country, that the war in Vietnam would continue." Ronald Reagan, who was then the governor of California, disagreed with Kennedy, saying,

> I definitely think the demonstrations are prolonging the war in that they're giving the enemy, who I believe must face defeat on relative comparison of the power of the two nations, they are giving him encouragement to continue, to hold out in the hope that division here in America will bring about a peace without defeat for that enemy.[12]

This exchange between Kennedy and Reagan is an example of how politics was changing in the 1960s. Where Kennedy saw no correlation between an expression of free speech and the war effort, Reagan believed that the actions of Americans exercising that right were empowering the enemy.

Kennedy, however, was not clear when he was asked if the war in Vietnam was an "illegal war." He said he did not agree with that characterization. "I have some reservations as I've stated them before about some aspects of the war, but I think that the United States is making every effort to try to make it possible for the people of South Vietnam to determine their own destiny," he said. Reagan agreed with this, saying, "This country of ours has a long history of non-aggression but also a willingness to befriend and go to the aid of those who would want to be free and determine their own destiny." However, when it came to the draft, the two of them disagreed.

Reagan was challenged by a student asking whether "draft dodgers" and conscientious objectors had the right to express their beliefs through those actions. Reagan said that there were some who were using technicalities in the language to avoid service, which he did not agree with. There were others, however, whom he understood on religious grounds. That said, he continued with his response:

> But I believe if government is to mean anything at all, that all of us have a responsibility, once the action has been decided upon and supposedly by the majority will, that we then, while reserving our right to disagree, we support the collective or the unified effort of the nation…. We give up certain individual freedoms in the interest of—well, I suppose it comes from our own Constitution our idea that every American or every person has the right, is born with the right to life, liberty and the pursuit of happiness.

Robert Kennedy disagreed. "I don't think that we're automatically correct or automatically right and morality is on our side or God is automatically on our side because were involved in a war," he said. "I don't think that the mere fact that the United States is involved in the use of force with an adversary makes everything that the United States then does absolutely correct."[13]

Kennedy's response continued to empower those who spoke out against the war. "So I—the idea that we're involved in this kind of a struggle, if there are those within the United States that feel that the struggle could be ended more rapidly with less loss of life, that the terror and the destruction would be less if we took a different course, then I think that they should make their views known," he said. In fact, Kennedy stressed that people had an obligation to speak out if they disagreed in American society. "I don't think they're less patriotic because they feel that. In fact, I think that they would be less patriotic if they didn't state their views and give their ideas, just because the United States is involved in this kind of a conflict as we are at the present time." He concluded, "Not to state any opposition, or say that we can't state an opposition because of the—the fact that we're involved in a struggle I think is an error."[14] The exchange is an example where Kennedy was willing to accept, even welcome, a dissenting opinion in the hopes of finding a solution on Vietnam. To be sure, Kennedy wanted an end to the war, but he also wanted there to be elections in South Vietnam, despite the outcome. He made that clear on the Senate floor a few months later.

By August 1967 the growing division in the nation regarding Vietnam started to gain momentum. As the Johnson administration continued efforts to have an election in South Vietnam, Robert Kennedy and other senators spoke out on the nature of the elections amid the current state of the war. From the floor of the Senate, Kennedy said that the "ruling Junta in South Vietnam is making a fraud and farce" of the election. When the idea of sending observers to South Vietnam was introduced, Kennedy disagreed. He said that the United States needed the "assurance that the present trend will be reversed so that our moral position in Vietnam will not be further eroded." He said that the military junta in South Vietnam had made it nearly impossible to have a free election. "If there is no free election, if somebody asks 'what are you doing in South Vietnam?' what can one possibly argue? What is the remaining argument that can be made for what we are doing there?"[15]

Kennedy went further to articulate his position and that America's commitment was to the people of South Vietnam, "not to any Government, not to any generals, not to a powerful and privileged few." If the vote for the government was fraudulent in any way, "the rulers of South Vietnam will have denied their people the very right for which more than 12,000 Americans have died ... [and] we would no longer have a common purpose with the Government of Vietnam."[16] In November Kennedy did more to sharpen his position on the war for the public.

On November 16, 1967, Kennedy appeared on CBS's *Face the Nation*. In the interview Kennedy said that he planned to support Johnson if he were nominated for the 1968 campaign and downplayed any notions that he was going to run for the presidency. "I think one of the problems in the country at the moment is the fact that there is not communication between races and between various groups in the country, that there is not real dialogue about Vietnam," he said. "We have taken to the streets, there is violence, there is lawlessness ... we frequently will not let those who disagree with us speak." After being asked about his position on Vietnam, Kennedy said, "I think that what we are doing at the present time in Vietnam is a mistake."[17]

When asked whose interests the war served, Kennedy pointed to self-determination and said that the nation was making an effort in the region "so that the people would have their own right to decide their own future and could select their own form of government, and it wasn't going to be imposed on them by the North Vietnamese, and we had the support of South Vietnam." He emphasized that while he was in office with both his brother and Johnson, that was how he viewed the conflict. The war, however, since that time had turned into something else. What started as a fight for self-determination morphed into a protracted war that involved both the nation's defense and halting the spread of communism. Kennedy said that the United States' intentions had changed. "Now we've changed and switched," he said.

> Maybe they don't want it, but we want it. So we're going in there and we're killing South Vietnamese; we're killing children; we're killing women; we're killing innocent people because we don't want to have the war fought in American soil, or because they're twelve thousand miles away and they get to be eleven thousand miles away.[18]

Kennedy's comments are a testament to how he saw the war in 1967. To be sure, this was the war that he and his brother had talked about four or five years prior.

Beyond the change in strategy, Kennedy, like King in his comments on the war, saw the moral issues in the war and how it was contradictory to American ideals. He posed the question to the moderator, "Do we have the right here in the United States to perform these because we want to protect ourselves, so that ... it is not a greater problem for us in the United States?" He responded to his own question, saying, "I very seriously question whether we have that right.... I think other people are fighting it, other people are carrying the burden ... but this is also our war." In this instance,

Kennedy and King shared a common belief in where they saw the Vietnam War headed.

> Those of us who stay here in the United States, we must feel it when we use napalm, when a village is destroyed and civilians are killed. This is our responsibility. This is the moral obligation and moral responsibility for us here in the United States. And I think we have forgotten about that.

Kennedy went further with this notion of a moral issue saying that the United States had done more than just kill the enemy or the Vietcong: "We are also responsible for tens and tens of thousands of innocent casualties, and I think we are going to have a difficult time explaining this to ourselves."[19] This moral position on the war was something that he and King agreed on, and it did a great deal to demonstrate to the nation that there were some people who considered the moral questions in times of war. The war did a great deal to unite Kennedy and King in the public eye. While they approached it from a different perspective, they both had a similar vision that empowered many of the rights movements in the late sixties.

III

"This is a war for the allegiance of the people."

Robert Kennedy published a book titled *To Seek a Newer World* in 1967 that brought together some of his speeches and thoughts on the issues of the 1960s. It was, most likely, a means to get his views out there for the voters if he decided to challenge Lyndon Johnson for the nomination, which some people were asking him to do. One of the topics that he addressed was Vietnam. "It is dangerously easy, even seductive, to concentrate on what we know best: conventional warfare, bombing from the air, technology and armies that do not meddle in politics," he wrote. "But to do this is to ignore every past lesson of this war, and all of the "new wars" of the last twenty years. "For if these conflicts are called wars, and have deep international consequences, they are at the same time not wars, and their outcomes are determined by internal factors." Kennedy concluded, "Their essence is political."[20] Kennedy had stressed since his time in the White House that the goal in Vietnam should be focused on the political elements and not the military. To be sure, counterinsurgency programs were what he believed could assure victory in Vietnam. Furthermore, he saw this as the only way to win in Vietnam. Once the elections were done and a government was chosen by the people, then it was time for the United States to leave the territory.

Kennedy argued in his book that a superior military was not the best way to win in Vietnam. He said that the use of advanced weapons was not conclusive for several reasons. One of those reasons was the character of a military force that only destroys. Ultimately, he wrote, "the inadequacy of military power is that it can give not hope. Force is neutral; it has no program." Hope was a pervasive factor in Kennedy's plan in Vietnam. "Every insurgent movement lives not primarily on force, but on a dream—of independence, of justice, of progress, of a better life for one's children. For such dreams, men will undergo great hardship and sacrifice."[21] In his book, Kennedy stressed that there was the "other war" in Vietnam, one which he believed should be the focus of efforts in the region.

Kennedy wanted the United States to embrace a policy that aimed at changing the political course in Vietnam. "Since 1966," he wrote, "it has been referred to as the 'other war,' to distinguish it from the active large-unit combat operations, fought principally by American troops." He believed that this was where the war could be won. This "other war" was "the political contest for the allegiance of the people of Vietnam, that is in fact *the* war. And this 'other war' has been lost repeatedly in the last two decades." Kennedy argued that the French involvement in the 1940s and 1950s followed by the successive governments have failed at this "other war." He stressed that the lessons they had learned at that point were that Vietnam taught the United States "that a government must command the willing allegiance of its people, and make itself a vehicle for the satisfaction of their national and personal aspirations."[22] It seems clear that Kennedy's commitment to fair elections to determine the government in Vietnam stemmed from his commitment that the effort to win the war should begin by focusing on the "other war."

Kennedy also commented on the election process that took place in September 1967 in Vietnam. While that effort was something that would address the "other war" in Vietnam, it also demonstrated that the government in Vietnam was reliant on American troops. "The elections may have given a paper veneer of respectability to the ruling group that survives by the strength of American arms. They have not affected the allegiance of the South Vietnamese people; though they may, if we so desire, allow us to delude ourselves." Kennedy stressed that the elections of 1967 "thus appear as another event in the long history of missed opportunities, failures of essential political action, which at each turn of the road have had to be rescued by the application of greater military force."[23]

In his book he stressed that if there were not true elections then there was not a commitment of the South Vietnamese people to the government. He quoted President Kennedy, who said in 1963, "It is their war. They are the ones that have to win it or lose it. We can help them, we can give them equipment, we can send more men out there as advisers, but they have to win it, the people of Vietnam against the communists." Getting the people of Vietnam to believe in their government and a commitment to government other than communism was essential to winning the war in Vietnam according to Kennedy's book. "This is a war for the allegiance of the people," he wrote.

> If after thirteen years of American involvement, and over two years of major combat participation, the "other war" has failed to attract the allegiance of the people of Vietnam, we must ask ourselves whether all the sacrifice—the scars of which will still be borne twenty and more years from now by Vietnamese children and American young men—will have been for the benefit of forgotten generals and a selfish elite.[24]

Kennedy's thoughts on Vietnam speak to his commitment not only to find a solution to the conflict but also begin to address the aftermath of the war that had ravaged the countryside for so many years. It is an example of how his evolution as a politician in his own right in the wake of his brother's assassination had come to full fruition. To be sure, his presidential campaign in 1968 continued that journey, only to be halted suddenly and tragically by an assassin's bullet.

IV

"Somehow this madness must cease."

As 1967 came to a close, Martin Luther King continued with his comments on the Vietnam War and his commitment to peace. The Canadian Broadcast Cooperation invited King to give a series of talks as part of the Massey Lectures that would be broadcast on their radio network. Coretta Scott King wrote in 1968, just after King's death, that "the assignment was for him to talk about anything he considered of importance, of relevance not only to the United States, but the world at large." King wrote that her husband chose topics that were

> uppermost in his mind during the past years and months: his conclusion that nonviolent protest had evolved in to actions of civil disobedience; his conviction that our role in the Vietnam war demanded closer scrutiny and stronger resistance; his thoughts about the role which our awakened youth—both black and white—might play in the shaping of a new world.[25]

These are topics that were pervasive in the 1960s. His lectures serve as a final treatise of sorts on his vision for the nation, indeed the world. His final lecture, which took place from his pulpit at Ebenezer Church in Atlanta, Georgia, was titled a "Christmas Sermon on Peace."

In his remarks King addressed the people who said that he was foolish to try and make a connection between the Vietnam War and the civil rights movement. "Why you?" they asked. "Peace and civil rights don't mix. Aren't you hurting the cause of your people?" he said. "And when I hear such questions, I have been greatly saddened, for they mean that the inquirers have never really known me, my commitment or my calling." His address concentrated on his reasoning for making a comment on the Vietnam War, saying that he "remained perplexed ... by the complexities and ambiguities of Vietnam."[26] From there he outlined the same reason that he decided to make a comment on the war as he did in other public comments. "If we continue, there will be no doubt in my mind and in the mind of the world that we have no honorable intentions in Vietnam.... Somehow this madness must cease."[27]

Like Kennedy, King's message was to get away from war and focus on other efforts to win the war in Southeast Asia. King believed that a "positive revolution of values is our best defense against Communism." He concluded, "War is not the answer. Communism will never be defeated by the use of atomic bombs or nuclear weapons." He finished the address saying, "We must find new ways to speak for peace in Vietnam and justice throughout the developing world, a world that borders on our doors." King believed that a commitment to this kind of peace was the only way to find a solution in Vietnam. "If we do not act, we shall surely be dragged down the long, dark, and shameful corridors of time reserved for those who possess power without compassion, might without morality, and strength without sight."[28]

The final lecture was broadcast on Christmas Eve 1967. King's comments were centered around peace on earth. "We have neither peace within nor peace without," King started the sermon. "Our world is sick with war; everywhere we turn we see its ominous possibilities.... If we don't have goodwill toward men in this world we will destroy ourselves by the misuse of our own instruments and our power. Wisdom born of experience should tell us that war is obsolete." King believed that survival of humankind was contingent on leaders embracing peaceful measures in the world. "And so, if we assume that life is worth living, if we assume that mankind has the right to survive, then we must find an alternative to war."[29] King went on to discuss those alternatives to war and ushering in peace.

King believed that the concept of nonviolence should be used to address these problems as they were to combat racial issues in the South. "It really boils down to this: that all life is interrelated. We are all caught in an inescapable network of mutuality, tied in a single garment of destiny. Whatever affects one directly, affects all indirectly." This was the essence of his message for peace. "We are made to live together because of this interrelated structure of reality." King believed that until the world recognized this idea that they were all interrelated there would never be peace on earth.[30] King used a very eloquent argument on how many leaders in history looked for peace while at the same time they perpetrated some of the worst wars.

King saw the fact that the great military geniuses of the world spoke about peace as the ends to their means of destruction.

> The conquerors of old who came killing in pursuit of peace, Alexander, Julius Caesar, Charlemagne, and Napoleon, were akin in seeking a peaceful world order. If you will read Mein Kampf closely enough, you will discover that Hitler contended that everything he did in Germany was for peace. And the leaders of the world today talk eloquently about peace. Every time we drop our bombs in North Vietnam, President Johnson talks eloquently about peace.

King saw this as a problem for the world. Humankind's commitment to peace should be a process, not an end to destructive means. "We must pursue peaceful ends through peaceful means," he said.[31] King continued with his sermon, pointing to the nonviolent methods that he believed the world needed to embrace to usher in peace on earth. It all led up to a discussion of his dream that he shared on the steps of the Lincoln Memorial in 1963.

Martin Luther King, Jr.'s "I Have a Dream" speech is an iconic moment in the civil rights movement. On the eve of his last Christmas on earth, King reflected on his dream in this sermon. "I must confess to you today that not long after talking about that dream I started seeing it turn into a nightmare," he began, addressing the violence of the movement in late 1963 and the impoverished conditions of the nation that he confronted in the next phase of the movement.

> I remember the first time I saw that dream turn into a nightmare, just a few weeks after I had talked about it. It was when four beautiful, unoffending, innocent Negro girls were murdered in a church in Birmingham, Alabama. I watched that dream turn into a nightmare as I moved through the ghettos of the nation and saw my black brothers and sisters perishing on a lonely island of poverty in the midst of a vast ocean of material prosperity, and saw the nation doing nothing to grapple with the Negroes' problem of poverty.[32]

These were moments in the movement that had a profound impact on King. To be sure his vision for the nation was best exemplified in that speech from 1963. On the threshold of 1968, amid the Vietnam War and continuing racial strife, King wanted to do more to change the nation and usher in an age of goodwill and peace.

King also reflected on the tension that was so pervasive within the Black community in the nation. "I saw that dream turn into a nightmare," he said, "as I watched my black brothers and sisters in the midst of anger and understandable outrage, in the midst of their hurt, in the midst of their disappointment, turn to misguided riots to try to solve that problem."[33] The riots and violence were something that he hoped he could confront with love and nonviolence. Despite the setbacks, King never faltered in his vision.

The Vietnam War was something that in 1967 King was committed to speaking out on, contributing to a nationwide discussion on war and violence. "I saw that dream turn into a nightmare as I watched the war in Vietnam escalating, and as I saw so-called military advisors, sixteen thousand strong, turn into fighting soldiers until today over 500,000 American boys are fighting on Asian soil," he said. But despite these issues and the growing violence that he was fighting, King was not going to quit on his dream.

> Yes, I am personally the victim of deferred dreams, of blasted hopes, but in spite of that I close today by saying I still have a dream, because, you know, you can't give up in life. If you lose hope, somehow you lose that vitality that keeps life moving, you lose that courage to be, that quality that helps you go on in spite of all. And so today I still have a dream.[34]

What followed was a stirring sermon on how his dream could still be realized. To be sure, that vision is something that drove many Americans to work toward peace and hopefully find solutions to the issues that had plagued the nation in those fateful days of the sixties.

King finished his sermon with a positive rendition of a dream speech that looked to empower his followers as they entered a new year. "I have a dream that one day men will rise up and come to see that they are made to live together as brothers," he said.

> I still have a dream this morning that one day every Negro in this country, every colored person in the world, will be judged on the basis of the content of his character rather than the color of his skin, and every man will respect the dignity and worth of human personality.

This was not a new dream, but the original speech realized anew amid new hardships that had developed in the nation and the world. When King gave that first speech in 1963, he was an up-and-coming leader in the movement. Now, with a Nobel Peace Prize and two major acts of Congress that he had helped usher into American law, he was an affirmed force that had the ability to make change in the nation. He finished his sermon saying, "With this faith we will be able to speed up the day when there will be peace on earth and good will toward men. It will be a glorious day, the morning stars will sing together, and the sons of God will shout for joy."[35]

Martin Luther King and Robert Kennedy had a clear vision for the nation as they entered the final months of their lives. The year 1968 would prove to be a turning point for the nation. Kennedy and King were in the forefront of that change only to be taken suddenly before they had the opportunity to follow those ideals to full fruition. Their deaths marked a moment in history where it seemed that America would never come back from those fateful days that played such an enormous role in reshaping the American identity and ushering in an era where the American people were wary of the government and wanted to take back power for themselves. Indeed, it was a revolution that proved to last into the twenty-first century. The racial tension and military conflicts that played such a prominent role in the sixties came back to characterize the early part of the twenty-first century.

16

1968

I

"I shall not seek, and I will not accept."

At the beginning of 1968, the war in Vietnam took a major turn that would affect the nation. On January 30, 1968, the North Vietnamese attacked several major points in South Vietnam that would be known as the Tet Offensive. The attacks ranged from the demilitarized zone to the Ca Mau Peninsula, the southern tip of Vietnam.[1] This attack was something that the U.S. military forces in Vietnam did not expect. William Westmoreland's intelligence officer later said, "Even had I known exactly what was to take place, it was so preposterous that I probably would have been unable to sell it to anybody."[2] Walter Cronkite was said to comment, "What the hell is going on? I thought we were winning the war!" George C. Herring writes, "Televised accounts of the bloody fighting in Saigon and Hue made a mockery of Johnson and of Westmoreland's optimistic year-end reports, widening the credibility gap, and cynical journalists openly mocked Westmoreland's claim of victory."[3]

An editorial in the *New York Times* said, "In three days of astonishingly sharp and sustained attack, the Vietcong and their North Vietnamese allies have overrun and isolated wide areas of Saigon, including the United States Embassy grounds, for an agonizing six hours." The *Times* mentioned that U.S. officials had dismissed the offensive as a "'one shot effort,' a 'psychological gambit,' a 'diversionary tactic' and anticipated 'fireworks'" by the Vietcong. While the editorial acknowledged that it was unclear what impact this attack would have on the war, "it is evidently far more serious than any or all of these assessments acknowledge." Like many other news organizations, the *Times* acknowledged the inefficiency of the American military leadership and how that played a role in the attack. "The scope, the intensity and the tenacious thrust of the Communist attacks clearly caught a supposedly alerted allied command badly off balance. Initial Communist successes throw doubt on recent official American claims of progress in the war."[4]

Robert F. Kennedy had been contemplating whether he should challenge Johnson for the nomination. He had always believed that Johnson could not carry on the vision that he and his brother had for the nation, and he felt it was time to challenge his presidency. There was some debate among Kennedy's advisers whether he should go against an incumbent. Walter Cronkite interviewed Kennedy on March 13, 1968, and asked about the senator's intentions of running for the presidency. Kennedy said that he was "giving it thought." One of his main issues was how the administration continued with the policy in Vietnam where he said after hearing Dean Rusk speak, "We're going to continue the same policies and the same programs that we followed over the period of the last few years, which I think can lead to a catastrophic ending."[5]

In addition to Vietnam, Kennedy expressed concern over President Johnson's reaction to the Kerner Commission Report, which looked into the racial riots from the previous summer, and there was no response from Johnson. The report concluded, "Our nation is moving toward two societies, one black, one white—separate and unequal." The report stressed that this racial division in the nation was not inevitable. "The movement apart can be reversed," it said. "It is time to make good the promises of American democracy to all citizen—urban and rural, white and black, Spanish-surname, American Indian, and every minority group."[6] The report was something that drove not only Kennedy but many other people who believed that there needed to be something to end the racial tension.

"These are grave crises," Kennedy said, "crises that are facing this country internally and in our relationship to Southeast Asia." When asked if the Democratic Party was divided over these issues, Kennedy responded, "Yes, I think it's divided. I think that's demonstrated. I felt that it was divided and I felt that there was this—and that people were very disturbed across the country and I think that the primary in New Hampshire proved that."[7] Kennedy's reference was to the New Hampshire primary where Johnson only received 49 percent of the Democratic vote when he was predicted to get two-thirds. His challenger, Eugene McCarthy, won 42 percent.[8]

Kennedy made it clear to Cronkite that if he entered the race he would be committed to winning. Kennedy said that he felt strongly about his own generation, but it was future generations that compelled him to run against Johnson, saying, "What we do now and the policies that we put into operation, the programs we effectuate—they're going to have ... tremendous bearing on the next generation of Americans and the young children." He concluded, "So we have a responsibility to them—and I feel that strongly—and I am distressed at the direction we are moving, both at home and around the rest of the world."[9] Kennedy did not wait much longer to make his decision to run for the presidency.

In the Caucus Room of the Old Senate Office Building, the same room where his brother, John F. Kennedy, announced his candidacy for the presidency, Robert F. Kennedy stood before the cameras, with his family by his side, to tell the nation that he intended to challenge Lyndon Johnson for the Democratic nomination. He wore a blue suit with his *PT 109* tie clip that was given out during the campaign in 1960.[10] It was a long road from that moment at Hickory Hill when he heard that his brother had been shot and it could be fatal. In his eyes, he was reclaiming the mantel that his brother was supposed to pass on to him.

"I do not run for the Presidency merely to oppose any man but to propose new policies," Kennedy said. "I run because I am convinced that this country is on a perilous course and because I have such strong feelings about what must be done, and I feel that I'm obliged to do all that I can." He cited many of the issues that had plagued the nation since the assassination of his brother. "I run because it is now unmistakably clear that we can change these disastrous divisive policies only by changing the men who are now making them. For the reality of recent events in Vietnam has been glossed over with illusions."[11] Kennedy made the argument that it was time for change, and he wanted to lead it into the next decade.

In his statement Kennedy pointed to both his past experience and the issues that were clearly in the media. He cited the Kerner Commission Report saying that it had been "largely ignored" by Johnson. In addition, he talked about his time on the National Security Council as attorney general, the Cuban missile crisis and the issues in Berlin that he advised President Kennedy on in 1961 and 1962. In that role and as a senator he told the room that he had "seen the inexcusable and ugly deprivation which caused children to starve in Mississippi, black citizens to riot in Watts, young Indians to commit suicide on their reservations because they've lacked all hope and they feel they have no future." He was running on those issues. "I cannot stand aside from the contest that will decide our nation's future and our children's future."[12] Kennedy's last campaign started in that room. His entrance into the race seemed to mark the end of the Johnson era.

The Tet Offensive would prove to be a defining moment in the presidency of Lyndon Baines Johnson. On March 30, 1968, Johnson addressed the nation regarding the war in Vietnam and his presidency. "We are prepared to move immediately toward peace through negotiations," Johnson said after outlining what the administration had done in the months leading up to the speech. "So, tonight, in the hope that this action will lead to early talks, I am taking the first step to deescalate the conflict. We are reducing—substantially reducing—the present level of hostilities." Johnson ordered troops to stop any offensive in the North, with the exception of a few areas. "Our purpose in this action is to bring about a reduction in the level of violence that now exists. It is to save the lives of brave men—and to save the lives of innocent women and children. It is to permit the contending forces to move closer to a political settlement."[13] Johnson went on with what he had planned to do to bring about peace talks in Vietnam. Then at the end of the speech he told the nation that he had not planned to run for reelection in 1968.

It was a shock to the nation. Johnson started his announcement quoting John F. Kennedy, a fitting way to make the announcement, since it was in the wake of Kennedy's death that he took office. "There is division in the American house now," he said. "There is divisiveness among us all tonight. And holding the trust that is mine, as President of all the people, I cannot disregard the peril to the progress of the American people and the hope and the prospect of peace for all peoples." Johnson was a great statesman, but the Vietnam War had done a great deal to make his time in office difficult to the point where it hampered his vision of a Great Society.

> Fifty-two months and 10 days ago, in a moment of tragedy and trauma, the duties of this office fell upon me. I asked then for your help and God's, that we might continue America on its course, binding up our wounds, healing our history, moving forward in new unity, to clear the American agenda and to keep the American commitment for all of our people.[14]

Johnson affirmed that he was committed to finding a way to help America move forward.

Johnson believed that the war and finding a peaceful solution should occupy his days, not a political contest. "With America's sons in the fields far away, with America's future under challenge right here at home, with our hopes and the world's hopes for peace in the balance every day," he said, "I do not believe that I should devote an hour or a day of my time to any personal partisan causes or to any duties other than the awesome duties of this office—the Presidency of your country." With that in mind he made the announcement that very few presidents have done, especially given his landslide victory in 1964. "Accordingly, I shall not seek, and I will not accept, the nomination of my party for another term as your President."[15] With that statement, the road to the presidency would be much easier for Robert F. Kennedy.

II

"Because I've been to the mountaintop."

Martin Luther King was gearing up for the next phase of his movement in the opening months of 1968. He planned another march on Washington, to take place in April. This was a part of what he called the "Poor People's

Campaign." According to King, the goal of this march was to get Congress to pass legislation that helped Americans gain employment or disability benefits. He believed that finding some level of relief for African Americans would help maintain his vision of a nonviolent movement. King was at odds with the militant groups regarding his philosophy of nonviolence. President Johnson responded to this new effort, saying, "We'll do all we can to work with all groups, see that their views are heard, considered and acted upon."[16] King would go into the last month of his life with a vision that hoped to empower not only African Americans but also the impoverished, disenfranchised citizens of the country.

On March 4, 1968, King unveiled what he called the "Nonviolent Poor People's March on Washington." He said the date was planned for April 22, 1968, and it would include a march through the state of Alabama. He also continued to link the war in Vietnam to the civil rights movement, saying he wanted "the honorable end" to the conflict. "We believe the highest patriotism demands the ending of that war and the opening of a bloodless war to final victory over racism and poverty," he said. "Flame throwers in Vietnam fan the flames in our cities," he said, steadfast in his belief that the two issues were inextricably tied together. "I don't think the two matters can be separated, as some people continue to feel." King also commented on the Kerner Commission Report saying that it was a "physician's warning of approaching death [of American society], with a prescription to life. The duty of every American is to administer the remedy without the regard for the cost and without delay."[17]

In the month of March, King went around the nation recruiting people to march on Washington. He made a stop in New York, speaking to people in Harlem and Queens. "We need an alternative to riots and to timid supplication. Nonviolence is our most potent weapon," King told a group in Harlem. He visited a high school in Long Island and commented on the war in Vietnam, saying, "We've got to de-escalate and end that evil, unjust war. The hour has come for the President, Dean Rusk and the Administration to say we made a mistake in Vietnam."[18] King continued his efforts for his Poor People's Campaign by supporting a strike of sanitation workers in Memphis, Tennessee, later that week.

King marched in Memphis on March 28, 1968, with sanitation workers who were looking for fair wages. They made $1.70 an hour and wanted a fifteen-cent raise. The mayor of the city offered eight cents. The march was met with violence, and King, who was in the lead, was taken out of harm's way when the violence erupted. Sixteen-year-old Larry Payne was killed by police in the midst of the protests. Allegedly the African American youth was caught "looting" and attacked a police officer with a "butcher knife."

The violent end to the march cast doubt on King's ability to successfully make the march on Washington that he proposed in April.[19]

The day after the violence in Memphis, King reassured people that he was committed to showing that he could have a nonviolent march. He acknowledged that the march may have been "miscalculated." King told the group, "If I had known there was a possibility of violence yesterday I would not have had that particular march." In an effort to address the people who believed that there would be similar outbreaks of violence in Washington, King said, "We are fully determined to go to Washington. We feel it is an absolute necessity." The sanitation workers continued to strike. They carried placards that read in large letters, "I am a Man."[20]

King came back to Memphis in early April. On April 3, 1968, he delivered what has been referred to as his "Mountaintop" speech at Mason Temple. In a reflective way, King spoke about time and how if he had the opportunity he would go back through the ages to witness the great achievements and rhetoric throughout history. He acknowledged that there was something happening in the world. "The masses of people are rising up," he told the audience. "And wherever they are assembled today, whether they are in Johannesburg, South Africa; Nairobi, Kenya; Accra, Ghana; New York City; Atlanta, Georgia; Jackson, Mississippi; or Memphis, Tennessee—the cry is always the same: 'We want to be free.'"[21] He was grateful that he was alive to see this civil rights revolution. History has characterized this speech as almost prophetic. It would be his last major address to the people.

King stressed to the audience that the time had come for African Americans to take charge of their own destiny. "We mean business now, and we are determined to gain our rightful place in God's world. And that's all this whole thing is about," he stressed. Empowering the people, he said that he planned to march again, to bring his nonviolent protest to the masses. "We aren't going to let any mace stop us. We are masters in our nonviolent movement in disarming police forces; they don't know what to do." To be sure, the police and authorities of the 1960s were perplexed over how to deal with King and his followers, who would rather go to jail than pay a fine, who would rather be beaten than fight back. Indeed, this was a revolution, and King was the leader. "We don't have to argue with anybody," King said, stressing that another riot would not be productive for the movement. "We don't have to curse and go around acting bad with our words. We don't need any bricks and bottles. We don't need any Molotov cocktails."[22] He asked the people to continue a boycott of goods in Memphis. This was a protest at all levels in the hopes of bringing the Memphis leadership to its knees so that it gave in to the demands of the sanitation workers.

On another level, this movement was about legitimizing the use of nonviolent protest as a means to gain equal standing in the eye of the law. King stressed the sacrifice that they needed to make in order to keep this movement alive:

> Now, let me say as I move to my conclusion that we've got to give ourselves to this struggle until the end. Nothing would be more tragic than to stop at this point in Memphis. We've got to see it through. And when we have our march, you need to be there. If it means leaving work, if it means leaving school—be there. Be concerned about your brother. You may not be on strike. But either we go up together, or we go down together.

King was not only sending a message to the people; he was also recruiting them to march for justice and jobs and poor people everywhere. As King moved into the final thoughts of this speech, he spoke about stories from the Bible, empowering the crowd with steadfast determination to make the nation better. "Let us rise up tonight with a greater readiness. Let us stand with a greater determination. And let us move on in these powerful days, these days of challenge to make America what it ought to be. We have an opportunity to make America a better nation."[23]

In this speech, King recalled an attempt on his life in New York City. He was autographing a book that he wrote when a woman came up to him and asked him if he was Martin Luther King. "And I was looking down writing, and I said, 'Yes.' And the next minute I felt something beating on my chest. Before I knew it I had been stabbed by this demented woman." King was rushed to the hospital where they did X-rays. "And that blade had gone through, and the X-rays revealed that the tip of the blade was on the edge of my aorta, the main artery. And once that's punctured, your drowned in your own blood—that's the end of you," he said. He told the crowd, the *New York Times* wrote the next day that if he had sneezed, he would have died. He recalled a little girl writing to him saying, "I read that if you had sneezed, you would have died. And I'm simply writing you to say that I'm so happy that you didn't sneeze."[24]

King went on, reflectively again, that he was happy that had not sneezed. If that were the case he would not have been there for all the success of his movement starting in 1960 with the sit-in movement to the 1961 Freedom Riders to the 1963 events that galvanized the nation and brought him a Nobel Peace Prize to Selma in 1965 and finally to Memphis. "I'm so happy that I didn't sneeze." he also shared a story of his flight to Memphis and how they needed to make sure that the plane was free of any threats. "And then I got into Memphis. And some began to say the threats, or talk about the threats that were out. What would happen to me from some of our sick white brothers?"[25] This led into his stirring last words that have served as his final thoughts on the movement.

With a level of uncertainty, but also acceptance that things were out of his control, King said, "Well, I don't know what will happen now. We've got some difficult days ahead. But it really doesn't matter with me now, because I've been to the mountaintop. And I don't mind." King's words that followed demonstrated how he gave all of himself to the movement, how he was certain that he was not going to survive the days ahead and accepted it as long as the people he was leading understood that there was hope.

> Like anybody, I would like to live a long life. Longevity has its place. But I'm not concerned about that now. I just want to do God's will. And He's allowed me to go up to the mountain. And I've looked over. And I've seen the Promised Land. I may not get there with you. But I want you to know tonight, that we, as a people, will get to the promised land!

He concluded that he was happy that night. "I'm not worried about anything. I'm not fearing any man! Mine eyes have seen the glory of the coming of the Lord!"[26] King stepped away from the microphones into the arms of Ralph Abernathy.

III

"Make gentle the life of this world."

On April 4, 1968, Robert F. Kennedy was in Indianapolis, Indiana, when he heard about the assassination of Martin Luther King, Jr. John Lewis was among the people who met him at the airport that day. "I'm sorry, John," Kennedy said over a two-way radio as he made his way to the site where he was supposed to give a speech. "You've lost a leader. We've lost a leader," Kennedy said.[27] He addressed a predominantly African American crowd from the back of a pickup truck wearing an overcoat. He gave one of his most stirring speeches of his life, one that was historic and serves as evidence that he shared a vision for the nation with Martin Luther King. After asking members of the crowd to put down the signs, he told the crowd what had happened earlier in the day. "I have bad news for you, for all of our fellow citizens, and people who love peace all over the world, and that is that Martin Luther King was shot and killed tonight."[28] There were gasps and screams as Kennedy gave the news to the crowd.

"Martin Luther King dedicated his life to love and to justice for his fellow human beings, and he died because of that effort," he said. Like King, who took time to write a book on where the movement was headed, Kennedy said the same of the nation. "In this difficult day, in this difficult time for the United States, it is perhaps well to ask what kind of a nation we are and what direction we want to move in." Kennedy wanted to embody the ideals of King in his message to the crowd. He offered them a choice.

> For those of you who are black—considering the evidence there evidently is that there were white people who were responsible—you can be filled with bitterness, with hatred, and a desire for revenge. We can move in that direction as a country, in great polarization—black people amongst black, white people amongst white, filled with hatred toward one another.

Kennedy stayed true to King's vision and what he wanted for the nation and the world. Like the debate in the movement over militancy versus nonviolence, Kennedy stressed King's belief in nonviolence to the crowd. "Or we can make an effort, as Martin Luther King did," Kennedy said, "to understand and to comprehend, and to replace that violence, that stain of bloodshed that has spread across our land, with an effort to understand with compassion and love."[29]

Robert Kennedy rarely spoke about the death of his brother in public. In the moment, and amid a great crisis, he used that experience to make a connection with them. "For those of you who are black and are tempted to be filled with hatred and distrust at the injustice of such an act, against all white people," he said,

> I can only say that I feel in my own heart the same kind of feeling. I had a member of my family killed, but he was killed by a white man. But we have to make an effort in the United States, we have to make an effort to understand, to go beyond these rather difficult times.[30]

The fact that he considered the loss of his brother as the same as losing King for the African American group demonstrated that he had a level of compassion in 1968 that was not there when he began his journey in public life.

Kennedy quoted a passage from a poem by Aeschylus that embodied some of the grief that he experienced when his brother was assassinated, going back to that time when he found solace in Greek literature. He followed that up with a statement to the people of what he believed the nation needed in their time of grief.

> What we need in the United States is not division; what we need in the United States is not hatred; what we need in the United States is not violence or lawlessness; but love and wisdom, and compassion toward one another, and a feeling of justice toward those who still suffer within our country, whether they be white or they be black.

He asked the crowd to return home and say a prayer for Martin Luther King's family, "but more importantly to say a prayer for our own country, which all of us love—a prayer for understanding and that compassion of which I spoke."[31]

Kennedy continued with his speech, on the verge of tears, imploring the people to find it in themselves to get through that moment. "We can do well in this country," he said. "We will have difficult times; we've had difficult times in the past; we will have difficult times in the future. It is not the end of violence; it is not the end of lawlessness; it is not the end of disorder." He wanted them to look to the future, to look into the potential of the United States. "But the vast majority of white people and the vast majority of black people in this country want to live together, want to improve the quality of our life, and want justice for all human beings who abide in our land."

Kennedy concluded his speech harking back to the Greeks, a source of strength and solidarity for him. "Let us dedicate ourselves to what the Greeks wrote so many years ago: to tame the savageness of man and make gentle the life of this world. Let us dedicate ourselves to that, and say a prayer for our country and for our people."[32] With that he left, leaving behind his impassioned message of hope for the people. There were no riots in Indianapolis that night. However, there were riots throughout the nation. The next day Kennedy canceled all rallies and campaign stops. His only speech would address the death of Martin Luther King. He called Coretta Scott King and chartered a plane for her to go to Memphis. He said he would attend Dr. King's funeral.[33]

The next day Kennedy's speech was devoted to talking about the violence that had plagued America. He spoke at the Cleveland City Club. He was focused on the death of King and the riots that took place in the wake of his death. His usual speechwriters helped him with the draft, but he also had help from Ted Sorensen, his brother's main speechwriter, with the final version.[34] "This is a time of shame and sorrow," he started, very deliberately and slow, making each word count, each idea resonate with the people he was speaking to. "It is not a day for politics. I have saved this one opportunity to speak briefly to you about this mindless menace of violence in America which again stains our land and every one of our lives."[35] The violence that Kennedy was talking about was something that he had experienced too often in his adult life. It was something that he wanted to confront as he continued his evolution as a leader for the nation.

Robert Kennedy believed that violence was something that plagued the nation universally. It was necessary to confront that issue, especially in the wake of a tragedy like the death of King. "It is not the concern of any one race," he said.

> The victims of the violence are black and white, rich and poor, young and old, famous and unknown. They are, most important of all, human beings whom other human beings loved and needed. No one—no matter where he lives or what he

does—can be certain who will suffer from some senseless act of bloodshed. And yet it goes on and on.

He asked the question to the audience of why this has been case in American history. "What has violence ever accomplished? What has it ever created? No martyr's cause has ever been stilled by his assassin's bullet. No wrongs have ever been righted by riots and civil disorders." He concluded, "A sniper is only a coward, not a hero; and an uncontrolled, uncontrollable mob is only the voice of madness, not the voice of the people." His words demonstrate not only extreme sorrow in the wake of King's death, but also a leader who was trying to make sense of the violence that had plagued the nation in the 1960s. He wanted solutions to these problems in these last months of his life.

In many ways, Kennedy's speech emulated King's life work to embrace nonviolence and the fact that the nation was connected. In the spirit of John Donne and Dr. King, Kennedy said, "Whenever any American's life is taken by another American unnecessarily—whether it is done in the name of the law or in the defiance of law, by one man or a gang, in cold blood or in passion, in an attack of violence or in response to violence—whenever we tear at the fabric of life which another man has painfully and clumsily woven for himself and his children, the whole nation is degraded."[36] Indeed, this was a reference to the notion that we are all interrelated and connected in some way. He quoted Abraham Lincoln and commented on society's acceptance of violence.

To some extent, Kennedy argued, society had tacitly accepted violence as something that was commonplace, even celebrated. "We calmly accept newspaper reports of civilian slaughter in far off lands. We glorify killing on movie and television screens and call it entertainment. We make it easy for men of all shades of sanity to acquire weapons and ammunition they desire," he said. This was the heart of his comments. The American people had accepted violence into their lives as commonplace, something to live with. Kennedy and King wanted to get away from that notion and embrace a peaceful coexistence with one another.

Kennedy told the group that he knew the next phase, the thing that they needed to do as a society. "It is to achieve true justice among our fellow citizens.... The question is whether we can find in our own midst and in our own hearts that leadership of human purpose that will recognize the terrible truths of our existence," he said. To that end, Kennedy was committed to finding solutions, creating a path that would eventually make the nation stronger, more accepting and willing to embrace the diversity that made the nation strong. "We must admit in ourselves that our own children's future cannot be built on the misfortunes of others. We must recognize that this short life can neither be ennobled or enriched by hatred or revenge."³⁷

This was the doctrine that he ran on for presidency. He was determined to approach the problems that plagued the nation with a new attitude, one that would have an impact on the world as well as the nation, much like Dr. King. "Our lives on this planet are too short and the work to be done too great to let this spirit flourish any longer in our land. Of course we cannot vanish it with a program, nor with a resolution," he said knowing that the problem was systemic, something that had grown for a long time and needed to be approached in the same manner, not with some program or legislative agenda. Bobby Kennedy knew that the nation would have to work at solutions to the problems that led to King's death and his own death two months later. He believed in people and the determination to foster change.

> But we can perhaps remember—even if only for a time—that those who live with us are our brothers, that they share with us the same short movement of life, that they seek—as we do—nothing but the chance to live out their lives in purpose and happiness, winning what satisfaction and fulfillment they can.³⁸

This brotherhood and belief in the good in humanity was something that he left for the world in the wake of his death.

Kennedy finished his speech invoking the notion that the nation had the potential to embrace a common bond, something that could propel it into the next phase of the healing process. "Surely this bond of common faith, this bond of common goal, can begin to teach us something," he said. "Surely we can learn, at least, to look at those around us as fellow men and surely we can begin to work a little harder to bind up the wounds among us and to become in our hearts brothers and countrymen once again."³⁹ With this speech Kennedy's rhetoric took King's death and tried to bring positive change in the wake of such a tragedy.

Bobby Kennedy's campaign for the presidency embraced many of the qualities that were a part of both his and King's vision for the nation. In addition to speaking out on the racial tension in the nation, he was committed to ending the war in Vietnam, confronting poverty in the inner city and reforming welfare to name a few of the issues he spoke about in the two months after the death of Dr. King. When Kennedy was gunned down by Sirhan Sirhan on June 5, 1968, a victim of the violence that he wanted to end in the nation, he was still trying to make that dream, that vision for the nation, a reality. Both he and King shared a vision, and it is clear that as long as America continued to embrace those ideals that dream still had a chance to thrive and grow even larger.

Epilogue—Selma, 2015

"We know the march is not yet over."

On the site where Robert Kennedy gave his speech on Martin Luther King's death in Indianapolis there is a statue commemorating the event. The statue is a depiction of both Robert Kennedy and Martin Luther King, their arms outstretched to one another across a path, hoping to make a connection in death as they had in life. The two men lived parallel lives beginning with their ascent to public life in the 1950s and their untimely deaths by an assassin's bullet only two months apart from each other. The statue is the only living memorial to that shared vision that these men had for the nation. That said, their words, certainly their ideas, are another memorial to the vision that they shared.

President Barack Obama, the first African American to hold the post of president of the United States was awarded the Nobel Peace Prize in 2009. It was not lost on him how the power of that prize helped shape the civil rights movement, but also that King's efforts were a major reason why he was able to be there that night. "In 1964, when Dr. King received this prize, the course of the civil rights movement was still uncertain," he said.

> How that would play itself out was not yet entirely known. And for a Baptist preacher from the South to be lifted up on the international stage, to highlight the fact that this was not simply a parochial struggle but was rather a struggle for the ages, a struggle for the hearts and minds not just of the American people but of the world, and how we thought about each other and how we thought about minorities in countries everywhere, what extraordinary power that had. And as a consequence, I think it's fair to say that it helped to put the wind behind the sails of a movement that is largely responsible for both Michelle and my presence here tonight.[1]

Obama understood the power that King had in paving the future for himself and other African Americans.

Upon accepting that Nobel Peace Prize, Obama pointed to President

Kennedy's philosophy on how to consider the issues in the world. "Concretely, we must direct our effort to the task that President Kennedy called for long ago. 'Let us focus,' he said, 'on a more practical, more attainable peace, based not on a sudden revolution in human nature but on a gradual evolution in human institutions,'" he said.[2] This was a philosophy that Robert Kennedy embraced as he considered the issues in Vietnam and other parts of the world. Obama believed that the path to peace lay in the philosophies of the Kennedys, which was something that Robert Kennedy fought to uphold.

In his acceptance speech, Obama also pointed to the nonviolent philosophies of Gandhi and King. He said, "As someone who stands here as a direct consequence of Dr. King's life work, I am living testimony to the moral force of nonviolence. I know there's nothing weak, nothing passive, nothing naive in the creed and lives of Gandhi and King." He went further, saying that the philosophy of nonviolence "may not have been practical or possible in every circumstance, but the love that they preached, their fundamental faith in human progress, that must always be the North Star that guides us on our journey."[3] He invoked the remarks that King made when he was awarded the prize.

> As Dr. King said at this occasion so many years ago: "I refuse to accept despair as the final response to the ambiguities of history. I refuse to accept the idea that the 'isness' of man's present condition makes him morally incapable of reaching up for the eternal 'oughtness' that forever confronts him." Let us reach for the world that ought to be, that spark of the divine that still stirs within each of our souls.[4]

Obama understood that King's vision reached beyond those days in the sixties when he and Kennedy were trying to make sense of a time where people wanted, indeed needed leadership.

On March 7, 2015, fifty years after the march on Selma, Alabama, President Barack Obama joined Representative John Lewis on the stage to commemorate the event that led to the passage of the Voting Rights Act of 1965. "In one afternoon 50 years ago, so much of our turbulent history," Obama said to a crowd of nearly 40,000 people, "the stain of slavery and anguish of civil war, the yoke of segregation and tyranny of Jim Crow, the death of four little girls in Birmingham, and the dream of a Baptist preacher—all that history met on this bridge." Obama pointed to the power of the people who were there on that historic moment. "We gather here to honor the courage of ordinary Americans willing to endure billy clubs and the chastening rod, tear gas and the trampling hoof; men and women who despite the gush of blood and splintered bone would stay true to their north star and keep marching towards justice."[5]

Obama's words were meant to reflect on the sacrifice, on the violent nature of race relations in the 1960s. "The Americans who crossed this bridge, they were not physically imposing, but they gave courage to millions," he said. "They held no elected office, but they led a nation. They marched as Americans who had endured hundreds of years of brutal violence, countless daily indignities." He pointed to the fact that the very act of marching in Selma was what America was all about, this notion that ordinary people led the nation and stood up for rights.

> That's what makes us unique. That's what cements our reputation as a beacon of opportunity. Young people behind the Iron Curtain would see Selma and eventually tear down that wall. Young people in Soweto would hear Bobby Kennedy talk about ripples of hope and eventually banish the scourge of apartheid.

He spoke of Kennedy and his speech in South Africa. That notion, that hope that Kennedy was trying to convey to the world converged with President Obama, on Edmund Pettus Bridge, almost fifty years later. It speaks to the power of Kennedy's vision and the impact it had on a movement that focused on the rights of people.

Robert Kennedy was not the only person mentioned in that speech. Indeed, Martin Luther King's vision was also with them that day. The mere fact that they met on the bridge where he led people to stand up to segregation was a testament to his influence. "Their endeavors gave the entire South the chance to rise again, not by reasserting the past, but by transcending the past," Obama said. "What a glorious thing, Dr. King might say. And what a solemn debt we owe." Understanding that the work they started fifty years before was incomplete, Obama said, "We know the march is not yet over. We know the race is not yet won. We know that reaching that blessed destination where we are judged, all of us, by the content of our character requires admitting as much, facing up to the truth." Obama celebrated America's uniqueness and finished, saying, "We honor those who walked so we could run. We must run so our children soar. And we will not grow weary, for we believe in the power of an awesome God and we believe in this country's sacred promise."[6]

Robert F. Kennedy and Martin Luther King's rhetoric inspired generations of Americans. Their vision for the nation was something that shaped future politicians and brought into sharp focus the issues that remained important. Poverty and racial tension have consistently created barriers within American society that held people back from attaining their full potential in a society that championed such social mobility. Kennedy and King were trying to break down those walls of oppression. Their words in the wake of the assassination of John F. Kennedy helped the nation come to grips with that tragedy by invoking a message of hope. In addition to those issues, both men wanted to address the morality of war.

The war in Vietnam, with all of its issues, was something that these two men wanted to address. They were both looking for the correct response and hoped to find a solution that gave hope to the people. Their words, actions and vision were something that they shared in those final years of their lives. That type of rhetoric, looking to bring out the good in human nature in the hopes of finding progressive solutions, is a very powerful force in American society. The 1960s was a moment in American history where people wanted leadership. Kennedy and King filled that void only to be violently taken away at a critical moment. Their vision, however, was something that people took into future generations and helped to define what truly mattered in America as leaders continue to move forward and the ever-changing American culture, that has made the nation so distinct, continues to influence the world.

Chapter Notes

Prologue

1. Martin Luther King, Jr., to Senator Robert F. Kennedy, March 2, 1966, "Letter to Senator Kennedy from MLK," The King Center Digital Archives, http://www.thekingcenter.org/archive/document/letter-senator-robert-kennedy-mlk.
2. Senator Robert F. Kennedy to Martin Luther King, Jr., March 31, 1966, The King Center Digital Archives, http://www.thekingcenter.org/archive/document/letter-robert-f-kennedy-mlk-2.
3. Arthur M. Schlesinger, Jr., *Robert Kennedy and His Times* (New York: Houghton Mifflin, 2002), 607–608.
4. Schlesinger, *RFK and His Times*, 150.
5. Ibid., 165.
6. Taylor Branch, *Parting the Waters: America in the King Years, 1954–63* (New York: Simon & Schuster, 1988), 166; David J. Garrow, *Bearing the Cross: Martin Luther King, Jr. and the Southern Christian Leadership Conference* (New York: Quill William Morrow, 1986), 60–61.
7. Harris Wofford, *Of Kennedys and Kings: Making Sense of the Sixties* (Pittsburgh: University of Pittsburgh Press, 1980), 19.
8. Ibid.
9. Evan Thomas, *Robert Kennedy: His Life* (New York: Touchstone, 2000), 101.
10. Ibid., 101–102.
11. Ibid.
12. Address by the Honorable Robert F. Kennedy, Attorney General, to the University of Georgia Law School, 5/16/61, Robert F. Kennedy AG Papers, Speeches, Box 1, University of Georgia Law 5/6/61, JFKL.
13. Ibid.
14. Raymond Arsenault, *Freedom Riders: 1961 and the Struggle for Racial Justice* (New York: Oxford University Press, 2006), 234–235.
15. Philip A. Goduti, Jr., *Kennedy's Kitchen Cabinet and the Pursuit of Peace: The Shaping of American Foreign Policy, 1961–1963* (Jefferson, NC: McFarland, 2009), 100.
16. Philip A. Goduti, Jr., *Robert F. Kennedy and the Shaping of Civil Rights, 1960–1964* (Jefferson, NC: McFarland, 2013) 153–155.
17. Goduti, *Kennedy's Kitchen Cabinet*, 176–196.
18. *Foreign Relations of the United States 1961–1963, Volume XI: Cuban Missile Crisis and Aftermath*, ed. Edward C. Keefer, Charles S. Sampson, and Louis J. Smith (Washington, DC: United States Government Printing Office, 1996), 270–271.
19. Ibid.
20. Robert F. Kennedy recorded interview with Burke Marshall by Anthony Lewis, p. 496, 12/4/1964, John F. Kennedy Oral History Project of the John F. Kennedy Library.
21. Ibid., 497.
22. Ibid., 81–82.
23. Robert F. Kennedy Address to the North Carolina Cold War Seminar, 5/17/1963, Robert F. Kennedy AG Papers, Speeches, Box 2, 5/13/63–5/17/63, JFKL.

Chapter 1

1. Thomas, 277.
2. David Talbot, *Brothers: The Hidden History of the Kennedy Years* (New York: Free Press, 2007), 2.
3. Edwin Guthman, *We Band of Brothers: A Memoir of Robert F. Kennedy* (New York: Harper and Row, 1971), 244.
4. Thomas, 277–278.
5. Jeff Shesol, *Mutual Contempt: Lyndon Johnson, Robert Kennedy and the Feud That Defined a Decade* (New York: Norton, 1997),12.
6. Schlesinger, *RFK and His Times*, 205.
7. Shesol, 44.
8. Ibid., 45.
9. Robert F. Kennedy recorded interview by Arthur Schlesinger, p. 618, 2/27/1965, John F. Kennedy Oral History Project of the John F. Kennedy Library.
10. Ibid.

11. *Ibid.*
12. *Ibid.*, 618–619.
13. *Ibid.*, 618.
14. *Ibid.*, 618.
15. *Ibid.*, 619.
16. Shesol, 41.
17. *Ibid.*
18. Robert A. Caro, *The Years of Lyndon Johnson: The Passage of Power* (New York: Knopf, 2012), introduction.
19. Robert F. Kennedy recorded interview by Arthur Schlesinger, p. 622–623, 2/27/1965, John F. Kennedy Oral History Project of the John F. Kennedy Library.
20. Shesol, 9.
21. Shesol, 3.
22. Shesol, 7; Doris Kearns-Goodwin, *Lyndon Johnson and the American Dream* (New York: St. Martin's Griffin, 1991), 54.
23. Shesol, 8.
24. Shesol, 107.
25. *Ibid.*, 114.
26. Caro, chapter 12.
27. *Ibid.*
28. *Ibid.*
29. *Ibid.*
30. *Ibid.*
31. Shesol, 115.
32. Caro, chapter 13.
33. *Ibid.*
34. *Ibid.*
35. Garrow, *Bearing the Cross*, 307.
36. Nick Kotz, *Judgement Days: Lyndon Baines Johnson, Martin Luther King, Jr. and the Laws That Changed America* (New York: Houghton Mifflin, 2005), chapter 1.
37. *Ibid.*
38. Garrow, *Bearing the Cross*, 307.
39. Shesol, 116.
40. *Ibid.*
41. *Ibid.*
42. Lyndon B. Johnson: "Remarks upon Arrival at Andrews Air Force Base," November 22, 1963, online by Gerhard Peters and John T. Woolley, *The American Presidency Project*, http://www.presidency.ucsb.edu/ws/?pid=25976.
43. Caro, chapter 13.
44. Schlesinger, 611.
45. Robert F. Kennedy recorded interview by John Barlow Martin, p. 187, 4/13/1964, John F. Kennedy Oral History Project of the John F. Kennedy Library.
46. Robert F. Kennedy recorded interview by John Barlow Martin, p. 316, 5/14/1964, John F. Kennedy Oral History Project of the John F. Kennedy Library.
47. Shesol, 118–119.
48. Robert F. Kennedy recorded interview by John Barlow Martin, p. 316, 5/14/1964, John F. Kennedy Oral History Project of the John F. Kennedy Library.
49. Thomas, 278–279.
50. Schlesinger, *RFK and His Times*, 627.
51. William Manchester, *The Death of a President: November 20–November 25 1963* (New York: Little, Brown, 2013), chapter 8.
52. Shesol, 119.
53. Schlesinger, *RFK and His Times*, 627.
54. Shesol, 120.
55. Schlesinger, *RFK and His Times*, 627.
56. Shesol, 120.
57. MLK "Ebenezer Church Bulletin," November 24, 1963, Atlanta, Georgia, The King Center Digital Archives, http://www.thekingcenter.org/archive/document/ebenezer-church-bulletin-and-president-kennedys-eulogy.
58. Description of the funeral services are based on video "Funeral Services for President John F. Kennedy: November 1963: 23–25," Accession Number WHN:28, JFKL, Boston, MA.
59. *Ibid.*
60. Thomas, 281.
61. Description of the funeral services are based on video "Funeral Services for President John F. Kennedy: November 1963: 23–25," Accession Number WHN:28, JFKL, Boston, MA.
62. Thomas, 282.

Chapter 2

1. Zachary Karabell and Jonathan Rosenberg, eds., *Kennedy, Johnson and the Quest for Justice: The Civil Rights Tapes* (New York: Norton, 2003) 203–204.
2. *Ibid.*
3. Remarks by MLK at the Freedom House Annual Dinner, Waldorf Astoria Hotel, November 26, 1963, The King Center Digital Archives, Atlanta, Georgia, http://www.thekingcenter.org/archive/document/remarks-mlk-freedom-house-annual-dinner.
4. *Ibid.*
5. *Ibid.*
6. *Ibid.*
7. *Ibid.*
8. *Ibid.*
9. *Ibid.*
10. *Ibid.*
11. President Lyndon B. Johnson"s Address to Congress, November 27, 1963, MP505, LBJ Library Video upload to YouTube, 2012, https://-www.youtube.com/watch?v=LF0TxpxIMA0.
12. Robert Dallek, *An Unfinished Life: John F. Kennedy 1917–1963* (New York: Little, Brown, 2003), 54; Kearns-Goodwin, 172.
13. Kearns-Goodwin, 175.
14. Lyndon B. Johnson, "Address before a Joint Session of the Congress," November 27,

1963, online by Gerhard Peters and John T. Woolley, *The American Presidency Project*, http://www.presidency.ucsb.edu/ws/?pid=25988.
  15. Caro, chapter 16.
  16. Lyndon B. Johnson, "Address before a Joint Session of the Congress," November 27, 1963, online by Gerhard Peters and John T. Woolley, *The American Presidency Project*, http://www.presidency.ucsb.edu/ws/?pid=25988.
  17. *Ibid.*
  18. Caro, chapter 16.
  19. Guthman, 246.
  20. Guthman, 247.
  21. Schlesinger, *RFK and His Times*, 631.
  22. *Ibid.*
  23. *Ibid.*
  24. *Ibid.*
  25. MLK, "Our New President," draft for *New Amsterdam News*, December 27, 1963, King Center Digital Archives—Note: This source comes from a manuscript and handwritten notes, http://www.thekingcenter.org/archive/document/new-york-amsterdam-news-our-new-president.
  26. Martin Luther King, Jr., Address at the Pilgrimage for Democracy, December 15, 1963, King Center Digital Archives, http://www.thekingcenter.org/archive/document/mlks-address-pilgrimage-democracy.
  27. MLK, "Our New President," draft for *New Amsterdam News*, December 27, 1963, King Center Digital Archives—Note: This source comes from a manuscript and handwritten notes, http://www.thekingcenter.org/archive/document/new-york-amsterdam-news-our-new-president.
  28. *Ibid.*
  29. Guthman, 254.

Chapter 3

  1. Guthman, 249; Schlesinger, *RFK and His Times*, 634.
  2. Schlesinger, *RFK and His Times*, 634.
  3. Guthman, 249.
  4. Schlesinger, *RFK and His Times*, 634.
  5. Guthman, 249–250.
  6. *Ibid.*
  7. Guthman, 250.
  8. *Ibid.*
  9. Schlesinger, *RFK and His Times*, 635.
  10. *Ibid.*, 637.
  11. Thomas, 290–291; Robert F. Kennedy recorded interview by John Barlow Martin, p. 317, 5/14/1964, John F. Kennedy Oral History Project of the John F. Kennedy Library.
  12. Guthman, 254.

  13. *Ibid.*, 257.
  14. Guthman, 258.
  15. *Ibid.*, 259.
  16. *Ibid.*, 259.
  17. Robert F. Kennedy recorded interview with Burke Marshall by Anthony Lewis, p. 425, 12/4/1964, John F. Kennedy Oral History Project of the John F. Kennedy Library.
  18. Speech Given by the Attorney General at the Second Annual Awards Dinner of the Joseph P. Kennedy Foundation in New York on February 5, 1964, AG Files, Speeches, Box 255, JFKL.
  19. *Ibid.*
  20. Thomas, 285–286.
  21. *Ibid.*, 287.
  22. *Ibid.*, 288.
  23. Guthman, 267–268.
  24. Address by Attorney General Robert F. Kennedy to the Friendly Sons of St. Patrick of Lackawanna County, Scranton, Pennsylvania, on March 17, 1964, AG Files, Speeches, Box 255, JFKL.
  25. Guthman, 269.
  26. Guthman, 270.
  27. *Ibid.*, 269.
  28. *Rocky Mountain News*, AG Files, Box 73, JFKL.
  29. *Ibid.*
  30. Harvard College Library Clipping Sheet, "Paar's Interview with Bob Kennedy," March 31, 1964, AG Files, Speeches, Box 255, JFKL.
  31. MLK, "Statement to the Second Precinct Clergymen's Association," Washington, DC, March 26, 1964, The King Center Digital Archives, http://www.thekingcenter.org/archive/document/mlk-second-precinct-clergymens-association.
  32. Thomas, 280.
  33. Lyndon B. Johnson, "Annual Message to the Congress on the State of the Union," January 8, 1964, online by Gerhard Peters and John T. Woolley, *The American Presidency Project*, http://www.presidency.ucsb.edu/ws/?pid=26.
  34. *Ibid.*
  35. Statement of the Honorable Robert F. Kennedy, Attorney General of the United States, before the House Committee on Education and Labor in Support of HR 10440, the Economic Opportunity Act, April 7, 1964, AG Files, Speeches, Box 255, JFKL.
  36. *Ibid.*
  37. *Ibid.*
  38. *Ibid.*
  39. Senator Edward M. Kennedy Speech in Support of the Civil Rights Bill on the Floor of the United States Senate, April 8, 1964, USA Congressional Record Proceedings and Debates of the 88th Congress, Second Session,

Volume 110—Part 6, April 7, 1964 to April 20, 1964, pp. 7375–7380.
40. Edward M. Kennedy, *True Compass* (New York: Twelve, 2009), 214.
41. *Ibid.*, 216.
42. Senator Edward M. Kennedy Speech in Support of the Civil Rights Bill on the Floor of the United States Senate, April 8, 1964, USA Congressional Record Proceedings and Debates of the 88th Congress, Second Session, Volume 110—Part 6, April 7, 1964 to April 20, 1964, pp.7375–7380.

Chapter 4

1. Address by Attorney General Robert F. Kennedy to the Canadian Press, as Delivered, Royal York Hotel, Toronto, Canada, April 14, 1964, AG Files, Speeches, Box 255, JFKL.
2. *Ibid.*
3. *Ibid.*
4. *Ibid.*
5. *Ibid.*
6. *Ibid.*
7. Branch, *Parting the Waters*, 839.
8. Robert F. Kennedy recorded interview by John Bartlow Martin, p. 90, 1/29/1964 and March 1, 1964, John F. Kennedy Oral History Project of the John F. Kennedy Library.
9. Excerpts from Remarks by Attorney General Robert F. Kennedy at a Panel Discussion "After The Civil Rights Bill, What?," American Society of Newspaper Editors, 1964 Convention, Washington, DC, April 16, 1964, AG Files, Speeches, Box 255, JFKL.
10. *Ibid.*
11. *Ibid.*
12. *Ibid.*
13. *Ibid.*
14. *Ibid.*
15. *Ibid.*
16. *Ibid.*
17. Address by Attorney General Robert F. Kennedy at the Herbert H. Lehman Human Relations Award Dinner of the American Jewish Committee Appeal for Human Relations, Plaza Hotel, New York City, April 16, 1964, AG Files, Speeches, Box 255, JFKL.
18. *Ibid.*
19. *Ibid.*
20. *Ibid.*
21. *Ibid.*
22. *Ibid.*
23. John F. Kennedy: "Special Message to the Congress on Civil Rights and Job Opportunities," June 19, 1963, online by Gerhard Peters and John T. Woolley, *The American Presidency Project*, http://www.presidency.ucsb.edu/ws/?pid=9283.

24. Clay Risen, *The Bill of the Century: The Epic Battle for the Civil Rights Act* (New York: Bloomsbury Press, 2014), chapter 5.
25. Guthman, 271.
26. Address by Attorney General Robert F. Kennedy to a Joint Meeting of the Kanawha Country Parent-Teachers Council and Members of Action for Appalachian Youth, Inc., Civic Center, Charleston, West Virginia, April 29, 1964, AG Files, Speeches, Box 255, JFKL.
27. *Ibid.*
28. *Ibid.*
29. Lyndon B. Johnson: "Special Message to the Congress Proposing a Nationwide War on the Sources of Poverty," March 16, 1964, online by Gerhard Peters and John T. Woolley, *The American Presidency Project*, http://www.presidency.ucsb.edu/ws/?pid=26109.
30. Address by Attorney General Robert F. Kennedy to a Joint Meeting of the Kanawha Country Parent-Teachers Council and Members of Action for Appalachian Youth, Inc., Civic Center, Charleston, West Virginia, April 29, 1964, AG Files, Speeches, Box 255, JFKL.
31. *Ibid.*
32. *Ibid.*

Chapter 5

1. Address by Attorney General Robert F. Kennedy, University of Chicago Law School, Chicago, Illinois, as delivered, May 1, 1964, AG Files, Speeches, Box 255, JFKL.
2. John F. Kennedy: "Remarks at Amherst College upon Receiving an Honorary Degree," October 26, 1963, online by Gerhard Peters and John T. Woolley, *The American Presidency Project*, http://www.presidency.ucsb.edu/ws/?pid=9497.
3. Address by Attorney General Robert F. Kennedy, University of Chicago Law School, Chicago, Illinois, as delivered, May 1, 1964, AG Files, Speeches, Box 255, JFKL.
4. Address by Attorney General Robert F. Kennedy, Bellevue Stratford Hotel, Philadelphia, Pennsylvania, May 6, 1964, AG Files, Speeches, Box 255, JFKL.
5. *Ibid.*
6. *Ibid.*
7. *Ibid.*
8. Martin Luther King, Jr., address titled "Love and Forgiveness" at the American Baptist Convention Meeting, May 5, 1964, The King Center Digital Archives, http://www.thekingcenter.org/archive/document/love-and-forgiveness.
9. *Ibid.*
10. *Ibid.*
11. *Ibid.*

12. Address by Attorney General Robert F. Kennedy to the Anti-Defamation League accepting the B'nai B'rith Award, New York City, May 19, 1964, AG Files, Speeches, Box 255, JFKL.
13. *Ibid.*
14. Address by Attorney General Robert F. Kennedy to the Young Israel of Pelham Parkway, Concourse Plaza Hotel, New York City, May 20, 1964, AG Files, Speeches, Box 255, JFKL.
15. John F. Kennedy: "Commencement Address at San Diego State College," June 6, 1963, online by Gerhard Peters and John T. Woolley, *The American Presidency Project*, http://www.presidency.ucsb.edu/ws/?pid=9259.
16. Address by Attorney General Robert F. Kennedy to the Young Israel of Pelham Parkway, Concourse Plaza Hotel, New York City, May 20, 1964, AG Files, Speeches, Box 255, JFKL.
17. *Ibid.*
18. Remarks by Attorney General Robert F. Kennedy at the dedication of the John F. Kennedy Interfaith Chapel, West Georgia College, Carrollton, Georgia, May 26, 1964, AG Files, Speeches, Box 255, JFKL.
19. *Ibid.*
20. *Ibid.*
21. MLK, Statement regarding School Desegregation 10 Years After, May 7, 1964, The King Center Digital Archives, http://www.thekingcenter.org/archive/document/school-desegregation-10-years-later.
22. Martin Luther King, Jr., Address at the Convocation of Equal Justice Under Law of the NAACP Legal Defense Fund, May 28, 1964, The King Center Digital Archives, http://www.thekingcenter.org/archive/document/convocation-equal-justice-under-law.
23. *Ibid.*
24. Address by Attorney General Robert F. Kennedy, Commencement Exercises, Marquette University, Milwaukee, Wisconsin, June 7, 1964, AG Files, Speeches, Box 255, JFKL.
25. *Ibid.*
26. "The Opening to the Future," Address by Attorney General Robert F. Kennedy to the California Institute of Technology, Pasadena, California, June 8, 1964, AG Files, Speeches, Box 255, JFKL.
27. *Ibid.*
28. *Ibid.*
29. *Ibid.*
30. *Ibid.*; see also John F. Kennedy, "Remarks Prepared for Delivery at the Trade Mart in Dallas," November 22, 1963, online by Gerhard Peters and John T. Woolley, *The American Presidency Project*, http://www.presidency.ucsb.edu/ws/?pid=9539.
31. *Ibid.*
32. Robert F. Kennedy recorded interview by Arthur Schlesinger, p. 619, 2/27/1965, John F. Kennedy Oral History Project of the John F. Kennedy Library.
33. Memorandum from Robert F. Kennedy to President Lyndon Johnson, June 5, 1964, AG Files Box 73, JFKL.
34. *Ibid.*
35. *Ibid.*
36. *Ibid.*
37. Lyndon B. Johnson, "Radio and Television Remarks upon Signing the Civil Rights Bill," July 2, 1964, online by Gerhard Peters and John T. Woolley, *The American Presidency Project*, http://www.presidency.ucsb.edu/ws/?pid=26361.
38. *Ibid.*
39. Taylor Branch, *Pillar of Fire: America in the King Years, 1963–1965* (New York: Simon & Schuster, 1998), 387.
40. Lyndon B. Johnson, "Radio and Television Remarks upon Signing the Civil Rights Bill," July 2, 1964, online by Gerhard Peters and John T. Woolley, *The American Presidency Project*, http://www.presidency.ucsb.edu/ws/?pid=26361.
41. Garrow, *Bearing the Cross*, 338.
42. Schlesinger, *RFK and His Times*, 645.
43. Shesol, 165.
44. *Ibid.*; Schlesinger, *RFK and His Times*, 645.

Chapter 6

1. Statement by Attorney General Robert F. Kennedy, June 23, 1964, AG Files, General, Box 2, JFKL.
2. Arrival Statement, Berlin, by Robert F. Kennedy, June 26, 1964, AG Files, General, Box 2, JFKL.
3. "Berlin Visit of U.S. Attorney General Robert F. Kennedy," Official Text Service of Berlin Senate—U.S. Mission (USIS), Free University of Berlin, June 26, 1964, AG Files, Speeches, Box 255, JFKL.
4. *Ibid.*
5. *Ibid.*
6. *Ibid.*
7. *Ibid.*
8. *Ibid.*
9. Guthman, 274.
10. *Ibid.*, 275.
11. *Ibid.*, 276–277.
12. Statement by Attorney General Robert F. Kennedy, on Departure from Poland, July 1, 1964, AG Files, Speeches, Box 255, JFKL.
13. Statement by Attorney General Robert F. Kennedy, London, England, July 1, 1964, AG Files, Speeches, Box 255, JFKL.
14. Robert F. Kennedy on the Luncheon

with Anatoly Dobrynin, July 7, 1964, AG Files, Personal, Box 97, JFKL.
15. *Ibid.*
16. *Ibid.*
17. Schlesinger, *RFK and His Times*, 657.
18. Robert F. Kennedy on the Luncheon with Anatoly Dobrynin, July 7, 1964, AG Files, Personal, Box 97, JFKL.
19. Martin Luther King, Jr., Public Statement at the Mississippi Freedom Democratic Party, July 22, 1964, The King Center Digital Archives, http://www.thekingcenter.org/archive/document/public-statement-mississippi-freedom-democratic-party.
20. Paul L. Montgomery and Francis X. Clines, "Thousands Riot in Harlem Area," *New York Times*, July 19, 1964.
21. Martin Luther King, Jr., Public Statement on the New York Riots, July 27, 1964, The King Center Digital Archives, http://www.thekingcenter.org/archive/document/mlk-statement-about-new-york-riots.
22. *Ibid.*
23. *Ibid.*
24. The Rev. Dr. Martin Luther King, Jr., Sermon: "A Knock at Midnight," Tape Recorded Remarks at Riverside Church in New York City, August 9, 1964, The King Center Digital Archives, http://www.thekingcenter.org/archive/document/knock-midnight.
25. *Ibid.*
26. *Ibid.*
27. *Ibid.*
28. Address by Attorney General Robert F. Kennedy to the Fifth General Assembly World Assembly of Youth, University of Massachusetts, Amherst, Massachusetts, August 7, 1964, AG Files, Speeches, Box 255, JFKL.
29. *Ibid.*
30. American Experience, *RFK*, documentary, directed by David Grubin (2004; USA; PBS), DVD.
31. Statement by Attorney General Robert F. Kennedy, Gracie Mansion, New York City, August 25, 1964, AG Files, Speeches, Box 255, JFKL.
32. *Ibid.*
33. *Ibid.*
34. The description of Robert Kennedy before the speech was in papers at the JFKL, AG Files, Speeches, Box 255.
35. Address by Robert F. Kennedy, Tribute to John F. Kennedy at the Democratic National Convention, Atlantic City, New Jersey, August 27, 1964, AG Files, Speeches, Box 255, JFKL.
36. *Ibid.*
37. American Experience, *RFK*, documentary, directed by David Grubin (2004; USA; PBS), DVD.
38. Lyndon B. Johnson, "Radio and Television Report to the American People Following Renewed Aggression in the Gulf of Tonkin," August 4, 1964, online by Gerhard Peters and John T. Woolley, *The American Presidency Project*, http://www.presidency.ucsb.edu/ws/?pid=26418.
39. Johnson Library, National Security File, NSC Meetings, Vol. 3, Tab 20. Top Secret; Sensitive; For the President Only. Drafted by Bromley Smith, August 4, 1964, quoted from Foreign Relations of the United States, 1964–1968, Volume I, Vietnam, 1964, Document 278.
40. Source: Johnson Library, Meeting Notes File, August 4, 1964, no classification marking, drafted by Walter Jenkins of the President's Staff, quoted from Foreign Relations of the United States, 1964–1968, Volume I, Vietnam, 1964, Document 280.
41. *Ibid.*
42. *Ibid.*
43. *Ibid.*
44. Lyndon B. Johnson, "Special Message to the Congress on U.S. Policy in Southeast Asia," August 5, 1964, online by Gerhard Peters and John T. Woolley, *The American Presidency Project*, http://www.presidency.ucsb.edu/ws/?pid=26422.
45. Department of State, Presidential Correspondence, Lot 77 D 163, no classification marking. The Russian text of the signed original, which was handed to Ambassador Kohler at 9 p.m. on August 5 is quoted from Foreign Relations of the United States, 1964–1968, Volume I, Vietnam, 1964, Document 295.
46. *Ibid.*
47. Department of State, Presidential Correspondence, Lot 77 D 163, no classification marking, also published in Declassified Documents, 1978, 315B, quoted from Foreign Relations of the United States, 1964–1968, Volume I, Vietnam, 1964, Document 302.
48. Johnson Library, National Security File, Aides Files, McGeorge Bundy, Meetings on Southeast Asia, Vol. 1, Top Secret, drafted by McGeorge Bundy, quoted from Foreign Relations of the United States, 1964–1968, Volume I, Vietnam, 1964, Document 307.
49. *Ibid.*
50. Lyndon B. Johnson, "Remarks upon Signing Joint Resolution of the Maintenance of Peace and Security in Southeast Asia," August 10, 1964, online by Gerhard Peters and John T. Woolley, *The American Presidency Project*, http://www.presidency.ucsb.edu/ws/?pid=26429.

Chapter 7

1. Shesol, 285.
2. Guthman, 284.
3. *Ibid.*, 285.

4. Schlesinger, *RFK and His Times*, 668.
5. *Ibid.*, 669.
6. *Ibid.*, 670.
7. *Ibid.*
8. *Ibid.*, 671.
9. Guthman, 307.
10. *Ibid.*, 308.
11. Schlesinger, *RFK and His Times*, 672–673.
12. Schlesinger, *RFK and His Times*, 673.
13. *Ibid.*, 674.
14. Robert F. Kennedy, Remarks at the Columbia/Barnard Club, New York City, October 5, 1964, as quoted in C. Richard Allen and Edwin O. Guthman, ed., *RFK: Collected Speeches* (New York: Viking, 1993),125.
15. *Ibid.*
16. *Ibid.*, 126–127.
17. *Ibid.*, 127.
18. *Ibid.*
19. *Ibid.*, 128.
20. *Ibid.*
21. *Ibid.*
22. *Ibid.*, 129.
23. Schlesinger, *RFK and His Times*, 674.
24. *Ibid.*
25. Guthman, 309.
26. *Ibid.*, 310.
27. *Ibid.*
28. *Ibid.*, 1250.
29. Schlesinger, *RFK and His Times*, 675–676.
30. Shesol, 295.
31. MLK, "Comments on JFK at the Berlin Festival," Berlin, West Germany, September 13, 1964, The King Center Digital Archives, http://www.thekingcenter.org/archive/document/comments-john-f-kennedy-mlk-berlin-festival.
32. *Ibid.*
33. *Ibid.*
34. "MLK Accepts the Nobel Peace Prize," Oslo, Norway, December 10, 1964, The King Center Digital Archives, http://www.thekingcenter.org/archive/document/mlk-accepts-nobel-peace-prize-0.
35. "Statement from MLK Returning from Receiving Nobel Prize," New York, NY, December 18, 1964, The King Center Digital Archives. http://www.thekingcenter.org/archive/document/statement-mlk-returning-receiving-nobel-prize.

Chapter 8

1. Warren Weaver, Jr., "Kennedy (D-NY) Gets a Back Seat," *New York Times*, January 5, 1965.
2. Joseph Palermo, *In His Own Right: The Political Odyssey of Robert F. Kennedy* (New York: Columbia University Press, 2002), 8–9.
3. Guthman, 319.

4. *Ibid.*
5. Palermo, 10–11.
6. Garrow, *Bearing the Cross*, 358.
7. *Ibid.*, 359.
8. John Herbers, "Alabama Vote Drive Opened by Dr. King," *New York Times*, January 3, 1965.
9. *Ibid.*
10. David J. Garrow, *Protest at Selma: Martin Luther King, Jr. and the Voting Rights Act of 1965* (New York: Open Road Integrated Media, 2015), chapter 2.
11. Lyndon B. Johnson, "Annual Message to the Congress on the State of the Union," January 4, 1965, online by Gerhard Peters and John T. Woolley, *The American Presidency Project*, http://www.presidency.ucsb.edu/ws/?pid=26907.
12. Garrow, *Bearing the Cross*, 378–379.
13. John Herbers, "67 Negroes Jailed in Alabama Drive," *New York Times*, January 20, 1965.
14. Warren Weaver, Jr., "At Inaugural Moment, Some Stand by Kennedy's Grave," *New York Times*, January 21, 1965.
15. Lyndon B. Johnson: "The President's Inaugural Address," January 20, 1965, online by Gerhard Peters and John T. Woolley, *The American Presidency Project*, http://www.presidency.ucsb.edu/ws/?pid=26985.
16. *Ibid.*
17. *Ibid.*
18. "MLK Speech at Nobel Peace Prize Recognition Dinner," Atlanta, Georgia January 27, 1965, The King Center Digital Archives, http://www.thekingcenter.org/archive/document/mlk-speech-nobel-peace-prize-recognition-dinner.
19. *Ibid.*
20. *Ibid.*
21. Marjorie Hunter, "Senate Approves 1.1 Billion in Aid for Appalachia," *New York Times*, February 2, 1965.
22. Thomas, 304–305.
23. Schlesinger, *RFK and His Times*, 780.
24. Garrow, *Protest at Selma*, chapter 2.
25. Garrow, *Bearing the Cross*, 382–383.
26. Garrow, *Protest at Selma*, chapter 2.
27. Lyndon B. Johnson, "The President's News Conference," February 4, 1965, online by Gerhard Peters and John T. Woolley, *The American Presidency Project*, http://www.presidency.ucsb.edu/ws/?pid=27196.
28. Garrow, *Protest at Selma*, chapter 2.
29. Branch, *Pillar of Fire*, 579.

Chapter 9

1. Garrow, *Protest at Selma*, chapter 2.
2. John Herbers, "Taunted Sheriff Hits

Rights Aide," *New York Times*, February 17, 1965.

3. John Herbers, "Dr. King Urges Selma Negroes to Wage a More Militant Drive," *New York Times*, February 18, 1965.

4. John Herbers, "Negroes Beaten in Alabama Riot," *New York Times*, February 19, 1965.

5. John Lewis, *Walking With the Wind: A Memoir of the Movement* (New York: Harvest, 1998), 328.

6. John Herbers, "2 Inquiries on Racial Clash in Alabama Town," *New York Times*, February 20, 1965.

7. "Statement from MLK Regarding the Death of Malcolm X," February 21, 1965, The King Center Digital Archives, http://www.thekingcenter.org/archive/document/statement-mlk-regarding-death-malcolm-x.

8. Branch, *Pillar of Fire*, 597.

9. Garrow, *Bearing the Cross*, 393.

10. Roy Reed, "Alabama Victim Called a Martyr," *New York Times*, March 4, 1965.

11. *Ibid*.

12. *Ibid*.

13. John Herbers, "Dr. King, Back in Alabama, Calls for March on Capital to Push Voting Drive," *New York Times*, February 22, 1965.

14. Garrow, *Protest at Selma*, chapter 2.

15. John Lewis and Silas Norman, "Letter from SNCC Executive Committee to MLK," March 7, 1965, The King Center Digital Archives, http://www.thekingcenter.org/archive/document/letter-sncc-executive-committee-mlk.

16. Garrow, *Protest at Selma*, chapter 2.

17. Roy Reed, "Alabama Police Use Gas and Clubs to Rout Negroes," *New York Times*, March 8, 1965.

18. *Ibid*.

19. Garrow, *Protest at Selma*, chapter 2.

20. "Dr. King Announces Plan for New Walk and Assails Attack," *New York Times*, March 8, 1965.

21. Garrow, *Protest at Selma*, chapter 3.

22. Kearns-Goodwin, 228.

23. Garrow, *Bearing the Cross*, 401.

24. *Ibid*., 402.

25. Transcript, Nicholas D. Katzenbach Oral History Interview I, 11/12/68, by Paige E. Mulhollan, Internet Copy, LBJ Library, p. 21.

26. Garrow, *Bearing the Cross*, 402.

27. *Ibid*., 403.

28. Garrow, *Bearing the Cross*, 403–404; *Protest at Selma*, chapter 3.

29. Garrow, *Bearing the Cross*, 404–405.

30. Lyndon B. Johnson: "Statement by the President on the Situation in Selma, Alabama," March 9, 1965, online by Gerhard Peters and John T. Woolley, *The American Presidency Project*, http://www.presidency.ucsb.edu/ws/?pid=26802.

31. Garrow, *Bearing the Cross*, 405–406.

32. "Dr. King's Statement," *New York Times*, March 12, 1965.

33. *Ibid*.

34. Lyndon B. Johnson, "The President's News Conference," March 13, 1965, online by Gerhard Peters and John T. Woolley, *The American Presidency Project*, http://www.presidency.ucsb.edu/ws/?pid=26804.

35. *Ibid*.

36. "Alabama: Racism vs. Reason," *New York Times*, March 14, 1965.

37. *Ibid*.

38. Nan Robertson, "In the Capital, Sermons on Courage in Selma," *New York Times*, March 15, 1965.

39. Ben A Franklin, "Dr. King Says He Did Not Intend to March to Montgomery Tuesday," *New York Times*, March 12, 1965.

40. *Ibid*.

41. Roy Reed, "Selma March Held after U.S. Court Arranges Accord," *New York Times*, March 16, 1965.

42. Lyndon B. Johnson, "Special Message to the Congress: The American Promise," March 15, 1965, online by Gerhard Peters and John T. Woolley, *The American Presidency Project*, http://www.presidency.ucsb.edu/ws/?pid=26805.

43. *Ibid*.

44. Lewis, *Walking with the Wind*, 353–354.

45. Garrow, *Protest at Selma*, chapter 3.

46. "Dr. King Praises Voting Bill But Urges Continued Protests," *New York Times*, March 17, 1965.

47. Martin Luther King, Jr., "Address at the Conclusion of the Selma to Montgomery March," Montgomery, Alabama, March 25, 1965, as quoted in *A Call to Conscience: The Landmark Speeches of Dr. Martin Luther King, Jr.*, ed., Clayborne Carson and Kris Shepard (Grand Central Publishing: New York, 2001), 114.

48. *Ibid*., 119–120.

49. *Ibid*., 120.

50. *Ibid*., 120–121.

51. *Ibid*.

52. *Ibid*., 121.

53. *Ibid*., 125.

54. *Ibid*., 126.

55. *Ibid*., 128.

Chapter 10

1. Department of State, Bundy Files, Lot 85 D 240, February 1965, Top Secret, Controlled Dissem, Limited Distribution. The Central Intelligence Agency and the intelligence organizations of AEC, NSA, and the De-

partments of State and Defense participated by the Director of Central Intelligence and concurred in by all the members of the U.S. Intelligence Board, except for the Assistant to the Director of the FBI, who abstained on the grounds that the subject was outside his jurisdiction. As quoted in *FRUS* 1964–1968, Volume II, Document 111.

2. Johnson Library, National Security File, Memos to the President, McGeorge Bundy, Vol. VIII, Secret, as quoted in *FRUS* 1964–1968, Volume II, Document 124.

3. Johnson Library, Papers of McGeorge Bundy, no classification marking. The notes were handwritten by Bundy for his personal use and were not an official record of the meeting. No other record of the discussion has been found. Attending the meeting were the President, Rusk, McNamara, Thompson, William Bundy, McGeorge Bundy, and Ball. The information on the time and attendance was taken from the President's daily diary. As quoted in *FRUS* 1964–1968, Volume II, Document 128.

4. Johnson Library, National Security File, Memos to the President, McGeorge Bundy, Vol. IX, Secret, Personal and Sensitive, as quoted in *FRUS* 1964–1968, Volume II, Document 183.

5. *Ibid.*

6. "Improved Education for Puerto Ricans Urged by Kennedy," *New York Times*, March 1, 1965.

7. For a more detailed explanation of these two instances, see Warren Weaver, Jr., "Senate Takes Up New Haven Problem," *New York Times*, March 3, 1965; "Senate Gets Bill on Scenic Hudson," *New York Times*, March 7, 1965.

8. "The Nation," *New York Times*, March 7, 1965.

9. Robert F. Kennedy, Speech to the National Council of Christians and Jews, April 28, 1965, Chicago, Illinois, as quoted in *RFK: Collected Speeches*, 155.

10. *Ibid.*, 156.

11. *Ibid.*

12. Robert F. Kennedy, Speech on the Floor of the Senate, May 6, 1965, Washington, DC, as quoted in *RFK: Collected Speeches*, 272.

13. *Ibid.*, 272–273.

14. *Ibid.*, 273.

15. *Ibid.*, 274.

16. Shesol, 501, Macbook.

17. John D. Morris, "Kennedy Critical of Johnson Move," *New York Times*, May 8, 1965.

18. Robert F. Kennedy, Commencement Address at Queens College, New York City, June 15, 1965, as quoted in *RFK: Collected Speeches*, 133.

19. *Ibid.*, 133.

20. *Ibid.*, 134.

21. *Ibid.*

22. "Kennedy's Speech Urging Pact to Check Nuclear Weapons Spread," text of his speech, *New York Times*, June 24, 1965.

23. *Ibid.*

24. *Ibid.*

25. *Ibid.*

26. *Ibid.*

27. *Ibid.*

28. *Ibid.*

29. "Kennedy Speaks Out," *New York Times*, June 25, 1965.

30. Tom Wicker, "Kennedys and Johnson," *New York Times*, June 24, 1965.

31. Robert F. Kennedy, "America's Approach to Wars of Liberation," Washington, DC, July 9, 1965, as quoted in *RFK: Collected Speeches*, 275.

32. John F. Kennedy, "Remarks at West Point to the Graduating Class of the U.S. Military Academy," June 6, 1962, online by Gerhard Peters and John T. Woolley, *The American Presidency Project*, http://www.presidency.ucsb.edu/ws/?pid=8695.

33. Robert F. Kennedy, "America's Approach to Wars of Liberation," Washington, DC, July 9, 1965, as quoted in *RFK: Collected Speeches*, 276.

34. *Ibid.*, 277.

35. *Ibid.*

36. *Ibid.*, 279.

37. "Kennedy Urges Political Stance," *New York Times*, July 10, 1965.

38. Palermo, 11–13.

39. Palermo, 14.

Chapter 11

1. Martin Luther King, Jr., Transcript from "Meet the Press," March 28, 1965, Washington, DC, King Center Archives, http://www.thekingcenter.org/archive/document/mlk-interview-nbcs-meet-press.

2. *Ibid.*

3. *Ibid.*

4. Martin Luther King, Jr., Address to the American Jewish Committee, May 20, 1965, Americana Hotel, New York, NY, King Center Archives, http://www.thekingcenter.org/archive/document/address-mlk-american-jewish-committee.

5. *Ibid.*

6. *Ibid.*

7. James T. Patterson, *The Eve of Destruction: How 1965 Transformed America* (New York: Basic Books, 2014), 124.

8. "Dr. King Declares U.S. Must Negotiate in Asia," *New York Times*, July 3, 1965.

9. John Herbers, "Civil Rights and War: Peace Movements and Negro Groups Seen as Forming Closer Relationship," *New York Times*, July 5, 1965.

10. Lyndon B. Johnson, "Commencement Address at Howard University: 'To Fulfill These Rights,'" June 4, 1965, online by Gerhard Peters and John T. Woolley, *The American Presidency Project*, http://www.presidency.ucsb.edu/ws/?pid=27021.
11. *Ibid.*
12. *Ibid.*
13. Garrow, *Bearing the Cross*, 433–434.
14. Austin C. Wehrwein, "Dr. King Attends Winnetka Rally," *New York Times*, July 26, 1965.
15. Austin C. Wehrwein, "Dr. King's Drive Ends in Chicago," *New York Times*, July 27, 1965.
16. William G. Weart, "Dr. King's Philadelphia's Visit Assailed," *New York Times*, August 1, 1965.
17. William G. Weart, "Dr. King Assails Policy at Girard," *New York Times*, August 4, 1965.
18. "Economic Freedom for Negroes Stressed by King," *New York Times*, August 5, 1965.
19. John Herbers, "Dr. King to Fight Bias in the North," *New York Times*, August 6, 1965.
20. Lyndon B. Johnson, "Remarks in the Capitol Rotunda at the Signing of the Voting Rights Act," August 6, 1965, online by Gerhard Peters and John T. Woolley, *The American Presidency Project*, http://www.presidency.ucsb.edu/ws/?pid=27140.
21. *Ibid.*
22. E.W. Kenworthy, "Johnson Signs Voting Rights Bill, Orders Immediate Enforcement; 4 Suits Will Challenge Poll Tax," *New York Times*, August 7, 1965.
23. *Ibid.*
24. Peter Bart, "New Negro Riots Erupt on Coast; 3 Reported Shot," *New York Times*, August 13, 1965.
25. Peter Bart, "2,000 Troops Enter Los Angeles on Third Day of Rioting; 4 Die as Fires and Looting Grow," *New York Times*, August 14, 1965.
26. *RFK Collected Speeches*, 158.
27. Robert F. Kennedy, "Reflections on the 1965 Watts Riots: State Convention, Independent Order of Odd Fellows," Spring Valley, New York, August 18, 1965, as quoted in *RFK Collected Speeches*, 159.
28. *Ibid.*, 160.
29. *Ibid.*, 162–163.
30. Martin Luther King, Jr., "MLK Speaks to the People of Watts," August 19, 1965, The King Center Digital Archives, http://www.thekingcenter.org/archive/document/mlk-speaks-people-watts#.
31. Martin Luther King, Jr., "MLK Press Statement Regarding Riots in Watts," August 20, 1965, The King Center Digital Archives, http://www.thekingcenter.org/archive/document/mlk-press-statement-regarding-riots-los-angeles.
32. *Ibid.*
33. *Ibid.*
34. Garrow, *Bearing the Cross*, 448.
35. Schlesinger, *RFK and His Times*, 783.
36. Robert F. Kennedy, "A Program for the Urban Crisis, a Series of Three Speeches" New York, NY, January 20, 21 and 22, 1966, as quoted in *RFK: Collected Speeches*, 164–165.
37. *Ibid.*, 166.
38. *Ibid.*, 167.
39. *Ibid.*
40. *Ibid.*, 169.
41. *Ibid.*, 172.
42. *Ibid.*, 173.
43. *Ibid.*, 174–176.

Chapter 12

1. Martin Luther King, Jr., Address to the American Committee of Africa, Hunter College, NY, December 10, 1965, The King Center Digital Archives, http://www.thekingcenter.org/archive/document/mlks-address-about-south-africa.
2. *Ibid.*
3. Donald Janson, "Drive in Chicago Begun by Dr. King," *New York Times*, January 8, 1966.
4. Martin Luther King, Jr., "Chicago Plan," January 7, 1966, The King Center Digital Archives, http://www.thekingcenter.org/archive/document/chicago-plan-0#.
5. Austin Wehrwein, "Dr. King Occupies a Flat in Slums," *New York Times*, January 27, 1966.
6. Austin Wehrwein, "Dr. King to Help Police in Chicago," *New York Times*, January 28, 1966.
7. Ralph Blumenthal, "Brooklyn Negroes Harass Kennedy," *New York Times*, February 5, 1966.
8. Robert F. Kennedy, "Redirecting Government, Solving Problems," Utica, NY, February 7, 1966, as quoted in *RFK: Collected Speeches*, 208–209.
9. *Ibid.*, 210–211.
10. Schlesinger, *RFK and His Times*, 734.
11. *Ibid.*, 735.
12. Robert F. Kennedy, "Admitting the Enemy into the Political Process," Press Release, February 19, 1966, as quoted in *RFK: Collected Speeches*, 282.
13. *Ibid.*, 284.
14. *Ibid.*, 284–286.
15. *Ibid.*, 287–288.
16. E.W. Kenworthy, "Kennedy Bids U.S. Offer Vietcong a Role in Saigon," *New York Times*, February 20, 1966.
17. Schlesinger, *RFK and His Times*, 736–737.
18. *Ibid.*, 738.
19. David S. Broder, "Kennedy's Vietnam Plea Spurs Popularity on Democratic Left," *New York Times*, February 21, 1966.

20. Schlesinger, *RFK and His Times*, 739.
21. Dr. Martin Luther King, Jr., to Senator Robert F. Kennedy, March 2, 1966, "Letter to Senator Kennedy from MLK," The King Center Digital Archives, http://www.thekingcenter.org/archive/document/letter-senator-robert-kennedy-mlk.
22. Gene Roberts, "Dr. King Stirs Chicago But Still Lacks a Program," *New York Times*, March 24, 1966.
23. Garrow, *Bearing the Cross*, 466.
24. Martin Luther King, Jr., "Remarks of Dr. Martin Luther King, 'En Granslus Kvall Pa Operan,'" March 31, 1966, Stockholm, Sweden, The King Center Digital Archives, http://www.thekingcenter.org/archive/document/mlks-remarks-swedish-audience#.
25. *Ibid.*
26. "South African Visa Denied to Dr. King," *New York Times*, March 25, 1966.
27. Roy Reed, "Kennedy Cheered in Ole Miss Talk by Crowd of 5,500," *New York Times*, March 19, 1966.
28. Robert F. Kennedy, "University of Mississippi Law School Forum," Oxford, Mississippi, March 18, 1966, as quoted in *RFK: Collected Speeches*, 136–137.
29. *Ibid.*, 137–138.
30. *Ibid.*, 138.
31. *Ibid.*, 138–139.
32. *Ibid.*, 139.
33. Schlesinger, *RFK and His Times*, 780.
34. *RFK Collected Speeches*, 232–233.
35. *Ibid.*, 234.
36. *Ibid.*, 236.
37. Robert F.Kennedy, Day of Affirmation Speech, University of Capetown, Capetown, South Africa, June 6, 1966, JFK Library, Speeches of Robert F. Kennedy, audio and full transcript, http://www.jfklibrary.org/Research/Research-Aids/Ready-Reference/RFK-Speeches/Day-of-Affirmation-Address-as-delivered.aspx.
38. *Ibid.*
39. *Ibid.*
40. *Ibid.*
41. *Ibid.*
42. *Ibid.*
43. *Ibid.*
44. "America and Apartheid," *New York Times*, June 8, 1966.
45. "Kennedy Invited Back to South Africa," *New York Times*, June 8, 1966; see also, Taylor Branch, *At Cannan's Edge*, 475.

Chapter 13

1. Taylor Branch, *At Canaan's Edge: America in the King Years*, 1965–1968 (New York: Simon & Schuster, 2007) 476.
2. "Kennedy Saddened," *New York Times*, June 8, 1966.
3. Martin Luther King, Jr., "MLK's Speech in Yazoo, Mississippi," June 21, 1966, The King Center Digital Archives, http://www.thekingcenter.org/archive/document/transcript-mlks-rally-speech-yazoo-city-mississippi#.
4. *Ibid.*
5. Branch, *At Canaan's Edge*, 487.
6. *Ibid.*, 490–491.
7. Gene Roberts, "Why the Cry for 'Black Power,'" *New York Times*, July 3, 1966.
8. Austin C. Wehrwein, "Dr. King and CORE Chief Act to Heal Rights Breach," *New York Times*, July 11, 1966.
9. Martin Luther King, Jr., Transcript of Speech, "Speech at Chicago Freedom Rally," July 10, 1966, The King Center Digital Archives, http://www.thekingcenter.org/archive/document/speech-chicago-freedom-movement-rally#.
10. *Ibid.*
11. *Ibid.*
12. Branch, *At Canaan's Edge*, 501.
13. Austin C. Wehrwein, "Dr. King Declares Daley Balks Him," *New York Times*, July 12, 1966.
14. Branch, *At Canaan's Edge*, 502–503.
15. Austin C. Wehrwein, "Negroes in Chicago Clash with Police; 2 Hurt by Gunfire," *New York Times*, July 14, 1966.
16. Donald Janson, "4,000 Called Up," *New York Times*, July 16, 1966.
17. Martin Luther King, Jr., "A Statement by Dr. Martin Luther King, Jr." Chicago, Illinois, July 17, 1966, The King Center Digital Archives, http://www.thekingcenter.org/archive/document/statement-dr-king.
18. Robert F. Kennedy, "The Goals of American Foreign Policy: Columbus Day Dinner," Waldorf-Astoria Hotel, New York City, October 11, 1966, as quoted in *RFK Collected Speeches*, 261–262.
19. *Ibid.*, 262.
20. *Ibid.*, 263.
21. *Ibid.*, 263–264.
22. "Dr. King Declares Race Rioting Hurts Civil Rights Drive," *New York Times*, October 1, 1966.
23. Gene Roberts, "Dr. King Weighing Plan to Repudiate 'Black Power' Bloc," *New York Times*, October 10, 1966.
24. Branch, *At Canaan's Edge*, 538–539.
25. "Dr. King Endorses Racial Statement," *New York Times*, October 15, 1966.
26. Martin Luther King, Jr., "Statement by MLK," October 14, 1966, The King Center Digital Archives, http://www.thekingcenter.org/archive/document/statement-mlk#.
27. *Ibid.*

28. *Ibid.*
29. *Ibid.*
30. "Dr. King Clarifies His Racial Stand," *New York Times*, October 17, 1966.
31. Branch, *At Cannan's Edge*, 539–540; Garrow, *Bearing the Cross*, 534.
32. Richard Reeves, "Project to Aid Brooklyn Slums," *New York Times*, October 18, 1966.
33. RFK Collected Speeches, 140.
34. "Excerpts From Kennedy Speech on Coast," *New York Times*, October 24, 1966.
35. *Ibid.*
36. *Ibid.*
37. *Ibid.*
38. *Ibid.*
39. *Ibid.*
40. Warren Weaver, Jr., "Kennedy Deplores Racism of a 'Few' Negro Leaders," *New York Times*, October 24, 1966.
41. "Dr. King to Assist Voters in Chicago," *New York Times*, December 3, 1966.
42. Dr. Martin Luther King, Jr., "Statement to the Press," Chicago, Illinois, December 2, 1966, The King Center Digital Archives, http://www.thekingcenter.org/archive/document/chicago-freedom-movement-mlk-address.
43. Dr, Martin Luther King, Jr., "Statement to the Senate Subcommittee on Urban Reorganization," Washington, DC, December 15, 1966, The King Center Digital Archives, http://www.thekingcenter.org/archive/document/senate-subcommittee-urban-reorganization-statement.
44. *Ibid.*
45. Robert B. Semple, Jr., "Dr. King Scores Poverty Budget," *New York Times*, December 16, 1966.
46. "Dr. King Will Write a Book During Leave," *New York Times*, December 14, 1966.
47. Robert F. Kennedy, "Launching the Bedford-Stuyvesant Restoration Effort," Brooklyn, New York, December 10, 1966, as quoted in *RFK Collected Speeches*, 186.
48. *Ibid.*, 189.
49. *Ibid.*
50. Steven Roberts, "Redevelopment Plan Set for Bedford-Stuyvesant," *New York Times*, December 11, 1966.

Chapter 14

1. W. Granger Blair, "Kennedy Charms Oxford Students," *New York Times*, January 29, 1967.
2. "Aide Terms White House Puzzled by Kennedy's Remark on the War," *New York Times*, January 31, 1967.
3. Schlesinger, *RFK and His Times*, 765–766.
4. *Ibid.*, 766.
5. *Ibid.*
6. "Kennedy Assesses Atlantic Policies," *New York Times*, February 3, 1967.
7. "U.S. Prestige Drop Found by Kennedy," *New York Times*, February 5, 1967.
8. "Hanoi Said to Give Kennedy a Signal It's Ready to Talk," *New York Times*, February 6, 1967.
9. Shesol, 364–365.
10. Schlesinger, *RFK and His Times*, 767.
11. Shesol, 365.
12. *Ibid.*, 366.
13. Transcript, Nicholas D. Katzenbach Oral History Interview, II, 11/23/68, by Paige Mulhollan, Internet Copy, LBJ Library.
14. Shesol, 366; Dallek, 447.
15. Shesol, 366; Dallek, 448.
16. John W. Finney, "Kennedy Sees President; Denies Bringing Feelers," *New York Times*, February 7, 1967.
17. Shesol, 367.
18. Dallek, 448.
19. "New China Policy Urged by Kennedy," *New York Times*, February 9, 1967.
20. *Ibid.*
21. Shesol, 369; Schlesinger, *RFK and His Times*, 770.
22. "Kennedy Is Critical of Raid Resumption," *New York Times*, February 14, 1967.
23. "Kennedy Planning an Early Statement on Vietnam Policy," *New York Times*, February 18, 1967.
24. "Kennedy Bids Nation Heed Youths on War," *New York Times*, February 25, 1967.
25. Schlesinger, *RFK and His Times*, 770.
26. Palermo, 47.
27. Robert F. Kennedy, "A Break with the Administration and a Plan for Peace," Washington, DC, March 2, 1967, as quoted in *RFK: Collected Speeches*, 292–293.
28. *Ibid.*, 294–295.
29. *Ibid.*, 297–299.
30. "Excerpts from Kennedy Speech and Texts of Rusk Statement and Johnson Letter," *New York Times*, March 3, 1967.
31. Hedrick Smith, "Kennedy Asks Suspension of U.S. Air Raids on North; Administration Unmoved," *New York Times*, March 3, 1967.
32. "Goldwater Rebukes Kennedy on Call for End of Bombing," *New York Times*, March 3, 1967.
33. "The Vietnam Debate," *New York Times*, March 3, 1967.
34. Gladden Hill, "Dr. King Advocates Quitting Vietnam," *New York Times*, February 26, 1967.
35. *Ibid.*
36. *Ibid.*
37. *Ibid.*

38. "Dr. King to Press Antiwar Stand," *New York Times*, March 24, 1967.
39. "Dr. King Leads Chicago Peace Rally," *New York Times*, March 26, 1967.
40. John Herbers, "Dr. King's Aides Score Asia War," *New York Times*, March 31, 1967.
41. Douglas Robinson, "Dr. King Proposes a Boycott of War," *New York Times*, April 5, 1967.
42. Martin Luther King, Jr., "Beyond Vietnam," Riverside Church, New York, NY, April 4, 1967, as quoted in *A Call to Conscience*, 140.
43. *Ibid.*
44. *Ibid.*, 141–142.
45. *Ibid.*, 142–143.
46. *Ibid.*, 143–144.
47. *Ibid.*, 154–155.
48. *Ibid.*, 157.
49. *Ibid.*, 159.
50. *Ibid.*, 159–160.
51. *Ibid.*, 162.
52. *Ibid.*, 162–163.

Chapter 15

1. "Dr. King's Error," *New York Times*, April 7, 1967.
2. "NAACP Decries Stand of Dr. King on Vietnam," *New York Times*, April 11, 1967.
3. "Letters to the Editor of The Times," written by James Bevel, "Dr. King Backed," *New York Times*, April 11, 1967.
4. "Letters to the Editor of The Times," written by Benjamin Spock, "Civil Rights and War," *New York Times*, April 14, 1967.
5. "Dr King Supported on Warning on War," *New York Times*, April 15, 1967.
6. Douglas Robinson, "100,000 Rally at U.N. against Vietnam War," *New York Times*, April 16, 1967.
7. "Dr. King Starts Peace Crusade," *New York Times*, April 24, 1967.
8. Tom Wicker, "Westmoreland Tells Congress U.S. Will Prevail," *New York Times*, April 29, 1967.
9. Lyndon B. Johnson, "Remarks at a Luncheon for General Westmoreland," April 28, 1967, online by Gerhard Peters and John T. Woolley, *The American Presidency Project*, http://www.presidency.ucsb.edu/ws/?pid=28222.
10. "Dr. King Accuses Johnson on War," *New York Times*, May 1, 1967.
11. "Dr. King Rebukes Critics of His Stand on War in Vietnam," *New York Times*, May 11, 1967.
12. Robert F. Kennedy Speeches, "The Image of America and the Youth of the World," with Gov. Ronald Reagan, CBS Television and Radio, May 15, 1967, JFKL, https://www.jfklibrary.org/Research/Research-Aids/Ready-Reference/RFK-Speeches/Town-Meeting-of-the-World-The-Image-of-America-and-the-Youth-of-the-World.aspx.
13. *Ibid.*
14. *Ibid.*
15. Hendrick Smith, "Senators Deplore 'Fraud' in Vote Drive in Vietnam," *New York Times*, August 12, 1967.
16. "Vietnam," *New York Times*, August 13, 1967.
17. Robert F. Kennedy, interview on "Face the Nation," November 26, 1967, as quoted from *RFK Collected Speeches*, 302.
18. *Ibid.*
19. *Ibid.*, 303.
20. Robert F. Kennedy, *To Seek a Newer World* (New York: Doubleday, 1967), 172.
21. *Ibid.*, 173–175.
22. *Ibid.*, 178–179.
23. *Ibid.*, 192.
24. *Ibid.*, 193.
25. Coretta Scott King, in the foreword of the 1968 edition, Martin Luther King, Jr., *The Trumpet of Conscience* (Boston: Beacon Press, 2010), xiii.
26. Martin Luther King, Jr., *The Trumpet of Conscience* (Boston: Beacon Press, 2010), 21.
27. *Ibid.*, 31.
28. *Ibid.*, 33–34.
29. *Ibid.*, 69.
30. *Ibid.*, 71–72.
31. *Ibid.*, 73.
32. *Ibid.*, 78.
33. *Ibid.*
34. *Ibid.*, 79.
35. *Ibid.*, 79–80.

Chapter 16

1. George C. Herring, *America's Longest War: The United States and Vietnam, 1950–1975*, 2nd ed. (New York: McGraw Hill, 1986), 189.
2. *Ibid.*, 189–190.
3. *Ibid.*
4. "More Than a Diversion," *New York Times*, February 2, 1968.
5. "Transcript of Interview with Kennedy," *New York Times*, March 14, 1968.
6. "Text of Summary of Report by National Advisory Commission on Civil Disorders," *New York Times*, March 1, 1968.
7. "Transcript of Interview with Kennedy," *New York Times*, March 14, 1968.
8. Robert Dallek, *Flawed Giant: Lyndon Johnson and His Times, 1961–1973* (New York: Oxford University Press, 1999), 527.

9. Transcript of interview with Kennedy," *New York Times*, March 14, 1968.
10. John Herbers, "Scene Is the Same, But 8 Years Later," *New York Times*, March 17, 1968.
11. "Kennedy's Statement and Excerpts from News Conference," *New York Times*, March 17, 1968.
12. *Ibid.*
13. Lyndon B. Johnson, "The President's Address to the Nation Announcing Steps to Limit the War in Vietnam and Reporting His Decision Not to Seek Reelection," March 31, 1968, online by Gerhard Peters and John T. Woolley, *The American Presidency Project*, http://www.presidency.ucsb.edu/ws/?pid=28772.
14. *Ibid.*
15. *Ibid.*
16. Walter Rugaber, "Civil Rights," *New York Times*, February 11, 1968.
17. Ben A. Franklin, "Dr. King to Start March on the Capital April 22," *New York Times*, March 5, 1968.
18. C. Gerald Fraser, "Dr. King Takes 'Poor People's Campaign' to Groups in Harlem and Queens," *New York Times*, March 27, 1968.
19. Walter Rugaber, "A Negro Is Killed in Memphis March," *New York Times*, March 29, 1968.
20. Walter Rugaber, "Dr. King to March in Memphis Again," *New York Times*, March 30, 1968.
21. Martin Luther King, Jr., "I've Been to the Mountaintop," delivered at Bishop Charles Mason Temple, Memphis, Tennessee, April 3, 1968, as quoted in *A Call to Conscience*, 208.
22. *Ibid.*, 214–215.
23. *Ibid.*, 217–219.
24. *Ibid.*, 220–221.
25. *Ibid.*, 221–222.
26. *Ibid.*, 222–223.
27. Lewis, 406.
28. Robert F. Kennedy, *Robert F. Kennedy Speeches*, "Statement on Assassination of Martin Luther King, Jr.," Indianapolis, Indiana, April 4, 1968, transcribed from the news release version, JFKL, https://www.jfklibrary.org/Research/Research-Aids/Ready-Reference/RFK-Speeches/Statement-on-the-Assassination-of-Martin-Luther-King.aspx.
29. *Ibid.*
30. *Ibid.*
31. *Ibid.*
32. *Ibid.*
33. *RFK Collected Speeches*, 358.
34. *Ibid.*, 358–359.
35. Robert F. Kennedy, *Robert F. Kennedy Speeches*, "Remarks to the Cleveland City Club, "April 5, 1968, transcribed from the news release version, JFKL, https://www.jfklibrary.org/Research/Research-Aids/Ready-Reference/RFK-Speeches/Remarks-of-Senator-Robert-F-Kennedy-to-the-Cleveland-City-Club-Cleveland-Ohio-April-5-1968.aspx.
36. *Ibid.*
37. *Ibid.*
38. *Ibid.*
39. *Ibid.*

Epilogue

1. Barack Obama, "Remarks at the Nobel Banquet in Oslo," December 10, 2009, online by Gerhard Peters and John T. Woolley, *The American Presidency Project*, http://www.presidency.ucsb.edu/ws/?pid=86977.
2. Barack Obama, "Remarks on Accepting the Nobel Peace Prize in Oslo," December 10, 2009, online by Gerhard Peters and John T. Woolley, *The American Presidency Project*, http://www.presidency.ucsb.edu/ws/?pid=86978.
3. *Ibid.*
4. *Ibid.*
5. Barack Obama, "Remarks Commemorating the 50th Anniversary of the Selma to Montgomery Marches for Voting Rights in Selma, Alabama," March 7, 2015, online by Gerhard Peters and John T. Woolley, *The American Presidency Project*, http://www.presidency.ucsb.edu/ws/?pid=109728.
6. *Ibid.*

Bibliography

Books

Allen, C. Richard, and Edwin O. Guthman, ed. *RFK: Collected Speeches*. New York: Viking, 1993.

Arsenault, Raymond. *Freedom Riders: 1961 and the Struggle for Racial Justice*. New York: Oxford University Press, 2006.

Branch, Taylor. *At Canaan's Edge: America in the King Years, 1965-1968*. New York: Simon & Schuster, 2007.

_____. *Parting the Waters: America in the King Years, 1954-63*. New York: Simon & Schuster, 1988.

_____. *Pillar of Fire: America in the King Years, 1963-1965*. New York: Simon & Schuster, 1998.

Carson, Clayborne, and Kris Shepard, ed. *A Call to Conscience: The Landmark Speeches of Dr. Martin Luther King, Jr*. New York: Grand Central Publishing, 2001.

Caro, Robert A. *The Years of Lyndon Johnson: The Passage of Power*. New York: Knopf, 2012. ebook.

Dallek, Robert. *Flawed Giant: Lyndon Johnson and His Times, 1961-1973*. New York: Oxford University Press, 1999.

_____. *An Unfinished Life: John F. Kennedy 1917-1963*. New York: Little, Brown, 2003.

Garrow, David J. *Bearing the Cross. Martin Luther King, Jr. and the Southern Christian Leadership Conference*. New York: Quill William Morrow, 1986.

_____. *Protest at Selma: Martin Luther King, Jr. and the Voting Rights Act of 1965*. New York: Open Road Integrated Media, 2015. ebook.

Goduti, Philip A., Jr., *Kennedy's Kitchen Cabinet and the Pursuit of Peace: The Shaping of American Foreign Policy, 1961-1963*. Jefferson, NC: McFarland, 2009.

_____. *Robert F. Kennedy and the Shaping of Civil Rights, 1960-1964*. Jefferson, NC: McFarland, 2013.

Guthman, Edwin. *We Band of Brothers: A Memoir of Robert F. Kennedy*. New York: Harper and Row Publishers, 1971.

Herring, George C. *America's Longest War: The United States and Vietnam, 1950-1975*, 2nd ed. New York: McGraw-Hill, 1986.

Karabell, Zachary, and Jonathan Rosenberg, ed., *Kennedy, Johnson and the Quest for Justice: The Civil Rights Tapes*. New York: Norton, 2003.

Kearns-Goodwin, Doris. *Lyndon Johnson and the American Dream*. New York: St. Martin's Griffin, 1991.

Kennedy, Edward M. *True Compass*. New York: Twelve, 2009.

Kennedy, Robert F. *To Seek a Newer World*. New York: Doubleday, 1967.

King, Martin Luther, Jr. *The Trumpet of Conscience*. Boston: Beacon Press, 2010.

Kotz, Nick. *Judgement Days: Lyndon Baines Johnson, Martin Luther King, Jr., and the Laws That Changed America*. New York: Houghton Mifflin, 2005. ebook.

Lewis, John. *Walking with the Wind: A Memoir of the Movement*. New York: Harvest, 1998.

Manchester, William. *The Death of a President: November 20-November 25 1963*. New York: Little, Brown, 2013. ebook.

Palermo, Joseph. *In His Own Right: The Political Odyssey of Robert F. Kennedy*. New York: Columbia University Press, 2002.

Patterson, James T. *The Eve of Destruction: How 1965 Transformed America*. New York: Basic Books, 2014.

Risen, Clay. *The Bill of the Century: The Epic Battle for the Civil Rights Act*. New York: Bloomsbury Press, 2014. ebook.

Schlesinger, Arthur M., Jr. *Robert Kennedy and His Times.* New York: Houghton Mifflin, 2002.
Shesol, Jeff. *Mutual Contempt: Lyndon Johnson, Robert Kennedy and the Feud That Defined a Decade.* New York: Norton, 1997.
Talbot, David. *Brothers: The Hidden History of the Kennedy Years.* New York: Free Press, 2007.
Thomas, Evan. *Robert Kennedy: His Life.* New York: Touchstone, 2000.
Wofford, Harris. *Of Kennedys and Kings: Making Sense of the Sixties.* Pittsburgh: University of Pittsburgh Press, 1980.

Primary Source Collections

Peters, Gerhard, and John T. Woolley. *The American Presidency Project* [online]. Santa Barbara, CA: University of California (hosted), Gerhard Peters (database). Available at http://www.presidency.ucsb.edu/ws.
Foreign Relations of the United States, 1961–1963, Volume XI: Cuban Missile Crisis and Aftermath, ed. Edward C. Keefer, Charles S. Sampson, and Louis J. Smith. Washington, DC: United States Government Printing Office, 1996. eBook.
Foreign Relations of the United States, 1964–1968, Volume I: Vietnam, 1964–1968, ed. Edward C. Keefer and Charles S. Sampson. Washington, DC: United States Government Printing Office, 1992. eBook.
Foreign Relations of the United States, 1964–1968, Volume II: Vietnam, 1964–1968, ed. David C. Humphrey, Ronald D. Landa, and Louis J. Smith. Washington, DC: United States Government Printing Office, 1996. eBook.
Katzenbach, Nicholas, recorded interviews. President Lyndon B. Johnson Oral History Project, Lyndon B. Johnson Library, Austin, TX.
Kennedy, Robert F. Attorney General Papers. John F. Kennedy Library, Boston, MA.
Kennedy, Robert F. Recorded interviews, John F. Kennedy Oral History Project of the John F. Kennedy Library, Boston, MA.
Kennedy, Robert F. Robert F. Kennedy Speeches. John F. Kennedy Library, Boston, MA. https://www.jfklibrary.org/Research/Research-Aids/Ready-Reference/RFK-Speeches.aspx.
The King Center Digital Archives. Atlanta, Georgia. http://thekingcenter.org/archive.
USA Congressional Record Proceedings and Debates of the 88th Congress, Second Session, Volume 110, Part 6.

Audio / Visual

"Funeral Services for President John F. Kennedy: November 1963: 23–25." Accession Number WHN:28, John F. Kennedy Library, Boston. MA.
American Experience, *RFK,* documentary, directed by David Grubin (2004; USA; PBS) DVD.
"President Lyndon B. Johnson's Address to Congress," November 27, 1963. MP505. Lyndon B. Johnson Library, Austin, TX. Video upload to YouTube. 2012. https://www.youtube.com/watch?v=LF0TxpxIMA0.

Index

Abernathy, Juanita 145
Abernathy, Ralph 17, 149, 151, 154, 276
Apartheid 7, 12, 200, 201, 217, 220, 283
Arlington National Cemetery 7, 37, 71, 138

Ball, George 32, 207
Barnett, Ross 18, 70
Bay of Pigs 16–18
Bedford-Stuyvesant 7, 202, 232, 237, 296
Belafonte, Harry 256
Bevel, James 202, 256, 297
Birmingham, Ala. 12, 40, 155, 159, 222, 230, 266, 282; and the 1963 demonstrations 8, 20, 134, 136, 138, 144, 163, 193
Black Panthers 87, 158, 159
"Black Power" 87, 158, 195, 222, 223, 229–232, 258
Brown v. Board of Education (*Brown* decision) 47, 69, 84, 136, 141
Bundy, McGeorge 32, 35, 167–169, 207

Carmichael, Stokely 2, 222–224, 258
Castro, Fidel 16
"Chicago Plan" 201, 202
Civil Rights Act of 1964 6, 8, 31, 41, 42, 47, 55, 64, 74, 75, 84, 87, 94, 97, 98, 109, 111, 131, 132, 144, 148, 150, 157, 163, 196, 288
Clark, Jim 136–138, 143, 144, 146, 147, 149, 152–154, 158, 160, 196, 202
Communist Party 23, 55, 96, 97, 102, 103, 105, 114, 119, 167, 168, 171, 173, 189, 206, 217, 243, 244, 264, 269
Congress of Racial Equality (CORE) 17, 224, 229
Connor, Eugene ("Bull") 8, 19, 20, 134, 136, 149, 202
Constitution of the United States 16, 29, 98, 157, 185, 187, 199, 215, 235, 259
Cuban Missile Crisis, 1962 19, 91, 113, 116, 172, 176, 207, 271

Daley, Richard 189, 223–226
Declaration of Independence 80
Doar, John 99, 152–154
Dobrynin, Anatoly 19, 104–106

Edelman, Peter 196, 198
Eisenhower, Dwight D. 105
Emancipation Proclamation 74, 110
Evers, Charles 123
Evers, Medgar 21, 40, 123, 221

Face the Nation 207, 261
Farmer, James 152
Federal Bureau of Investigation (FBI) 13, 23, 52, 95, 96, 147, 210
Fifteenth Amendment 136, 141, 161, 191
Forman, James 152–154, 238
Freedom Rides 8, 17, 18, 54, 275
Freedom Summer 8, 87, 94, 107, 134, 137, 141, 221

Georgia 16, 47, 85, 250, 264, 274
Goodwin, Richard 45, 244
Gulf of Tonkin 6, 114, 116, 118–120, 127, 167
Guthman, Edwin 24, 50, 51, 56, 103, 113, 122, 123, 130, 135, 136

Hamilton, Edith 53, 67
Hickory Hill 13, 24, 28, 204, 271
Hoffa, James R. 14, 15, 45, 51, 169
Hood, James 20
Hoover, J. Edgar 13, 23, 28, 52, 95, 96
Housing Discrimination 61, 109, 113, 125, 126, 128, 191, 194, 195, 197, 198, 201, 202, 226, 238, 255
Howard University 23, 186
Humphrey, Hubert 38, 184, 207, 235, 257

Jackson, Jimmy Lee 147, 148, 156
Johnson, Frank (Judge) 152–154, 159, 160
Johnson, Lyndon B. 2, 5, 6–10, 36, 39, 42–48, 51, 56, 62, 64, 72, 94–96, 104, 112, 127, 130, 132, 133, 140, 141, 184, 186–188, 220, 224, 235; and assassination of JFK 24–33; and Civil Rights Act, 1964 38, 41, 67, 97–99; and Great Society (War on Poverty) 58–61, 74–76, 78–84, 142; and Gulf of Tonkin 114–120; and Inaugural Address, 1965 138, 139; and relationship with MLK 38, 184, 185, 191, 236,

301

247, 252; and relationship with RFK 25–35, 45, 46, 48, 52, 57, 58, 105–107, 122, 124, 129, 130, 177–181, 205–208, 242–245, 260–262; and selection as vice president 24–27; and Selma 137, 142–145, 154–158, 161, 162, 164, 167; and Vietnam War 114–120, 135, 136, 167–169, 171–174, 205–208, 239, 241–247, 252, 251, 257, 258, 260–262, 269–273; and Voting Rights Act, 1965 137, 138, 191, 192; and withdrawal from 1968 election 272, 272
Joint Chiefs of Staff 117
Justice Department 13, 17, 45, 51, 52, 55, 69, 78, 83, 84, 95, 122, 123, 132, 152, 153, 155, 192, 196, 256

Katzenbach, Nicholas 18, 29, 30, 69, 147, 148, 153, 242
Kennedy campaign, presidential 1960 15, 16, 75
Kennedy, Edward M. (Ted) 13, 15, 16, 56, 57, 63, 64, 68, 75, 73, 178; and maiden speech on the Civil Rights Act, 1964 62–64
Kennedy, Jacqueline 5, 7, 29, 30, 32–34, 36, 37, 53, 57, 102, 213
Kennedy, John F. (JFK) 4–7, 9–25, 29–36, 39–44, 46, 50, 51, 57–62, 64, 68, 69, 73–75, 80, 85, 86, 88, 91, 93, 94, 98, 101, 103, 113, 114, 116, 117, 123, 128, 131–133, 135, 138–140, 142, 148, 156, 161, 170, 172, 173, 176, 179, 180, 233, 252, 271, 272, 282, 283; and assassination 23; and choosing vice president 25, 26, 28; and funeral 35–37; and PT 109 17
Kennedy, Joseph P., Jr. 24
Kennedy, Joseph P., Sr. 9
Kennedy, Robert F. 1–10, 11, 12, 65–68, 90–94, 116; and Anatoly Dobrynin 19, 104–106; and Bedford-Stuyvesant 202, 203, 232, 237, 238; and civil rights 126, 128, 170, 171, 233–235; and Civil Rights Act 1964 68–74, 84–86, 97–99; and Cuban Missile Crisis, 1962 19, 91, 113, 116, 172, 176, 207, 271; and "Day of Affirmation" speech 213–220; and death of JFK 13–14, 17–21, 23–25, 28–30; and Democratic National Convention, 1964 112–114; election for senate, 1964 112, 122–131; election of 1960 15, 16; funeral for JFK 35–37; and inauguration, 1965 138–140; and interview with Jack Paar 57; and maiden speech to the Senate 176–178; and Nuclear Test Ban Treaty, 1963 91, 132, 177; and Ole Miss 18, 210–212; and poverty 58–62; 74–81, 142, 196–199, 227, 228; presidential nomination, 1968 270; and "Rackets Committee" 14; and relationship with LBJ 25–35, 45, 46, 48, 51, 52, 57, 58, 105–107, 122, 124, 129, 130, 177–181, 205–208, 242–245, 260–262; and St. Patrick's Day speech, 1964 53–56; and selection of LBJ as vice president 24–27; and South Africa 200, 212–220; and speech on MLK's death 276–278; and *To Seek a Newer World* 262; and trip to Asia 49, 50; and trip to Europe 100–104; and urban crisis 196–199; and Vietnam War 104–106, 126–128, 171–174, 179–182, 204–208, 239–246, 257–264; and violence in Mississippi 94–97; and Watts Riots 193, 194, 197; and youth 79–81, 83, 89–91, 174–176, 217–220, 235
Kerner Commission 270–273
Khrushchev, Nikita 15, 17–19, 104, 106, 118, 119, 278
King, Coretta Scott 14, 15, 31, 145, 264, 278
King, Martin Luther, Jr. 1–8, 11, 14–21, 57, 58; and the assassination of JFK 31, 32, 35, 39–42, 131–133; and "Black Power" 222–224, 229–232; and Chicago 188–190, 196, 200–202, 208, 223–227, 235, 236, 248; and Civil Rights Act, 1964 87, 88; and Freedom Summer 107; and "Love and Forgiveness" speech 81–83; and "Meet the Press" 183–185; and "Mountaintop" speech 274–276; and Nobel Peace Prize, 1964 133, 134, 140–142; and relationship with LBJ 38, 46, 47, 184, 185, 191, 236, 247, 252; and riots in Harlem 1965 107–111; and school desegregation 86; and Selma Campaign 135–138, 143–156, 159–162, 202; Selma to Montgomery March 162–166; and South Africa 200, 201, 209; Vietnam War 185, 186, 190, 236, 246–258, 264–267, 273; and Voting Rights Act, 1965 192; and Watts Riots 194, 195; and *Where Do We Go from Here* 237
Ku Klux Klan (KKK) 17, 95, 134, 109, 194, 209

"Letter from a Selma Jail" 144
"Letter from the Birmingham Jail" 20
Lewis, John 2, 17, 21, 137, 138, 147, 149, 150, 162, 163, 186, 187, 276, 282
Lincoln, Abraham 4, 8, 33, 41, 93, 132, 192, 279

Malcolm X 87, 145, 147, 148, 150, 156, 158, 223
Malone, Vivian 20
March on Washington 8, 39, 68, 272, 273, 274
Marshall, Burke 20, 67, 69, 94, 99, 196, 197
Marshals, U.S. 17
Martin, John Bartlow 68
McCarthy, Eugene 246, 270
McCarthy, Joseph 15, 57
McClellan Committee (Rackets Committee) 14, 15, 25, 57, 135
McCone, John 24, 115
McNamara, Robert S. 19, 28, 32, 34, 44, 115, 116, 120, 169, 206, 244
Meet the Press 183, 207
Meredith, James 18, 210, 212, 221, 223, 229
"Meredith March" 221, 223, 229
Mississippi 12, 18, 40, 57, 82, 87, 94, 95, 96, 107, 108, 109, 123, 134, 136, 141, 158, 209, 210, 221–223, 271, 274
Montgomery, Alabama 4, 14, 17, 133, 147, 149, 151, 153, 154, 159, 160, 162–165, 170, 183, 201, 225, 230

Montgomery Bus Boycott 8, 14
Moore, Cecil B. 189, 190

National Association of the Advancement of Colored Peoples (NAACP) 87, 88, 123, 186, 189, 190, 255
National Guard 18, 192, 226
National Liberation Front (NLF) 206, 207, 252
"New Frontier" 2, 5, 9, 13, 23, 24, 40, 42, 43, 45, 46, 50–53, 56, 59, 60, 67, 74–76, 78, 90, 102, 114, 123, 130, 142, 170, 171, 174, 176
New York Times 108, 123, 135, 138, 144, 146, 147, 151, 158, 173, 178, 181, 186, 189, 206, 220, 221, 223, 229, 230, 241, 246, 247, 255, 256, 269, 275
Newsweek 106, 241
Nixon, Richard M. 10, 15
Nuclear Test Ban Treaty, 1963 91, 132, 177

Obama, Barack H. 2, 134, 166, 281–283
O'Donnell, Kenneth (Kenny) 24, 30

Pleiku 9, 135, 167, 171
"Poor Peoples Campaign" 272, 273, 275
Profiles in Courage 213

Rackets Committee, Senate see McClellan Committee
Randolph, A. Philip 230, 231
Reagan, Ronald 258, 259
Reeb, James J. 155, 156, 160
Reuther, Roy 99
Robertson, Ian 212–214
Roosevelt, Franklin 4
Roosevelt, Theodore 90, 219
Rusk, Dean 34, 115, 116, 120, 169, 206, 241, 243, 245, 258, 270, 273
Rustin, Bayard 21

Schlesinger, Arthur M. 27, 45, 50, 122, 124, 129, 207, 212
Seigenthaler, John 15, 17
Selma, Ala. 6, 8, 58, 134–147, 149–165, 167, 169, 170, 183, 192, 194, 202, 223, 230, 275, 281–284
Shakespeare, William 28, 114
Shriver, Sargent 15, 35
"Sit-in" demonstrations 15, 89
Sorensen, Theodore 278
South Africa 7, 12, 198, 200, 201, 209, 212–214, 216, 217, 239, 274
Southern Christian Leadership Conference (SCLC) 8, 87, 88, 134, 136, 143, 145–147, 149, 150, 152–154, 157, 160, 162, 185, 201, 223, 225, 226, 229, 230–232, 248, 249
Spock, Benjamin 256, 257
Student Non-Violent Coordinating Committee (SNCC) 17, 87, 88, 137, 147, 149, 150, 152–154, 157, 159

Taylor, Maxwell 169, 206, 244
Tet Offensive 6, 269, 271
Truman, Harry S. 173, 183

University of Mississippi (Ole Miss) 18, 87, 221

Vietnam War 1, 4, 6–13, 23, 33, 48, 59, 69, 71, 72, 82, 91, 93, 97, 104–106, 109, 114–119, 121, 126–128, 135–137, 139, 141, 145, 149, 166–169, 171–173, 176–181, 185, 186, 190, 195, 200, 205–208, 225, 227, 229, 230, 235, 236, 238–267, 269–273, 280, 282, 284
Vivian, C.T. 20, 146, 147
Voting Rights Act, 1965 6, 8, 31, 160, 183, 191, 192, 196, 282

Wallace, George C. 20, 47, 69, 70, 136, 137, 147, 149, 151, 152, 154, 158, 196
Watts Riots 192–194, 196, 197, 202, 209, 215, 234, 271
Westmoreland, Willam 257, 258, 269
Wilkins, Roy 186, 230
Williams, Hosea 150–152, 163
Wofford, Harris 15

Young, Andrew 143, 202, 208

www.ingramcontent.com/pod-product-compliance
Lightning Source LLC
Chambersburg PA
CBHW051209300426
44116CB00006B/491